Disunion, War, Defeat, and Recovery in Alabama

Endowed by
TOM WATSON BROWN
and
THE WATSON-BROWN FOUNDATION, INC.

Disunion, War, Defeat, and Recovery in Alabama

The Journal of Augustus Benners, 1850–1885

Edited by Glenn and Virginia Linden

Mercer University Press

Macon, Georgia

© 2007 Mercer University Press
1400 Coleman Avenue
Macon, Georgia 31207
All rights reserved

First Edition.

Books published by Mercer University Press are printed on acid free paper that meets the requirements of American National Standard for Information Sciences—Permanence of Paper for Printed Library Materials.

Library of Congress Cataloging-in-Publication Data

Benners, Augustus, 1819 or 20-1885.
Disunion, war, defeat, and recovery in Alabama : the journal of Augustus Benners, 1850-1885 / edited by Glenn and Virginia Linden. — 1st ed.
    p. cm.
Includes bibliographical references and index.
ISBN-13: 978-0-88146-056-8 (hardback : alk. paper)
ISBN-10: 0-88146-056-7 (hardback : alk. paper)
1. Benners, Augustus, 1819 or 20-1885—Diaries. 2. Plantation owners—Alabama—Diaries. 3. Slaveholders—Alabama—Diaries. 4. Plantation life—Alabama—History—19th century. 5. Alabama—History—Civil War, 1861-1865—Personal narratives. 6. United States—History—Civil War, 1861-1865—Personal narratives, Confederate. 7. Reconstruction (U.S. history, 1865-1877)—Alabama. 8. Alabama—Social life and customs—19th century. 9. Alabama—History—1819-1950. 10. Greensboro (Ala.)—Biography.
    I. Linden, Glenn M., 1928- II. Linden, Virginia. III. Title.
F326.B46A3 2007
976.1'05092—dc22
                                            2007019735

Contents

Acknowledgments	ix
Editing	x
Introduction	1
Summary of Augustus Benners's Life	4
Chapter 1. Prelude to War: 1850–1860	25
Chapter 2. The Civil War Years: 1861–May 1865	58
Chapter 3. The Reconstruction Years: May 1865–1877	138
Chapter 4. The Later Years, 1878–1885	263
Bibliography	341
Index	345
About the Editors	359

Acknowledgments

We owe thanks to many people who helped us with this book. In spring 1998, John Westbrook, one of my students, showed me parts of a plantation journal written by Augustus Benners, his great-great-grandfather. He asked if I would be interested in editing it for publication. I took it home and showed it to my wife, Virginia, and we agreed to edit the journal. We also thank the owners of the journal, Katharine Regester Westbrook and her brother Howard William Regester, Jr., for allowing us complete freedom in the editing process. Early in our work, Nicholas Cobbs, a lawyer and historian in Greensboro, Alabama, and Guy Hubbs, archivist at Birmingham-Southern College, were asked to help us in this work. They were gracious in their support of the project over the next seven years. Their understanding of the history of Greensboro and the events of mid-nineteenth-century Alabama were invaluable in our efforts.

Brenda Cooper and Julie Stewart typed the first draft of the original 1,000-page single-spaced manuscript. We are grateful to Southern Methodist University for providing financial support for this work, and especially James Breeden and James Hopkins. We also want to thank Kitty Grey Long of Uniontown, Alabama, for her research on county records; Neal Faulkner for his interest in and financial support of the project; and Bettie Gray House for her editorial work.

Editing

Augustus Benners's journal has been typed almost as is, with spelling and punctuation as it appears in the journal. Periods have been added when needed to understand the sentence and the one that follows. Commas and periods have been added when needed for clarity. It was often difficult to distinguish between a period and a dash. If the thought was incomplete, the dash was used. Capitalization has been left as he wrote it. It was often hard to tell the difference, so if a capital was required it was used.

Benners had a very large vocabulary, including Latin and Greek words, and was an excellent speller. However, he spelled Tuesday as "Teusday"—especially noticeable in the years 1884 and 1885, so this was corrected since the word appeared so often and would have been irritating to the reader. His friends' names are occasionally spelled with variations—Reid, Reed, Herran, Herrin. He consistently spelled the names of his good friends such as D. F. McCrary as McRary and J. L. Tunstall as Tunstal. These spellings have been left in the manuscript as is, with a footnote for explanation.

Augustus Benners, 1818–1885
Courtesy of Nicholas H. Cobbs, Greensboro, Alabama

Jane Hatch Benners,
wife of Augustus Benners, ca. 1866

Augustus Benners and daughter Fanny, ca. 1853

William (Willie) Haywood Benners

Graham Benners, ca. 1888

Jane (Jennie) Benners, ca. 1876

Alfred Hatch Benners in later years when he was judge of Chancery Court in Alabama, ca. 1940

William "Willie" Benners

Margaret (Maggie) Jones Benner (February 2, 1871),
wife of Alfred Hatch Benners

Hamilton Graham Benners and Elizabeth (Liz) Benners, ca. 1880

Augustus Benners and family at home

Introduction

Augustus Benners: Witness to a Time of Torment

The world smiled on Augustus Benners. As a young and middle-aged man, he was a major cotton planter who lived handsomely on the labor of dozens of slaves. He had no qualms about that. It does not seem that he treated them with cruelty, but he did not hesitate to buy, sell, and rent them. His neighbors respected and trusted him, so they made him their political representative. He was a farmer who observed soil, rain, cold, drought, heat, and crops and governed his days accordingly. He had a large mind and closely followed news from the North, from Europe, and from Asia. He married happily, and his wife bore many children.

But the world frowned on Benners as well. He watched the sectional crisis with growing apprehension, and when it came, it destroyed the system that had treated him so well. He was too old to fight, and during the war, he mourned the loss of fellow white Southerners who died in slavery's defense. After it, he also mourned black former slaves whose lives had been wrapped around his. He watched some of his children die and saw others suffer in their adulthood. After his wife had spent decades at his side, she went off to Texas to visit a grown child, despite Benners's apprehensions about the trip. He was right to fear. On her way home, she died from an attack of dysentery. Benners was a diarist, and he recorded it all.

The diary he kept is very rich, about both public events and his own life. Benners was an important man in his own time. But he was no James Henry Hammond of South Carolina, seeking fame and urging the cause of Southern separation, or Jefferson Davis of Mississippi, presiding over a failed attempt at nationhood. Before and during the war, Benners never doubted the rightfulness of the social order into which he was born. Nor, when that order crashed, did he doubt the rightfulness of men like himself remaining in charge and taking care of their own interests. He was a keen and influential politician, but in his county seat and in the state capital of Montgomery rather in Washington. He was a legislator and state convention delegate, not a congressman, senator, or even governor. The only exception was his call to the national capital to testify during the disputed presidential election that put Rutherford B. Hayes rather than Samuel J. Tilden in the White House in 1877.

We know far too little about men like Benners. We ought to know more. We need to understand the rhythm of their lives. Historian T. H. Breen has demonstrated that most eighteenth-century Virginia planters were governed far more by the daily routine and the perceived large significance of growing tobacco than they were by public disputes on taxation and liberty. Benners's slaves grew not tobacco but rather cotton, corn, wheat, vegetables, and a little sugar. Clearly, the daily routine absorbed him most of the time, even during the war. In 1863, he did not even note the Emancipation Proclamation, though he surely heard about it. He was much more interested in the rain, the wind, and the two "thoroughbred & pure" Chester pigs that he bought in order to "procure a breed that would fatten kindly." Two years later, when the Southern cause was finally lost, he did not bother to describe the day that slavery ended.

Another reason for getting to know Benners is his perspective on the great events of his time. He endorsed secession, but he voted in the Alabama legislature against the taxes that the Southern cause needed. He suffered during the war but to nothing like the extent of Mississippians who endured the siege of Vicksburg or Georgians in the path of Sherman's invading army. After it was over, he regained both position and wealth, and he began to travel. Benners paid several visits to New England, the heart of pre-war abolitionism, and apparently became fond of the region. He worked for election victories by the "Democratic & Conservative Party," but he showed no surprise that former slaves were solidly for the Republicans, whom he called "radicals." He disliked the

Republicans' control of the presidency, but he mourned the death of Republican president and Union veteran James A. Garfield.

Benners's diary gives us the perspective of one man who enjoyed real privilege but not overwhelming wealth, who took part in major decisions but never wielded great power, and who witnessed destruction but was not himself destroyed. The Old South's leaders have long been the subject of study. We have learned a huge amount about its African-Americans in bondage, in struggle, and in freedom. We still know far too little about its nonslaveholding "plain folk." And we know less than we ought to know about men of its upper middle rank, such as Augustus Benners. The diary that he lovingly and carefully kept is not a "neutral" source, but it is very valuable. Thanks to generations of his descendants, the diary was preserved. Thanks to Glenn and Virginia Linden's careful editing, the diary and the world it reveals are now available for anybody who wishes to see. Whoever reads it will see a lot about Benners himself and about the time through which it was his fate to live.

—Edward Countryman
Southern Methodist University
June 2003

Summary of Augustus Benners's Life

In 1839, Augustus Benners—recently graduated from University of North Carolina at Chapel Hill and soon to be a successful lawyer, planter, and legislator in Alabama—decided to keep a daily journal. He began with a quote from William Shakespeare—"Let's take the instant by the forward top—for we are old—and on our quick'st decrees / The inaudible noiseless foot of time / Steals ere we can effect them." Though his original reasons for keeping a journal were as much amusement and recreation as history, in the first entry he explained in flowery detail his reasons for this new effort:

> To my own amusement this book (now blank) I appropriate—As a recreation from the fatigue of severer duties. And to occupy moments which cannot be more usefully employed I intend it. And while it answers this purpose—whilst it serves for my amusement—perhaps improvement—for the time present—it will perhaps at a future day be looked into with interest—as a repository of the thoughts & feelings—hopes and fears of other times, of days "which shall too soon have fleeted"—when hope was young—when the buds of promise had scarcely begun to expand. And when sorrow herself was beautified with the bright gilding of hope—A book of this description is like a rock projecting from the surface of a lake—which catches whatever may be floating past—before it is swept away into the ocean—the huge oak unprotected by the storm—And tossed upon the bosom of the water here finds an anchorage. And the flower too tender to withstand the rude blast & blown by it from the stem that had nurtured it here finds a resting place—the rock which was at first a mere point becomes in time an island—An island composed of strange materials

too—for trees shrubs fruits and flowers—have promiscuously floated around—And what would have been floated away and lost in the immensity of the ocean is here preserved. Thoughts which in the stream of time would be floated away here find a fixed habitation—And inconsiderable in themselves by constant accessions they swell into a pile of reminiscences—interesting and important.

During the next few years, Benners made occasional entries in which he expressed anxiety about friendships, politics, and lady friends; the death of his mother was a severe blow. However, his decision to move to Alabama changed his life. There he met and married Jane Hatch, who would be the mother of his twelve children, and became a successful lawyer, planter, slaveholder, and legislator. In early 1850, he began to make regular daily entries about his life and the events of the times. He called the journal a "Brief Memorandum of Crops, Seasons, Temperatures—rains—and events: Begun this 18th day of June AD 1850." It continued for the next thirty-five years.

Augustus Benners was born at New Bern, North Carolina, on Christmas Day 1819. His father was Lucas Jacob Benners IV, his mother Frances Batchelor. His father died on 27 May 1819, seven months before his birth. Augustus received his education in North Carolina, graduating from the University of North Carolina at Chapel Hill in 1837. His brother Edward Graham Benners studied law in Franklin at Spring Grove Academy. In spring 1837, Edward left New Bern for Alabama where he remained for two years. Then he returned home and convinced Augustus that he also should move to Alabama. In early 1840, they moved to Linden, Alabama, and subsequently formed a law partnership.

Augustus refers to his decision to move and his anxieties over the future in his journal entry of 10 February 1840. It was a pivotal experience in his life. For the first time, he was away from family and friends:

On the 13th day of January 1840 I left Newbern to seek a new home in the West. A step I doubt not which will have its effects for weal or woe on my whole future life. Oh what gloomy feelings rushed upon my mind as I thought of the days that were past—of leaving what once was my happy home—the scenes of my childhood & youth—endeared to me by the tenderest ties—I above all: when I reflected that I was leaving perhaps forever the friends who were so dear to me—all upon whose kindness or concern for my welfare I had any right to depend. My bosom was full—almost to bursting—The world was before me. I had my own fortune to make & my only confidence was that the same overruling providence who had made it necessary for me to depart would protect & provide for me in a strange land—I have reached the terra incognita—and must reserve my judgement until I am longer & better acquainted with the habits, manners &c of the people.

The most perplexing point to a person in my situation I find is where ought I to locate? What place combines the most advantages? After deliberation upon these important questions my brother & myself have concluded that Greensboro is the spot—And so it certainly must be if our calculations have been accurate—At any rate I shall try it & may heaven smile upon our efforts—My Journey which was very tedious & tiresome I was 15 days in completing. Having been detained a day in Milledgeville in consequence of the stage breaking down & another day (sunday 13 Jan) in Columbus. And I was detained two days longer than I ought to have been on the creek shoals in the Ala river. After arriving at prairie bluff & refreshing myself with a nights sleep I took a horse to Wootens (saturday) and after dinner was surprised & delighted to see my brother ride up. Questions innumerable [have] been asked & answered—he was obliged to go on next day to court & I concluded to await his return, which kept me 3 days longer away from this place. On tuesday Jan 27 we rode over to Linden together and here I am.

During the next few months Benners boarded at John Rains's house in Linden. Then in March, the brothers moved to Greensboro where they boarded with the Harveys for several weeks. The following week the two brothers took possession of William Huntington's house at a monthly cost of $16. This arrangement continued for several years until Edward left for Mobile in 1844.

In the following years, Augustus continued to build his law practice and became associated with William M. Murphy, one of Greene County's most successful lawyers. He met Jane Hatch of Greensboro and married her in November 1846. Their first child, Fanny, was born the next year on 23 August. Two years later, Alfred Hatch Benners was born. There would eventually be twelve children—nine boys and three girls of whom only four boys and the three girls survived past early childhood.

The 1850s

During the 1850s, Benners was an active planter, an effective legislator, and a busy lawyer. Most of his time was spent in planting, harvesting, and worrying about the cotton, corn, peas, and farm animals. There was seldom enough rain, frosts could damage the crop, and high winds were always a danger. He had two plantations—Walker Place and Cheney Place, a total of 715 acres. Each had to be visited and eighty-two slaves supervised.[1] On 31 October 1854, he visited the two plantations. He found that they had commenced gathering corn and had packed eighty-five bales cotton at Cheney Place and sixty-three bales at Walker Place, a total of 148 bales. The key to success was good weather, reliable labor, and a trustworthy overseer of the slaves.

In 1853, Benners received a letter informing him of his nomination to the state legislature. He accepted it, campaigned in July, and was elected by the largest number of votes of any candidate—941. The following year, Benners served in Montgomery, during which time he helped defeat a bill to issue state bonds of $8,000 per mile for railroad

---

[1] US Bureau of the Census, 1860 US Census, schedule, slave inhabitants, Scott's beat, page 55, Perry County, Alabama.

construction. He argued that the state already had too large a debt, and with the help of other legislators, he was able to defeat the bill. Another bill, authorizing a geological and agricultural survey of the state, a bill that Benners suggested, easily passed. Though successful as a legislator, he declined to be renominated. He would not serve again until 1861.

During these years, Benners expressed his views on political events taking place at the national level. The death of Zachary Taylor was especially disturbing. For days, he hoped it had not happened—"account being telegraphed is disbelieved by some." Nevertheless, it was true. During 1850, Benners followed the Compromise of 1850—Clay's bill, Webster's speech, and the Texas boundary question. He also noted that the new president, Millard Fillmore, intended to maintain the authority of the western states in New Mexico "from which a civil war may be apprehended." He ignored the Kansas-Nebraska Bill and the violence in Kansas but became alarmed at the possibility of John C. Frémont, a "black Republican," being elected president in 1856. A staunch Whig no longer belonging to a major party, he finally decided to vote for James Buchanan, the Democratic candidate, who supported "the true doctrine on the slavery issue non interference by Congress." Several years later, in August 1858, Benners and his wife visited Washington, DC. They called on President Buchanan and were pleased with the visit. Undoubtedly, Buchanan assured them that slavery would be allowed to expand into the western territories. Two years later, on 29 December 1860, Benners realized that there was a serious possibility of secession and civil war. South Carolina had seceded and Alabama was planning a meeting to decide whether or not to follow its example. In the next few weeks, he watched the unfolding drama, noting the secession of the lower Southern states, including Alabama, on 11 January. He did not attend the Alabama Secession Convention but supported their efforts to leave the Union. The next month, Benners and a friend, Judge Sydenham Moore, traveled to Selma on the way to the first meeting of the Provisional Congress of the Confederacy in Montgomery. When they found that the sessions were secret, they returned home. The inaugural address of Abraham Lincoln appeared to Benners to be "very warlike," and he noted that "the prospect of war is very imminent."

The Civil War Years

In the early months of the war, Benners was confident of Confederate victory. The "glorious news" of the Southern victory at Manassas on 21 July 1861 filled him with pride. The enemy was routed and there were few Southern casualties. But as the war continued, he began to have serious misgivings. The federal blockade cut off supplies and prices began to rise. By spring 1862, "everything sold at war prices," he wrote. Also losses at Forts Henry and Donelson, Shiloh, and New Orleans forced him to recognize that "a long and cruel war is the fate of the country."

As the war progressed, Benners kept a close watch on significant events as they occurred. On 5 September, he noted that "God had blessed the Confederate armies with a signal victory on the plains of Manassas [29, 30 August 1862]." A few weeks later he recorded, "The news from Gen Lees army in Maryland is conflicting and unsatisfactory. There was a severe battle at Sharpsburg on the 16th and 17th Septr—victory claimed by both sides." The next year he continued to record and reflect on the great events of the war—Lincoln calling for three million conscripts, England declining all efforts at mediation, Lee's victory at Chancellorsville, the siege of Vicksburg and its fall, Gettysburg, and the battles of Chickamauga and Chattanooga. In June 1863, he expressed his growing anxiety over the war—"We are all anxious for the war to close but there seems no prospect of such a desirable event—The South cant stop and the North wont. May God overrule it for the good of the country."

Throughout the war, Benners spent considerable time in Montgomery, the capital of Alabama. As an elected legislator, he was called there often for both special and regular sessions. In fall 1861, he fought hard to stop the creation of a new bank and the effort to "flood the country with spurious currency." A year later, as chairman of the judiciary committee and a member of the ways and means committee, he tried to block efforts to give $2,000,000 to families of indigent soldiers and $2,500,000 for the defense of Alabama—"The Extortion Bill was one of the most important measures passed to which I was opposed." His efforts to resist tax increases were in vain. In fall 1863, he attended a "disagreeable session for two weeks." Three months later, Benners attended another legislative session—also hurried and unsatisfactory in which little legislation was passed. He continued to serve in the legislature as late as December 1864.

In the last months of 1864 and early 1865, Benners spent considerable time in Montgomery. He was busy with his legal practice and occupied with the disposal of the Planters Insurance Company. The trustees decided to close it down and he received $1,818 for his services. He noted that the Confederate Congress had passed a bill to seize the cotton and tobacco. On 4 February 1865, he wrote, "I hope it is untrue—Robbing and violence can not produce peace and that is what we need."

Later in the month, Benners lamented Sherman's march north into Georgia and North Carolina. The Federals would accept no terms but submission, and the Confederates would not listen to that. "In the meantime our husbandry is neglected and at Richmond they are on the eve of starvation," he wrote. There was a rumor that the recognition of the Confederate states by the French might take place after 4 March 1865. Benners dismissed it as impossible.

His final entry about the war was not until 5 May 1865, a month after the war ended. Then he briefly summed up the last days of the war but made no mention of Lincoln's assassination: "Gen Lee's army of Northern Va surrendered to Gen Grant on [April] the 9th at Appomattox Court house under an apple tree—this was followed by news of an armistice between Sherman and Johnston to settle differences.... Our condition is a very sad one—the money of Confederacy has ceased to have any purchasing value and want of provisions is getting to be a very serious matter. What distresses are still in store for us God only knows. May he give us strength to endure whatever may befall."

The Reconstruction Years

On 17 May 1865, Augustus Benners wrote of his frustration with post-war conditions: "The sadness of these times can scarcely be described." There was a great cloud of gloom hanging over the South because of the destruction of the old labor system. The Freedmen's Bureau required that contracts be made with the freedmen; thus, it was difficult for Benners to have a reliable labor force. A number of his former slaves were discontented, and this troubled him—"Virgil & Rhoda are anxious to leave and want a contract with me. Jenny dont know whether she will or will not & Delia do [ditto]." The Negroes were working slowly and it seemed impossible to produce a good crop. Also his favorite horse, Sunbeam, had been illegally impressed. Times had changed and the future looked very uncertain.

Over the next few years, political conditions continued to trouble him. Southern states were not quickly readmitted to the Union, and the conflict between President Johnson and Congress grew worse. The passage of the Civil Rights Bill over Johnson's veto meant trouble. "I can not see how civil war will be averted," Benners wrote. There had been hope for peace but "the radical party are apparently determined to carry on the war." The passage of the Reconstruction bill dividing the South into five military districts under a major general with military forces caused him even more anxiety. Now the South was in fact a conquered province.

His economic situation did not improve in these years. The weather remained severe and unpredictable. In spring 1867, a cold snap killed the peaches and peas. Corn and potatoes were also damaged. The price of cotton continued to decline. As agricultural conditions worsened, Benners began to rely more heavily upon his legal practice for a regular income. In summer 1865, he sent in an application for amnesty, which was granted. Then, he successfully applied to practice law in US District Courts in Alabama. Busy with his law practice, Benners made few entries in his journal in the years 1868 to 1871.

However, his interest in politics was revived by the election of 1872. Following the campaign closely, he felt that Grant could be beaten, saying, "Great hopes were entertained of a change in the government," but it was not to be. Grant won easily and continued to support reconstruction in the South. It was a bitter pill for him to swallow. It was not until fall 1874 that Benners finally received good political news: the Democratic and Conservative parties defeated the Republican Party in

Alabama. Now Southerners in Alabama were once more in control of their destiny.

He reentered politics in June 1875, being nominated as a delegate to the Alabama Constitutional Convention by the Democratic and Conservative party. He accepted and made a short speech to the convention. The next month he campaigned in support of the Constitutional Convention, but the vote went against the convention, and he lost by 873 votes. However, in spring 1876, Benners went to the state convention in Montgomery as a delegate from the Democratic and Conservative party of Hale (formerly Greene) County. There he met old friends and was offered several leadership positions including the state executive committee, all of which he declined. He enjoyed seeing his friends but was no longer interested in political office.

The same year, the election of Democrat Samuel Tilden as president seemed certain. "If Indiana can be carried for Tilden then his election is sure," Benners wrote. Still there were riots near Hamburg, South Carolina, and trouble with the Negroes, which bothered him. In an effort to help the Tilden-Hendricks ticket, he made a speech in their behalf on 16 October.

On 7 November 1876, the election was held. Early results favored Tilden, but soon news came that his election was doubtful. For the next several months, Benners watched the controversy, the appointment of a special commission to resolve the difference over the vote count, and its struggle with the decision.

Then, on 27 January 1877, Benners received a telegram to appear before the Senate committee on privileges and elections. He arrived in Washington, DC, the next week, where he witnessed the counting of the electoral votes for Tilden and Hayes. Later, he attended a meeting of the special commission on electoral votes. He wrote on 11 February, "It is considered that the decision of the commission is purely a partisan one—and that all the other rulings will be of the same character and that Hayes will come in." Benners was examined by the Senate committee on 13 February regarding Democrats' successes in recent elections in Alabama and the election of 1876. He said there had been no intimidation, though relations were not always cordial.

He returned home to Alabama, where on 3 March 1877, the announcement of Hayes election was received. His response was bitter: "The vote on the Commission was a party one from first to last & was disgraceful to them."

In the next month and a half, Hayes removed all Federal troops from the last Southern states, thus restoring control to the states. He made an effort to conciliate the South in his inaugural speech and actions. Benners would have none of this: "Poor Hayes his little day will be flaunted out in stolen finery and if not forgotten he will be censured by posterity for his crime." Benners's last entry on the election of 1876 and the end of Reconstruction was on 26 April 1877: "The troops are removed from N. O. [New Orleans]."

The Later Years

In the remaining eight years of his life, Benners continued to manage his properties, keep a close eye on the price of cotton, and raise his family. He found it difficult to find reliable renters. Often, it took weeks or even months to find a suitable person. The Mellown property was idle for several months, and then the renter left before the end of the year. It was not an easy time for him since many owed him money and wanted to extend the time for their repayment. The price of cotton remained at a low level through most of these years. His only choice was to hold his cotton off the market until he could sell it at a better price. It was a gamble, not always successful. Still Benners continued to make money, though fearing that his wealth would soon be lost.

His children, particularly Ed and Willie, caused him great pain. Ed tried to raise cotton but found it too difficult; he wanted to be like his father but to no avail. Finally, in December 1879, Ed began to have mental problems. He was unable to sleep and believed that others were trying to kill him. Gathering friends together, Augustus and Jane considered the choices and decided to have Ed committed to the state mental asylum. It was traumatic for Jane and for Augustus, who grieved for him for the rest of his life: "My poor heart bleeds when I think of my son." Willie was a continuing problem since he could not find a satisfactory job. Augustus helped him to find several opportunities, but they did not work out. Willie remained at home and Benners agonized over his future: "Willies case is a hard one nothing to do and no ability to do anything or rather no desire."

Benners's father-in-law, Alfred Hatch, died in 1879. Jane, Benners's wife of thirty-five years, died in 1881. These were crushing blows. Alfred had helped his son-in-law in the early years, even giving him a house in Greensboro. He also aided him in becoming a cotton planter and continued to help him for the next twenty years. He was sorely missed. Jane had gone to Dallas to visit their son Alfred and on the way home at a brief visit at Benners's brother in Jefferson, Texas, she died. He grieved for her for months: "Her death leaves a great void in my life which recurs to my mind continuously." He spent hours walking on the paths where he and Jane had found peace and comfort. Slowly, he regained his composure and peace. Two of his daughters, Fanny and Liz, aided in the healing process. Fanny, the eldest, helped raise the children, took care of the grounds, accompanied him to various functions, and wrote many of his letters. Liz took over the role of housekeeper, helping in the kitchen and sewing and knitting for the family. These two daughters comforted him for the remainder of his life.

He continued to follow the political scene. The election of 1880, with James Garfield running against Winfield Hancock, especially interested him. At first, it appeared that the Democrat, Hancock, had a chance to win, but Benners feared that the radical Republicans would win since "money is power and the radicals have it." Garfield won a narrow election and once again Benners was disappointed. Still, he hoped his party would win the presidency again, and in 1884, the Democrats elected a president for the first time since 1856. Grover Cleveland ran against James G. Blaine in a hotly contested race. Benners did not participate in the campaign since he was no longer interested in the day-to day-political combat, preferring to give advice and watch the campaign unfold. The race was so close that it finally came down to the vote of the state of New York. Democrats won by a narrow margin, though it took a week of recounting to be certain of the vote. There was great rejoicing in the South. Benners was overjoyed, writing, "Great gratification as news of count closed in N. York...Blaine giving it up."

In the last year of his life, Benners continued to balance his account books, collect rents from his tenants for the previous year, and rent lands for the new year. When pressed, he often loaned money to those in need. The possibility of war between England and Russia made him uneasy since the price of cotton could be affected by such a conflict. There were also persistent reports of Grant's ill health. On 21 March, Benners made his first reference to Grant's health: "Gen Grants condition is not supposed to have improved any." For the next few months, he closely followed Grant's deteriorating physical condition.

In May, Benners health worsened. On 11 May, he complained, "My dyspepsia is right bad." He began to take quinine, which soon became a daily necessity. Although he was feeling poorly, Benners decided to go to Jenny's graduation exercises in Montgomery. He made the trip, attended the ceremony, but was unable to hear her read her own composition—"one may smile & smile & be a villain." Still, it was a satisfying day for Benners, who was accompanied by Fanny and Liz, and all rejoiced at Jenny's success.

In the last full month of his life, Benners suffered greatly but continued to keep abreast of national and international affairs. He noted that the strike of cab drivers in Chicago was finally over, that "Indians are murdering citizens in Kansas," that there was a stir of anger in London over the sale of girls for immoral purposes, and Russia and England were again talking about war. He continued to worry about the price of cotton and about his children and their lives. Ed was never far from his thoughts—"My heart grieves for him."

On 21 July, Benners wrote that he stopped eating fruit and vegetables. He also took a daily tonic, which was "a bitter dose." However, he remained active and alert. On 3 August, he went to church for a service and communion in the morning and to a lecture in the afternoon. The next day he worked in his office and completed the sale of Walker Place. On 7 August, he played backgammon and made his final journal entries. His last two sentences were: "Grants corpse has reached New York and is lying in state at City Hall. Cholera is very bad in Spain & France." He died later in the same day of apoplexy (a stroke) at the age of sixty-five. He was buried in the family plot in Greensboro, Alabama, next to his wife, Jane.

Benners's Family and Friends

Jane Hatch Benners, daughter of Elizabeth Blount Vail and Alfred Hatch, was born in 1826 in North Carolina. She moved to Alabama in 1840 with her parents. Six years later, on 26 December 1846, she married Augustus H. Benners. She bore twelve children, nine boys and three girls. In the antebellum and Civil War years, she lost five children, all boys. She was frequently ill. Her life in the 1850s was largely concerned with raising the children and entertaining many guests since her lawyer husband had become a planter and was beginning a political career. She traveled regularly with her children to her father's large Arcola plantation near the Warrior River. She died 23 May 1881, while returning from a visit to her son, Alfred in Dallas, Texas, having stopped off in Jefferson, Texas, to see Augustus's brother, Edward.

Alfred Hatch—Jane's father—was born in Craven County, North Carolina, near New Bern, on 14 October 1799. He married Elizabeth Vail and moved to Alabama in 1840, where he built the Arcola plantation of 5,000 acres with over 200 slaves. The census of 1850 lists six children: Alfred P. Hatch, born in 1825 in North Carolina; Jane Hatch, born in 1826; Lemuel Hatch, born in 1834; Mary, born in 1836; Caroline, born in 1841; and Benjamin Francis Hatch, born in 1843. All of these children survived the Civil War and are mentioned frequently in the journal. His wife passed on at the end of the Civil War, and Alfred married a younger woman, Victoria Jones Walker, a widow thirty-two years of age. They had a daughter Evalina Hatch (called Lena) in 1871. His health declined considerably in the late 1870s, and he died on 30 January 1879 and left the bulk of his estate to his wife, causing considerable ill feelings among children of the first wife.

Edward Graham Benners, Augustus's only brother, was born 13 February 1814, in North Carolina. He studied law in Franklin, North Carolina at Spring Grove Academy. In spring 1837, he left New Bern for Alabama and returned in May 1839. The same year, he and Augustus returned to Alabama, and in 1840, he formed a law partnership with

Augustus. In 1844, he moved to Mobile, Alabama, and in December of the same year he married Helen Donaldson. On 4 August 1850, he left Mobile, arriving in Jefferson, Texas, on 9 September 1850. From 1851 to 1857, he practiced law in Marshall, Texas, and then he returned to Jefferson and continued his law practice. In 1868, after the death of all his children during an epidemic, he retired from the bar and began preparing for the ministry. He took charge of Christ Church at Jefferson in 1869 where he was a minister until his death on 18 March 1894.

Children of Augustus and Jane Benners

Fanny Benners was born in Greensboro on 23 August 1847. The eldest of the Benners's children, she and Alfred were enrolled in a school in fall 1855. In the next few years, she traveled with her father to the family plantations and to Arcola, her grandfather's plantation. During the Civil War, she "acquitted herself well" in presenting a play by the young ladies of the Greensboro Female to a number of young soldiers. She remained in school until graduation and continued to live with her parents after the war. She enjoyed going to concerts, dances, dinners, and to Blount Springs for the annual family vacation. After her mother's death, Fanny, now in her mid-thirties, began to play a more important role in the family. As the eldest daughter, she took the place of her mother, writing letters, taking care of the grounds, accompanying her father to important functions, and taking the younger children to school and cultural activities. In the last years of his life, Augustus found her to be of great help in his efforts to raise the family. She never married and died in 1896.

Alfred Hatch Benners was born on 22 February 1849, in Greensboro, Alabama. He graduated from Southern University in 1868 and practiced law in Greensboro, Alabama. He married Margaret Jones, daughter of Colonel Allen C. Jones, in 1871. In 1875, he moved to Dallas, Texas, where he practiced law until 1885, when he returned to Greensboro upon his father's death. In 1890, he located permanently in Birmingham. In 1905, Governor Jelks appointed him chancellor of the northwest division of Chancery Court of Alabama. In the latter years of his life, he wrote a historical sketch called *Slavery and Its Results*.

Edward Graham Benners, born on 11 December 1852, was a sickly child, regularly suffering from croup and coughing. He did not travel regularly to the family plantation or to Arcola, his grandfather's plantation, as any bad weather made it more difficult. Throughout the Civil War, he had extended periods of ill health. After the war, he had little sense of direction but finally tried to grow cotton in order to please his father. According to his father, Edward was "in great perplexity" about what to do. However, he began to have mental problems, and it became an unbearable family situation. Finally, he consented to go to the Alabama state mental hospital in Tuscaloosa to get help. It was a heartbreaking decision for his father and mother, but it proved to be the right one. He remained there until his death in 1911.

Elizabeth (Liz) Benners was born in 1855. She enrolled in Mr. Cabels school at Dorman's Hall in Greensboro where she graduated in 1873. During the next few years, Liz visited other churches, often the Presbyterian church, and spent time visiting her friends and relatives. In 1881, she traveled to Atlanta with the Jeffries family to an exhibition. When her mother died, Liz took over the role of housekeeper, often cooking for the family, though they had a regular cook. She was busy sewing and knitting for the family—quilts for her father and dresses for her younger sister Jenny. Augustus came to depend upon her and was unhappy when she was away. In November 1881, he wrote "I parted with her with regret. She is so kind and tries so hard to please and be helpful." Several years later, Liz decided to go to Texas to visit her brother. This greatly disturbed her father—"What shall I do—she is housekeeper." After her father's death, she married A. C. Evans.

William Haywood Benners (Willie) was born on 11 January 1860. He studied three years at Southern University, Greensboro, and then he completed a business course in Atlanta, Georgia. He moved to Dallas, Texas, in 1881, where his older brother was practicing law. He married Eleanor Davidson on 25 December 1885. They had six children. He was assistant to the publisher of the *Dallas News*, later *Dallas Morning News*, when he retired in 1947. He died in 1951 at the age of ninety-one.

Jane (Jenny) Benners was born in 1866 in Greensboro, Alabama. She often visited friends, went to parties, and traveled to Arcola and

Blount Springs. Her favorite game was Bezique, which she played regularly with her father. In 1882, her father sent her to Hamner Hall, an Episcopal school in Montgomery. The spread of yellow fever delayed her enrollment, but she attended the school for three years, especially enjoying music, French, and dancing lessons. When she came home, she attended Mary Avery's school. She graduated from Hamner Hall in June 1885. Her father attended the ceremony and was pleased with her performance—she read a composition of her own writing. She received an award for her performance. She died in 1932.

Hamilton Graham Benners (Graham) was born in Greensboro on 11 May 1868. He became a lawyer and married Annie LeVert Poellnitz. He bought the old *Alabama Beacon* newspaper in 1892, worked for John Turpin in the Alabama legislature, and worked in Washington, DC for his closest childhood friend, US Representative Richmond Pearson Hobson, a hero of the Spanish American war. Returning to Greensboro, he wrote an entertaining "Benners Diary" column for many years for the *Greensboro Watchman*. He died in February 1951.

Children who died at an early age were Augustus, 1851–1854; Lucas, 1857–1860; James Marbury, 1858–1860; John, 1861–1865; and Charles, 1864–1865.

Friends

Colonel Allen C. Jones (1811–1893) was the son of Colonel Cadwallader Jones and Rebecca Long. He became a wealthy planter on the Black Warrior River in Greene (later Hale) County, Alabama. When the Civil War broke out, he was a state senator and captain of the Greensboro Guards, a volunteer company. The guards became Company I in the 5th Alabama Regiment in May 1861. Allen Jones was elected Lieutenant Colonel of the regiment. The guards were at the Battle of First Manassas, but they saw little action. On 27 April 1862, Colonel Jones was replaced and the guards became Company D of the reorganized 5th Alabama Regiment. Jones left the service and later served in the Alabama legislature.

Henry Watson graduated from Washington College of Hartford Connecticut in 1828. He attended law school at Harvard for one year, moved south in December 1830, and taught for a year in Erie, Alabama. He returned home, completed his law studies, and was admitted to the Connecticut bar. He then returned to Greensboro where he became a partner of John Erwin, one of its leading citizens. He purchased a plantation at Newbern and became a cotton planter. He married Sophia Peck, a Southerner, on 18 February 1845. By 1848, he considered himself a Southerner, and by 1854, he owned 2,000 acres and 101 slaves. He founded the Planters Insurance Company, a bank, the same year.

When the war broke out, Watson returned to the North. He had become a Unionist and was opposed to the war. Uncomfortable in the North, he was still sympathetic to the South, so he took his family to Europe, first Germany and then France, where he remained throughout the war. He returned to Northampton, Massachusetts, on 5 September 1865 and then to Greensboro in December 1865. He was welcomed back by many, but he was no longer comfortable in the South. He kept his Greensboro house until 1870, making regular visits each winter. Finally, in 1870, no longer enjoying life in the South, he sold off his lands and moved North where he lived for the rest of his life. Being one of Benners's best friends, he continued to visit him into the mid-1880s.

John G. Harvey was born in Beaufort County, North Carolina, in 1807. He attended West Point and graduated in the class of 1831 along with Jefferson Davis. He spent two years in the army, but because of his wife's ill health, he resigned and settled in Greensboro in 1837. First a merchant, then a student of law, he became the editor of the *Alabama Beacon* in Greensboro. Although opposed to the war, he went with his state when it seceded.

Colonel Isaac Croom was a well-known Greensborian and a good friend of Benners. He was a planter in Greene County and president of both the Alabama Agricultural Society and the Alabama Historical Society. Benners gave the eulogy at Croom's funeral in 1863.

Sydenham Moore was born in Tennessee on 25 May 1817. He attended the University of Alabama from 1833–1836, was admitted to the bar, and practiced in Greensboro. He was judge of the circuit court in 1857 and was often referred to as judge. He served two terms in the House of Representatives, 4 March 1857 until 21 January 1861, when he withdrew from Congress. He was a colonel and commanding officer of the 11th Alabama Regiment and was wounded at the Battle of Seven Pines on 31 May 1862 and died in August of that year.

Other friends included James D. Webb, a lawyer who practiced in Greensboro, served in the legislature, and was killed in the Civil War at the Battle of Chickamauga. His brother was William P. Webb, a lawyer who practiced in Eutaw. J. H. Y. Webb was a planter who lived in Greensboro; his brother was William T. Webb, a doctor who also lived in Greensboro. Henry Webb was a doctor who lived and practiced in Greensboro; Henry Y. Webb, a doctor in Eutaw. Most of these Webbs were born in North Carolina. William Inge, C. E. (Charley) Waller, and Thomas Roulhac were fellow lawyer friends of Benners. Church friends included C. L. Stickney, a tanner and lay reader at St. Paul's Episcopal Church and Richard Hooker Cobbs, rector of St. Paul's. His father was Bishop Nicholas Hamner Cobbs, Alabama's leading Unionist who hoped he would never live to see Alabama secede; he died in 1861 shortly before the war broke out. Relatives of Augustus and Jane included the names Kornegay, Vail, Hatch, Haywood and Daves.

Greensboro

Alabama was admitted to the Union in 1819. Four years later, Greensborough, a small town with few residents, asked for and received incorporation. The common practice of dropping the last few letters resulted in its being known as Greensboro.[2] By the 1830s, the great cotton plantations that surrounded Greensboro were fully developed, and for the next thirty years, Greensboro was their major trading center. As wealth poured into the area, goods were transported in and out of the area and the city grew into one of the most important in Alabama. In cotton production, it ranked as third or fourth in the state.

At the same time, its citizens had learned to work together to "promote commerce, establish fraternal organizations and churches and push for moral and educational reforms."[3] The Freemasons aided in this

---

[2] Guy Hubbs, "Guarding Greensboro, A Confederate Company and the Making of a Southern Community" (Ph.D. diss., University of Alabama, 1999) 12.

[3] Ibid., 38.

process with their emphasis on honesty, moral rectitude, and active moral benevolence. They appealed to those citizens who wanted to build a better community. Their message was received favorably by many in Greensboro, resulting in a significant growth in their membership and in a new attitude toward their own community. Many churches sprang up in the 1820s and 1830s. The Greensboro Methodist church began in 1822, the Baptist church in 1819, the Presbyterian church in 1823, and the Episcopal church in 1830. This resulted in a vibrant religious life by the 1850s with all of the churches participating in celebrations honoring Sabbath School students. These celebrations included "prayers, ministerial addresses, and hymns."[4]

During these years, Greensboro had a number of private schools, the best known of which was the Greensboro Female Academy, chartered in 1841 and run by William S. Barton, an educational reformer. Efforts to open public schools were more difficult since Henry Tutwiler founded the Greene Springs School in nearby Havana. Many Greensborians sent their children to this highly regarded school.[5] Tutwiler had many progressive ideas, one of which was to allow students to choose subjects that interested them.[6]

In the 1850s, efforts at reform in Alabama resulted in the establishment of a modern public school system along the lines of the system created by Horace Mann in Massachusetts. With the support of John Harvey, editor of the Greensboro *Beacon*, and Allen Jones, state senator from Greene County, the decision was made to open public schools in Greensboro in 1858: "Miles Hassell Yerby, a graduate of the state university at Tuscaloosa, came to Greensboro and taught at its first public school."[7] With the help of concerned town leaders, public schools were now in place in Greensboro.

The Greensboro Temperance Society, organized in 1842, soon had a membership of 322 people—"175 men and 147 women."[8] The society

---

[4] Ibid., 54.
[5] Ibid., 61.
[6] Ibid., 61.
[7] William Edward Yerby, *History of Greensboro, Alabama from its Earliest Settlement* (Montgomery AL: The Paragon Press, 1908) 80.
[8] Hubbs, "Guarding Greensboro," 56.

helped decrease the amount of drinking in Greensboro. In 1849, a chapter of the Sons of Temperance was formed that demanded total abstinence. In the next few years, Greensboro temperance advocates became prohibitionists. Their greatest success came when the city decided to attract a new Methodist school—Southern University—to Greensboro. In order to do this, a coalition—"town boosters, businessmen, religious leaders and reformers"[9]—cooperated in raising over $168,000 and pledging that no alcohol would be sold within five miles of the city if the university would come to Greensboro. They were successful in beating the offers of rival cities, and in January 1857, the largest crowd ever seen in Greene County assembled to celebrate its success. It was, in the words of Guy Hubbs, "a public recognition that Greensborians could collaborate to build together what their individual efforts could not have done separately.["][10]

Greensboro had come a long way by the late 1850s. It had outgrown the rampant individualism of its frontier past and was proud of its many volunteer associations. Greensboro in the 1850s had beautiful houses, many distinguished citizens including two former governors, and confidence in its political and economic future. This was the world that Augustus Benners entered by marrying Jane Hatch, daughter of Alfred Hatch, wealthy slaveholder and planter. As Guy Ward Hubbs has written, "By entering an existing family network, [Southerners] were getting a headstart; and by building their homes near each other, neighborhoods became identified with families."[11]

Benners was not wealthy and, despite the support of his father-in-law, needed to find his own path. He decided to pursue the profession of law, a choice that opened the door to his future success. Greensboro had few lawyers and Benners quickly made a reputation for himself. Like many other Southerners, he found that the practice of law had many natural advantages, including ready access to information and the decision-making process and an insider's knowledge of an "area's

---

[9] Ibid., 58–59.
[10] Ibid., 69.
[11] Ibid., 37–38.

economic possibilities."[12] He found it was not difficult for a young lawyer to make a name for himself. Many young lawyers across the South were doing the same thing. A newspaper editor complained that "lawyers monopolized local offices...and the legal profession was a mere preparatory school for the training of politicians" and as such created "a sort of aristocracy."[13] Benners did not see himself as an aristocrat, but he saw opportunity for success and worked hard as planter, slaveholder, lawyer, and politician. He was also a family man and active in the Episcopal church. But it all began in the city of Greensboro where he lived and kept his journal for thirty-five years until his death in the summer of 1885.

---

[12] William L. Barney, *The Secessionist Impulse: Alabama and Mississippi in 1860* (Princeton NJ: Princeton University Press) 52.
[13] Ibid., 53.

Chapter 1

Prelude to War: 1850–1860

1850–1853

In the summer of 1850, Augustus Benners began a regular journal that he called a "Brief Memoranda of Crops, Seasons, Temperatures—rains and events." The first entry was 18 June, and he continued for the next thirty-five years until his death on 7 August 1885.

In the first three years, 1850—1852, his entries were abbreviated and usually about the weather, crops, and—occasionally—local events. At first, they were very short: "Saturday [June] 22. Ther. 3. oclock P.M. 90"; "Tuesday July 9th Ther. at 8 oclock, 76°. had heavy rain on Saturday and on Monday." Other entries were more detailed but largely about economic matters related to his plantation. Exceptions were his mentioning the conflict in Congress over the issue of slavery in the compromise of 1850 and the death of President Zachary Taylor. The next two years were very similar—many concerns about cotton, hot weather, and his slaves. In 1852, he began his diary at the beginning of the year rather than starting in June as in the two previous years. This time he referred to legal cases, the state Supreme Court, and his vacation at Bladen Springs.

Then, in 1853, he entered the wider world of politics. He was notified on 21 April that the Whig party nominated him for the Alabama legislature. Two months later, he began his political career.

June 25, 1853…. Our canvass commences on Monday at Newbern and will probably occupy 15 days—It will be a tiresome & disagreeable business. The disaffection of the Anti Liquor Whigs is likely to effect my defeat—

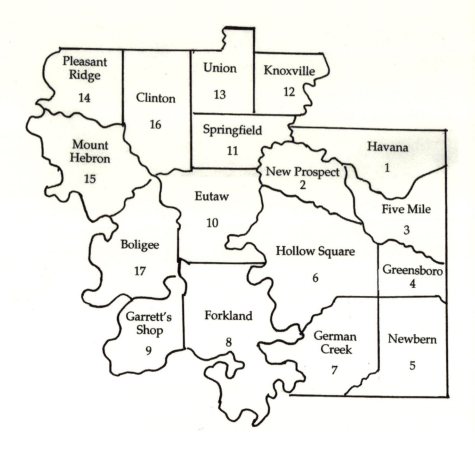

Precincts of Greene County, Alabama, 1858
Based on 1858 map by V. Gayle Snedecor

July 20, 1853. Having accepted the nomination of the Whig party for the lower house in the legislature—we commenced our canvass at Newbern on Monday the 27th day of June—there was quite a large company assembled, a good deal of interest having been excited on the Liquor selling question—Messrs Webb & Hunt were the Candidates for the Senate[1]—and Mr Inge & myself the Whig candidates for the House & Judge Coleman, the Democratic candidate for the house.[2] We were all called out on the Ala Liquor Law to know if we would support it & we each refused to do so or to advocate its claims and were told by the faction that if we did not agree to advocate it or its principles—they would have candidates of their own after us with a sharp stick. accordingly on tuesday the 28th of July Mr [Caswell C.] Huckabee appeared at Greensboro and announced himself a candidate for the senate and Mr Francis H. Hawks a candidate for the lower house[3]—The latter commenced the speaking in the morning in Kennedy's yard and stated in substance that as there were now no issues between the two parties he was a candidate not as a Whig or a democrat but as an advocate for what he called the majority principle i.e. that the Legislature should pass an act to give to the people in each county & beat the right by a majority vote to regulate the liquor traffic in their beats. which I opposed on the grounds that in the first place it was unconstitutional and could not be legally enacted—and that if it could it would be productive of more harm than good to the cause of Temperance. It was unconstitutional because the Constitution has provided that the legislative or Law making power should be vested in the senate and house of Representatives and has not conferred upon them the authority to delegate said power—That if the Legislature should pass such an act they have not passed an act which regulates the

---

[1] James D. Webb, lawyer; R. S. Hunt, grocer, Greensboro, Alabama (V. Gayle Snedecor, *A Directory of Greene County for 1855–6* [Mobile AL: Strickland & Co., 1856; ed. and indexed by Franklin Shackelford Moseley, Eutaw AL: *The Greene County Democrat*, 1957] 28, 45).

[2] Richard F. Inge and Wiley Coleman practiced law in Eutaw, Alabama. Ibid., 12, 24. Coleman was elected judge of county court of Greene County in 1846.

[3] Caswell C. Huckabee, planter, and Francis H. Hawkes, principal, Newbern Female Academy, Newbern. Ibid., 23, 21.

liquor traffic but have attempted to confer upon a majority in the beats the right to do so and thus to make a Law which by the Constitution can be done only by the two houses of the Legislature. That even if it were constitutional it would be productive of immense evil to the cause of Temperance because individuals being by this prohibitory law prevented from getting liquor by the glass or quart as they saw proper would furnish themselves with whiskey by the barrel and being thus furnished in large quantities would drink more than they now do. And that the multiplication of private barrels of whiskey in this way would greatly aggravate the evils of our negroes being furnished with spirits—my argument was by many considered a successful refutation of his positions—on Wednesday we spoke to a small company at Oak Grove—and here Mr Huckabee dwelt prominently on the fact that he was a planter & made good corn the best proof of which he said was the fact that it staid in his crib all the year round—The crop being very short in this neighborhood one of the neighbors is said to have come to him after his speech & endeavored to get some corn which Cass agreed to sell to him at 40 cts a bushel, about 60 cts under the market price—he did not get one vote at this precinct.

On Thursday we spoke at Havana—there seemed to be quite a favorable feeling to the Liquor law candidates at this box—But I think it was greatly less after the speaking than before—we spent the previous night at Mr Owens from Havana, from Havana we went to Mr Tutwilers at Greene Springs and the appearance of the old place where I had spent some happy days when I was younger brought them very forcibly to my mind—[4]

The next day friday we spoke at the flat woods—this was the place where the liquor law men had organised a league—Jim Anderson was warmly in their favor. He however did me the justice to say that my argument vs Hawks was as fair as he had ever heard[5]—That night we

---

[4] Professor Henry Tutwiler established Greene Springs Academy for Boys in 1847. Ibid., 68.

[5] James A. Anderson, planter, Clinton. Snedecor, *Greene County*, 6.

staid at Mr Wymes [Wemyss] & on Saturday spoke at Hollow Square—[6] The company was not very large—and Webb made a very good speech—I was also flattered with many compliments—from Hollow Square we went to Eutaw. Mr Webb and I, travelling as before in his buggy together. Sunday we remained in Eutaw and staid at Fields Hotel. On Monday being the 4th July we went to Springfield and spoke—there was a good turn out and we dined at Mr Clevelands. I was delighted with the Whig feeling I found prevailing here—Made many acquaintances—from Springfield we went to Tyrees & staid all night and the next day spoke at Knox's to a pretty good crowd.... A fight occurred as Cas [Huckabee] was speaking and he was left almost alone in his glory—we started with Mr Aquilla Hardy for his house where he had invited us to stay all night and were very lucky in getting over the worst road in Greene county to our destination just in time to escape a furious storm of rain wind thunder & lightning. Hunt[,] Hardaway[,][7] Webb & myself staid here all night—and the next day spoke at Union—dined with Billy Miller was much annoyed by a jack braying incessantly while I was speaking[8]—and lest someone else should say it for me desired him to be still and let us take it "one at a time." from Union we went to Clinton to Mrs Harkness hotel & the next day spoke at Pleasant ridge. There the Turn out was very small and we spoke in the open air under a tree. Pullam Carver a candidate who to use the language which was imputed to him could not read or write but was death on ciphering and was a candidate for Pickens County and was called out and made a speech after I finished mine—he commenced with the Pig & Puppy story which Cas had so frequently told and could not understand why we were so much diverted before he got to the funny part of it—Mr Philemon Kirkland invited Mr Webb and myself home with him where we spent the night and the next day spoke at Mt Hebron—Si Collins, Arnold Jolly & Ceph

---

[6] J. A. Wemyss was a commisson merchant in Mobile, Alabama, and Benners was a cotton factor. He was Jane Benners's uncle.
[7] Aquilla Hardy, farmer in Talladega County. 1860 US Census Talladega County, Alabama, population schedule, Court Hill post office, page 896, National Archives Micropublication M653, roll 24; William R. Hardaway, proprietor of the Exchange, Greensboro, AL. Snedecor, *Greene County*, 20.
[8] William Miller, commission merchant, Union and Mobile. Ibid., 31.

Wilson democrats had made a good deal of smoke here for the liquor law—appearing greatly to favor it[9]...—we felt much discouraged as to this box but the results shewed our fears were unfounded. We dined here with Dr Webb and after the speaking went to Mrs Harkness' Hotel in Clinton—Major Barry as good a Whig as the county can shew treated us very cleverly and we enjoyed fine bathing at his running over well.[10] We spoke the next day at Clinton and were much flattered by the reception of our speeches.

That night I staid with Mr Webb at the home of his brother Wm P. Webb Esq. at Eutaw and the next day (being sunday) I suffered all day from a violent headache—on Monday we spoke at Eutaw to a very large crowd in the Court house—and staid that night at Fields hotel—on tuesday morning we rode to Bradly Ridgeway's to breakfast and rode from there to Boligee where they had prepared a splendid barbecue[11]—The rain interrupted the speaking for a short time in the morning but being over the speaking proceeded—The ladies were in attendance at this precinct & they had a dance at Johnsons house after the speaking—Mr Webb & I went Home with Dr Perrins and the next day Wednesday spoke at Forkland—The company was not a very large but was a very intelligent one. I spoke first after dinner and immediately thereafter bid Webb & Mr Hatch[12] good bye and came home in my carriage which Jane had sent there to meet me—Mr Hardaway rode home with me. I found all well having been gone on the canvass just a fortnight.

On Saturday the 23rd day of July we had a speaking at Drakes Landing. Mr Hawks opened and I followed and then Judge Coleman & then Inge. Dr W. T. [Hendon] was present and placed himself very

---

[9] Pullam Carver, farmer. US Bureau of the Census, 1860 US Census, Pickens County, AL, population schedule, Olney post office, page 829, National Archives Micropublication M653, roll 20. Arnold Jolly, planter, Mt. Hebron; Cephas L. Wilson, planter, Mt. Hebron. Snedecor, *Greene County*, 25, 47.

[10] Major A. P. Barry, commission merchant, Mobile, Clinton. Ibid., 7.

[11] Bradley H. Ridgway, planter, commissioner of roads and revenue, Boligee, Eutaw. Ibid., 37.

[12] Alfred P. Hatch, Benners's father-in-law and a wealthy plantation owner with over 200 slaves, supported Augustus Benners in the early years of his career.

conspicuously in front of the speakers—He asked Inge some questions which he answered very much to the Dr's discomfiture. I rode home that evening & on Monday the day of the election I was at Clinton—staid at Mrs Harkness hotel—There was a very hard rain on the morning of the election, and the vote was a small one. I was however much gratified with the support I got which would have been greater but for the impression which got out among the democracy that the contest would be between Coleman & me causing them to take me off of their ti[c]kets and to put Hawks on. I was satisfied that I would be elected but was very agreeably surprised when I was waked up at Eutaw monday night of the Elections and told that I had rec'd 240 at Greensboro. I returned home tuesday night having got the printed return—before leaving.

The result of the Election was in the aggregate as follows

Hawks		228 in Greene County
Inge		895
Coleman		706
Benners		941*
Webb	(for senate)	921
Hunt		503
Huckabee		139

I was very much pleased with the vote I rec'd & especially with the vote given me at Greensboro & Hollow Square & 5 Mile—…

Benners regularly visited his two plantations—Cheney Place and Walker Place. They were ten miles from his home in Greensboro. He employed an overseer who was responsible for raising the cotton and supervising the work of his "hands"—he never referred to them as slaves. Often the weather was severe and the slaves ill.

August 22. I visited my plantation on saturday and before that on monday being the 7th Aug & saturday 20th Aug. The rains have been incessant and the misfortune is they still continued on the 7th it rained while I was there a flood & on saturday 20 again it rained in torrents.

How can the cotton stand such continued rains—The best I have is shedding the forms & squares and the bolls are rotting in addition to which the worm is quite numerous from all which I conclude that it is impossible to make a fair crop. Pitts wants to leave my employment—on account of wages he says but I think partly because the cotton crop is going to be short and he dont like to stay & bear the name of it. I consider it by no means good treatment to want to leave me at this time—I think he should have at least waited till the crop was housed—if not till the end of the year—Gray Huckabee[13] has enticed him from me by a promise of larger wages—which conduct is more in keeping with a selfish low live character than a gentleman.

September 7. Mr Hilliard Smith set in as overseer on the 27 aug. Jane and the children visited plantation with me last Monday and staid 3 days—all kept well and were much pleased with the trip. The cotton is much injured by the rain and worms—the red lands will make no top crop. I think if the present rainy weather continues I shall not make more than 175 bags—if that. Corn good—left Wash at Cheney place when we came away—he was of so little service under the management he had that I thot it best to remove him from the company of my children. [14]Mr Hatch came over to the Cheney Place when we were down there.

September 27. Visited Plantation on this day & returned next day—There are about 75 bales gathered Mr Smith thinks he will not get more than 160 bales—The cotton which in the spring was very promising was much injured by rain & worms. The uplands are very poor the bottoms have a good crop—they were gathering corn at Cheney place Aggy was sick—Emily about to be confined—Lewis sick—and Charles sick.

October 7. Visited the plantation on Tuesday morning and returned Wednesday. Found the hands at Walker Place gathering corn—the Pick

---

[13] Gray Huckabee, planter, Newbern. Ibid., 23.
[14] Among Benners's slaves, there is Big Wash, Wash, and Little Wash. In the unedited journal, Wash's name appears frequently as a driver who takes supplies to the two plantations. After the war, he remains with Benners and his last name is Grant.

room full of cotton. Lydia and Ellen sick. At Cheney Place found Smith sick—Aggy & Margaret were also sick—the rest of the hands were picking cotton. Pickroom nearly full—only six bales having been packed out since I was down here. The cotton is certainly the meanest I ever saw before frost and the crop will inevitably be a very light one—the corn gathering very well so the overseer says. My horse was taken sick from eating pumpkins & corn and I returned to plantation and drenched him with ash water. There is more rotten cotton than I ever saw before and very little top crop—only 60 bales packed and I suppose about 80 bales out.

In October, the family was struck with a tragedy—Gus Benners, three years of age, died.

October 27, 1853. We had a white frost on the morning of the 24—at 1/2 past 2 on that day my little boy Gus died. He had been seized with croup the night before, about 8 o.clock. My wife came down stairs and informed me that he had symptoms of it and I went immediately upstairs where he was sleeping to see him—he shewed some signs of it in his breathing but we were not alarmed at it—we applied a snuff plaster to his breast and greased and greased his little feet—it was a dreadful night—being unable to find Virgil[15] I started off in a hard rain for the Doctor, not that I considered him bad off but fearing that something might come of it. upon Doctor Webbs[16] arrival he manifested great alarm and administered an emetic of alum which operated promptly but did not relieve him. I was still of the opinion he was not very sick—again & again was he vomited but no relief his symptoms shewed little or no abatement. Spirits of turpentine was applied to his breast till it was raw—but no relief—I still did not permit myself to consider him dangerous—about 12 o'clock the Dr told me if he did not get relief in six

---

[15] Virgil was a house servant. He was one of five slaves listed in the 1860 slave census for Greene County who lived on Benners's property in Greensboro. Virgil remained with Benners after the war and was one of the drivers on the annual trip to Blount Springs.

[16] There were two Dr. Webbs in Greensboro: William T. and Henry.

hours he could not recover—oh my God how my heart sank at the announcement and how I watched the time—day came the six hours had passed and my sweet little Gus was still gasping with the horrid croup. Dr Osborne was called in to consult[17]—but could give no assistance & told me he would certainly die—oh how my heart chilled as I was told again & again there was *no change* in him—my poor little boy gasped on till after two o clock when I was told he was most gone. I hurried to his little crib and sure enough he was breathing his last the Dr was closing his eyes. my poor wife was weeping near him my little darling breathed a few small breaths and ceased to breathe forever—May God have mercy on us. he took our little cherub to himself. I know it was for his good and ours but oh how bitter to loose [*sic*] my little darling His smart little prattle will no more gladden my heart on earth never again will his fat little feet paddle out to meet his pa and give him a hug and a kiss—but God be praised he is still our child in Heaven—He was buried in the town graveyard on tuesday at Two oclock. Mr Hatch performed the service....

It was a sad Christmas for all the family, and especially for the father, who continued to grieve.

December 26, 1853.... Christmas was a cold day but clear. I missed my dear little Gus very much—and every thing reminded me of him. I try to think of him as an angel in Heaven. Betsey Vail, Mary Hatch and Parker Hatch who had been spending several days with us spent Christmas at my house. This is my birth day and how different are the feelings with which I note its return from those I once felt. Now I *feel* that each succeeding one brings me nearer to my lifes end. May I be ready and may my dear children profit by their fathers advice the result of experience—to learn early to obey God & keep his Commandments.

---

[17] Thomas C. Osborn, physician and druggist, Greensboro, AL . Snedecor, *Greene County*, 34. The doctor's name is misspelled Osborne in his drugstore ad in Snedecor, 80.

1854

For six weeks in January and early February of 1854, Benners served in the state legislature in Montgomery. The session involved state aid to railroads and the establishment of a system of free public schools in Alabama. He opposed any loans to the railroads and helped defeat the bill 54-40. Worried over the efforts to divert monies from the townships and put additional power in the hands of the superintendent of schools of Alabama, he brokered a compromise bill that provided funding for the public schools. He was already making a mark for himself as a leader in the legislature.

March 1, 1854. I left Greensboro on the 6th January to return to the Legislature at Montgomery which reassembled on the 9th having had a recess of 19 days during the christmas.... We arrived (Mr Webb & self) at Montgomery on the Emperor (Kirks boat) on the 7th took lodging at the Madison house at 12 a week—The session commenced on Monday—and continued till the 18th. The prominent and leading question during the session was State aid to Rail Roads. The first proposition known as the omnibus was for the Governor to issue State bonds to each of [the] roads at the rate of $8000 a mile which complied with the terms of the bill. This proposal gave great concern to the members who were opposed to the state incurring any additional liabilities—and its success was for a long time regarded as probable—& many speeches were made for it. I opposed it and made a speech against it in reply to Mr Curry of Talladega Chairman of the Com. of internal improvements.[18] after considerable parliamentary tactics we came to a vote and the bill was defeated by a vote of 54 nays to 40 ayes. The main reasons of my opposition to the bill were that the State already involved with a large debt should not whilst it was so considerable incur additional liabilities—and because from the geographical structure of the Country if The principle of indorsing bonds were initiated there was great reason to apprehend that in future all legislative freedom would be

---

[18] Jabez L. M. Curry was a Baptist minister, college president, professor, author, legislator, Congressman, and director of the Peabody Fund for Education. William Warren Rogers, et al., *Alabama: The History of a Deep South State* (Tuscaloosa: University of Alabama Press, 1994) 248.

destroyed by the coalition of the roads interested in getting more aid. The more especially as it would not be very difficult to persuade the people that future burthens which were now so useful to them would be no great incubus as the payment was to be so distant not less than 10 nor more than 20 years—After the defeat of the main bill, the attempt was made to divide out by an omnibus all the money in the treasury at the rate of $8,000 a mile to Railroads this passed the Senate and was defeated in the House. The Mobile & Ohio road received a loan of $400,000 for two years on mortgage & personal security. This I voted for considering it in a business view as proper—the security not only being ample but readily convertible into the money without embarrassing the operations of the Company—they having a great quantity of property which could be sold for the money before the loan would be needed. The other roads applying for aid having nothing with which to secure the State for advances but anticipated profits. I voted against loans to them.

The bill to establish a system of free public schools appropriating about $200,000 per Annum including 16th Section monies was also of great general importance. The feature of the bill diverting the 16th Section moneys from the townships to which it belonged I considered wrong as also the immense discretion vested in the superintendent. I for these & other reasons voted against the bill. The Bill introduced by me as a substitute for the Committee bill on the Statute of Limitations, to repeal Section 2502 of the code. After a hard battle over it was finally passed in both houses and is become the law—

The bill for a geological & agricultural survey of the State was also one of the general bills which I considered valuable—

Mr Webb and I left on friday night the 17th [13th] on the Magnolia & arrived at home on Saturday night the 18th February—having rode over a very bad road between Cahaba river & Hamburg—I found Alfred[19] quite sick when I reached home but recovering—and was much more delighted to get away from Montgomery than I had been to go there....

---

[19] Alfred Hatch Benners, eldest son of Augustus and Jane Benners, was born on 22 February 1849 in Greensboro, AL. He was five years old.

Benners worried about the individual slaves on his plantation, especially when they became ill. One of his favorites was Ned, who became ill in the spring of 1854. Benners contacted Dr. Hendon, a local physician, who treated him for several weeks. During that time, Benners watched closely as Ned fought for his life. Gradually, he got better, and Benners ceased to mention his name again until September when he wrote, "Ned carried down the mules on Sunday" to welcome back the Benners family from their vacation at Blount Springs.

May 12. Heard that Ned was very sick and went to plantation the morning of the 6th. I returned in the evening. found him very low with Pneumonia but something better than he had been....

May 15. Having rec'd a note from Dr Hendon that Ned was no better.[20] I went to the plantation on yesterday in the carriage and returned last night—found Ned very ill—respiration hurried pulse 120 tho some stronger than before—very weak—in his senses and wanting to eat something—hope he may recover but think that the chances are against him....

May 16. Rec'd word from Dr this morning that Ned on yesterday morning was no worse—and that if he got no worse to day he ought to recover—doubt it....

May 18. ... Ned was better and without a relapse likely to recover....

May 22. ... Ned is reported to be getting well—& Parker....

June 7. ... Ned is still very weak....

The deaths of his sister, Fanny, in July 1855, and William Murphy, a former law partner, in November 1855, saddened him deeply. Each had played an important part in Benners's life and he grieved deeply.

1855

July 17, 1855. Sister Fanny is dead! I had started in the Stage for Newbern on a visit to her when a letter from Isaac handed to me in the Stage as it tarried a short time at the hotel informed me of the fact.

---

[20] Dr. Benjamin F. Hendon, physician, Newbern. Snedecor, *Greene County*, 21.

Bitterly does my heart grieve for her loss—for during infancy, childhood & youth she was my dear, my constant unwearied friend & benefactress, and in her whole life no trace of selfishness was discerned—it was devoted to others—how much do I regret it was not permitted me to see her once more.... My Dear Sister farewell—Thou art gone to a fathers home—where the happiness in store for his children will compensate for all the cares, privations & afflictions of this mortal life. May the memory of thine excellence ever stimulate & encourage me to do good—and may God in his infinite mercy reunite us in his Heavenly kingdom for Christ's sake. She had been attacked with paralysis last August and her recovery was always considered improbable—but a few weeks since I rec'd a letter from Isaac saying that she was materially improved—on Friday before her death she was attacked with severe sick stomach and suffered much from it all that night and on saturday was considered better—on sunday she seemed to grow worse until tuesday 10th July when at 1/2 past one she died—Isaac's letter to me was a very short one and the foregoing are all the particulars of her death related—I have written to Edward [Benners] to day informing him of her death—and sent it to him at Jefferson Texas....

November 8, 1855.... heard to day of the death of Wm M. Murphy Esq. Poor fellow he had some noble traits and the death of no one would have caused more sorrow than of him, of a friendly disposition no one ever called on him for succor or assistance in vain. Alas poor Murphy—...[21]

1856

Benners rented, bought, and sold slaves during the 1850s. At the beginning of each year, he rented a number of slaves for work around his house; a contract was drawn up, usually about $130–$140 for the year. At the same time, he purchased and sold slaves. On occasion, he sold an entire slave family. Though

---

[21] William Murphy was a partner with Benners for several years in the 1840s.

Benners profited from the slavery system, he still considered it to be a "troublesome business."

January 1, 1856. The new years day has been on the whole a pleasant one tho quite cool part of the day cloudy and wet under foot. Not a great many people have been in town and I have hired only one negro to day. Mr Webbs Joe at $150 and he is to be allowed once in a while to come to town. Orris from Jno B Williams at $150 and Margaret & Phillis at $190 are all hired up to this time....[22]

February 21.... verily planting is a troublesome business—an everlasting want to supply—an everlasting fuss to settle—ever settling—ever giving. Never settled—never satisfied—I could wish I had never seen a negro—and dont in the least doubt I would have been more of a man if not a better one if I had never owned one—...

May 24. Sold Silvey and her five children on 21st May, Bonaparte, Frank, Wm. Henry, Jacob & Melissa to J. O. K. Mayfield[23] for $2,500—of which 1,600 was paid in a northern check and $900 in a draft accepted by the Palmers. And gave bill of sale signed by self & Wm. P. Webb as trustees—Payt for them was made by C. S. Bray as agent for Mayfield and I went up to the house opposite Southern University grounds where B. D. Palmer lives and where sd negroes were and there delivered them to said Bray as agent for Mayfield—He told Beckham to keep them for Mayfield till he called for them. Sent the bill of sale at Brays request to W. P. Webb to have registered and returned to him. delivery of negroes was made on 24th May 1856....

---

[22] Benners hired a few slaves each January, often the same ones.
[23] J. O. K. Mayfield bought Benners's slave family. Caswell S. Bray, planter and miller, Five Mile, Harrison, received the money. The slaves were kept by B. D. Palmer until the owner came to get them. It was a simple business transaction between two Greensboro planters and a planter from Harrison. Caswell Bray acted as the broker for the transaction, and William P. Webb, a lawyer and notary in Eutaw, registered the change of ownership.

The death of the wife of an overseer and the murder of a fellow planter depressed Benners. There had been few murders in Greensboro.

March 29, 1856. I went to the funeral of Mrs Boyd the wife of my overseer on the 28th March—she was taken on the 15th of March had a miscarriage and died on thursday 27th at one oclock and was buried in the Presbyterian burial ground on yesterday 28th at 12 oclock—she was a pious faithful industrious woman and her loss will be greatly felt by her husband and 4 little children whom she has left behind her—Before I reached Newbern I met a white boy riding—who informed me that Thomas R. Borden had been shot the night previous—in his bed asleep—thro the window with balls.[24] I found immense excitement in Newbern on account of it and went to the house where the murder had been committed and examined the place from which he was shot—he was lying on the bed, the head of which was between the front windows in the right hand room on the first floor—and the gun was fired thru the lower panes of glass of the side window—about 3 1/4 yards from where he lay—the balls entered his head making as I was told a large hole and scattering the brains. A number of men under Frank Hawks as magistrate were sitting as Coroners inquest in the office in the yard when I was there about Eleven oclock in the morning. Some one the night before he was shot had thrown a brick at the window as was said and shortly there after another brick was thrown upon which a gun was fired by Jim Borden. It was said that the dogs which were very ferocious made no noise—a strong suspicion existed that Jim Borden was the man who had done the deed—Mr Borden was buried on Saturday at 10 clock about which time Jim left.

April 2, 1856.... Jim Borden was arrested at Lauderdale Springs in Miss—and brought here yesterday evening—was before the magistrate today and trial put off till tomorrow—...

The approaching election in fall 1856 forced Benners to consider the possibility that a "black Republican" might be elected president. A

---

[24] Thomas R. Borden, planter, Newbern. Snedecor, *Greene County*, 8.

life long Whig, he had to choose between James Buchanan (Democrat), John C. Frémont (Republican), and Millard Fillmore (American party and Whigs). It forced Benners to change parties, and he became a Democrat.

October 21, 1856.... News of election in Pennsylvania is still very conflicting the Buchanan party claiming a triumph by a small majority & the Fil[l]more & Frémont fusionites also claiming that they have carried it. intense interest is felt in the result....[25]

November 3, 1856.... Tomorrow is the day for election of president & vice president of U States—intense interest is felt in the result. the South dreading the possible success of J. C. Frémont who is the candidate of the Black republicans. Filmore who is supported by the American party stands we think no chance and the best opinion is that Buchanan & Brackenridge will be elected. I shall vote for them, the destruction of the Whig Party by the formation of American party a know nothing party—having left me as it were without a party—and besides other objections to it believing that the American party has been measurably free soilized. I have felt it my duty to support the Democratic candidates believing that their platform of principles contains the true doctrine on the Slavery issue—non interference by Congress with the subject—May God in his mercy overrule the election to the good of our people....[26]

---

[25] Pennsylvania was a key state in the election of 1856. James Buchanan, the Democratic nominee, was from that state and needed a victory in order to win the election. Millard Fillmore, a former Whig president, was the candidate of the former Whig party and what was left of the American party. John C. Frémont was the choice of the Republican Party in their first effort to win the presidency; he hoped to attract former Democrats. The two parties agreed to combine; that is, to fuse in an effort to defeat Buchanan. The fusion effort was unsuccessful.

[26] Benners had no other choice since his stand on slavery required that it be protected from any interference by Congress or the federal government. He voted for James Buchanan who received 45 percent of the popular vote, 174 electoral votes, and won the election.

Benners was a successful cotton planter. He closely watched the price of cotton as it rose and fell. When the Panic of 1857 began in late September, many banks suspended operation and credit dried up. Benners feared that the price of cotton might fall. His answer was to hold on to his cotton until there was a fair price. He did not want to exchange his cotton for worthless currency.

1857

October 22, 1857.... Cotton has declined from 16 to 8 cts and in fact is reported dull of sale at that—this in consequence of the financial embarrassments which have put a stop to almost all kinds of business and the end of which no man can tell—all the Banks in New York have suspended—all in the N. East & the N. West and many in the South, the Central, the Commercial & Savings Bank in this state and Mobile, Southern & others are expected to follow. Negro men it is said have declined to $1000 and a great fall in all kinds of property is expected. I am determined not to sell my cotton until a change occurs—In fact we cannot get it to Mobile—the river being as low as it ever gets. A strange exemplification this present state of affairs of the treacherous character of outward appearances—but a short time since everything was inflated and every kind of property was commanding the most extravagant prices—negro men selling at 1600 and women at 12 and 1500—cotton at 16 cts and every outward appearance indicated a long continuance of this seeming prosperity—the sea which but a short time since was unruffled even by a ripple has been swept by a storm & many a tall craft foundered by its violence—and still it rages—and still Bank after Bank suspends and firm after firm is proving infirm and much distrust and fear for the future have taken the place of confidence & hope. I do not think that the Banks can speedily resume. I do not think they can act with sufficient concert & without this none can safely resume—but I do think cotton will improve and for a guess I will venture that it will sell for 10 cts by July next & crop be 3,100,000 bales....

October 30, 1857. The financial pressure is still severe and the gloomiest forebodings are indulged for the coming winter. The immediate question seems to be will the Mobile Banks suspend—and in either case of doing so or refraining there can be but little doubt that much trouble is ahead. It is said they are able to pay all their notes in specie—but while specie is in so much demand they dare not loan their notes for fear of a drain of specie—Now to suspend will relieve them from a fear of a drain and they could lend their notes and save the merchants if those who are the creditors of the merchants would take them, but this is only asking the planter to give his cotton which is specie for Bank notes which are rags—and which will certainly deteriorate—nor can it permanently relieve the pressure because it is too much to expect the state of inconvertibility to remain always—and whenever the bank prepares to resume she must bear on her customers & the extension of the loan has only been the extension of the trouble—but say you in the meantime the cotton will come in & the planter can pay the merchant and the merchant can then pay the bank—this is true but—what will the paper be worth which the planter who dont owe the Bank will get for his cotton—certainly less than par and he is coolly desired & requested to contribute to sustain the credit of the merchant by taking like a goose rags for specie, i.e. cotton—...

1858

During the 1850s, Benners practiced law but wrote little about his cases. He recorded ten visits to various courts in Alabama, chancery court in Eutaw, Perry county court in Marion, and Marengo county court. He does not provide any details except one entry on 12 April 1852: "Returned from Eutaw cir. co. on Sat. 10th aft. having been there since Monday 5th. Jury found no bills in case of Dillards negro. Civil case continued. Had much int. & excitement in case of Alexander vs Graham and Chapman." We do not learn what the excitement was. Dissatisfied with his law practice in the last years of the 1850s, he changed offices hoping for a "large practice."

January 9, 1858—on the last day of the last year I gave up the office of Dr Williams I had been occupying for 8 years and had my things carried home. on the 7th of Jany I moved into Gen R. D. Huckabees office for which I am to pay him sixty dollars for joint occupancy with him—on yesterday evening I hired Nancy from Dr Hill on trial for one month and if I like her am to give him $50. for the year....[27]

May 24, 1858.... I have agreed to give $600 for the office this side of J. D. Webbs & Owens is to have the title made to me by Dr Peterson who has never made a title to Stokes & Dupré from whom I purchase....

June 11, 1858. Having purchased the office lately owned by Dupre & Stokes, I had it put in order: I employed Bob Johnson to put up book cases and made Sip white wash and Virgil paint it. I waited several days for the smell of paint to get out of it and on yesterday I moved in. It is not altogether as pleasant a place as the office of Huckabee's but I did not like to feel in the way of the owner & two lawyers ought not to practice together unless in partnership, and preferred to occupy by myself—what will be the issue I know not, I can only hope for the best. I would be willing to do a large practice at the Law, but the prospect is not flattering.

Early in 1858, Benners visited his brother, Edward, in Jefferson, Texas. The trip to New Orleans, then Jefferson, and back to Greensboro took five weeks. It was full of new sights, adventure, and near disaster. He survived with exciting experiences to recount to his family.

February 17, 1858—on Monday the 11th day of Jany I started on horseback to Withers Ldg[28] to take the steam boat to Mobile on the way to New Orleans where my brother [Edward] had promised to meet

---

[27] Robert D. Huckabee, lawyer, Greensboro; Alabama Legislature Greene County 1857, 1859.

[28] Robert W. Withers operated a landing at Millwood on the Warrior River. He was most identified with the artesian wells of Alabama that were a sensation around the United States in the years before the Civil War. These wells played a significant role in the early prosperity of the Black Belt. Nicholas H. Cobbs, Jr., "Alabama's 'Wonder of the Earth,'" presidential address, Alabama Historical Association, Selma, AL, 16 April 1994.

me—It had rained very hard the night before I started and we found the roads very sloppy—and at the bridge before getting to the ldg a little difficult. the bridge being out of repair we kept the causeway—on reaching the landing I found the S. Boat Warrior had just arrived on her upward trip to Tuscaloosa and reported the Vivian had broke a flange and would not come up so I concluded to take the Warrior and at Capt Mays invitation went on her to Tuscaloosa[29]—it was quite tedious but I had an opportunity by going to see the country along the river and was very much pleased with the Warrior bottom lands tho the water being very high, they were not quite as attractive as they would be under other circumstances. We got back to Withers ldg and left there on the down trip on Wednesday about dinner time—and reached Mobile friday morning about 10 o clock. We had a very hard blow and rain as we went into Mobile—much damage was done by it to the shipping at Orleans and Galveston. I went to the Battle House thro the rain and staid til Saturday 2 o clock when I left on California for New Orleans. We had a very pleasant passage across. Bat Peterson of Barbour was going out to look for lands in Arkansas and one or two with him. I knew none of the other passengers, reached New Orleans Sunday morning 17th Feby [January] and stopped at Oviatts, where I found my brother. I was truly delighted to see him and more especially as he seemed to be in fine health and spirits. We enjoyed ourselves prodigiously going about & seeing what was to be seen—the performing elephants, the bearded woman, Siamese twins, Swiss Warblers—and King Lear—and the cemetery, the Cathedral & shopping & walking & riding generally. We attended Bishop [Leonidas] Polks church on Sunday and to my agreeable surprise Mr Dunn preached the sermon—on Wednesday evening we took the Caddo Belle for the town of Jefferson. I was much pleased with the magnificent estates on the Miss river—and can readily understand why their owners are unwilling to part with them, the strange appearance is presented all along here of a river higher than the country.

---

[29] James T. May, steamboat captain and warehouse keeper, Hollow Square voting precinct. Snedecor, *Greene County*, 29.

The Levee is about 4 or 5 feet high and 12 feet at its base—carriage & horses behind it can hardly be seen in some places by reason of the great depression of the country—the Red river which comes into the Miss about 250 or 300 miles from New Orleans takes its name from the color of the water which is red and arises from the color of the soil along its banks which is as red as red ocre. And the finest cotton lands I ever saw. I got pretty tired of my trip as we did not reach Jefferson till Wednesday Morning 27th Jany—We arrived before day and Edward and I left the boat and walked to his house about a mile—his family were all asleep but were soon aroused, a fire kindled in the parlor and we had a glorious reunion. Sister H looked very well tho the extraction of her teeth imperiled her good looks.[30] The breakfast being dispatched, Edward went to the Wharf in his buggy to send up our baggage & freight—and on its arrival the opening and distribution was delightful. he had bot a great many knicknacks and articles for presents for one and another and I had gotten a little carriage for my namesake Augusta Edwena and we all enjoyed it hugely. I spent two days & a half very pleasantly with my brother and could scarcely realise the fact that after so many long years of separation we were together once more at so distant a place as Jefferson [Texas]. There were two of his children with them, Henry and Augusta the infant. They were all well and in good health—I remained with them until friday 12 o clock—when I took passage on the Sunbeam for New Orleans. I need not say how sad I felt as I looked after my brother whom I was leaving on the shore—a thousand thoughts rushed thro my mind and with a heart full to overflowing I hastened out of sight. We had a disastrous trip but as all is well that ends well, I feel truly thankful for my escape and experience—Instead of keeping the regular navigation down the red river our capt Denslow concluded to go in by Red Bluff thro Bayou Pierre, a way steam boats had never before been and a pretty bad time we had of it—almost all the way the overhanging trees threatened to carry off our chimneys and at one place a raft which had been 30 years accumulating threatened to turn us back but the capt determined to force it. The boat was backed for a good start and with a

---

[30] His sister-in-law was Helen Donaldson Benners.

full head of steam stove into it—The crashing and parting of the huge logs of which the raft was composed gave proof of the prodigious power in requisition, again and again she stove into it and the third time she broke thro it—a shout of triumph greeted the parting of the raft and we were thro—again we stuck in the bayou wedged fast at the head & stern & middle in attempting to make a point which was too short for our boat & had to work 6 or seven hours before we got off. Our mate was knocked off the hurricane deck by an overhanging limb and nearly killed; at last we got to Point republic on Bayou Pierre—here we took 310 bales cotton and 30,000 staves and a passenger (Carlton) who pretended that he knew the bayou and could pilot us out—we left the Point about day break. the bayou seemed to improve and get wider affording good room for our boat which of itself was a great improvement on the narrow places we had gone thro—all hands felt much more cheerful and it really seemed as if we were going to come through—but alas for our poor short sightedness—we had scarcely seated ourselves at the breakfast table when a thundering crash—which scattered plates & saucers & almost threw us from our seats—apprised us we had struck a stump. I went immediately through to my state-Room to look out and see what was the matter, when on looking towards the bow of the boat I saw that the cotton was tumbling off and floating down the Bayou—I gathered my carpet bag and went up on the Hurricane deck—she was sinking—they attempted to launch the yawl—it sunk in the rapid current—The men declined to go in the boat on account of the rapidity of the current[.] at length the engineer and one of the hands took a line and tried to go ashore—they failed—this was with the captains gig. The negro cook and another man again made the attempt and this time without rope succeeded in getting to the shore—a line was thrown to them from the boat and by this a rope was hauled ashore and then the hawser. The yawl was now gotten up and the water got out of it and again launched—and I got into it by a line from the Hurricane deck. We succeeded in reaching the shore thro a very formidable current. We landed 5 at a time. The weather had got from bad to worse. What had been a rain had turned to a sleet and snow and this with the mud we had to stand in was very disagreeable. We kindled a fire, the full benefit of which we were prevented from receiving on acct of the high wind which smoked us considerably. We put up a tarpaulin but the thick smoke rendered it untenantable and a good many of the hands having come ashore and taken possession of our fire to cook their breakfast we had a very uncomfortable time—We remained at this fire about 1-1/2 hours and concluded by this time that it would be impossible for us to remain safely where we were and we must look out for shelter—We accordingly determined to move. Leslie the old french pilot who was presumed to know the country better than any one else said we could not get out that the high water had filled all the bayous in such a way that we could not possibly pass without swimming, but this could hardly be worse than standing still so we started—and a pretty rough time we had. the country was covered with water and occasionally we encountered smaller bayous making into the main one & there we had to wade across—sometimes to our breasts.

About six miles from our starting point we succeeded in making a man hear us across the Bayou and he came over and to our great satisfaction undertook to pilot us to the ferry which after wading 2 long miles we reached about dusk—here we came near another trouble—the woman on the other side of the Bayou who owned the ferry mistaking us for a parcel of drunken rowdies at first refused to let the ferrymen cross us but after a considerable parley our pilot who was known to her made fair weather for us and she told the hands to bring us the flat—and we crossed the wide and rapid Bayou safely. We were still two miles from any house and cold and wet but on we trudged and arrived at the house of a man named Silas about dark and just as it again commenced raining—he didnt want to take us but finally consented—& glad enough we were to stop. I got from him an old red flannel shirt and pair of drawers and shared a bed with an old schoolmaster who had already gone to sleep—and had a glorious nights sleep of it—in the morning I procured the two horse wagon of my host and went in it to Grand Ecore on the red river—here we waited 5 hours at a hotel kept by a negro man and his wife when the St Boat Empress came along and we took passage on her for New Orleans where we arrived safely on Saturday evening. I remained till Monday evening at the City hotel rooming with my fellow passengers of the Empress, 8 beside myself and as they drank and swore considerably it was not as congenial or agreeable as it might have been tho they were very clever and polite to me. I reached Mobile tuesday morning and left tuesday evening on the Wallis—and arrived at Eastport before day on thursday morning—took a carriage and got home at 9-1/2—road was pretty bad & mules dull—found all well. Children having all had the measles in my absence and gotten well of it.[31]

In summer 1858, Benners took a long trip to his childhood home in North Carolina and then to Washington DC. Two of his children, Fanny and Alfred, plus many members of the Hatch family accompanied him. The visit to New Bern brought back painful memories. He also attended a wedding of a cousin Mary Daves to the governor-elect of North Carolina, Judge Ellis, and called on President James Buchanan in Washington DC before returning home.

August 25, 1858. Wednesday. After an absence of one month I reached home on yesterday evening. I left home on the 25th of July on a visit to North Carolina—Mr Hatch & his sons and his daughters Caroline & Mary and my children Fanny and Alfred accompanied me. We all left my house in Hacks at 3 o clock in the Morning and reached Marion in time for the train at 8-1/2 o clock; reached Selma by Railroad at 12-1/2 o clock, found the Coosa Belle there and went immediately on board for Montgomery and reached there about 12 o clock at night. laid over at Montgomery until evening to wait for Richd W Hatch & party who left with us in the cars for West Point at 9-1/2 o clock on Monday evening. We reached Augusta on tuesday evening and remained there...till Wednesday morning—leaving Augusta on Wednesday morning at 8 o clock we reached Columbia same evening. left Columbia Wednesday evening at 7 o clock and by the way of Charlotte—Salisbury, Hillsboro, reached Raleigh thursday morning 7 oclock. The rest of the party proceeded on to Newbern. I remained over with the Children until Friday morning having dined at Cousin Jane Haywoods and taken tea there, we stopped at Yarboroughs Hotel, on friday morning we left for

---

[31] This trip lasted thirty-six days, from 11 January to 16 February 1858.

Newbern at 9 o clock and reached there at 4 o clock by the Rail Road. I found Newbern so much altered I should not have known it but for knowing I was in *that* Town. The old houses looked very much dilapidated and not repaired or cared for and not many good new ones had been erected. the principal change was at and about the depot & Rail Road—the Houses are back of the old Stephens house & have very much changed the appearance of that part of the town. It looked very strange & unnatural to ride thro the streets of Newbern on a Rail Road—at the foot of the street one of the best bridges I ever saw, spans Trent river which is here a half of a mile wide—we stopped at the Gaston House where we found our party had arrived and put up the night before. The first place I went to before sunrise on the following morning was to the grave of my mother—and here in solemn silence I seemed to hold communion with my dear departed Mother. Here I lingered and in all the truthfulness of reality seemed that I could see her dear face and hear the tones once more of her affectionate voice that was to me always the voice of love—How many scenes rushed upon my memory—how I prized that Love she had shown to me and how forcibly I felt the truth—that whatever I was—of good under God I owed it to her—May God give me grace to walk in this world so that I may meet her in her heavenly Home—Here too in an adjoining lot are the remains of my beloved sister Fanny for whom I always entertained the warmest affection and from whom during her life I never heard any other than words of tenderness & affection. Peace to her—the best of Women. Sister Sally lies buried next to my mother and I could fondly recall the words of kindness and goodness spoken by her. John Brame is buried next to his Mother—and oh how my heart swelled within me as I thought of other days passed with him. he was a gifted man—and a most excellent one. Well he did his duty on earth as he understood it and God has taken him early to himself in Heaven—Here were gathered the remains of what had been to me the dearest earthly objects—and here was all that was left on earth of those my soul loved well. oh what a mystery is life—what a mystery is death. Oh God of our Spirits give us strength to believe & trust—

I went to church on Sunday and as old times and the memory of my dear Mother came over me I could not restrain my feelings which gave themselves vent in tears—So few of the many familiar faces were there—it was painful—and in fact I was glad to leave Newbern there was so much of sadness to me in everything there. We spent 8-1/2 days at Beaufort and I returned on tuesday the 3rd August to Newbern. I enjoyed my trip to Beaufort very much. the fishing and sailing & bathing were fine. I went one day to sea fishing in an open boat and took Alfred along, he was very sick from the rolling of the billows. We got very wet from a hard rain returning. We visited the fort once or twice—and attended a pony penning about 15 miles from Beaufort. These marsh ponies as they are called are foaled from mares running loose & wild on the banks—the mares are put over there & breed there. at a certain day named[,] the folks all assemble and the mares & ponies are driven up in herds into a pen made of rails or poles. the scene is a very exciting one as the large herds are seen coming along from a great distance driven by the men, and as they approach others are overtaken and join the gang and some times when all penned they number 500—there were not more than 200, the day we were there.

We returned to Beaufort in a Steam boat—The fishing there is almost altogether with a lead line, a weight is attached to the end of the line & the hooks are placed just above it—this is run out till it reaches the bottom and as soon as a fish strikes it you can feel it and of course proceed to pull him up & throw out again. They bite very fast—we had many very pleasant sailing excursions & the bathing was delightful. In Newbern to which I returned on tuesday the 10 August I attended the wedding of cousin Mary McKinley Daves to Judge Ellis, the Governor elect of that State. The marriage took place in the Church. And I waited on Cousin Betsy Daves. After the marriage we had a very pleasant party at Cousin Betseys—we stopped during our stay in Newbern at the Gaston House and on friday the 13 August at 8-1/2 left in the cars for Old Point Comfort via Goldsboro—we paid from Beaufort to Newbern $2.00 from Newbern to Goldsboro $2.25. We went to Weldon to Dinner; on Saturday (fare 2.75); by the Seaboard & Roanoke Rail Road to Portsmouth fare $4.00 to Old Point. 50 cts which we reached

Saturday night to supper Aug 14th. Staid at Old Point Sunday & Monday & left Monday evening at 7 o clock for Washington City—at Old Point we were much pleased with the fine bathing &c it is a beautiful place tho not so accessible to breezes as Beaufort. the bathing is fine. We reached Washington to Dinner. on tuesday morning visited the Capitol & Presidents house same evening. Next morning visited patent office & Smithsonian institute and Presidents house. Called on the President Mr Buchanan—were much pleased with him and with our visit[32]—Alfred was particularly so—We left Washington City on our way home on Wednesday evening by the upper route as it is called. from Washington City we took a thro ticket to Montgomery for which we each paid $32. We went to Alexandria on S. Boat. From Alexandria to Gordonsville by the Alexandria & Orange Rail Road, thence to Richmond. Thence by the South side rail road to Lynchburg. From Lynchburg by Va & Tenn Road to Bristol by the way of Montgomery White Sulphur Springs where we stopped two days—I consider the country thro which we passed on this route as the most picturesque I ever saw and was delighted with the changing Landscape as we passed along—it is really a matter of wonderment that the enterprise should have ever been projected & completed of constructing a road thro these mountains which had in many places to be cut down to immense depths—and over which in places very high bridges had to be built—and thro which tunnels were dug, one of which was 660 yards thro—We passed the peaks of Otter—on the road—we were greatly delighted with the Springs and found Two blankets quite comfortable. Dr Taylor & Lady & Gov. Winston were the only acquaintances I met there. We left on Saturday the 21 August and came on by Wytheville Abingdon &c to Bristol which is on the line between Va and Tenn. here we took the E. Tenn & Va Rail Road to Knoxville. and thence the Ga & Tenn R. Road to Dalton and then the Western & Atlantic Rail Road to Atlanta—and there the W Point & Atlanta R Road to West Point, and there the Montgomery & West Point Rail Road to Montgomery and then the Stage to Selma. Rail Road to Marion. Stage home tuesday 24th Aug '58.

---

[32] James Buchanan served as the fifteenth president of United States from 1857–1861.

A number of comets passed near the Earth in the years from 1858 to 1860. Benners observed them and gained an interest in the operation of the solar system. Later in life he would often wake up his children in the middle of the night to observe a comet or a meteor shower. There was a spectacular Leonid meteor shower in Alabama the night of 12–13 November1833, which resonated in the consciousness of Alabamians many years afterward.[33]

July 10, 1858.... There [is a] comet visible or as Ed calls it a star with a tail to it—it is quite small...barely visible in N. West—[34]...

September 17, 1858.... The comet is reported as visible and was seen by many of our citizens last night and this morning....

October 7, 1858. There is now to be seen of an evening about 7 o clock a very brilliant and beautiful comet[35]—the appearance of which is striking and grand. It first was seen of an evening in the North West—now it is almost due West and seems to be moving very rapidly in a Southerly direction. It is supposed to be the one that returns at intervals of 300 years tho this is rather conjecture than certainty....

A continuing problem for Benners was the poor health of his family and slaves. They constantly needed medical attention, which was so inadequate that he lamented, "I fear the doctor as much as the disease." Early in 1860, a baby boy, William Haywood, was born; it was a happy occasion. Sadly, Benners lost two children to disease later in the same year, the first on 29 May and the second on his annual vacation at Blount Springs.

1860

January 20, 1860. I visited the plantation on Monday the 16th and came home on 17th having been detained the week before by my wifes being

---

[33] John C. Hall, "When Stars Fell on Alabama," *Alabama Heritage*, no. 55 (Winter 2000): 16–23.

[34] Comet C/1860M1 (Great Comet). Passed closest to Earth on 11 July. Gary W. Kronk, *Cometography, A Catalog of Comets*, 3 vols. (Cambridge: Cambridge University Press UK, 2004) 2:284–88.

[35] Comet C/1858L1. (Donati). Passed closest to Earth on 10 October. Kronk, *Cometography*, 2:268–76.

confined on 11th with a boy then born [William Haywood]—She is doing well up to this time and I trust will recover without her usual set backs....

June 4, 1860. Again it has pleased our Heavenly father to visit us with severe affliction by the death of our sweet little darling James Marbury Benners. He died at Arcola May 29 after a sickness of four weeks.[36] He was taken on the 1st May with dysentery—and the Doctor was called in—the violence of the disease seemed overcome and it changed to a form of low fever with dyarrhaea—his discharges being of a deep green color and of very strange odor—in vain were remedies applied—the darling child lay like a patient little sufferer ebbing his life away—and by his ineffable beauty & sweetness winding around our hearts if possible more strongly than ever. He was a great favorite with all—just beginning to talk and his little voice when he would say I, I Ride the last words he ever spoke—was melody itself He was 1 year and nine months old at the time of his death—he was brought up from Arcola on Wednesday the 30th May & buried in my lot in the town burying ground south of his little brothers grave—there my two sweet little ones await the last trump when they shall come forth to be clothed with immortal bodies. His early death has removed him from a world of sin and sorrow to a safe home in Heaven—and to the eye of reason we should not weep for him—but oh! the pang of parting with our darling little one is bitter—his death has made a large void in our home circle—and a heavy sorrow on our hearts—may we have Gods grace to enable so to live that when we come to die we my go to meet our dear departed children at Gods right hand—For Christ's sake Amen!

Vacations were important to Benners and his family. They took four extended vacations during the 1850s—to Mobile, Bladen Springs, and two to Blount Springs. The last one started off as a leisurely trip but ended up with the burial of a son, Lucas, on a hillside in Alabama.

---

[36] James Marbury Benners was born on 2 September 1858 and died on 29 May 1860. He was named for James Marbury, a former rector of St. Paul's.

October 12. On Tuesday the 24th day of July I started with my family from Greensboro for Blount County. My wife, six children and myself composed the white family[,] Emline, Celia, Mary, Jenny & Kit the negroes & Ed and Ned drove the wagons, one the six mule the other the two mule wagon and Virgil drove the carriage—I rode in my buggy—The summer had been oppressively hot—and it still continued so. We got off about 7 o clock—and after a very hot ride got to Turner Harpers 8 miles—where we made our first stop & took our breakfast. I was delighted at the prospect of getting with my wife and little ones to a cooler climate and little dreamed that our dear little Lucas would return with us no more. We dined at the 14 mile branch and camped at the Church. had a pleasant night and got a good start next morning—after breakfast. Wednesday 25 we dined at Harris spring and enjoyed our stay here very much—Camped that night at Howards near Centreville 40 miles from home. Thursday the 26th we stopped for dinner two miles from Scottsville—and were a good deal troubled at the sickness of one of our wagon mules and galding [galling] of another. Camped that night at Marshal, 19 miles from Centreville—Friday 27th we took dinner at Pattersons Spring—4 miles beyond Davis—and camped that night at Academy Spring near Jonesboro. Saturday 28 left camp after early breakfast and stopped in Jonesboro out of the rain, had to remain here till after dinner on acct of the creek getting up—started after dinner and after crossing creek, tongue of Little Wagon broke and we had to send back to Jonesboro & get it mended very hot, road heavy. Family went on to Smiths where we waited for wagons and there concluded to stay all night. Next day Sunday we dined at Hawkins plantation and as the night was rainy put up with Cliffs 15 miles. The next day Monday we took breakfast at Belchers—dinner at the river & travelled that night to L. D. Hatchs 24 miles next day to Valley Hill. We carried corn up with us but bot it along where we could & paid 1.50 cts in every instance & 40 cts for fodder. I found upon arrival that the rooms I had ordered built were not finished—but were nearly so. We got into one of them in about a week and to the other 3 weeks. Provisions were higher than the year previous chickens 12-1/2 & 15 cts—butter d[itt]o—Mutton 6, Eggs 12-1/2. The nights were delightful and I never enjoyed walking any where more than at Blount during my stay. We had of course some set backs but could have done finely—but our Heavenly Father in his wisdom & goodness took from us our dear Little boy Lucas.[37] He died 19th September having been sick abed only 5 days. his disease seemed to be a throat affection the ulcerations probably extending to his stomach. May God forgive me if I repined or grieved more than I ought but it was a bitter cup—Oh my Darling child how my heart still bleeds when I think we had to leave him behind. his little grave on the mountain's side. God's will be done—I know it is for the best—both for him and us, but oh how hard to give him up. Bless the Lord oh my Soul—who forgiveth thy sin & healeth thine infirmity. We started home from Blount Springs on Monday 1st October. Ed had had the croup Saturday & Sunday and we were very much perplexed as to the propriety of starting but the Dr (Mabry) advised to start—the weather was very unpromising—looked stormy and lowering but strange to say though it was damp warm drizzly and rainy Ed got better and we considered him nearly well when we reached home.

October 1st the first night out we stayed at Davenports, I slept in the tent—2nd at McWilliams—3rd at McMaths 4th at Howards—5th at the Church 6th home. This trip was an exceedingly disagreeable one on account of our uneasiness about Ed and by reason of the bad weather—and the only pleasant time was our stop at the church. We reached here about 2 o clock and I determined to halt and rest all hands we carried our mattresses into the church & had a fine rest as well as fine fare for the night—next morning we started for home—dined at Harpers left there at 3 & arrived at the end of our journey about sun down.

The Christmas season of 1860 was a hard time for Augustus Benners. He was still grieving—"My heart bled as I filled the little stockings, and thought of the missing ones." There seemed so little for which to be grateful. Many members of the family were ill, and the weather remained severe.

---

[37] Lucas Benners died on 19 September 1860. He was buried on the mountainside near Blount Springs. Benners lost two sons within four months.

Benners's mood had not improved when he made his last journal entry for 1860, in which he reflected on the sad state of affairs in the country and the growing possibility of war.

December 29, 1860.... The season is one of deep gloom—the election of Lincoln president of the U. States has produced such intense dissatisfaction in the Southern States that revolution is imminent. S. Carolina seceded on the 20th Dec and the news was rec'd by telegraph last night that the Fort Moultrie had been abandoned by Anderson and the U States officers and set on fire. we are on the eve of great events.[38] How they will terminate God only knows. in war and anarchy I much fear. In God is our trust.

---

[38] Major Robert J. Anderson was sent to Charleston to head the Union garrison at Fort Moultrie. He reported it to be undefensible against a land attack. The War Department gave him discretionary orders to move his men to Fort Sumter if he thought an attack was imminent. Fearing such an attack on the night of 26 December, he spiked Moultrie's guns and transferred to Sumter. The Confederacy immediately seized Moultrie and demanded that Northerners evacuate Charleston harbor. They refused and remained in Fort Sumter until 13 April 1861, when Anderson's garrison was permitted to depart after saluting the flag.

Chapter 2

The Civil War Years: 1861–April 1865

1861

January 7. The year has gone out & the new one been ushered in amidst the deepest excitement and gloom. The election of Lincoln by the Black Republicans of the North has been considered as the culminating of intended aggressions on the institutions of the Southern States.[1] S. Carolina by her convention seceded from the Union on the 20th Dec. and to day the convention of Alabama meets to do as I believe the very same thing—Civil war seems imminent every mail comes freighted with exciting intelligence and mens minds are filled with gloomy apprehensions for the future—The forts at Charleston have been taken, fort Sumter is besieged by S. Carolina and the forts of Ala have also been captured. Where it will end God only knows may he give us courage & wisdom to do our duty as men.[2]

January 16. The U. States sent the Star of the West to reinforce Major Anderson at fort Sumter—on the 11th she was fired into by S. Carolina from Morris Island and hit 3 times trying to get in—she retired—[3]The expectation is now that U. States will send more troops with larger ships of war and the battle will begin—It is hard to give any idea of the distressing gloom and sadness that pervades all classes.

---

[1] *Black Republicans* was a derogatory term applied to Northern antislavery Republicans by proslavery Democrats, who accused Republicans of seeking total equality for the African race.

[2] South Carolina, by a vote of 169–0, was the first state to secede.

[3] The *Star of the West* was a merchant vessel commissioned by the US Army to help fortify Fort Sumter. It was driven back by fierce fire from South Carolina troops.

Alabama seceded on the 11 Jany—Mississippi has also & Florida—our Company of L[ight] A[rtillery] Guards went last Sunday to Fort Morgan. it was a sad parting and many a brave spirit may be lost in battling for his countrys right[4]

February 11. I started with Judge [Sydenham] Moore on last Friday to Montgomery to attend Southern Congress which met on the 4th.[5] We got left by Cars at Newbern and I went to my plantation and spent the night. They were reported all well, but had had a tremendous rain friday previous 1st Feb. Herrin was sowing oats on the land between the well and the house—had received 50 bushels from Mobile via Selma. The roads were in bad condition—next day took cars to Selma and having learned sessions of Southern Congress were secret and being pretty well worn out in Selma waiting for a boat we returned on Sunday—Mr. [Francis Strother] Lyon from the legislature & Price were in the Cars.[6]

March 7. Commenced planting corn at plantation on Monday March 4th. On Wednesday March 6th we had a white frost and again this morning—much uneasiness is felt lest the fruit has been killed by the cold. Tom brot up a load of fodder on yesterday—Lincolns inaugural was received last night and is considered very warlike. Probably before new hostilities have begun—perhaps at fort Sumter—he denies the right of secession and says that he must collect the revenues and possess the forts—The prospect of a war is very imminent—[7]

---

[4] Fifty-seven members of the Greensboro Guards received orders to join the garrison at Fort Morgan. It was the larger of the two forts taken by Alabama troops on 5 January 1861—the other was Fort Gaines. Guy W. Hubbs, "Guarding Greensboro, A Confederate Company and the Making of a Southern Community"(Ph.D. diss., University of Alabama, 1999) 142–43.

[5] The first meeting of the Provisional Congress of the Confederate States of America was convened on 4 February 1861 in Montgomery, Alabama.

[6] Francis Strother Lyon, member of Alabama House of Representatives 1861 and the Confederate Congress 1862–1865. *Biographical Directory of the American Congress 1774–1949* (Washington, DC: US Government Printing Office, 1950) 1486.

[7] Abraham Lincoln's inauguration as the sixteenth president of the United States occurred on 4 March 1861 in Washington DC. During his address, Lincoln stated that although he was not opposed to slavery where it already existed, the secession of the Southern states was an act of war.

BY TELEGRAPH.
THE WAR BEGUN!

THE SURRENDER OF FORT SUMTER DEMANDED!

ANDERSON REFUSES TO COMPLY

Correspondence between Secretary Walker and Gen. Beauregard!

Matters have at last reached a crisis at Charleston. Our Government have formally demanded the surrender of Fort Sumter, and this demand Major Anderson refuses to comply with. The following is the official correspondence between Secretary Walker and Gen. Beauregard, who is in command of the Confederate States forces at Charleston, relative to the Fort:

No. 1. Gen. Beauregard's dispatch to the Secretary of War:

CHARLESTON, April 8, 1861.

To L. P. Walker:

Authorized messenger from Lincoln just informed Gov. Pickens and myself, that provisions will be sent to Sumter, peaceably, otherwise by force.

(Signed) G. T. BEAUREGARD.

No. 2. Reply of Secretary of War to Gen. Beauregard:

MONTGOMERY, April 10, 1861.

Gen. Beauregard, Charleston:

If you have no doubt of the authorized character of the agent, who communicated to you the intention of the Washington Government, to supply Fort Sumter by force, you will at once demand its evacuation; and if this is refused, proceed in such manner as you may determine to reduce it. Answer.

(Signed) L. P. WALKER.

No. 3. Gen. Beauregard to the Secretary of War:

CHARLESTON, April 10, 1861.

To L. P. Walker:

The demand will be made to-morrow at 12 o'clock.

(Signed) G. T. BEAUREGARD,
Brigadier General.

No. 4. The Secretary of War to General Beauregard:

MONTGOMERY, April 10, 1861.

General Beauregard, Charleston:

Unless there are special reasons connected with your own condition, it is considered proper that you should make the demand at an earlier hour.

(Signed) L. P. WALKER.

No. 5. General Beauregard to the Secretary of War:

CHARLESTON, April 10, 1861.

To L. P. Walker:

The reasons are special for twelve o'clock.

(Signed.) G. T. BEAUREGARD.

No. 6. Gen. Beauregard to the Secretary War:

CHARLESTON, April 11, 1861.

To L. P. Walker:

Demand sent at two. Allowed till six to answer.

(Signed.) G. T. BEAUREGARD.

No. 7. Secretary of War to Gen. Beauregard.

MONTGOMERY, April 11, 1861.

Gen. Beauregard, Charleston:

Telegraph reply of Anderson.

(Signed.) L. P. WALKER.

No. 8. Gen. Beauregard to the Secretary of War:

CHARLESTON, April 11, 1861.

To L. P. Walker:

Maj. Anderson replies:

"I have the honor to acknowledge the receipt of your communication demanding the evacuation of this fort, and to say in reply thereto, that it is a demand with which I regret that my sense of honor and of my obligation to my Government prevent my compliance." He adds, verbally, "I will await the first shot, and if it do not batter us to pieces, we will be starved out in a few days."

Answer.

(Signed) G. T. BEAUREGARD.

No. 9. Secretary of War to Gen. Beauregard:
                    MONTGOMERY, April 11, 1861.
Gen. Beauregard, Charleston:
  Do not desire, needlessly, to bombard Fort Sumter. If Major Anderson will state the time at which, as indicated by him, he will evacuate, and agree that in the meantime he will not use his guns against us, unless ours should be employed against Fort Sumter, you are authorized thus to avoid the effusion of blood. If this, or its equivalent, be refused, reduce the Fort, as your judgment decides to be the most practicable.
  (Signed)   L. P. WALKER.

No. 10. Gen. Beauregard to the Secretary of War:
                    CHARLESTON, April 12, 1861.
To L. P. Walker:
  He would not consent. I write to-day.
  (Signed)   G. T. BEAUREGARD.

No. 11. Gen. Beauregard to the Secretary of War:
                    CHARLESTON, April 12, 1861.
To L. P. Walker:
  We opened fire at four, thirty minutes.
  (Signed)   G. T. BEAUREGARD.
  Note. Intercepted dispatches disclose the fact that Mr. Fox, who had been allowed to visit Major Anderson on the pledge that his purpose was pacific, employed his opportunity to devise a plan for supplying the fort by force—and that this plan had been adopted by the Washington Government, and was in progress of execution.

PROGRESS OF THE BOMBARDMENT!

Nothing has transpired up to the hour of going to press, except that we learn MAJOR ANDERSON is returning the fire of GEN. BEAUREGARD. At last accounts the fleet had not been heard from.

Expressly for the Advertiser.

Important from Washington!

Departure of the Commissioners!

They Accuse the Administration of Perfidy!

                    WASHINGTON, April 12, 1861.
  The Southern Commissioners left here yesterday for the South, the Black Republican Administration having refused to receive them in a diplomatic character.

  The Commissioners, before their departure, wrote a letter to the Administration, saying that if hostilities between the two governments should occur, the responsibility will rest upon their heads. They repeat that they had almost daily indirect assurances that Fort Sumter would positively be abandoned, and the efforts of the government directed towards bringing about a peaceful termination of the difficulties which have caused the revolution now agitating the country; but under this pretext and assurance, an immense armada, with hostile intent, has been dispatched to provision and re-inforce the different forts within the confines of the Confederate States.

  The Commissioners boldly accuse the Administration of gross perfidy, and announce their intention of returning to the outraged people of the Confederate States, and expressing to them their firm conviction that war is inevitable.

WASHINGTON, April 10, 1861.

Sumner to-day called on Seward, and urged upon him the propriety of recognizing the independence of Hayti.

WASHINGTON, April 1[?]—[?] p. m.

Lincoln's reply to the Virginia Commissioners in writing, is to the effect that he will act according to the programme laid down in his inaugural address—that is, hold the public property, and defend it with all the means in his power. He disclaims any intention of waging war (?) against the seceding States, and says he intends to act on the defensive.

[SPECIAL DISPATCH TO THE ADVERTISER.]

CHARLESTON, April 13—1:30, p. m.

Major Anderson has hauled down the United States flag from Fort Sumter, and run up the white flag.

The Fort has been burning for several hours from the effect of shells. Two explosions have been produced by shells.

Maj. Anderson has ceased firing for some time, while the fire of all the batteries of Gen. Beauregard has been continued untill now.

Aids have been sent by Gen. Beauregard to Fort Sumter.

[EXPRESSLY FOR THE ADVERTISER.]

CHARLESTON, April 13—[?] p. m.

Fort Sumter has surrendered. Nobody is hurt on either side.

Valuable Recipes.

This is said to be worth $1000, to house keepers:

For Washing Clothes.—Take one pound of Soda, and half a pound of *unslacked* lime, put them in a gallon of water, and boil for twenty minutes. Let it stand till cool. Then drain it off and put it in a jug or other tight vessel for use. Soak your dirty clothes over night or until thoroughly wet. Then wring them out and rub on plenty of soap, and in one boiler of clothes, well covered with water, add one tea-spoonful of the above washing fluid, boil half an hour briskly, and then wash the clothes thoroughly through one suds, and rinse well through two waters, and your clothes will look better than the old way of washing twice before boiling. This receipe is invaluable, and every poor tired washerwoman should have the benefit of it. With a patent tub to do the little rubbing required, the washing will almost do itself.

To Clean Guns.—Wash your gun barrel in Spirits of Turpentine by dipping a rag or sponge into the liquid, fastened on the gun rod, and swob it out two or three times, when it will be cleansed from all impurities, and can be almost instantly used, as the Turpentine will evaporate and leave the barrel dry. And even if used a little moist, will not make any material difference. After being cleansed thus, there is no danger of rust, as when water is used.—*Scientific American.*

April 15th, 1861. I went to plantation on the 12th and returned on the 13th. Carried Fan with me. The corn had come up very pretty, Cotton was coming up but looked yellow, Oats looked tolerably well and potatoes were beginning to put up. Have had so far a very propitious time for planting. Had given out the shoes except a few which would not fit. The overseen reported that he had hauled all the cotton nine bales to the river — said he had rec'd two barrels flour from London. Hands were building bridges on the road across dry creek. To day is 1st day of court and a stormy day it is. Raining and blowing as if it would blow its last. I am expecting not to go till to morrow the river is very high. Lidia's child at Walker Place died of Pneumonia on 8th inst.

Benners made few entries in the critical months leading to the outbreak of war. Apprehensive and gloomy, he seemed uncertain as to what to write down. From 8 March to 14 April he clipped out articles from the Montgomery Advertiser *and pasted them in his journal. The clipped articles are included to give the reader an idea of what he was reading.*

For the next few months, Benners read about the war but made no reference in his journal until June 1861.

April 15. I went to plantation on the 12th and returned on the 13th Carried Fanny [his daughter] with me. The corn had come up very pretty & cotton was coming up but looked yellow. oats looked tolerably well and potato slips were beginning to put up. Have had so far a very propitious time for planting. Had given out the shoes except a pair which would not fit. The overseer reported that he had hauled all the cotton nine bales to the river—said he had recd two barrels flour from landing. Hands were building bridge on the road across dry creek. To day is 1st day of court and a stormy day it is. Raining and blowing as if it would blow its last. I am expecting not to go till to morrow the river is very high....

April 24. Visited plantation and returned on yesterday—Corn looks very well—fine stand cotton has been looking sickly from cold but was improving—have been over corn & chopped out right smart of the cotton—Give Burke a thrashing for impudence and coming up here—Sent down 7 pair shoes having taken back 5 pair [illegible] for Spring 62 pair—...

May 31. on the 28th I went fishing at Ke[a]ting lake. We had a very pleasant ride and took our dinner on the road at a meeting house 3 miles from Carthage. fine spring and pleasant place. Messrs Wemyss, Hill, Alfred & T. F. Witherspoon & Lem Hatch, were of the party—We stopped at Mr Browns in Carthage. Caught bait—and went to Keyton lake next morning—Mr Brown refused to take any pay from us and his hospitality & politeness made us quite ashamed as we expected to pay & behaved accordingly. The Wilsons went with us to the lake and promised boats but when we arrived we learned that these desired articles could not be procured—and I fished from the bank. The party caught 63. I, 12 trout & 1 cat, had many fine bites—lost 1 line—and one hook.[8] Stopped at Bordens coming home—got home thursday at 11 o clock.

In early June, Benners began to write with more regularity. His first reference to the war began on 6 June when an Alabama regiment was ordered to Virginia and he was asked to raise money for the support of the war. When the Confederacy won a major victory at Manassas in July, Benners was filled with elation—"too much praise cannot be bestowed upon the soldiers." On 5 August, he was elected to the Alabama House of Representatives and became an important leader in Alabama's war effort.

June 6. Rode to plantation on the 4th Tuesday and returned on Wednesday—Mr Wemyss accompanied me—and we fished a while in the Creek. I found the Gin house not yet raised and they were hauling some of the pieces preparatory to raising. The cotton looked very small and poor. on the red lands the stand has been much injured by the lice; found a few squares. The corn looks very finely and in a few places is commencing to Tassel.—Herrin reported that he had hauled from Ldg 8 Barrels pork and two of fish leaving 19 barrels pork there—on our return home we stopped at Hagans and got Dinner & met Col A. C. Jones and family on their way to N. Caro. The regiment of Ala No 5 has been ordered from Pensacola to Virginia;[9] Alexandria was invaded & taken possession of Friday week. El[l]sworth was killed by Jackson, for taking flag down 24th May[10]

---

[8] It is ironic that 140 years later, Greensboro has become the "catfish capital of the world." This section of the Southern black belt, the Canebrake, that produced more cotton than any other place in the South, has become the center of a lucrative business in catfish.

[9] The Fifth Alabama Infantry Regiment fielded 1,000 men in May 1861. Its first colonel was Robert E. Rodes. Allen C. Jones was elected lieutenant colonel and Eugene Lafayette Hobson took over as captain of the Greensboro Guards. James D. Webb, a secessionist delegate, was appointed regimental quartermaster. The regiment was in Pensacola, Florida, for three weeks before being transferred to Richmond, Virginia. Hubbs, "Guarding Greensboro," 153–56.

[10] As Union troops moved across the Potomac to occupy Alexandria. Virginia. Elmer Ellsworth of the 11th New York Regiment became the first Union fatality of

June 24. On Wednesday June 19th I carried Lt. Col. [Stephen] Hale to Newbern where he was to take the cars on his way to seat of War in Va. Col [Sydenham] Moore also went—and a company from Clinton—after the cars left I went to plantation they had no rain since 1st June when they had a rain at Walker Place but very light at Cheney Place. The corn is shooting very finely but needed rain and on uplands was suffering. The cotton is very small and still infested with grass hoppers tho a good deal of it is squaring well. I staid all night at Parkers and on thursday made a speech in Newbern on the loan of cotton to Confederate States. 195 bales were subscribed.[11] Came home in the evening on Saturday the 22 went to Havana with Messrs Waller[,] Wemyss & Hutchinson—had a fine day and splendid Basket dinner and got 417 Bales cotton subscribed to the loan.[12] Stopped at five mile with Waller & fished a little while—Got home about dark.

Yesterday Sunday evening we had clouds & thunder and a light shower here—we hear that south and west of this place there were good rains. I hope it rained at my place and I think it did. The news from the War is very conflicting and unreliable—It is certain we gained a victory at Bethel under Col McGruder—North Carolina troops under Col. Hill covered themselves with glory 250 of the enemy killed—and 1 of ours—It is reported that Harpers Ferry was captured on 17 by our troops....[13]

---

the war when he was shot and killed by James Jackson while attempting to take down a Confederate flag from a hotel roof.

[11] Under the Produce Loan Act of 16 May 1861, the Confederate Congress authorized the issue of $50,000,000 in 8 percent bonds. Later, the amount was increased to $100 million, which could be paid for in specie, military supplies, manufactured goods, or agricultural products. Prominent men spoke in favor of the loan throughout the South. Benners was successful in raising money for the war. Grady McWhiney, Warner O. Moore, and Robert E. Pace, eds., *Fear God and Walk Humbly, the Agricultural Journal of James Mallory, 1843–1877* (Tuscaloosa AL: University of Alabama Press, 1997) 583–84.

[12] Waller, R. B., lawyer, Greensboro. V. Gayle Snedecor, *A Directory of Greene County for 1855–6* (Mobile AL: Strickland & Co., 1856; ed. and indexed by Franklin Shackelford Moseley, Eutaw AL: *The Greene County Democrat*, 1957) 44.

[13] On 18 April 1861, the Federal authorities abandoned Harpers Ferry armory and arsenal after setting fire to its shops and the building in which 17,000 finished muskets were stored. The muskets were destroyed, but the shops were saved with

June 27. I visited Havana on Saturday last with Messrs Wemyss, Waller & Hutchinson to get subscriptions for loans of cotton proceeds to Confederate States. We had a very favorable reception—a fine dinner and got 417 Bales subscribed—on yesterday Messrs Webb & [T. Crawford] Clark came here and presented the same subject to the people and they procured a subscription of 127 Bales.[14] In the afternoon a flag was presented by the young ladies of the female academy to the young rebels. Fanny presented it—and acquitted herself very well. Elliott Hutchinson responded for the boys, and the occasion altogether was a very interesting one. We have had fine showers falling around commencing on last Sunday 23. I understand there was a good rain at my plantation last night. The Missouri news about the capture of Lyon is not confirmed. The blockading squadron have got inside of Ship Island and captured 3 schooners. We are most anxiously looking for a great conflict—...[15]

July 8. on friday July 5th I attended a public meeting at 5 mile church & made a speech to procure promises to loan proceeds of cotton to Confederate States in March. We had a pleasant day and a fine dinner and got 83 Bales. I went up with Mr J. J. Hutchinson. There is a very beautiful comet visible in N. West bright star of 1st Magnitude for the head and a fan shaped tail going off from the comet.[16] It gets very bright by 9 oclock. Grow has been elected Speaker of H of R at Washington

---

their machinery, tools, and large quantities of material. By 18 June, all of this was evacuated. When the Confederate forces captured it in late June they made the armory the core of their Confederate ordnance effort. E. B. Long with Barbara Long, *The Civil War Day by Day and Almanac, 1861–1865* (Garden City NY: Doubleday Press, 1971) 84.

[14] T. Crawford Clark of Eutaw was a law partner of Stephen F. Hale, who had just left for the war.

[15] General Nathaniel Lyon, angered over attempts by the Missouri state government to undermine federal authority, met with state officials in St. Louis on 11 June 1861. He was not captured by Confederates but died in action at Wilson's Creek on 10 August 1861. Confederate troops were on Ship Island in the Mississippi Gulf until 16 September when these forces were evacuated. The North used Ship Island as an operating base for action along the Gulf Coast.

[16] Great Comet, also Tebbutt, C/1861 J1. Passed closest to Earth on 30 June 1861. Gary W. Kronk, *Cometography, A Catalog of Comets*, 3 vols. (Cambridge: Cambridge University Press UK, 2004) 2:293–302.

and Ethridge of Tenn. Clerck,[17]—Abe will ask that his acts be sanctioned and more also—say men 1/2 million. Money 200 million. Well we shall see great things in our day. But the subjugation of the South never—...

July 20. I went on yesterday to a muster and barbecue in Mr Madison neighborhood at an academy 12 miles north East of Greensboro. Mr Harris went with me in my buggy. There was a very fair gathering of people. Mr Madison was called to the chair and Mr Ramey Secy. I addressed the meeting on the cotton loan to Confederate States in a speech of about one hour—was followed by Mr Hutchinson—after which we got subscriptions to amt of about 75 Bales and 150 pairs of socks to be knit by women for the soldiers. Mr Harris made a speech after dinner for members of his company—and after him Mr Hutchinson and before he concluded a rain came up. We left the ground about 4 oclock—and got home 8 min before 6—name of the meeting place was brush heap.

July 24. Wednesday—I rode to plantation yesterday evening and returned this morning.... On our way thro Newbern Dr. W. T. Hendon told us that the glorious news of a great battle had been rec'd near Manassas—in which 4000 of our side were killed & 10,000 federals, and enemy routed with real slaughter—running like sheep—this on top of the fight at Bull Run a few days ago (18th) in which we are said to have killed 960 with a loss of 142 is very encouraging—4 Batteries were taken—and 1-32 pounder brass siege piece Johnson commanded on the left, Beauregard on the right and [blank space] the Center—Patterson was there—Scott & Patterson & McDowell commanded the federals. It is reported that only 200 of five Zouaves are left from the Slaughter. Davis telegraphed Congress as follows—Manassas Sunday night July 22 P.M. Night has closed on a hard fought field. Our forces have won a glorious victory. The enemy was routed and fled precipitately,

---

[17] Galusha Aaron Grow was a Free Soil Democrat and became a Republican. He served in the US House of Representatives from March 1853–March 1863 and was speaker of the house from 1861–1863. Emerson Etheridge, a Whig representative from Tennessee, served from 1853–1857 and 1859–1861. He was elected clerk of the house 1861–1863.

abandoning a very large amt of arms, munitions, knapsacks and baggage. The ground was strewed for miles with those killed. And the farm homes and the ground around are filled with the wounded. The pursuit was continued along several routes towards Leesburg & Centreville until darkness covered the fugitives. We have captured several field Batteries of Artillery and Regimental stand of Arms and one U States flag. Many prisoners have been taken. Too high praise cannot be bestowed, whether for the skill of the principal officers or for the gallantry of the troops. The Battle was mainly fought on our left several miles from our field works. Our force engaged did not exceed 15,000. That of the enemy is estimated at 35,000 (signed) Jeff Davis.[18]

July 29. Monday—I went to the plantation yesterday evening in my buggy & returned this morning—Herrin had commenced pulling fodder the previous Monday and had fine weather for it. The corn does not look as well as I thought it would—and I apprehend it will be injured to some extent by pulling off the fodder. The Cotton is well loaded with bolls & squares on the slough and black land but the red land is a failure—Hannahs child is still quite sick & I found on getting home that Alfred was still unwell his arm hurt last friday week by falling from a tree being considerably swollen—…

Hopes that the war could be won in a few months gave way to serious concerns about the blockade and questions about Jefferson Davis's leadership. Benners felt a growing uneasiness about the conduct of the war.

October 7. We have had last week a spell of warm weather—say 2, 3, 4, 5 of Oct yesterday evening it rained and again this morning—it is cloudy and unsettled—We had a report yesterday that Gen Lee in Western Virginia had defeated Rosencrantz & he was in full retreat for

---

[18] On 21 July 1861, the Battle of Bull Run ended in a Southern victory for Johnston, Beauregard, and Jackson, the latter receiving the nickname of "Stonewall" because of his courage in this battle. The Confederate forces numbered 32,000, the Union forces, 35,000. Confederates suffered 387 casualties and 1,582 wounded, while Union troops, under the command of McDowell, lost 460 men and 1,124 were wounded.

Wheeling.[19] The suspense about the movements in the Potomac is awful—it really seems that every day tends to demoralize the army and unless there is some good reason for not advancing a defeat there would overthrow Davis in the good opinion of his people—Why dont they move is asked but not exactly answered. The yankees are threatening the coast & to come down the Miss with a great force—When oh when will this ever end? Meat is getting very scarce.

October 18. I went to the plantation on the 10th with my wife and returned on 11th having spent the night at Parkers. They were hauling corn at Cheney Place. The great quantity of sickness had checked the cotton picking very much—there being only 23 Bales packed out at Cheney Place and 18 reported ginned—at Walker Place there were reported 40 Bales packed—we have determined to store it under sheds on the Plantations to preserve it from the possible destruction of Lincolnites if carried to the cities before the blockade is raised, the prospect of which at present does not seem very flattering—[20]It is hard to give an idea of the uneasiness and apprehensions of our people from the customary supplies of pork being cut off from the west, the greatest trouble is apprehended from this source. There is yet no decided movement on the Potomac—action there is eagerly looked for.

October 23. I visited the plantation last Saturday evening and returned on Sunday morning the 20th Oct. Herrin had packed out 48 Bales at Walker Place and 38 at Cheney making 86 in all. said he had out about 100. Expect to get 150 or 160 say Walker 100 Cheney 60. Priscy was sick and so was Mr Herrin & daughter. I have hired Herrin for next year at $450. John is to stay at Walker Place and I give 100 for his negro man per annum while I keep him. I am to find meat & bread—either

---

[19] On 1 August 1861, Davis sent Robert E. Lee to West Virginia to replace General Garnett and General William S. Rosecrans led a successful Union attack on Confederate forces at Carnifex Ferry, Virginia, on 10 September 1861. By 25 September, the troops under Lee and Rosecrans advanced on the Kanawa Valley in western Virginia.

[20] Jefferson Davis and Confederate Generals Beauregard, Smith, and Johnston met at Centreville, Virginia, on 1 October 1861. Owing to an insufficient number of troops and provisions, they waited until spring of 1862 to begin a new offensive against the North.

party quits at pleasure. I sent the cotton subscription to Mr Mem[m]inger to day[21]—expecting to leave for Newbern on my way to Montgomery this evening—as a member of the house of Representatives—the Gov. having called it for 28th of this month....

Benners was elected to the Alabama House of Representatives on 5 August 1861, receiving 670 votes, more than the other four candidates combined. He was called to Montgomery for numerous special and regular sessions during the war. A state representative in the 1850s, Benners emerged as an important leader in the extra thirty-day session ending on 11 December. His main concern was to preserve the credit of Alabama, and he opposed all efforts to expand the amount of money available—"to create new banks & flood the Country with spurious currency."

December 24. on Wednesday Oct 23rd I left home in my Carriage on my way to Montgomery—staid at night at Parkers and next morning took the cars for Selma reached Montgomery on friday to Dinner. Extra Session commenced on Monday. Walter H. Crenshaw was elected speaker. A. B. Clitheral, Clerck. The business of the extra session was mostly preparatory—the principal bill passed was to authorize the volunteers in the army to vote wherever they might chance to be—for President and Members of Congress. the act being clearly unconstitutional—as the constitution provided that no elector should be entitled to vote except in the city, County or town in which he resided at the time of his election. I voted against it. After the adjournment of the extra session the same officers were elected for the regular session—and a difficult and disagreeable time we had of it, being both on the judiciary & Committee of Ways & Means I was almost constantly engaged either in the house or in the Committees. There was a great disposition to create new bank[s] & flood the Country with spurious currency. this I opposed at every step of its progress, and it was no easy task as the pressure for money caused a great many to lend a willing ear to anything

---

[21] Benners refers to Christopher Memminger, Confederate secretary of the treasury, and the cotton subscription that the Confederate government asked for support of the war effort.

which seemed to relieve for the present. The committee of ways & means proposed a series of relief measures—viz The State to assume the war tax and borrow the money from the banks—which had suspended and which desired that suspension [be] legalised—To pass a stay Law—to suspend the State taxes till next meeting of the legislature and to reduce salaries 25 percent. The senate with Sam Rice at their head were very anxious to pass the treasury note bill as it was called—to authorise the Gov to issue 5,000,000 treasury notes to be advanced to planters on their cotton—said notes to be receivable in payt of all taxes & public dues. To this the objections were so many that I opposed it. It would deplete the treasury—it would destroy the credit of Alabama and it would produce jealousies and heart burnings against the class who were singled out for State relief—and it would ruin the currency of the Banks—and of the Confederate States.

The bill was brought from the Senate to our house on the last day of the session and failed by a refusal to order it read a second time forthwith 4/5ths not voting to suspend the constitutional rule—and a glorious thing for Ala was its defeat. We had a hard time resisting the efforts to establish free banks & suspend them before hand. The Senate bill provided that the same privileges which were conferred on the Bank of Selma, Montgomery & farmers Bank should be extended to every free bank that should come into existence in the next 90 days—and how many would have come into being no man could tell. The great abundance of confederate bonds which were the basis for the issue rendered it highly probable that there would be a large number—and the Country would be filled with irredeemable paper trash—the bill was defeated in our house by refusing to suspend. I introduced and had passed a bill to prevent corporations from being stockholders in private bank[s], the main object was to prevent the Insurance companies & Railroads from being banks. I also introduced and passed a law to prevent the exportation of what salt there was in the State of Ala under a penalty of $5000—The Senate passed it and then reconsidered and substituted a bill to authorize the Gov to seize all the salt and appropriated $150,000 to pay for it—Our house passed a bill to make advances on cotton a lien—the senate rejected it. They passed a bill extending the salt Law to all necessaries of life—we rejected it—They refused to pass our bill suspending taxes till November and extended the time for tax collectors to make returns till 1 May—They passed bill to legalise suspension of the Planters Bank at Gainesville—and Bank at Tuscaloosa and Bank of Alabama—we rejected it.[22] The session expired by limitation at 12 o clock on tuesday 11 dec. having lasted 30 days. I came down the river same night and reached home Wednesday evening at 9 o clock. Mrs Hatch & family were at my house—she was quite invalid and had been there 5 weeks—Sam, Julia, horses &c now in attendance. Mrs Hatch left for home on Monday 30th of Dec.

December 26. Yesterday was a pleasant mild day—attended church in the morning. Congregation was small and church dressing quite handsome. Mrs Hatch was at my house and the children got more in their stockings from Santa Claus than they expected. I could not restrain a tear as I thought of my dear departed ones. They are safely arrived at their fathers house while we are still exposed to the peltings of the pitiless storm. Windsor, Milly, Edward, Dred came up—Presents were very scarce as times are very hard—what shall we do for meat—God only knows—…

1862

The new year began with a continuing naval blockade, a crisis between the North and Great Britain over the Mason-Slidell Affair, and a worsening economic situation. Benners hoped for European intervention to break the blockade and end the war.

January 14. The first day of the present year was a very mild pleasant day—there was comparatively little business transacted in town in consequence of the derangements resulting from the War and the blockade. It being impossible to buy meat or to ship cotton to Europe. The Mason & Slidell affair have engrossed the public attention and it was greatly hoped from the boastings of the yankees about their capture

---

[22] Benners fought every effort to allow soldiers to cast absentee ballots for Congress. He vigorously opposed the creation of new banks or paper money, which he believed would destroy the credit of Alabama and the Confederacy. In this session, he supported unsuccessful efforts to suspend taxes until November 1861.

of them from the British steamer Trent that they would refuse to surrender them. But with a degree of pusilanimity which could hardly have been expected even from them they surrendered them on demand—and made fools of themselves by the frivolous reason assigned therefor—to wit: that as Com Wilkes did not take the Trent before a prize court the capture as contraband could not be considered as finished—or rather by the release of the vessel must be considered as in [illegible] or abandoned and therefore he gives em up—...[23]

February 5. On Wednesday morning Jany 29th I rode to Plantation—road very bad and rain several times—Report all well. Herrin was ditching at the creek. I went at night to Parker's and staid all night and took cars next morning for Selma. reached there 10-1/2 and went to Harrisons Warehouse, collected the money for 5 Bales cotton sold for me the previous saturday @ 8 cts. Attended a large sale of groceries—and purchased only a few articles viz 2 boxes sperm candles @ 40 cts a pound and 1 doz madeira wine. A sack of coffee @ 51 cts—which I let Lawson have. Everything sold at war prices—Gunpowder $5. a pound, shot from 8 to 12 a bag and tin at $5.00 a pound, old rusty bacon @ 28 cts—I returned on friday evening and came home next morning.

Herrin yesterday sent up 37 hams from plantation—viz 10 from Cheney place and 27 Walker P. 5 or six of them are sour—and I fear I shall lose *them* perhaps more—as we are having a warm rainy time—I have ordered them to be cut up and put in charcoal and salt—if salt can't save them perhaps charcoal may—

February 12. After a very protracted spell of mild rainy weather it turned off cool Sunday night & the Ther was at 23° monday morning 10th Feby—

Herrin killed 18 hogs at Walker Place that day and sent up the lard and some spare ribs and 2 hams on tuesday 11th. The night last was quite cold and I hope I shall have better luck with this killing than the last. There is a great gloom over our people from the bad news of the taking by the federals of Roanoke Island and 3000 men—also the capture

---

[23] On 8 November 1861, the USS *San Jacinto* stopped the British mail ship *Trent*, removed James Mason and John Slidell—Confederate commissioners to Great Britain and France—and carried them to a Union prison in Boston.

of fort Henry in Ten[n] and the advance to Florence & Tuscumbia in Lauderdale County Ala. There is considerable gloom in our Community on acct of these things and all sorts of evils are anticipated, among them that the army of Feds may March down on Tuscaloosa—another that they may capture Mobile and come up the river. These things are very depressing and the truth is manifest that we have fallen on evil times.

February 14. After 4 bright days 3 of which were cold, it turned warm yesterday and last night we had a rain with thunder lightning and wind and this morning the wind is at the North and cold—and raining—the bad news gets no better—Elizabeth City has been shelled and burnt in N.C. and the enemy are pressing for Norfolk and the Town of Weldon—They are reported to have returned from Florence down the Tennessee river to Fort Henry—doubtless for reinforcements. To what straits we may yet be reduced no one can guess—they have the malice and energy of the devil and we are illy [ill] furnished to cope with them—God only knows what will be the issue.

The loss of Forts Henry and Roanoke Island were severe blows to Benners, but the fall of Fort Donelson was the real disaster—"God grant it may not be true." Unfortunately for him, it was true.

February 17. There was a cold snap Friday night & a sleet. Saturday melted very little. Sunday still cold Sunday night heavy rains with Thunder and lightning. This morning it rained again and is still (4 o clock) very cloudy Edward came up Saturday from plantation—news that there had been a good deal of sickness principally bad Colds. Tom White, William & Kit—Priscys child had been very sick and Annes was not expected to live. The news from Fort Donelson is that on thursday the Federals made an attack—were repulsed with 500 killed. on friday attack was renewed and they were driven with cold steel beyond their tents—but that they had been reinforced and the Battle was still raging on friday up to 11 1/2—God forbid that we should meet with a disaster there—…

February 19. Rain more rain—It rained yesterday it rained last night it has rained to day and now at 1 o clock it is still raining and distant thunder signifies another hard shower—while the skies are so lowering the news is also bad—Johnston fell back from Bowling Green last Wednesday and the town was burnt by Yankees. They attacked fort Donaldson [sic] on the Cumberland river last thursday and were repulsed—Battle was renewed on friday and they were again defeated and driven from their positions—and again on saturday we are said to have defeated them—There is a rumor to day that it has fallen and that Nashville is in the hands of the yankees.[24] God grant it may not be true—the story is that they have taken 18,000 of our men—some doubt attaches to the story—

1.10 o clock—we have had a tremendous rain—and it still rains—I presume this must be the clearing up showers.

February 21. Friday. This has been a gloomy sad day in the village by reason of the news from Fort Donaldson which was taken on Monday. The fight continued thro thursday, friday, saturday, sunday—on all which days we are reported to have had success but on Monday the enemy poured in with immense reinforcements said to have been 100,000 men and the fort surrendered—6000 prisoners are said to have been captured and among them Buckner.[25] Every nerve must be strained to sustain ourselves as the Cause is ruined.

Yesterday was a bright day Herrin came up and I pd him $200 on his wages. May God in his mercy give me strength to do my duty in this trying time—

February 22. Washington's birthday—and upon it how different are our feelings and prospects from former days, then with proud exultation we recalled the virtues of the illustrious man who with such signal success illustrated the excellence of human nature and carried his Country safely thro the storms of the revolution and bequeathed to us

---

[24]At Nashville Tennessee, General Buell's Federals took over and the Confederate cavalry troops under General Nathan B. Forrest were forced to retreat.

[25] On 13 February 1862, U. S. Grant with 17,000 soldiers attacked Fort Donelson, and after four days of fighting, General Buckner asked for the terms of surrender. Grant's reply was simple and soon made him famous: "No terms except an unconditional surrender and immediate surrender can be accepted. I propose to move immediately upon your works." Buckner surrendered Fort Donelson and his 13,000 Confederate soldiers.

the priceless boon of freedom—now our country invaded and that freedom sought to be wrested from us by the fierce and relentless foe. No news this morning and we are still in an agony of suspense about the battle at fort Donelson—and the subsequent catastrophes—We are to have a muster to day and a town meeting to take into consideration the defences on the River in case the enemy should possess themselves of Mobile—also providing for indigent families of absent volunteers—God knows where our troubles will end. The prospects are truly gloomy enough. This is also Alfred's birthday—...

February 28. This last day of the winter has been as bright and balmy as May—and the Heavens have been propitious and the birds joyous—but oh how distressingly sad have been the hearts of our people—It was a day of Humiliation and fasting & prayers. I went to church—[Fort] Henry, Donelson, Nashville all gone—and the enemy pressing hard upon us at Mobile—We are very much depressed & the uneasiness arises from our want of preparation and arms and ammunition—

March 1. Saturday. This first day of the spring opens upon us an afflicted and distressed people—provisions scarce meat not to be had at any price—and all articles sold for cash—our ports blockaded—Mobile & New Orleans not yet in possession of the federals but both threatened—our people discouraged by reverses at Donaldson [*sic*] Henry & Roanoke—without the means of procuring the necessary arms and ammunit[ion]—a well equipped army of 700,000 men bent on Robbery and subjugation—What the end of all will be God of Heaven only knows—without his aid—we are ruined[,] with it all may yet be well. Muster to day & every saturday—people excited—uncertain—anxiety in every face, and withal the morning cloudy & threatening rain—

March 6. Thursday—The news to day by the Selma paper is that Gen Johnston is falling back on the Charleston road at Decatur—the Federals are in possession of Nashville and their pickets are said to be 20 miles this side—Genls Bragg & Withers have gone from Mobile to Tennessee and there is much anxiety felt about Mobile in consequence—Tho a large part of the Federal force have gone from

Ship Island—and it is said there are only 1500 men there—The prospects of the federals are certainly brightening and a long and cruel war is the fate of the Country—what the issue will be no one can foretell—England & France so far decline all interference and unaided the Southern States have to defend themselves. Wemyss Company was organised on tuesday last and he was elected captain[26]—C. Stewart[27] 1st Lieut. A. H. Hutchinson 2nd Knight 3rd.

Confederates were being pushed back, more men needed to be raised to fight, and Benners's daughter Liz was near death. These were difficult times for Benners.

March 11. The Gov of Ala has issued a Proc. that he will soon call for a large draft of men from 14 counties including the County of Greene Marengo & Perry—but will accept 60 companies to go to Mobile armed and equipped at their own expense. The Confederates have evacuated Columbus and fallen back to Island No 10.[28] There has been a battle last saturday 8th near Newports [Newport] News between the steam marine iron battery Virginia (Merrimac) and three confederate gunboats and the federal frigate[s] Cumberland & Congress—the Cumberland was sunk and Congress run ashore. Two large frigates supposed to be Min[n]esota and Colorado went towards Newport News when the batteries from Sowells point opened on them damaging them considerably.[29]

A fight is reported in Arkansas near Fayetteville. Confederates had 26,000—Federals 38,000—Confederates are reported victorious.[30]

---

[26] J. A. Wemyss, a cotton factor in Mobile, organized the new company and became its captain. Hubbs, "Guarding Greensboro," 180.

[27] Charles Stewart, planter, Greensboro. Snedecor, *Greene County*, 41.

[28] On 8 April 1862, John Pope's army of 20,000 with the cooperation of the Navy was able to take Island No. 10, its 7,000-man garrison, and 123 guns.

[29] On 9 March 1862, in a battle of special significance to naval warfare, the CSS *Virginia* and USS *Monitor* clashed at Hampton Roads. The battle turned out to be indecisive.

[30] The battle of Pea Ridge in Northern Arkansas on 6–8 March 1862 pitted General Sam Curtis with 12,000 men against Sterling Price with his 16,000 soldiers including one Creek and two Cherokee infantries. The Federals held their lines

April 6. on Saturday March 22nd my daughter Liz was taken sick—sick stomach vomiting and slight fever—we did not consider that it was a very serious attack and gave her some simple medicines—she continued sick without any alarming symptoms until Monday when we discovered that her lungs were very much implicated & sent for a physician—he pronounced it to be Pneumonia—and seemed to consider it a pretty decided case—he administered small doses of Calomel[,] cupped her and applied leaches—and a blister—this produced considerable relief—but when the blister healed up all the bad symptoms returned & in addition a very distended abdomen and pains in the stomach—he applied another blister on the other side and with good effect—she is better and I hope and trust will continue to mend—nothing can exceed the importunity with which she begs for something to eat. I can't stand it.

April 4. The order for 200 men from this regiment for the defence of Mobile was rec'd here two weeks since 94 men have volunteered and six more have to be had to day by draft or other wise—there is considerable excitement and great uneasiness felt in some quarters on account of the large number removed from the county. Capt. Milton May commands the Company.[31]

April 8.... Tuesday evening—Dr Osborn has just called to ask a consultation with H. Webb as to Lizzie—her respiration is hurried and she has a hectic irritating fever—Poor Liz would to God I could relieve my little darling—

The news to day is that there has been a battle at Corinth—and we have gained a victory—Particulars not known—A. S. Johnston Major General in command is said to be slain.

April 9. My child is still lingering and I fear no better. Her case is very critical in my opinion. She still has fever and is being dosed with

---

against fierce attacks and drove the Confederates from the field. Of the 11,250 Union troops, there were 1,384 casualties; of the 14,000 Confederates engaged there were 800 casualties.

[31] Milton May was a warehousekeeper living in Hollow Square voting precinct before the war. Snedecor, *Greene County*, 29.

Turpentine mixture every 3 hours. Dr Webb was in consultation last night—

The news of the fight [at] Corinth is confirmed this morning—A. S. Johnston is killed—Gladden had his arm shot off. We took 2000 prisoners and drove the enemy to Tennessee river.

April 10. cool morning. Lizzie is a little better her respiration last night was better and she slept well—No news by paper of Corinth Battle driver says we took 9000 prisoners and killed 6000—

April 11. Visited plantation yesterday evening on horse back and returned this morning—the road in places was very bad—and rough—the corn is generally up where it has been planted & a good stand. The Walthal bottom up to the big gate not yet broke up on account of the wet. Were planting ground peas to day—wheat looks pretty well. cotton is up at Walker Place planting some at Seabrooks—Got home at 11 found Lizzy better—tho very weak—The news from Corinth to day is not so glorious as before—the Confederates pursued the federals to their gunboats and retired—having destroyed the tents[,] equipage &c they had taken—being unable to carry it—Buell is reported killed Robert Armistead is killed—General Albert S. Johnston is also killed—it has been since ascertained that General Wallace & not Buell of the Lincolnites was killed—Gen Prentiss & about 4000 others were taken prisoners our loss about 500 killed and 2500 wounded.[32]

The fall of New Orleans saddened Benners and the entire South. It was so unexpected. At the same time, there were rumors of large numbers of Federal troops approaching Alabama, and Liz, his daughter, remained very ill.

April 17. on Monday the 14th I went to Eutaw to settle account as adm of Haywood. found the river high and road in the swamp very bad returned home tuesday 3 o clock. Judge Coleman did not make his

---

[32] The battle of Shiloh occurred 7–8 April 1862. The first day while urging his troops to go forward, General Albert Sidney Johnston was hit in the leg and soon bled to death. It was a tragic loss for the Confederacy. General Beauregard was given command of the troops on 8 April. He did not receive reinforcements and lost heavily the next day. Losses for the North were 13,047; for the South, 10,694.

appearance and there was no Cir. Co. while in Eutaw heard that fort Pulaski near Savannah had surrendered—383 prisoners taken—[33]on reaching home Huntsville & Decatur were reported captured by Federals and Kirby Smith is said to have started that way with 20,000 men. The times are gloomy and this dreadful war brings death & destruction on all our prospects—There is an immense effort to induce our planters to raise little or no cotton and to send hands to destitute families.

April 18. Report in town to day that Federals are approaching Tuscaloosa with 8000 men—a courier was sent by Fowler to Selma to telegraph Gov Shorter at Montgomery and Gen Jones at Mobile to permit Fowlers artillery to remain and to send him additional reinforcements—the large number of prisoners at Tuscaloosa is thought to make it probable—there are about 1200 there—There is also a rumor that the Govt is about to remove from Richmond—

April 21. rode in the buggy to plantation yesterday evening and returned this morning. Aggy & Little Frances are sick—Wm Henry is complaining of his hip—The corn is growing finely and is very promising—the wheat is rusted in the blade and beginning to head—a hard rain on last sunday prevents the Walthal bottom from being broken up as yet—have set out one planting of potato drawers.

April 28. The news reached here yesterday by telegraph from Mobile to Selma that Orleans had fallen. The gunboats were reported to have passed Fort Jackson on thursday and 14 had reached New Orleans—It has been since reported that the city had four days allowed to capitulate.[34] The news was entirely unexpected—and is an important step in the progress of affairs. My daughter Lizzie still continues very low and improvement if any is very slight. Poor little thing she has had a

---

[33] The Union assault on Fort Pulaski in Savannah, Georgia, proved successful on 10 April 1862. Long-range guns and penetrating shells made the difference. Confederates surrendered at 2:00 PM and 360 were taken as prisoners.

[34] David Farragut planned and led the campaign to take New Orleans, culminating in its surrender on 29 April 1862. The Confederacy lost eight ships and sixty-one men, the Union one ship and thirty-six men. It was a stunning victory for the Union.

hard time of it—and her lingering a long long time—she is a little more sprightly to day—

April 30. Mr Hatch came up last night and we had about supper time a rain and right smart wind. The river having risen again being the fifth time this season is still very high. The federals have possession of New Orleans—the troops under Lovell retired to Camp Moore and the Mayor informed Faragut that he could not defend the City but declined to remove secession flags—I dont know whether the Commodore will accept the surrender in the way it was made. The Confederates Burnt 10,000 bales of cotton & rolled sugar and molasses into the river. These things will try the Confederate fortitude very much it is said the ... forts were not captured but were turned by a bayou—there is much conjecture & divers rumors on the subject.

Lizzie still lies in a very low state—fever last night and Dr twice a day—

Ed commenced with Dr Avery yesterday—

May 3. There is a despatch in the Mobile Tribune to day that Forts Jackson & Phillip have been taken—this seems to make complete the possession of New Orleans and the Miss River and is a great blow to the Confederates[35]—What will be the next point of attack it is difficult to conjecture—perhaps Mobile—this is said to be poorly defended and will in all probability have to surrender—

May 5. Mrs Elizabeth Willis[36] and six children arrived last night at my home having made her escape from Newbern [North Carolina] the day the Confederates were defeated there—she lost every thing except a few clothes—The stages failed to come last night and there is great uneasiness as to the cause. The forts below New Orleans are surrendered to the federals—a fight has taken place at Cumberland Gap and the federals repulsed—but were reinforced with 8 Regiments and no news since.

---

[35] Forts Jackson and St. Phillip held out for three days after New Orleans fell. The forts were outflanked and the way to Vicksburg was open.

[36] Elizabeth L. Benners Willis, 1829–1868, daughter of Lucas Jacob Benners V and Evalina Rowe Tomlinson, was Benners's niece. Paul G. Scott, *The Family Benners* (College Park GA: self-published family genealogy, 1990) 33.

May 7. Rode to plantation yesterday morning and returned to day. Stopped at the Walker Place found all well—and corn doing finely Cotton is such a drug I did not think or care much about it. The wheat is rusted but will make some. At Cheney Place stand of corn is good and growing off very finely. Wheat at Seabrooks place is badly rusted but I hope will yield a little[,] the clover is very fine. There are reported 100 head of hogs at Walker Place and there are 12 fattening hogs in stable lot at Cheney place & 7 or 8 in Pasture. The news from Virginia last night is that our forces have fallen back from Yorktown[37]—it was yesterday reported that fighting had commenced at Corinth—...[38]

Union forces under General McClellan were on the outskirts of Richmond at the end of May 1862. Benners carefully watched the efforts of Joseph Johnston and his replacement, Robert E. Lee, to save the Confederate capital. The Greensboro guards acquitted themselves well in the fierce fighting, while suffering large casualties. Then Lee won a major victory in the Seven Days Battle in late June, driving McClellan back to Harrison's Landing. Benners hoped this would lead to European recognition.

May 24. We are having this morning a fine rain—it was much needed to enable us to set out the potato and on the sandy land to start off the corn. The papers to day report that on the 22nd there was heavy skirmishing at Corinth and that the battle was expected the next day but as it is reported to have rained there—the expected event may be delayed. Intense anxiety is felt as to the results of the fight at Corinth and in Virginia—and the greatest uneasiness prevails. There is also some speculation as to the intervention of France, from the visit of their

---

[37] George B. McClellan with an army of 100,000 took one month to force the Confederate army of 17,000 to evacuate Yorktown. On the night of 3 May 1862, General Johnston withdrew toward Richmond.

[38] They continued to fight around Corinth where the Confederates had an army of 70,000. Henry Haleck replaced Grant assuming command of a force of 110,000 and spent almost a month slowly advancing toward Corinth. Beauregard realized that he had to retreat to save his army. He escaped the night of 29–30 May 1862. Halleck was called east to advise Lincoln and Grant was given command of the Union forces in Western Tennessee and Northern Mississippi.

Minister to Richmond—These calculations will prove illusory until the Confederates obtain some signal victory—when foreign intervention may be expected....[39]

June 3. We had news on yesterday that a battle was raging 7 miles from Richmond on Chicahominy swamp between the Creek & Williamsburg road—and that the Confederates had driven the federals 1-1/2 miles.[40] Last night we rec'd the news that there was a cessation to bury the dead—also that Col Syd Moore was seriously wounded below the knee—and L Col Hale[41] slightly, D Gus Montris is killed and Alonzo Chapman & 15 of the Greensboro Company wounded—Dr Ramsey, Scott McCall, Alfred Ward, T. Nutting, David Barnum J. W. Crowell, R. H. Adams, A. J. Coleman, Wm Lanier, W. Haden, J. Sanders, E. Foster, I. Sheldon, Jas. Jack, Davis Williams.[42] This unnatural & cruel war brings death and mourning to many a hearth stone. How long shall these things be. Intelligence to night is eagerly looked for—The fight is reported now to have lasted two days. Saturday & Sunday—May 31 and June 1 1862—

June 6. I rode to the plantation yesterday morning and carried Miss Kate Borden to Newbern—returned to day. Herrin reports that there

---

[39] France supported the Confederacy but was unwilling to intervene without Great Britain's support. Benners was correct in believing that only a significant military victory would result in foreign intervention on behalf of the Confederacy.

[40] On 31 May 1862, Joseph E. Johnston hurled two-thirds of his army against the Northern troops of George B. McClellan at Seven Pines, east of Richmond, Virginia. Unsuccessful the first day, Johnston had even less success the second day. The rebels had 6,000 casualties while the Union had 5,000. Johnston was wounded and Robert E. Lee took command. It was a fortunate turn of events for the Confederacy.

[41] Stephen F. Hale was a member of the Alabama legislature in 1843 and 1857–1861, served in the US Army during the Mexican War, and was a lieutenant colonel in the Confederate army in Civil War. He was wounded at the Battle of Seven Pines on 31 May 1862 and died two weeks later. The eastern half of Greene County was named Hale County when it was divided in 1867. See entry of 2 February 1867.

[42] The Greensboro company suffered at least seventeen wounded. Two were dead. The first to die at the enemy's hands was Gus Moore, a young physician in his twenties, and the second was Alonzo Chapman, a recent arrival in Greensboro. They were buried on the battlefield and a map drawn so that their bodies might later be taken home for reburial in the Greensboro cemetery. Hubbs, "Guarding Greensboro," 193.

has been some sickness. Paul had just got out and Big Hannah and Lewis were sick. I found there had been a hard rain on the road—a shower at Walker Place but none at Cheney P. the corn is beginning to tassel & needs rain. I gave out the shirts & pants to negroes at C. P. and frocks to the women and clothes to the children—it took for the children 36 yds and for the frocks 73. The report from the mill is that it works finely—There is no further news from Richmond. Jackson is reported to have gone into Maryland and been joined by 10,000. Beauregard has fallen back from Corinth 25 miles.[43] Vicksburg is not yet taken—and we hear very little from fort Pillow—

June 11. Visited plantation yesterday and returned to day—Phillis, Priscy & Bill sick[.] gave out clothes (Pants & shirts to men and frocks to women) to Walker hands[.] corn is tassling & needs rain—Tom was cutting oats—the Federals have taken Memphis & fort Pillow is evacuated—Vicksburg not heard from—Jackson has defeated Frémont in the valley—and is said to be pursuing Shields....[44]

June 23. Rode to plantation on Friday 20th & returned on 21st the hands were all well except little Wash—who had a chill—Morcea lost a baby born dead—was reported doing well—the drought continues and forward corn is failing—clover is beginning to die, gardens are suffering very much. Jane visited [Hatch] plantation on Wednesday and returned on friday—The prospect for a good corn crop is not good unless it rains soon. Public affairs are very depressing—the horrible war is raging and every thing is getting up to famine prices—what will become of us God only knows. And if to all the other horrors a failure takes place in the corn it will leave us very destitute—...

June 30, Monday. I rode to the plantation in the buggy with Alfred on the 28th and returned on the 29th had a very hot ride down having gone by the Jones road and returned same way. The corn is suffering dreadfully for rain—it fell on saturday the 28 all around but we got

---

[43] Stonewall Jackson fought in the Shenandoah Valley from 8 May until 9 June 1862. His army of 17,000 men marched 350 miles, fought four different battles against three armies twice its size, and inflicted heavy casualties on the Union.

[44] The Confederate troops at Fort Pillow near Memphis evacuated their position leaving the city helpless before the advancing Union army.

none—the corn on the uplands is used up and if the rain does not come soon we will be greatly cut off—it is really distressing to see it—have had no rain there since 24th of May. As we returned the road for 7 miles on this end was heavy from the rain that had fallen and I found it had rained in Greensboro. It is cause for thankfulness for we needed it bad. There is news last night that there has been another battle near Richmond—and the Confederates are said to have gained a victory—it is reported that they have driven them 6 or 7 miles and taken 3000 prisoners and many guns—the accts however are contradictory and unsatisfactory.[45] The [H]erald says that England & France have in contemplation an armed intervention to force a peace on the basis of a separation between the North & the South—

July 11. Friday—I rode with Fanny to Plantation on Wednesday morning and returned on friday morning—Fanny had a very hot fever at night and gave great uneasiness she is still sick but not so bad—There was a light shower at Cheney place on the 2nd July but there is great want of it on the corn much of which is killed outright from the drought—It is sad to see the fields—May 24th was the last good season and that not very hard. They had the loom up at Cheney place and it seemed to work pretty well, Martha Johnson had put in a piece of cloth for Mrs Herrin—and Susan Herrin was on a visit—I was greatly concerned about getting Fanny home next morning—fearing the ride would make her worse but it did not[.] we started before breakfast & came by John W. Waltons[46]—got home by 8 o clock—Alfred has gone to 5 Mile Creek with Virgil fishing. The Richmond battle has not resulted in the capture of the army as was expected. Lincoln calls for 300,000—...[47]

---

[45] The Seven Days Battle was Robert E. Lee's first victory as commander of the army that he named the Army of Northern Virginia. With the help of J. E. B. Stuart and Stonewall Jackson, he achieved a major victory. Confederate losses were greater—20,000, to the Federal 11,000 dead and missing. McClellan was driven away from Richmond and the way was open for Lee to invade the North.

[46] John W. Walton, planter, commissioner of roads and revenue, Newbern, Greensboro. Snedecor, *Greene County*, 44.

[47] President Lincoln responded to the request of Northern governors to be allowed to raise 300,000 new three-year volunteers. On 2 July 1862, Lincoln assigned each state a quota based on its population.

The next month Benners received the news that his close friend Judge Sydenham Moore, wounded in the Battle of Seven Pines, had died. A few days later, reports of another Southern victory at Manasses lifted his spirits. Now he hoped for an invasion of the North.

August 25. Took a ride with Alfred on Saturday morning 23rd and extended it to the plantation and returned yesterday morning—Anthony was Ironing the wagon body and the hands picking peas. We have had no rain yet and potatoes and peas are suffering badly—Mrs Herrin expected to go to Miss on to day—Emline has wove about 30 yds cloth—a very poor article—The timbers have been hauled up for the screw taps—Kit was complaining—I was quite unwell after breakfast with headache which passed off by dinner—we were all deeply pained at the intelligence of the death of Judge [Sydenham] Moore last friday morning—This sad news tho being expected fell with crushing weight on our hearts and to me his loss is very severe—he was a noble man a true friend—a brave & chivalrous patriot He has fallen in his countrys cause and in my judgment there is none left in our country who can fill his place exactly. May God have mercy on his bereaved family—

August 29.... Stewart [Jeb Stuart] has routed 5000 of Popes forces and taken his servants and horses and uniform coat—It is thot we are on the eve of great occurrences—It is I think probable if Popes army are defeated Jackson will advance into Pennsylvania & draw off some of the invading forces—and Bragg will attempt Nashville and perhaps invade Ky—we shall see—...

September 5. Telegraph reported on tuesday 2 that Gen Lee had reported to the Pres Davis That on the 28th one wing of the army under Longstreet and on the 29th the other wing under Jackson were attacked by the Federals and repulsed in each instance—and that on the 30th God had blessed the Confederate arms with a signal victory on the plains of Manassas—Augusta Sept 3rd Genls Ewing and Grimble are reported to be badly but not mortally wounded and General Taliaferro slightly—Six Hundred prisoners are reported taken in the 1st fight. On Saturday a large number of prisoners and valuable stores were captured. The destruction of federal stores was immense[48]....

September 10. Rode to Cheney place on sunday evening 7th to Walker Place on 8th returned home on tuesday 9th. Screw taps had been put up at C.P. and had commenced Ginning on Saturday 6th Septr. The cotton appears to have improved a good deal from the rain on 30th Aug as also the potatoes. Herrin thinks will make 40 bales in all. The new crib at W.P. is not yet finished—Kit is at my house assisting on Portico.[49] Mrs Herrin not yet returned. The confederates gained a victory near richmond in Ky. on Saturday 30th Aug. under Kirby Smith and are reported to have advanced to Cincinnati and demanded surrender on Friday 5. Septr. on the same day in Va on the plains of Manasses Gen Lee reports a great victory—The enemy having been repulsed with great slaughter—and retreated to Centerville & beyond—a great many incongruous rumors are afloat—as to our forces being at Arlington heights—and 40,000 having crossed into Maryland. This came in the papers night before last—no news last night— Gen Bragg is pressing on from Chattanooga to drive Gen Buell out of Tennessee. It is reported that the federals have evacuated Huntsville & N. Ala[50]—and Gen Price has advanced 30 miles to Corinth. The war steamer Florida ran in under the guns of fort Morgan last

---

[48] The second battle of Bull Run was fought between Generals Robert E. Lee and John Pope on 29–30 August 1862. The Confederacy won a significant victory: 9,197 casualties of 48,500 engaged, while the Federals lost 16,054 of its 75,000-man army. The way was open to invade the North.

[49] Kit was one of Benners's Negro playmates in the home of his childhood, New Bern, North Carolina. He became a carpenter and was brought to Alabama where he was sold to a Doctor Reynolds whose plantation adjoined Benners's. Kit became a persistent runaway, and Reynolds offered to sell him to Augustus Benners at a low price since runaways were unprofitable property. He became a favorite with Benners and remained with him for the rest of his life, repairing the house, and performing many carpentry jobs on the plantations. In his old age, he was taken care of, and when he died he was mourned by his master. Alfred Hatch Benners, *Slavery and Its Results* (Macon GA: J. W. Burke Co., 1923) 29–30.

[50] Braxton Bragg moved steadily north into Kentucky bypassing the Federal forces at Murfreesboro and Shepardsville, Kentucky. This action forced Federal forces to retreat.

Thursday—she carries 8 guns, is iron clad and was built in England. There are rumors of a fleet at the mouth of the Mi[ss] but not credited.[51]

Benners knew a great battle was fought in Sharpsburg (Antietam) on 17 September 1862. However, there were conflicting reports and he was uncertain about its outcome. It was not a Southern success, but the lack of accurate information caused him to hesitate. In fact, it was a victory for the North, which stopped Lee's invasion of the North and the intervention by Great Britain and France. They remained neutral. It would take a clear victory for the Confederacy to bring them into the conflict.

September 29. I rode in my buggy to plantation on thursday 28th and returned on 26th Herrin had packed out 8 bales cotton & 21 Bales fodder at the Cheney Place—Thought there were 12 more to pack there and 20 at Walker Place. He was hauling the corn off the cut by the well to use. The roads were very rough going and returning & I think there was not much choice in the roads. Celia had a daughter at the Cheney Place last Sunday—the 21st Sept—… The morning glory has taken the bottom at the Cheney Place and never in all my life have I seen any thing like the quantity.

The news from Gen Lees army in Maryland is very conflicting and unsatisfactory. There was a severe battle at Sharpsburg on the 16th and 17th Septr—the victory is claimed by both sides—Gen Lees forces are said to have recrossed into Va—Jackson had a battle with ten thousand federals at Shepardstown and routed them with great Slaughter—this is the last reliable intelligence we got—The truth probably is that Lee's army did not meet with the cordial reception in Maryland that was expected—In Ky Gen Bragg is said to have gotten within ten miles of Lewisville and the federals to have reoccupied Mumfordsville—& taken & paroled 400 of our sick left at Glasgow—There is great difficulty in forming a correct judg't as to the position of affairs by reason of the meagerness of the accts and unreliability & conflict of the various

---

[51] The Confederate privateer CSS *Florida* moved in and out of Mobile Bay under the protection of Fort Morgan. It was responsible for the capture and destruction of fifteen Federal ships during the war.

reports—The most intense anxiety prevails to hear from the armies—but communication is so intensified that we get but little & it not reliable.[52] The country is very much exercised about the scarcity of salt it is said to have sold for $100 a bushel—flour is $40 a barrel whiskey $16 a gallon—eggs 25 cts a dozen.

October 10. I went to plantation monday morning oct 8th returned Tuesday ninth. Franky's child died on monday evening. it was strangely affected seemed to be stuffed up with cold—Webb came & gave a dose of medicine—it lived two hours after. Herrin was gathering corn at both places—had one side full at Cheney Place and one crib full at Walker Place. No potatoes gathered yet. Jane was sick and Susan & Bill had been. Mrs Herrin was sick—Aggy shewed me the new cards which are already worn out—it is plain that the cloth can never be made with the present arrangement as the cards cost more than the cloth is worth.

There is no news from the seats of war of a decided character Price attacked the enemy at Corinth and drove them into entrenchments but was compelled to fall back the federals are said to number 40,000—if so Price & Vandorn will probably have to fall back to Columbus—which is being fortified.[53]

October 22. rode to plantation and returned in the evening—arranged for George & Charles to go to Owen Bluff by the way of Demopolis—Having hauled 2 loads of corn to Mr Witherspoon

---

[52] The battle of Antietam, fought on 17 September 1862, was the bloodiest single day of the war. Lee and McClellan fought a fierce fight—the Federals losing 12,410 of an army of 75,310 and the Confederates losing 13,724 of an army of 51,844. Benners followed the battle as closely as possible but did not know that the Greensboro Guards were participants in the battle. They had been ordered to hold Fox's Gap in South Mountain to prevent the movement of Federal troops into Sharpsburg. Their efforts proved futile as the Union army poured through the gap. They were captured by Union soldiers and remained prisoners until transferred to Fort Delaware, then to Camp Winder where they were exchanged, received thirty-day furloughs, and left for home. The Greensboro *Alabama Beacon* carried numerous articles about the Guards throughout the war. Mark Boatner III, *Civil War Dictionary* (NY: David McKay Co., Inc., 1959) 21; Hubbs, "Guarding Greensboro," 202–15.

[53] On 3 October 1862, the combined armies of Van Dorn and Price launched an attack against an equal number of Northern soldiers under Rosecrans at Corinth. Early success the first day was followed by vigorous Union resistance the next day, which cut the Confederates to pieces. They retreated southward.

ordered 4 more hauled to him—the loads hold 31 barrels—and the barrels hold 1 bushels, 2 qts. & 1 pt.—I told Herrin I would give him at the rate of 400 dollars a year—did not want Pensy—and would tell him hereafter if his other negroes could stay—he is to leave whenever I want to take charge or for any purpose see cause to dismiss him—

In the remaining months of 1862, Benners made few journal entries. These were difficult times with rampant inflation and few military victories. The Alabama legislature called a special session to appropriate money to continue the war. Benners fiercely resisted the financial measures, calling one of them "the extortion bill." It passed despite his opposition.

December 16. On the 24th day of November I went to Newbern in my buggy to take the Cars for Selma on my way to Montgomery to the Called Session—staid at Mr Hatch's and left next morning. Reached Selma about 10 o'clock and took the Stage for Montgomery which we reached about 11 o clock at night. Took board at Floyds @ $90 per month and remained in Montgomery 47 days—the Session was a very disagreeable one and especially so to me as I had a large bile under my arm for 4 weeks which was very painful and disabling—being chairman of the Judiciary Committee and also a member of the Committee of Ways & Means I had a very laborious time of it. $2,000,000 of dollars were appropriated to families of indigent soldiers and $2,500,000 to defence of Ala: The extortion bill was one of the most important measures passed to which I was very much opposed—it taxes the trader all his profits over 15 per cent nett [*sic*]. And the probable effect, will be to drive honest Law abiding men out of business and the unscrupulous who will set the Law at defiance, will add to their profits to cover their risks—The revenue bill raised the taxes very considerably particularly on negroes—which being unproductive—should not have been raised out of proportion at the present time. I left Montgomery after the close of the Session on the Ross and had to pay $8.00 for my passage to Selma and bad fare at that—took the Cars on thursday 11th Dec and found my Carriage waiting for me at Newbern and took Judge Coleman in and came home about 1/2 past 8. found all tolerably well—had been vaccinated and Alfred a little sick from it. Mrs Hatch was quite sick at my house & is still I very much fear she has the dropsy—I went to the plantation yesterday and returned to day. It rained last night and turned off cold and the road being muddy I had a tedious and disagreeable ride. Herrin has killed 29 hogs and has 50 more to kill, which with six barrels of pork is my only dependence for meat. Corn is very light and tho I made a good deal it is not much more than 1/2 it looks to be.

December 23. I went to Walker place on Saturday and vaccinated all the hands but 4 who were not there Came home in evening in Carry all—killed squirrel 5 blackbirds & 2 doves—Went to Plantation again on Monday evening and returned this morning tuesday 23rd vaccinated some of the men and women. stopped at Walker Place on way back. Herrin killed a duck which I brot home this morning also 1-1/2 [doz] eggs, and six partridges, the hogs at Walker place are quite poor and dont fatten kindly—before I came home Herrin killed 12 hogs at Cheney place and 17 at Walker Place—killed them on thursday Dec 4th they weighed—[space left blank] 2/3 of a barrel of Lard was made from fat sent up.

Rec'd Jany 16 from the above killing 50 hams—weather cold and snowy.

1863

Despite the unceasing demands of the war, Benners continued to run his two plantations, raising pigs and selling them for a profit, renting slaves for use in his household, and planning the spring planting. But news of the death of his close friend Colonel Croom saddened him, and the constant threat of military action against Alabama and stories of the willingness of the North to draft millions of men kept him in a state of anxiety.

January 1. This new years day is a lovely one clear and cold—there was frost & ice this morning—Herrin killed 38 hogs yesterday viz 25 at Walker place and 13 at Cheney place—and Edward brought up to day the lard, two hams, two shoulders, 3 heads, spare ribs and 18 back bones. This killing with the 29 heretofore killed makes 67 in all killed at both places—They were in poor order—Hogs killed up to this time at Cheney Place amount to 30 at Walker Place to 37—

I agreed to keep Gen Owen's negroes Phillis, Hanna & Margaret and her two children—on the same terms as last year that is to find them victuals & clothes & pay their taxes as I do my own.

Rec'd from this killing Feby 7th 54 hams—weather moderately cool and fair.

January 15. I purchased two chester pigs from Mr S. N. Steele of Macon Marengo Cty Ala & Virgil brought them home on the 8th of January '63.[54] They are reported by Mr Steele to be thorough bred & pure chesters—Their grandfather & grandmother were brought direct form Chester County Pa. some three years ago—and these pigs have been bred pure since their arrival—The father & mother of these pigs are extra fine and strictly thorough[bred]—being both out of chester sows & by chester boars—I gave $50 a piece for my pigs my object being to procure a breed that would fatten kindly. They are represented to be four months old and are large and fine—I sent the largest one of my Jones sows to Dr Parish's boar which is a chester—& she is to return home to day—and the other one of the Jones sows is to be sent—

Largest Sow brought 6 pigs May 5th '63

Smaller [Sow brought] 5 [pigs] May 7th 112 days

January 16. We had a rainy day yesterday and last evening the wind veered round to North West and I thought we would have had a fair day to day—but instead it snowed a little in the night and this morning there is a light covering of snow on the ground—it fell quite fast but the ground being wet melted very fast. There was a despatch last night that 5 gunboats had commenced an attack on fort Caswell below Wilmington N. Caro—and I presume they will take it, the object being to secure the railroad.[55] Their attempt to take Vicksburg by land did not succeed they

---

[54] S. N. Steel, merchant, Macon, Alabama. W. C. Tharin, *A Directory of Marengo County for 1860–61* (Linden AL: Farrow & Dennett, 1861) 35.

[55] Fort Caswell was occupied by the citizens of North Carolina on 10 January 1861 and seized by state troops on 16 April. There was an effort by Union forces to get it back in February 1863, but it remained in Confederate hands until it was destroyed and abandoned on 16 January 1865.

were repulsed with reported loss of 5000.⁵⁶ Wm Norwood⁵⁷ came here on Saturday last & returned on Monday he is in Prices army near Vicksburg and think it can't be taken—

Rec'd this morning from plantation 50 hams Weather cold and sunny—Edward also brought some fodder—roads bad—

February 10.—Mr Herrin sent up from the plantation on saturday Feby 7th 54 hams. I hauled at Mr Hatchs request fodder from Jane Randolph's place on monday 9th and this morning sent wagon to Joe Stickneys to change white corn for red to plant at Walker Place. sent down by Edward a bottle of Spirits Turpentine and a lot of fig trees to plant around hog lots. Col Croom died on Sunday 8th Feby at 3 o clock and was buried in the Town graveyard on yesterday Monday Feby 9th at 3 o clock. He was in his 69th year and tho from his age his disease pneumonia was likely to prove fatal—he died more suddenly than was expected. He had been in my office on the previous tuesday and spoke of having arrested a threatened attack by using [illegible] root tea. He had been to Selma and his plantation recently and is supposed to have exposed himself too much. His death is a great blow to me—for many years he has been my friend and companion and truly will I miss him. He was a man of a kind heart and genial disposition—always disposed to be pleasant and agreeable and never to look on the dark side of things. We have lost one of our most valuable citizens—and his loss will be long felt and deplored—He is gone to his long home—peace to his ashes—and may we hope to be reunited in a blissful immortality—

March 7. I left home in my buggy for Marion on tuesday evening March 3 to take the cars for Selma. Mr Tal[l]man⁵⁸ rode down with me—we took the cars next morning and reached Selma at 9-1/2. I

---

⁵⁶ William T. Sherman's assault on the Chickasaw Bluffs, three miles north of Vicksburg, began on 29 December 1862 and was a failure from the start. Sherman's troops suffered 1,800 casualties to 200 for the Confederates. It was not possible to take Vicksburg from the north.

⁵⁷ William W. Norwood, an overseer in German Creek and Greensboro, served with General Sterling Price, commander of the 2nd corps of Confederate department of Mississippi and East Louisiana in December of 1862; it was part of the defense force at Vicksburg.

⁵⁸ James A. Tallman, merchant, Greensboro. Snedecor, *Greene County*, 42.

attended the sale of Bonds of the Ala & Miss R.R.R. Co. they sold from 120 to 125—I bought none—the price being too high—returned same evening to Marion took Jack McDonald in my buggy and got home at 10 minutes after 8 o clock. We have had very high rivers and immense rains last week—and on wednesday and thursday morning we had a frost. I am pleased to see that my fruit trees are very backward in blooming and hope the cold will check without killing them—some persons have planted corn but I consider it is too cold & wet for it to do well yet. Herrin writes to me that he has bedded potatoes—The war still rages—and from present indications is likely to Harrass our people many years. the last excitement grows out of the offers of the French emperors offer to propose a council on neutral ground where the dissatisfied parties can present their respective grievances. Mr Sewards reply of the 5th of February very promptly and positively declines—and it is hoped by many he will now acknowledge the Confederate States and aid them.[59] There is very little movement of the armies. All is reported quiet on the Potomac where Gen Lee is holding the enemy in check and in Tennessee Gen Bragg is expecting the alliance of Rosecrans.[60] At Vicksburg they are awaiting an attack and it is said the immense armament which gathered for the Capture of Charl[e]ston have deferred their attack for the present.[61] Most likely they will attack Savannah[62]—the convention which met at Frankfort was dispersed by a

---

[59] On 6 February 1863, Secretary of State Seward informed the French government that Napoleon III's offer of mediation was refused by the Union. The British were not willing to be involved as mediators and the French could not do it on their own.

[60] Rosecrans won a victory over Bragg at Stones River, near Murfreesboro, Tennessee, in a three-day battle from 31 December 1862 to 2 January 1863. His job was to drive Bragg out of Central Tennessee, but he moved too slowly. There was no further military action until 24 June 1863 when Rosecrans, in one week at the cost of 560 casualties, pushed Bragg back into Georgia.

[61] There was an attack on Fort Sumter in Charleston Harbor on 7 April 1863. Battered by Forts Sumter and Moultrie cannons, the Federal fleet withdrew. Flag officer DuPont did not believe that Charleston could be taken by a naval force alone.

[62] Efforts to take Savannah were also unsuccessful. Though the CSS *Tennessee* was sunk, the attack on 3 March 1863 failed after eight hours of bombardment.

regiment of soldiers[63]—it is said there is great disaffection in the North West & it is very probable that parties will spring up in the southern confederacy on that issue—There are said to be no indications of an early attack on Mobile—and the fortifications there under the superintendance of Gen Buckner are represented as very formidable—Fifty feet of the raft at Choctaw-bluff are reported as gone—floated off and there is a call for 4000 hands for owen Bluff. Greene County for 330.

March 7. [second entry of this date] We had a hard rain again this morning before day and it is now raining again accompanied with hail. The news to day is that fort McAllister below Savannah was attacked on the 3rd at 5 oclock A.M. two men wounded and an 8 inch Columbiad dismounted which is said to have been replaced—from the north comes the news that all the gunboats have gone thro the cut off at Vicksburg—and they are preparing to attack Port Hudson.[64] Rain, Rain, Rain. This is a gloomy day—and there is no encouraging prospect. Mrs Hatch is no better....

March 11. We have had almost continual rains for some time and again last night it rained a flood. the wind sheered around to the North last night and it has cleared off fair & cool. Many croakers are predicting another drought this summer because of the excessive spring rains thereby endeavoring to meet trouble half way—The mails have failed to day in consequence of the swollen streams—and we have no news. Intense anxiety is felt about the posture of affairs[.] much uneasiness is felt and expressed as to the inability to feed the army and the prospect of doing so as far as we can see is certainly not good. The Lincoln Congress have expired—4th March and have passed a conscription bill placing at the command of the president all the males between 20 & 45 supposed

---

[63] A Democratic convention at Frankfort, Kentucky, was broken up by Federal authorities since the convention was said to be pro-Confederate.

[64] General Banks's federal force moved north from New Orleans to Baton Rouge and toward Port Hudson in an effort to cooperate with Grant's activities against Vicksburg. At the same time, a fake ironclad made of logs with pork barrels for funnels drifted down past the city and was subjected to fire from the Confederate batteries.

to amt to 3,000,000 of men, and appropriated $500,000,000 to carry on the war. These arrangements look very formidable.[65]

The conditions along the Mississippi River were growing more dangerous. Confederate soldiers were not being fed, the major forts were under attack, and Benners greatly feared that Vicksburg and Fort Hudson might soon be lost.

March 20. We have had a number of fine spring days and vegetation is advancing rapidly. The Peaches are in full bloom—and peas are high enough to stick. There is still a painful anxiety felt as to the issues of the War—there has been an attack on Port Hudson reported to have resulted in a victory for us. The Mississippi a fine steamer was burnt to the waters edge and two gun boats passed by in a crippled condition. This was very unlucky as it will probably cause much disaster from there to Vicksburg.[66] There is no news from Bragg's army—it is said to have been reinforced by the army of the Potomac—From fort Pemberton there has come news of a fight in which Federals were repulsed[67]—Confederate money is declining rapidly—it is quoted in Richmond at 450[68]—What will the end of all this be. Blind Tom the great musical prodigy was on exhibition last night at the Town Hall—my children went and were much delighted. I may go to night.

---

[65] The enlistment terms of ninety regiments of the nine-month men and forty regiments of the two-year men were to expire in mid-1863. There were few volunteers to replace them. Hence the need for the Enrollment Act of 3 March 1863, which made every able-bodied male a citizen, including aliens who filed for naturalization. All who were twenty to forty-five were eligible for the draft.

[66] Admiral Farragut led his Union squadron past the batteries of Port Hudson. The USS *Hartford* and *Albatross* succeeded but the USS *Monongahela* and *Richmond* were damaged and fell back. The USS *Mississippi* ran aground and was set on fire and abandoned, soon exploding in the river.

[67] The Confederates constructed Fort Pemberton on the Yazoo River to stop Yankee efforts to take Vicksburg. On 11 March 1863, the fort repelled the first of several attacks by Union gunboats. On 16 March, the Federals were forced to withdraw. Another of Grant's efforts against Vicksburg came to an end, defeated by geography and the Confederates.

[68] Most Confederates did not want to pay taxes. Thus the government began to print paper money. By 1863, it was clear that such printing was causing inflation. Benners was concerned with a price index of 450. Soon it would double to 900. By spring 1864, it took $46 to buy what one dollar had bought two years earlier.

March 21. Saturday morning—This is a cool rainy morning wind from the East. Affairs are distressingly precarious. The provision question looks ominous. It is said that one regiment at Vicksburg has offered to surrender their arms for the want of something to Eat! And government agents are impressing provisions thro the country from the citizens.[69] There is no news from Port Hudson—from Virginia there is reported a skirmish in the upper Rappahannock in which the Federals were repulsed.[70]

March 28. I went to the plantation on wednesday the 25th and returned on thursday the 26th on horseback. The road was much better than I expected to find & but for a few very bad holes would have answered for buggy driving—I found there had been a great deal of sickness—at both places. The boys Wright, Paul and Henry who returned some time since from Mobile had all of them been sick there—and have yet very bad coughs. Lewis had a desperate attack of Pneumonia and Caroline, Tom, White, Bryan, Little Tom and little Frances had all been sick—and still were except Tom White & Caroline—Webb has 40 cases of measles—and I do not doubt but that we shall have it. The corn was coming up very handsomely and the wheat looked well—oats ruined—potatoes have been planted, sorghum, and groundpeas. There is a rumor that Fort Pemberton at the mouth of the Tallahatchie river has been taken—The federals came in thro the Yazoo pass & came down the river. If true it will give them a great advantage as the Confederates have large stores of grain in that county which will be lost.[71] At Port Hudson they attacked the forts and retired

---

[69] The Impressment Act of 1863 was passed on 26 March 1863. Merchants and farmers who were unwilling to sell food and supplies to the army at prices set by the government nevertheless had those supplies impressed. The disparity between the impressment price and the market price widened greatly. Farmers who were reluctant to accept Confederate money at any price were given IOU receipts. At the end of the war, unpaid receipts valuing half a billion dollars were still outstanding.

[70] On 19 March 1863 at the battle of Kelly's Ford, Virginia, William Averell ordered an attack on the Confederate forces. He crossed the Rappahannock River and engaged in a small but hard-fought contest, resulting in his withdrawal late in the afternoon. Casualties were seventy-eight for the Federals and 133 for the Confederates.

[71] It was a false rumor.

except two which succeeded in passing up—and the Mississippi which was burned. Two boats are reported to have attempted the passage at Vicksburg—one sunk and one got thro[72]—they now have three in below Vicksburg—There is great gloom over everything.

Friday 27 was a day of fasting & Humiliation. Mary is still sick & likely to be for a long time.

March 31. We had a hard storm of wind accompanied by rain thunder and lightning on sunday morning 29th about 1 oclock A.M. DuBois[73] shop was struck by lightning and burnt up—as also Dr Osborns stable. the last two days have been raw cold drizzly—and to day it looks like clearing off but is quite cold and many are expecting the dreaded frost which usually occurs about this full moon in Easter—the two wagons came up yesterday with 50 [or 80] barrels of corn from the plantation which was delivered to A. M. Dorman[74]—all the sick reported better—little Tom, Frances child is still quite sick. There is still no news of a decided character[.] we are awaiting the attack at Vicksburg, Yazoo & Port Hudson. England declines all mediation. We have no friends—must go it alone. The selfishness of nations—...

April 28. There was considerable excitement in town on last friday evening Mr Hatch having brot the news from Demopolis that Federal Cavalry had made a raid thro Miss and were threatening Meridian and Enterprise. To day we have news that they retreated from Enterprise without fighting a passenger reports that they are moving for Baton Rouge.[75] There have been a number of Boats passed the batteries at Vicksburg and there are between 6 & 8 now below—The prospects of

---

[72] On 25 March 1863, the USS *Lancaster*, struck some thirty times, sank with most of the crew escaping. The USS *Switzerland*, badly disabled, floated down out of firing range.

[73] John DuBois and Joseph C. DuBois were gin makers in Greensboro. Snedecor, *Greene County*, 15.

[74] Amasa M. Dorman, grocer, Greensboro. Ibid., 15.

[75] In an effort to draw attention from Grant's offensive against Vicksburg, Colonel Benjamin Grierson headed south with 1,700 cavalry in a startling raid into Mississippi toward Pemberton's railroad supply line east of Jackson. His troops tore up fifty miles of railroad and lured a division of Confederate infantry into an unsuccessful effort to trap them. Sixteen days later and 600 miles from their start, they returned home with a loss of twenty-four men. It was a brilliant effort.

the Confederates in that quarter look bad. there is great uneasiness felt. We had a considerable rain last night—and cloudy this morning. Mrs Hatch & family left my house yesterday to try the waters at Newbern. I took a fishing pole on last Tuesday to Lewis Mills 3 miles from Carthage caught a good many fish—slept in the mill house and came home thursday. Randolph[,][76] Bill Wilson[77]—went and Tal[l]man joined us.

April 30. Thursday evening. I rode to the Plantation on yesterday and returned to day—The wheat is looking very fine—but there is rust in it which however has not yet attacked the stalk being confined to the blade—if it does not increase there is a prospect of a good crop, both at Walker and Cheney Place—There had been a hard hail at Newbern which fortunately did not reach plantation. Corn is doing well, the stand fine—Herrin has planted a good many potatoe drawers and the largest part of the Peas—sugar cane is coming up looks very little and not very promising. We have no news from Vicksburg—The raiders in Miss have gone to Baton Rouge.[78] The state of things is very distressing—every thing is very high—The uncertainty which hangs around the duration of the war—the ceaseless surmises and conjecture as to the intentions of the army—the long quietude—the hope deferred. God grant us patience—...

May 12, Tuesday. The council for the diocese of Alabama commenced its session in Greensboro on the 7th May being 1st Thursday and closed on Saturday—Messrs McClure of Marion and Pierce of Mobile of the clergy staid with us and Mr Addison Cobbs[79] a part of the time—Mr Thomas Cobb of Livingston of the laity—there was quite a full attendance of clergy and a respectable No of Lay delegates—considering the times—the high price of provisions and scarcity of every thing it passed off very well. Next time it sits at Montgomery. We had the pleasure among other persons present of

---

[76] Richard Randolph, planter, Greensboro. Snedecor, *Greene County*, 36.

[77] William B. Wilson, planter, Hollow Square, Greensboro. Ibid., 47.

[78] Grierson's troops skirmished at Brookhaven, Mississippi, on 29 April 1863. On the same day, Grant's troops moved southward. By noon the next day, they had crossed the Mississippi River south of Vicksburg and were preparing to move inland.

[79] Addison Cobbs, Episcopal priest, Montgomery, and brother of Richard Hooker Cobbs.

seeing Rev Mr Banister.[80] I rode to plantation yesterday and returned this morning—Wheat is rusting—and if it gets the stalk will injure it greatly—and the birds are very bad. The corn looks well—Webster gave me the blade for a cradle and I am going to have it stocked. Herrin mended the old one also—We had a great alarm last Monday from a report that the enemy were advancing on Tuscaloosa & had reached to within three miles of Elyton. The rumor proved to be false.[81] It probably originated from their having visited Blountsville and endeavored to get to Rosa—and were captured by Forrest with 550 men—the number taken was 1600[82]—Gen Lee gained a victory at Chancellorville last sunday and on next day attacked them near Fredericksburg and drove them across the Rappahannock[83]—John Cowin was killed & a number of our company wounded & taken prisoners—Capt Williams W. A. Simms and Alfred Ward were taken prisoners[84]—Gen Jackson was wounded and has since died[85]—we have news also that Van Dorn has been murdered by a man named Dr Peters[86]—we have very little news from Mississippi. The fate of the country is trembling in the balance—the Govt impressed horses here on thursday and impressed Sunbeam—I bought a horse ...

---

[80] The Reverend Mr. Banister was a former rector of St. Paul's in Greensboro.

[81] On 11 April 1863, Colonel A. D. Streight and his cavalry left Nashville on their way deep into Georgia. On 1 May, Federal forces skirmished at Blountsville on the east branch of the Big Warrior River in Alabama. The North did not reach Elyton, Alabama, until 7 March 1865.

[82] At Cedar Bluff, Alabama, on 3 May 1863, Colonel Streight's tired and discouraged band surrendered to Nathan B. Forrest after a skirmish. Streight was unable to destroy Southern railroads, which had been his main purpose.

[83] From 2–6 May 1863, Robert E. Lee defeated Joseph Hooker at Chancellorsville, Virginia. The Confederacy lost 12,821—22 percent of Lee's 60,892; the Federals lost 17,278—13 percent of their army of 133,868. It has been called Lee's greatest battle.

[84] The Greensboro Guards fought in this battle. Fourteen were taken prisoner, seventeen lay wounded, and perhaps as many as four received fatal wounds. Doctor John H. Cowin was hit in the leg, and despite efforts to apply a tourniquet, bled to death. Hubbs, "Guarding Greensboro," 235.

[85] Stonewall Jackson was wounded on 2 May and died a week later.

[86] General Earl Van Dorn was killed on 8 May 1863 at Springhill, Mississippi, by Doctor Peters, a resident of the neighborhood who stated in justification of his act that Van Dorn had violated the sanctity of his home. Van Dorn's friends denied the reason, saying that Van Dorn was shot in the back in cold blood and for political reasons.

for $475 and he was accepted as a substitute at $400—The coldest weather I ever felt in this month was thursday & Friday during Convention—7th & 8 May....

Benners's worst fear, the loss of Vicksburg, was coming true. General Grant was able to take his men below Vicksburg and cross the Mississippi River with the help of his Navy. Then, in the next eighteen days, Grant covering 200 miles, won five battles, captured eighty-eight cannons, took 4,500 prisoners, and surrounded Vicksburg. It was a campaign as brilliant as any of Napoleon's. Time was running out for Vicksburg, the last Confederate stronghold on the Mississippi River.

May 25. I went to plantation last thursday 21st Jane went with me and called in to see her Mother at Huggins—I found Herrin just commencing to cut the wheat at the Walker Place—and finding it not fully ripe he stopped till to day—I felt quite unwell at the plantation having had a very bad Cough and cold for a week which affects my digestion. The federals advanced from Grand Gulf and captured Jackson and burnt all the public buildings—including the Penitentiary since which they have advanced on Vicksburg under Grant—it is said with a column of fifty thousand men—They are reported to have made three assaults on Vicksburg and been repulsed.[87] Snyders Bluff is evacuated—and Yazoo City captured.[88] Great events are about happening.

May 27. There seems to be great difficulty in getting the truth from the military operations in Mi[ssissippi]. Grant is reported to have telegraphed to Stanton that he has carried the 1st line of Entrenchments before Vicksburg—while our despatches report that the Federals assaulted six times and were each time repulsed.[89] There is

---

[87] On 7 May 1863, Grant, joined by Sherman's corps, began to move toward Jackson, Mississippi. Seven days later, he occupied the capital. Then he moved west toward Vicksburg with an army of 45,000 men. He attempted two assaults—one on 19 May and the second on 22 May. Neither was successful, so Grant settled down into a siege.

[88] Yazoo City was captured on 20 May 1863.

[89] On the 22 May 1863, all three of Grant's corps launched a simultaneous attack along a four-mile front. They made temporary penetrations of the enemy works at

intense uneasiness felt about Vicksburg—Vallandingham who was arrested by a military authority and tried has been sentenced by the Pres to come South[90]—He is Democratic Candidate for Gov of Ohio & his arrest in any other govt would produce great trouble—I have not been to plantation since last thursday & friday—having bad cold & headache.

May 29. We are still without definite news as to the condition of things at Vicksburg. There is a private despatch which says all is well there—but it is difficult to express the intense uneasiness felt for its fate. Burnside is said to be mounting all his army so as to move rapidly—and the federals are said to be preparing 100,000 cavalry for raids. Valandingham has been sent south. We hear very little of the progress of the revolution in the North—Gov. Seymour of New York has denounced the administration[91]—If Vicksburg is held it may produce the crisis—but I dont think it will I have again been urgently solicited to be a candidate for Legislature We had a light rain last night which was very grateful—but not 1/2 enough—

June 3. We had a good rain here on saturday May 30th at the plantation we had a light rain on Thursday 28th not enough—Mr Herrin set out potatoes. On Saturday, 30 Edward brought up and delivered to A. M. Dorman 23-1/2 barrels of corn being the balance due him of the 200 bushels according to my contract for salt—Edward reported that nearly all the wheat had been cut at plantation. We are still without definite news of the fate of Vicksburg. The federals are reported to have made the 9th assault and been repulsed with great slaughter—it is said that 30,000 have been killed—we have lost 400[92]—the dead lie unburied and pestilence is feared. Gen Johnston is massing an army 5

---

several points but could not hold them. In the attacks of 19 May and 22 May, the Federals lost 4,200 men.

[90] Clement Vallandigham, a US congressman from Ohio and opponent of the war, was arrested on 5 May 1863 and banished to the Confederacy but was transferred by them to Canada where he conducted a campaign for governor of Ohio.

[91] Horatio Seymour, governor of New York, believing that the liberties of the people were being lost, condemned the decision to banish Vallandigham, arguing that it was cowardly, brutal, and infamous.

[92] These rumors were not true.

miles north of Jackson, has 30,000 men will move when he gets transportation.[93] Snyders Bluff is evacuated and Port Hudson is invested.

June 5, [6] Saturday. I went to the plantation yesterday morning & returned to day. Jane went down in the carriage and carried Willie & Johnny—We were much pleased to learn that Mrs Hatch thought she was better. Jane took dinner with her mother and came over after dinner. Herrin had cut all the wheat but the acre sowed last which is not yet ripe—he reports it as turning out very well—it has not yet been housed. They are needing rain—what fell on 28 May having been very light and is all dried up nearly—it did not stop the cracks in the ground, but the corn is looking very well & is tassling in places quite low—the sugar cane is growing vigorously but is too thick. The papers report a battle at Port Hudson on the 27th and say that the federals under Gen Sherman were routed by Kirby Smith.[94] What is really the truth of affairs at Vicksburg among conflicting reports is very difficult to decide. The Federals claim that they have reduced all the shore batteries and all the batteries above and below and that their upper fleet is within 3 miles of their lower one—and they have set some houses afire. the confederates report that Grant has made 9 unsuccessful assaults having been repulsed every time—with great slaughter placing the number killed at 30,000[95]—the dead bodies which were not buried are very offensive and a pestilence is apprehended—Johns[t]on when last heard from was massing his forces 5 miles from Jackson—and there is a rumor that Gen Walker of Ga had with 8000 men cut his way thro the federals to reinforce Gen Pemberton. This is only a rumor—there are many refugees from Miss passing thro here on their way to a safer place with their negroes. I have consented to be a candidate for the Legislature again. It will be unpleasant and a great sacrifice to me if elected—But I want to do my duty to my state & country if required.

---

[93] Joseph Johnston raised the strength of his army to 30,000, but most of the men were green troops for whom sufficient supplies and equipment were not available.

[94] General Sherman attempted to reduce Ford Hill with the aid of gunboats. The high point of the Confederate position allowed them to shell the gunboat USS *Cincinnati*. It sank with forty casualties. It is clear that Sherman was not routed by Kirby Smith.

[95] Another false rumor.

June 8. Jane returned with the children Billy & Johnny friday night—she took dinner at Henrys [Henry Watson] and reports that while she was there it rained a very good shower and the road was wet as far as Hills. It has rained here a little this morning & turned cool and it looks as if we might have a general rain. It will be very acceptable. We get no further news from the war to day—There was a rumor in town friday that Johnston had engaged the federals and captured 30,000 prisoners—of course it is very unlikely—We are all distressingly anxious for the war to close but there seems now no prospect of such a desirable event—The South cant stop & the North wont. May God overrule it all for the good of the Country. We are much encouraged with prospect of good corn crops—it is tassling low but looks healthy & strong.

June 10. There is still a distressing uncertainty as to the results at Vicksburg & Port Hudson. We learn that a rumor was in Jackson that a courier from Pemberton advised Johns[t]on that he need not be in a hurry on his account. Per contra the federals speak with great confidence of their ability to reduce the place—From Port Hudson we hear positively nothing. Kirby Smith was said to have crossed over with his forces—It is now said that it was Gen Taylor. We had a fine rain on Monday 8th presume it rained at Plantation from the direction of the cloud—The seasons so far have been propitious for crops—and now cloudy and promising rain.

June 12. Friday. I went to plantation on Wednesday Evening 10 and returned yesterday morning. It threatened rain all the way down and also on my return. There was a light sprinkle at Cheney Place—wednesday night—and a good rain from Newbern to Greensboro thursday morning causing my road to be heavy. Herrin says we had a good rain on monday 8th June which is the only one he has had of any consequence. He had commenced to haul in the Wheat but the appearance of rain induced him to desist. The Corn looks very fine the tassling low—potatoes are doing well and peas do [ditto]. There is still nothing decisive from Vicksburg. It is said to day that there has been no fighting there for 10 days. Grant is investing for a regular siege—and Gen Johnston is preparing to raise the siege. The federal forces of cavalry are said to have crossed the Rappahannock and driven back by Gen Stewart—Why these drivings back are not more conclusive & disastrous is a wonder—

June 13. Saturday. I carried Fanny to see her grandma at Newbern yesterday evening & left her there and went to the plantation and returned this morning—The wheat has not yet been hauled in—the corn looks very well—but the earliest corn on the road at the Walker Place has been injured I think by late plowing—Vacation has commenced with Alfred and Ed and the latter has gone to Newbern this evening with his grandpa and Alfred has gone fishing. We have no decisive news from Vicksburg. In fact it is so difficult to distinguish the truth from the false that we may be said really to know nothing about the State of affairs there—Johns[t]on is gathering an army to raise the siege. Whether his army will be large enough or in time is yet to be seen.[96]

June 16. I carried Alfred to the plantation yesterday and I returned this morning leaving Ed and Alfred there. They were hauling in Wheat when I reached Cheney Place but immediately after a heavy rain coming on they had to desist. The corn looks well but I think is overshooting itself. Mrs Campbell was at Walker Place. There is still no news from Vicksburg. The federals are reported to have sent 37 transports with troops down the river—it is said we have only 30 or 40,000 with Johns[t]on.

July 3. I carried Ed to the plantation on Monday 29 June and returned on Wednesday 1 July. We had a rain on Monday 15—again on sunday it rained very hard having also rained on the night previous—the creeks were put out of the banks and got over the Walker bottom—a hard wind blew the corn down very badly especially in the Walker bottom the ground being made rotten by the water. it must be very much injured as there was much water standing among it when I was there. Kit was working on the mill and the hands were all hoeing along ditch banks &c, the ground being too wet for ploughs. The corn crop was the finest in its promise of any I ever saw on the land. to what extent it will be injured by the water & wind I cannot tell tho it must be

---

[96] Johnston's army of 30,000 was twenty miles east of Vicksburg, but the men lacked sufficient supplies, weapons, and transportation. On 15 June 1863, Johnston reported to Richmond, "I consider saving Vicksburg hopeless."

considerable. The sugar cane is growing very luxuriantly but is too thick to yield to the best advantage. I bot a barrel of lime to put up my furnace for boiling syrup. It is a very troublesome business—and I shall be sick of it before it is through with—[97]

The news from Vicksburg is still contradicting and indecisive—it is reported that supplies have been thrown in from the other side of the river—the enemy sprung a mine—it is said to have been a failure killing some of their own men.[98] Gen Johns[t]on has not advanced at the last accts. Nothing from Port Hudson—from Tennessee it is reported that Rosecrans has advanced and our forces have fallen back from Shelbyville to Tallahoma—the Confederates suffered in the fight at Liberty gap. Rosecrans it is feared is more than a match for Bragg[99]—Confederate forces from Lee's army have gone into Maryland and Pennsylvania—and there is a rumor that we hold Harrisburg[100]—Col. Garrett was killed at Vicksburg on 17 June. There was concert at the college on the 1st July—didn't go—Barbecue at Newbern tomorrow and concert there to night. Got 12 bushels wheat ground at Waltons mill 358 pounds flour—sent Herrin nearly 1/2 of it.

July 13. I went to plantation with Fanny on Monday 6th and returned on 7th. The govt took 4 of my negro men viz George Henry Paul Wright to work on Selma. George and Wright carried shovels & Paul & Henry spades.[101] The press is finished and the sugar cane

---

[97] Benners raised sugarcane for the first time; perhaps he needed the money, but he was unhappy with the process.

[98] Probably not true, but several attempts were made to penetrate Confederate defenses at Vicksburg by mining. On 25 June 1863, 2,200 pounds of powder were exploded in a tunnel. Two regiments attempted to exploit the gap in the defenses to no avail. Another attempt on 1 July was also unsuccessful.

[99] Rosecrans, moving forward into the middle of Tennessee, fought Bragg's men at Liberty Gap, Tennessee, 24–27 June 1863. His Tullahoma campaign was successful.

[100] Robert E. Lee invaded Pennsylvania, and one of his corps commanders almost reached Harrisburg before being recalled to Gettysburg where the battle was fought on 1–3 July 1863.

[101] In fall 1862, public support for the conscription of slaves to relieve white soldiers had resulted in the passage of such laws. There was some resistance since slaves were important to an owner's livelihood. Benners was not happy with the practice but did not resist it.

ripening fast. While I was there the news came that Vicksburg had Capitulated on the 4 July saturday—17,000 men surrendered[102]—Grant has since moved on to Jackson and attacked Johnson and the fight was not decided sunday morning.[103] There is much perplexity and panic in the Country. The course of events is rapid and uncertain. Mrs Hatch & family came to my home last Monday—her health continues very bad. The fruit crop is unprecedented. I never had such fine peaches—cantelopes too are very fine Watermelons a failure with me so far.

With news of the fall of Vicksburg and the march of Sherman in pursuit of Joseph Johnston's troops in Jackson, Benners feared that the Union army would soon be in Alabama. Actually, Sherman was happy driving Johnston out of Jackson and never intended to follow him into Alabama. He completed the victory of Vicksburg by driving Confederate troops out of Mississippi. Benners need not have worried about Sherman. Instead of entering Alabama, the battles shifted to Tennessee.

July 17. I went to plantation on tuesday morning and returned Wednesday and again that Evening and returned on Thursday—They were beating out the Wheat at both places. There is great gloom and distress in the community by reason of the fall of Vicksburg and advance of the federal army to Jackson—the last accts are that Johnston is still fighting there. it is thought he will have to fall back to Meridian, Demopolis and Selma—

July 22. I went to plantation on Monday with Alfred and on tuesday morning we went to Selma and returned in the evening—staid all night at Parkers and came home to day. They were still thrashing out the wheat at both places. Sugar cane has fallen down very badly—Scip came

---

[102] Pemberton surrendered his 30,000 men on 4 July 1863. These soldiers were paroled, pledging that they would not bear arms again.

[103] Grant sent Sherman with his 50,000 soldiers to pursue Johnston's army, which had retreated to Jackson, Mississippi. Sherman began to surround the city in order to starve out the defenders, but Johnston withdrew leaving central Mississippi to the Federals.

on 21 to put up furnace for boiling juice. Johnston has fallen back to Chunby and his cavalry have readvanced to Brandon.[104]

August 1. Saturday. I went in the Buggy with Ed to the Plantation on Thursday evening 30 July and returned this morning. They were busy pulling fodder and grinding cane—about 1/3 of a barrel was made of syrup before I left there and they are working to day—the syrup is pretty good but will be better when the cane is older. My principal straight is the want of barrels I have not got them, and dont know where I shall get them. Edward went to Mr John S. Haywoods to day and to Mr Huggins[105] who have both promised me two a piece. Mr Hatch and family are at my house. I hear no further news from Charl[e]ston, the general opinion is it will fall.[106] Raids from N. Alabama are spoken of and the Conscript act is raised to 45. What is still coming on us God only knows.

September 2. Wednesday. On the 14 I left home for Montgy—staid at Parkers and left on the train on Saturday—reached Selma at 9, and left on the Duke for Montgy—reached there Sunday morning 16th breakfast. took board at Hall—had disagreeable session of two weeks—left on Monday evening Aug 31 on the Senator & reached Selma tuesday to breakfast—left in cars at 3 o clock reached Newern 5-1/2 and home on stage at 8-1/2 tuesday night found all well. Some scamp has cut off my apron & curtains from my buggy and stole one of my pigs. While in Montgomery I was informed by a message from Dr Hal Webb that his brother Lt Col Jas D. Webb my intimate friend and companion had died in the yankee lines in Tenn of a wound received in battle. A noble generous spirit has fled and sadly do I feel my personal bereavement.[107] May God protect and defend his widow and little ones.

---

[104] There was action at Brandon, Mississippi, a part of Sherman's Jackson campaign. They also scouted Danville, Mississippi.

[105] John S. Haywood, planter, Newern, Greensboro, and Jacob Huggins, planter, Newern. Snedecor, *Greene County*, 21, 23.

[106] There was severe bombardment of Forts Sumter and Charleston throughout the last months of 1863. Neither surrendered until Sherman's men came to Charleston on 18 February 1865.

[107] James D. Webb died in the Battle of Chickamauga. This battle on 18–19 September 1863 was an important tactical victory for the Confederacy. Still it cost

September 15. I went to plantation with Ed & Alfred on thursday morning and returned with Ed on friday morning, Sept 11. Went again on Sunday 13 & returned with Alfred on Monday 14. Herrin had made 9 barrels of molasses—Burke had been sick at Selma and returned on Thursday 10—Wright & George returned on Saturday 12th. Every one of their spades were taken away from them by the overseers in Selma—Bragg has fallen back to Dalton and federals have taken Chattanooga.[108]

Benners continued to lose his lawyer friends to the war—Colonel James D. Webb in Tennessee and Colonel Richard F. Inge at the Battle of Chickamauga. He longed for the "horrible strife" to end. Several months later, he traveled to Montgomery for another unsatisfactory legislative session. These were not the best of times for Augustus Benners.

September 31 [30]. Wednesday morning. I went to plantation on the 26th with Alfred and Ed and returned on Sunday 27th I went to Eutaw with Parker on the 28 and returned same day. Went to plantation on tuesday 29th & returned same day Fanny went with me—Had made 12-1/2 barrels molasses and were gathering Corn—Herrin informs me that he has 70 packed bales cotton at Cheney P. 19 at Walker Place...he has 100 bales fodder 35 bushels peas—and the wheat crop was at Cheney Place 83—at W.P. 100. I am grievously pained to hear of the death of Col R. Inge my intimate companion and friend high souled and chivalrous he has fallen a victim to this war. Most deeply do I deplore his death and sympathize with his widow & children. O. H. Prince was killed in same battle (of Chicamauga) fought on Saturday, Sunday, & Monday 19, 20, 21 Sept. Mr Hutchinson lost a son Joe and had another wounded—Lt. Col. T. H. Herndon was wounded and is here in town. he is reported improving. Bragg is said to have gained a victory—but dearly

---

the Confederates 18,454 casualties, nearly 30 percent of its forces. Union casualties were 16,170.

[108] The Confederates bottled up Rosecrans in Chattanooga in late September 1863. Only when the Union government decided to reinforce him, sending 17,000 troops under Sherman and 20,000 men from the Army of the Potomac under the leadership of General Grant, was the situation rectified.

did the Southerners suffer—and I do not think much was decided by it as the Federal troops under Gen Rosecrans fell back on Chattanooga and hold it and are fortifying. Oh my bleeding Country when oh when will this horrible strife close—

November 2. I went to plantation on 31 Oct & Ret. Sunday Nov 1. Herrin had built the pen at depot to deliver corn to Red Mountain Iron Works. they have agreed to take it there at 1.25 a bushel—ordered 3 sacks filled with corn 1 with wheat and 1 with potatoes for Grambles [or Grumbles] at Selma. The war still rages and a great battle is expected down at or near Chattanooga—Bragg having driven Rosecrans to Chattanooga seems to have the bull by the horns.[109] The federal[s] are reported to have crossed below at raccoon ford to flank him. prices are very high—a pair of boots fifty Dollars and cotton cards 75. Salt $90—gave all shoes except Ned, Hannah, Caroline & 2 small ones besides Mary & Celia.

December 10. I left home on the 6th Nov for Montgomery to attend the Legislature—staid at Parkers that night.[110] took the cars on Saturday morning at 6 o clock reached Selma at 9. Alfred & Fanny & Mary Quitman went with me to Selma and returned that evening. I left at night on the Steamboat King and reached Montgomery Sunday morning. Took board at Judge Phelans—Judge Coleman and Mr Chapman of Perry and Mr Powell of Tuscaloosa comprised our boarders. We had a very hurried and unsatisfactory session. Not much legislation of a general character—but unfortunately the first out croppings of a purpose to revive parties—R. W. Walker was elected senator—Judge Phelan Judge of Supreme Court. J. R. John Chancellor of Middle division—I voted for Mr Clay for senator—and on the last ballot where his name was withdrawn for Fitzpatrick. I left Montgomery on tuesday evening on the St Charles reached Selma Wednesday morning to breakfast. took the cars after dinner and reached Newbern at

---

[109] Benners did not understand the situation at Chattanooga. With Grant in charge and fresh troops available, a plan was set in motion that won a victory for the Union and forced Bragg out of Chattanooga. Bragg was replaced by Joseph Johnston.

[110] Benners had been reelected to the Alabama legislature and served during 1864.

six being the 9th day of Dec. Staid with Coleman all night at Parkers and came home this morning Dec 10 in my carriage—found all well except my wife who has been quite sick and is still very unwell. she has had fever frequently and complains of constant sick stomach. My chester sow had seven pigs while I was gone and one of my half chesters was stolen the night I left here....

1864

The new year brought in some of the coldest weather Benners had ever experienced. He lost his overseer and had to return several slaves to his friend General Owens. Gloomy about the war, he wrote, "The times are sadly out of joint."

January 2. Saturday—Christmas was quite a pleasant day as was the day after. Sunday we had rain no church. Monday it rained. Tuesday was a fair day. Wednesday was cloudy and in the evening it rained very hard. thursday it rained nearly all day—and thursday night the wind was very high—the old year went out in a perfect storm of wind—chopping round to North West. Friday New Years day was very cold. Ther[mometer] in the morning at my house being 16 when I came down to breakfast. This morning same time it was 14°. I am told that some thermometers indicated 7° this morning. I sent for Gen Owens negroes Phillis & Hannah and Margaret and her two children on Wednesday—delivered them to S. D. Owens agent on thursday.[111] There is a good deal of trouble among the men who have furnished substitutes by reason of the bill which has passed congress putting them into the army. The position of affairs for Confederate States is very gloomy. The U. States forces drove Braggs army from position around Chattanooga and they have gone into winter quarters near Dalton. Desertions are reported numerous and the army destitute of clothes and shoes—[112]

---

[111] Stephen D. Owen, broker, Greensboro, is listed in Snedecor's *Directory of Greene County* as Owens; he is Owen in the 1860 US Census.

[112] The Confederate forces under the command of Bragg suffered a devastating defeat at the hands of new forces under the command of Grant at the battle of

January 15—We have had since 1st of January one of the coldest spells of weather ever experienced here. It sleeted and froze and rained and the Ther° was down as low as 12° at my house—To day for the first time since we have a glimpse of sunshine—tho the weather is still cold and apparently not settled. I sent George[,] Henry and Charles to Selma on tuesday 5 Jany—Henry came back on wednesday ankle weak Sent Herrin word to send another—agreed with Herrin before christmas to stay with me at the rate of $400 a year, returned Gen Owens negroes on the 29th Dec to S. D. Owens—hated to do it but could not help it.

January 16. Mr Herrin sent up yesterday 56 hams 2 Turkeys—Butter and a shoat and bag ground peas. These are the hams of the first killing Dec. 1. 63—and are to be smoked at home—Edward represents the road as very bad indeed.

January 29. I rode in buggy to plantation on Monday 25 and returned next day—Emelines youngest child had been found dead in the bed—supposed to have been smothered—Herrin had had a fuss with William and Tom White—he caught hold of him and he resisted—I had him thrashed for it. At the gin house they had broke the lock and at Walker place broke the house and stole wheat and ground peas—no clue to the rogues.

February 15. I rode to my plantation in my buggy on Monday evening 8th and walked back on the 9th—Herrin informed me he wants to quit—and would do so in a few days—his wife was displeased at my finding fault that so little cloth was spun. I went down again on the 11th and returned same evening. he left that day and went to Gray Huckabees. I have now no over[seer] and there is great excitement about our army falling back in Miss and fears of the federal army destroying by raids.[113] The times are sadly out of joint.

February 18. I walked to the plantation yesterday and came back in my buggy in evening. there is great excitement among our people. news

---

Chattanooga between 23 and 25 November 1863. Confederate casualties numbered 6,667, while Union losses were 5,824.

[113] In early February 1864, with Union forces under Sherman approaching Meridian, Mississippi, from the west and William Sooy Smith's troops approaching from the north, the Confederate army under Polk fell back from their position in central Mississippi.

from Demopolis—Confederates falling back and federals advancing. The result no man knows. The negroes are getting along pretty well....

The next month Benners's spirits brightened—planting was going better, slaves were working well, and a new overseer was hired. He took time to list the names of his slaves, with a few duplications. It is not clear why some names were underlined and some circled. In all, he had 125 slaves, a testament to his financial success.

March 7. Monday morning. I went to the plantation on Saturday the 5 and returned on Sunday the 6th Commenced planting corn on Monday Feby 29th. The negroes are all well & getting on pretty well. I gave out the allowance while I was down there. I sent down last Monday the two little sows from here—and the white one went to Dick on Thursday & Friday the 3rd & 4th. There are 28 pigs at cheney place & 10 sows. Ned was grinding meal. He turned out on Saturday 12 bushels. Caroline planted the Castor beans on Saturday 5th I gave Lewis a shirt when I was down there and gave Mary 3 yds cloth to make another shirt—and two yds for back bands. The little black sow at home had 6 pigs March 2 and big white one had 11 pigs March 4 all died but one and that looks likely to die—

March 16. Wednesday evening. Thanks to our heavenly father my wife was safe delivered of a fine boy on tuesday night March 15—and is reported doing well as also the baby.[114] On Monday evening 16th I went to plantation to meet Capt Bass who was impressing meat. I rode down in my buggy in two hours—road very rough. He ascertained I had no surplus and impressed no meat took an ox I was fattening—I came home next evening it was bitter cold and last night Ther fell to 29° alas for the fruit. There is great stillness in war matters. The Currency Tax &

---

[114] Charles (Charley) Benners was born on 15 March 1864 and died on 23 August 1865. A delicate child, he had health problems all of his short life.

Military bill are the topic of conversation[115]—when oh when will we have peace—Wash was better.

March 17. Thursday. Another hard frost last nigh[t] & Ice. I fear fruit is killed.

Friday 18. Another frost this morning—the weather however has now moderated—yesterday & to day Assessor took income tax.

March 28. on Wednesday 23 march 64 I rode to my plantation in the buggy. In the evening Mr Scarborough came over—on the previous Saturday I engaged him as overseer of both places at the rate of $600 a year to be paid in currency after I shall have sold some of the crop of '64—and he is to leave whenever I choose or whenever he pleases. He came over and Ed Hauled his furniture the next day 24th from which time his service begins. On the next day Thursday I went to Selma & returned in the evening—let Burke go on a visit to his Mother. It rained on the way back and had a very disagreeable time getting to Parkers where I staid all night and came home next day in my buggy—The road was very bad and I got home on good friday at 11 o.clock The peaches appear to have been all or nearly all killed by the frost and corn will have to be replanted—having probably rotted in the ground.

List of the slaves' names includes duplications; italicized names were underlined in journal, underlined names were circled.

Lewis	Burke	Windsor
Tom Scott	Wash	Lewis
Ann	Big Frances	Daneas
Laura	*Bill*	Lucinda
John Potts	Ed	Frances
Priscy	Mary	Milly
Big William	Celia	*Godfrey*
Jane	Kit	Dilsy
Frank	Susan	Henrietta

---

[115] An act of the Confederate Congress suspended the writ of habeas corpus until 31 July 1864 in order to meet resistance to the conscription law and other disloyal activities.

Paul	*Ned*	*Primas*
Henry	Elisha	Celia
Nathan	Caroline	John Edwards
Aggy	Math	Hagar
Tom White	*Nick*	*Venus*
Caroline	Want	Old Sukey
Emline	Isaiah	Old Horace
Isaac	Morca	Old Diver
Big Hanna	Liddy	Wright
Cornelius	Sarah	George
Gus	*Harry*	Charles
Wm Henry	Bryan	
Little Francis	Alfred	
Money	Big Wash	
	Peter	

[*second list of slave names*]

<u>Priscy & John</u>	Hannah	Lucinda
Amy	Liny	Maria
Isabella	Mose	Windsor
Mage	Joe	Jim
<u>Ann & Tom</u>	Little Frances	<u>Frances</u>
Rosanna	Tom	Dick
Jim	Catherine	<u>Milly</u>
Nat	<u>Big Frances</u>	Castilla
<u>William James</u>	Charles	<u>Anthony</u>
Ed	Christina	Dan
Wily	Fed	<u>Anthony</u>
Mary	<u>Celia</u>	<u>Dils</u>
Bob	Mary	Stephen
Milly		Phebe
<u>Henry & Aggy</u>		Bacchus
John		<u>Hagar</u>
William		Lara
<u>T. White & Caline</u>		<u>Venus</u>

Elliah   Mary
Allen   Peter
Emline & [illegible]
Nancy

The weather remained cold and wet. Despite Benners's efforts to replant some of his crops, he had little success. There was too much rain. Spring came very slowly, and the military situation grew worse. And there was always more inflation—"Prices still rule very high."

March 30. Dr Jackson hauled to my house on the 25 March 1000 pounds of fodder in return for 1000 pounds of fodder packed and delivered by me for him at Newbern in payment of his tithe—[116]

April 5. We have had more rain and protracted cold weather peaches are all killed some time since and the spring is the most backward ever seen. There is reason to fear that the apples have also been cut off by the cold tho not having all bloomed some of them may be saved. Lovings division was expected to have gone through here to day but the news is now they will not come along until to morrow. The gloomy weather the backward spring and the horrible war still in all its fury raging leave no room for happiness or pleasant anticipations—I have not been to my place since Mr Scarborough took charge—

April 9. I rode to plantation in sulky on the 6th Wednesday—and returned on friday evening—I left home after Lovings division passed thro—the day had been very bright—but before night it clouded up and rained pretty hard in the course of the night and again on thursday night it rained very hard with high wind. Scarboro came to take charge on 25th March. I found him and his wife at the Cheney place. I am to pay him at the rate of $600 a year—he is to leave whenever I see proper & can quit when he chooses. The corn is coming up badly by reason of the protracted cold and constant rains. There is nothing like a stand and the ground soaked with water—Celia & Edward were sick. I found the road home very bad—very deep holes in Watsons lane & in Boardmans—and

---

[116] Reuben H.Jackson, physician, Greensboro. Snedecor, *Greene County*, 24. Jackson was a member of St. Paul's and Benners was a vestryman.

mud nearly all the way. sold to day 4-1/2 bushels groundpeas to Ramey[117] for $45—

April 14. I went to plantation in sulky on tuesday 12 and returned this morning found the Jones road almost impassable. The corn is coming up badly by reason of the backward spring and heavy rains & continued cold—there is not a good stand by any means and we are replanting in missing places. They were also planting groundpeas at cheney P. The wheat looks very indifferent—not a half a stand and the ridges broken by the water and drowned—white cow had a calf the morning I got there—no cholera yet among hogs but am fearful of a visit—no one seriously sick. Kit finished covering the dwelling house the day I got there, and commenced on the ploughs.

April 21. Thursday. I attended Cir. Co at Eutaw this week. went over in sulky Monday evening and returned in buggy with C. W. Hatch on Wednesday to Dinner. Percival Hatch came home in my sulky last night. I staid at Judge Colemans and had a very kind entertainment—Dined at W. P. Webbs[118] tuesday. Hatchs pistol selling cases were continued during the War and his liquor selling cases till next time—The backwardness of the spring is very striking in the forest—very little foliage and dogwood not yet in full bloom—a few honey suckles only to be seen and to day out of the shade it is quite cool. There is intense anxiety felt as to the issue of anticipated military movements in Va & in Tenn—Lee cavalry passed thro Tuscaloosa to reinforce Johnson and Longstreet is said to have gone to Va to reinforce Lee[119]...no good effect is yet visible from the currency acts. The 5s are no better than the 1s.

April 23. Saturday. I rode to plantation in my sulky on Thursday evening and returned friday. stopped at Waltons mill where Edward had left eleven bushels of wheat the day before to have ground. It turned out

---

[117] A. Rodolf Ramey, teacher, German Creek precinct, Greensboro. Ibid., 36.

[118] William P. Webb, lawyer, Eutaw, and planter, Greensboro. Ibid., 45.

[119] On 7 April 1864, Longstreet was ordered to move his army from Tennessee northward to join Lee's army in Virginia in anticipation of Grant's next move. Two days later, Grant put in place his strategy of advancing against the Confederate forces on several fronts by directing Meade to lead the Army of Potomac against Lee in Virginia and Sherman to advance against Johnston's troops in Georgia.

275 pounds extra flour 154 pounds super fine and 30 pounds shorts besides the bran making in all 459 pounds—or 41. 8/11 pounds to the bushel—besides the bran. I sent to Mr Scarboro 60 pounds ie 24 Extra[,] 36 superfine—and the 30 pounds shorts[120] I sent to be given to the negroes. I sent to depot at Newbern tithe meat reported by Edward to be 446 pounds side and shoulders and to day I sent 15 hams weighing 247 pounds to be delivered to Griggs. The corn is doing very poorly. It does not seem to have grown any in a week, and stand is poor—wheat stand very poor. Charles & George returned [from Selma] on last saturday night April 16 having been absent since Jany 4th 102 days.

April 26. I rode to plantation on yesterday monday & returned in the evening. The roads have improved very much. I sent up Dilse to nurse the baby and she brings her two youngest children with her. Delia went down this morning in the same cart Dilse came in. There is very little improvement in appearance of the crops. Corn looks very badly and stand is miserable—have done replanting—ploughed up none except in sugar cane land. Hatchs regiment of cavalry came here Saturday and went to Newbern this Morn[ing]. The indications are that a great battle will be fought in Va very soon—the crisis of the war seems to be at hand. Banks is said to have been defeated in La by Dick Taylor—and Forest took Fort Pillow[121]—There has yet been no perceptible improvement in the currency—Prices still rule very high—

April 30. Went to plantation in Buggy yesterday evening with Fanny and returned this Saturday morning. Corn is very poor, wheat poorer. Peas eat up by bugs and garden vegetables poor enough. Sold to Brumbalow for poor families 100 bushels corn for poor families in Randolph[Bibb County].

---

[120] Shorts—a byproduct of wheat milling that includes the germ, fine bran, and some flour.

[121] After forcing the withdrawal of Union forces led by Banks after the Battle of Sabine Crossroads in Louisiana on 8 April 1864, Confederate forces led by Richard Taylor were themselves driven back at Pleasant Hill on the following day by Banks's forces. On 12 April 1864, forces led by Nathan B. Forrest captured Fort Pillow in Tennessee, resulting in 231 Union casualties (mostly Black Northern soldiers) and only fourteen Confederate casualties.

May 5. Capt Hill impressed my grey horses on Monday, Joe & Jerry, and they were appraised at $1900 and carried towards Tuscaloosa—he signed his name to the certificate he gave me E. P Hill capt and Q. M. Rossi Brigade, Lee's Cavalry—My only horse Sunbeam was not taken being pronounced by Arbiters Jones & Harvey to be absolutely necessary to my business. Sears Brigade Mississippians passed thro yesterday on their way to Tuscaloosa last night they counter marched and went back thro town on their way to Montevallo 2500—There is a report in town to day that Taylor has captured Banks whole army at Grand Ecore.[122]

The spring campaigns of Grant and Sherman in Virginia and Georgia had begun. Grant attacked Lee in the wilderness, while Sherman pushed Joseph Johnston back from Chattanooga toward Atlanta. Benners considered this the "crisis of the war" that could bring it to an end. There continued to be considerable sickness on his plantation, but the crops were improving.

May 9. I went to plantation on Saturday with Alfred in Buggy and returned friday morning. Corn is looking very badly & stand is very poor—wheat miserable—peas eat up by the bug—rain badly needed—potatoes are sprouting in bed very scantily—planting prospects very gloomy—on Saturday Rossi's brigade Texan Cavalry passed thro town—Fighting in Va commenced 25 miles from Orange Court house on Thursday. Longstreet was wounded by his own men accidentally. The crisis of the War is or seems to be at hand. The large armies in Georgia and Va it would seem will decide the contest—[123]

---

[122] Banks withdrew his forces from Grand Ecore, Louisiana, on 21 April 1864. Despite harassment from Confederate troops at Wilson's Landing, Bayou Pierre, and Well's Plantation, Banks's retreating army arrived at Alexandria, Louisiana, in late April.

[123] The Battle of the Wilderness on 5–6 May 1864 marked the first direct confrontation between Lee and Grant. The dead, wounded, and missing of the Union forces totaled 17,666; Confederate losses numbered between 7,600 and 8,000. Despite the success of the Confederate forces, they failed to stop Grant's advance on Richmond. In this campaign James Longstreet was accidentally wounded by his own men.

I sent the black sow to plantation to day by Kit and the two english ducks—also 4 milk bowls—one of my sows at plantation had 7 pigs on last sunday—and one of the sows took the boar yesterday May 8th pigging time 27 Aug—Isaiah was to go to Selma this morning place of Lishe left—

May 10. the news this morning from Gen Lee is favorable to his success—on the left the enemy were driven from their rifle pits—it is also stated that Beauregard has whipped Burnside—on the peninsula.[124] We are having a light shower of rain.

May 13. We had a fair shower of rain on the night of Tuesday the 10th Lightning & thunder. I hurt my left foot by stepping off the back piazza in the dark. There is an ominous suspense as to army movements. No news at all from war in Va.

May 18. Wednesday. Went to plantation yesterday morning and returned this morning. Scarboro volunteered on Saturday and left on Monday 16th for Selma. Corn looks better. White heifer had a calf—wheat poor but improving. it is again very dry the light rain of [Wednesday] 11th May not having soaked the ground—

May 26. I went to plantation on Monday 23 and came home Wednesday 25—Lishe was very sick & Webb was tending on him. We had a nice shower Tuesday morning before day[break]—24th—The impressing officers took Two of my mules—Dave and Charlotte I had Charlotte released by giving Nelly. Commenced a cradle to shell corn—The crop is somewhat improved. Potatoes were set out on tuesday morning corn is growing off & wheat looks better—

May 28. Saturday. I went to plantation yesterday morning and returned in the evening. There was another light shower there on the night of the 26th and the corn seems to be improving. There is a good deal of sickness—sore throat among negroes. Lishe is very sick. Dr Webb attends him. Typhoid fever—Gave 16 bushels corn to two poor women from Shelby & Calhoun—Kit is making cradle for corn—Johnny my son is very sick Osborn is attending him.

---

[124] General Butler attempted to cut the Richmond and Petersburg railroad line on the peninsula formed by the Appomattox and James Rivers, but he was repelled by a small force of Confederates under the command of General Beauregard.

June 3. Friday—I went to plantation Monday morning May 30 and returned tuesday morning. Went again wednesday morning and returned again this morning—Alfred got home last saturday night from Selma with measles—and Milly[,] Castilla and Francis at the Walker Place have taken it. Lishe is reported better—Emline is in sick, mumps—I sent Edward to mill this morning with 20 bushels wheat and 12 bu corn—cradle for corn not yet done.

June 4. Edward came from the mill yesterday evening—his 32 bushels by Russels report was only 26-1/4 yielding 1045 flour 96 seconds sold Talman 245 Huggins 618. kept 182. Sent 96 lbs seconds to negroes—and 50 pounds flour from home to Mrs Scarboro.

June 7. Went to plantation yesterday evening with Alfred in buggy and returned this morning. Corn is growing finely tho getting fired—Tom is reaping the wheat at cheney Place—Rye has been reaped—Lishe is still sick. Dr yet. Dr Reynolds cut the stick out of Laura's arm. They are using the corn cradle Kit fixed.

June 16. Went to plantation on Wednesday 8th Shelled corn in the cradle. sent 171 sacks to depot for which recpt came and 25 for which I have yet got no recpt. Rains set in on saturday again and from exposure to same I was taken sick saturday night. the rain & bad roads and indisposition prevented me from returning till Wednesday 15. Sent balance of wheat to mill by Edward—say 24 bushels after it was passed thru the fan—got 854 pounds superfine flour & 112 pounds seconds. Sent of the last 65 to plantation and kept 47 home—let Nutting[125] have 100 pounds for which he pd me 75 in old currency & 22 to Mrs Nutting, not yet settled for. Gen Polk was killed in Georgia this week by a canon ball.[126] Gen Grant is reported to have divided his army and sent a part towards James river on both sides Chickahominy—means I expect Petersburg[127]—The fate of the country is quivering in the balance—the

---

[125] Samuel Nutting, carpenter, Greensboro. Snedecor, *Greene County*, 33.

[126] On 14 June 1864, General Leonidas Polk, Bishop of the Protestant Episcopal Church and Confederate Corps commander, was killed on the summit of Pine Mountain near Marietta, Georgia, by a Union shell fired by Sherman's forces.

[127] After the devastating loss of 7,000 men at the Battle of Cold Harbor on 3 June 1864, Grant decided to take Petersburg by moving his army across the James River. As a diversion, he sent Sheridan's cavalry west to Charlottesville.

decisive battle is yet unfought. Lee in Virginia retired in accordance with Grants movements—and Johnston in Ga in accordance with Shermans—who is fortifying Alatoona Heights.

June 23. Thursday I rode to plantation on tuesday and returned this morning—had more rain just after I got there—and the prospect of a clean crop gets less. I had 90 sacks corn shelled and hauled 177 bushels…Mrs Scarboro has the measles very bad and I expect it to go thro. Wheat will be all cut to day—injured by the wet I fear—was quite unwell at plantation and still have torpid liver & neuralgia. Army news indecisive—Grant is entrenching on the south side of James [river]—and Sherman stands confronting Johns[t]on—in Ga.[128]

June 27. Monday. I rode with Ed to P. on friday evening and returned on Sunday to B[reakfast]. Mrs S is still very sick with measles—and there are a great many new cases at Walker P. Want, Peter, Lewis, and Wash and a number of children have it. It makes the grass killing a very slow business. While I was down there—one of my finest sows died—brought forth 4 pigs and died. The wheat is all cut & shocked. Mrs Hatch & family left my house on saturday evening for Arcola. Johnny is still feeble and troublesome. There has been no news from Va armies since Thursday and great anxiety exists. it is supposed that the federal forces have cut off communication. No news from Johnstons army. Great issue undecided.…

Grant's efforts to take Richmond and Petersburg quickly ended in mid-June, and the nine-month siege of these two cities began. At the same time, Sherman with his 98,000 men pushed Joseph Johnston and his army of 55,000 men back toward Atlanta. Benners continued to follow these developments closely. Information was scarce, and he grew more restive. These were indeed stirring times.

---

[128] By 16 June 1864, the entire Union army of the Potomac had secretly left Cold Harbor and moved to the south side of the James River by way of hastily constructed roads and bridges. In Georgia, Sherman's forces continued to close in on Johnston's location near Marietta between 15 and 22 June 1864.

July 2. Again to day we have no news from Richmond[.] the federals have possession of the Communications between it and Petersburg and have also cut the Danville road. It is said that Hunter has been driven back from two miles of Lynchburg 27 miles—and is returning towards Beverly.[129] There is no further intelligence from Marietta—the last attack by the federals on the confederate left are reported to have been repulsed by Cheatham & Cleburn. Intense anxiety is felt for the issue. There is some probability of Johnstons falling back to Atlanta.[130]

July 6. I rode with Jane to plantation on yesterday and returned this morning. There is still a good deal of sickness—Little William & Emline at Cheney place have the measles and Want is very low at W.P. Delia has measles—had B[r]yan flogged for going to Henry's where a hog was killed. We are still ploughing the corn with sweeps—too late to do it any good but it has to be done. Rye is hauled in—wheat not yet. Oats cut at C.P. not yet at W.P.—Johnstons forces are reported falling back from Marietta—and Kauntz [Kautz] Raiders have been captured in Va—Raid reported coming from Vicksburg and Gov Clark has called out every able bodied man.

July 8. I went to Plantation yesterday morning and returned to day carried Alfred. Want is a little better and Carolines child Fanny—there are two or three new cases measles at W.P. and no new ones at C.P. Wheat stacked at W.P. Corn is not looking very well, is turning red. Peas fine—had a rain last sunday. Jackson raiders went back,—no news from Richmond or Ga.

July 14. I went down on Monday 11th and came back this morning—Caroline's child Fanny died this morning after 3 weeks sickness with whooping cough. There is a great deal of this disease at Cheney Place—but Except Emline and Little Wm no case of measles—Godfrey was out in that hard rain Monday all the evening—having just recovered from measles he came home sick and if

---

[129] Acting on orders from Grant, General David Hunter attempted to sever the Confederate railroad link to Richmond and to destroy the Lynchburg supply depot. Hunter's forces were repelled on 18 June by troops led by General Jubal Early.

[130] On 4 July 1864, Johnston pulled his army back to the Chattahoochee River to prevent Sherman from getting between his army and Atlanta.

he recovers it will be a wonder. Shelled corn Monday evening and sent 25 sacks to Griggs—again tuesday and sent 60 sacks. Wednesday morning cleaned out crib and rain coming up in afternoon shelled again. Wheat not yet hauled. Corn fired very badly but improved by rain—Johnston it is said has crossed Chattahoochie—and it is thot Atlanta will be given up[131]—no news from Va—12,000 are said to be in Jackson. Forrest is reported fighting [C. C.] Washburn at or near Okalona....

July 28. Went to plantation in Buggy on Monday 25. To Selma on 26 and back to Plantation on 27—and home to day. Francis child at Walker Place named Richard died this morning aged 9 mo.—Thrashed out Rye yesterday. 17 bu. Kit worked for A.P.H[atch]. on tuesday & wednesday. Caroline is quite sick at C.P. Measles are still spreading. There are no telegrams from Atlanta to day the federal forces were repulsed twice once with loss of 2000 prisoners and 18 guns—Johnston was relieved on 18th and Gen Hood placed in Command of Conf. Army. There is a rumor that the federals occupy Atlanta—[132]

July 30. Went to plantation yesterday with Ed and returned to day. Carolines infant child died at Cheney P this morning and she is very low—Priscy, John Potts, and Jane have measles—all the children have whooping cough & I never had as much sickness at one time—Windsor is sick charles is sick &c. I got 30 bushels salt yesterday from Mr Brame pay 7 to one in corn—hauled 12 barrels & 10 sacks making 73 34/56 bushels from cheney Place and Diver was to send corn to day from W.P. Great anxiety prevails by reason of not hearing from Atlanta 2 days—presume to be taken by federal forces.

August 6. Went to plantation with Alfred on tuesday the 3rd Aug. returned this saturday morning—Mrs Scarboro left there for Mr Campbells on yesterday—They had pulled some fodder at each place—stopped because corn was too green. Beat out wheat at cheney

---

[131] As Sherman prepared for an assault on Atlanta, Johnston moved his troops south of the Chattahoochee River on 8 July 1864.

[132] On 17 July 1864, President Davis replaced Johnston as commander of the Army of Tennessee with General John B. Hood. On 20 July, they began an aggressive attempt to defend Atlanta against the advancing forces of Sherman. Forrest fought in the Battle of Tupelo against A. J. Smith and his army.

Place. bearded wheat 52 bu.—white wheat 21. still whipping to day. Left the keys with Edward. The Confederates still hold Atlanta—there was a raid on Macon Ga. Federal forces have landed at Dauphin Island and Gun boats threaten fort Gaines.[133] 16000 reported at Holly Springs.

August 13. went to plantation in Buggy with Ed on Tuesday 9th and returned this morning. The federal fleet passed fort Morgan last week. The Tennessee was captured...& the Morgan escaped. Tennessee sunk. Fort Gaines surrendered, fort Powell blowed up.[134] We are pulling fodder and have had rain every day—Alas! Alas!

August 19. Friday. Went with Ed to the plantation on tuesday and returned this morning gathered fodder all the time—had light rains—grinding at W.P.—3/4 of a barrel made. The federal boats have gone over dog river bar to the obstructions and returned. it is believed that fort Morgan is invested—2nd Class militia are ordered to Mobile. The assaults on Hoods forces have been repulsed. Wheeler is reported in Shermans rear. No news from the valley....

Atlanta fell to Sherman on 2 September 1864, and Benners found it out three days later. In the following months, it was difficult for him to get accurate news about the war. His entries were about life on the plantation, his trips to Montgomery for a special session of the legislature, and his legal business.

September 5. Went to plantation with Ed last Monday Aug 29 and returned thursday went down friday and returned saturday—They have finished fodder at ch P. only 25 stacks—Walker P. 42 stacks. Grinding

---

[133] General Stoneman and 700 men were captured on the outskirts of Macon on 30 July. At Mobile Bay, Union troops attacked, but failed to capture Fort Gaines on Dauphin Island on 3 August 1864.

[134] On 10 August 1864 at the battle of Mobile Bay, Union Admiral David Farragut's fleet took control of the port by capturing or sinking the entire Confederate fleet. The ironclad ram CSS *Tennessee* surrendered on 5 August 1864 thus securing Mobile Bay for the Federals. The Union bombardment from the water led to the fall of Forts Gaines and Powell within a few days and Fort Morgan on 23 August.

cane—mill broke. grinding at Henrys—Jane came down on saturday—They say atlanta is evacuated.[135]

September 7. Went down yesterday and returned to day—Henry and Paul were working on road and Alfred & Lewis. Peter and Harry sick at W.P. and Burk & J. Potts. Chimney fell down—sent 16 bu corn to poor women from Shelby—Hauling and grinding cane 4 barrels out—Morgan is killed at Greenville[136]—Tommy Hatch at Atlanta—Atlanta was evacuated on 1st Sep. Confederate army at Lovejoy 26 miles South on Macon R.R. [Gov.] Watts has called Legislature—26th Sept.

September 12. Monday morning. I went to plantation Wednesday morning 7th and returned sunday 11. am still grinding cane—the molasses appears to be very good. Lever broke and had to get another. had wheat sunned. Sent Mr Cobbs 12 bu.[137] There is a good deal of weavil in it. There is no news from the armies since fall of Atlanta on the 1st Septr. Morgan was killed in Ten[n]. at Greenville. Vance was elected over Holden by a very large majority—McLellan and Pendleton were nom[inated] at Chicago.[138] The terrible effects of the war are very depressing. Prices are awful—negro shoes 35 to 40 dollars—and hard to get at that—there is a great disposition to barter.

September 16. Friday evenin. I rode in sulky to P on tuesday morning and came back this morning bringing Ed with me, by Waltons—are still grinding cane. Mr Drake agreed to enter with me as overseer as an experiment at rate of $1000. Ed & George started to move him this morning. Has a wife & 1 child—We are cutting pea vine hay—Kit had mules to run away and break wagon tongue—he is making another—There is still a good deal of sickness. Want had relapse and Diver is sick Ned is better—Wm Henry is sick.

---

[135] General Hood and the Army of Tennessee evacuated Atlanta on 1 September 1864, blowing up munitions and stores as they left.

[136] John Hunt Morgan, famed Confederate raider and cavalry leader, preparing for the attack in East Tennessee, was shot trying to rejoin his own men in Greenville, Tennessee.

[137] The Reverend Richard Hooker Cobbs became rector of St. Paul's Episcopal Church in 1861 and served for fifty years, until 1911.

[138] Union General George B. McClellan accepted the Democratic nomination for presidency of the United States on 8 September 1864. The vice presidential nominee was George Pendleton of Ohio.

October 10. Left for Montgy on friday 23 Sep. staid at Parkers—next morning to Selma left on the Duke and reached there sunday to Dinner. 1 day at the Hall $20—Went to Dinner on Monday at Judge Bibbs—Coleman & I staid there during the 2 weeks. adjourned friday evening Oct 7th came down the river on the Gertrude—Breakfast & dinner at Selma—Home that night by 10-1/2 o clock road pretty bad—

October 13. Went to Plantation on tuesday and returned this thursday morning road was *very* bad in places—Drake has paid my tax in kind of oats, wheat & Rye—I pd wool before—Also delivered two Bales cotton 1040 lb in payt of tax in kind on cotton—he had also hauled 285 bushels corn—smoke house is going up—Tom White's house and wheat house, prospects gloomy much corn rotted & crop will be very light. Lord bless us—

October 20. Went to Eutaw to court on Monday in sulky and returned Wednesday to dinner—State vs Hatch for retailing was found in fav Hatch and 3 other cases continued—staid at Judge Colemans—declined invitation to serve as solicitor. Horse bill $3 a day—

December 24. Left home Saturday Nov 12 for Montgy staid at Parkers Sunday and took cars Monday morning Nov 14. Reached Montgy Tuesday 15 remained till Wednesday Dec 14, took boat for Selma & reached there thursday 15 and home that night in stage—Boarded at Mrs Halls 20 days, at Mrs Wadsworths 10[,] board 12-1/2 & 15 a day.[139] Went to plantation Monday 19—staid till Wednesday—very cold & road very bad riding home. Killed 40 hogs Dec 12th average 195—corn not gathered—very backward—Drake nonplussed.

December 29. Christmas was a very disagreeable rainy day—We went to church and rode home in a hard rain added to which are the distresses of our bleeding country. oh that Peace could be vouchsafed once more. The roads are very bad and the river high.

---

[139] Benners attended a legislative session in Montgomery but made no mention of it. It is evident that he attended the month-long session—15 November–14 December. Usually he wrote about the proceedings, but this time it must have been an unpleasant experience.

1865

Benners's first mention of Sherman's March to the Sea came on January 9. By that time, Sherman had marched his 62,000 men from Atlanta to Savannah, arriving there on December 22. After resting for several weeks, he began his march north. Benners watched the march hoping for a favorable end of the war. Inflation grew worse, and the weather remained severe.

January 9. We have had much rainy weather and the roads are very bad. I have not been to my plantation since 19 Dec. The corn is reported gathered and a few acres of land ploughed but the ground is so wet it is impossible to do any thing—Drake had 7 pr shoes cut of the leather I bot—& made by Haywood. I killed a hog at my house on Saturday weighed 260 had him barrelled to day—It is a gloomy day raining hard and prospects bad. Hoods army have been defeated and crossed Tennessee. he lost his Pontoon bridges 1/3 of his men and a large no of mules[140]—Gen Sherman occupied Savannah on the [blank space] day of Dec.[141] The attack on the forts at Wilmington was not successful—[142]

January 10. yesterday was one of the rainiest days I ever saw and continued till 12 last night—when a heavy wind brought up a big shower and it emptied itself & has not rained since tho still cloudy—

February 4. Have still been unable to get to plantation in consequence of bad roads and more especially because I have been occupied in settling up Planters Insurance Company. We determined to divide out and close up—there was no chance for profitable business and there seemed to be no likelihood of the war coming to a close very soon. after selling assets it divided $208 to the share & 1 share bank stock in

---

[140] John Bell Hood lost 35,000 of his 50,000-man infantry in the battles of Franklin and Nashville in November and December 1864. Then he and his shattered army retreated across the Tennessee River on 26–27 December 1864, reaching Tupelo, Mississippi, in early January where he resigned his command.

[141] Sherman's army occupied the city of Savannah on 21 December 1864. Hardee's army had evacuated the city one day earlier, heading toward South Carolina.

[142] After unsuccessfully bombarding Fort Fisher at the port of Wilmington for two days, Union forces under the command of Butler withdrew on 21 December 1864.

Southern Bank to 4 shrs in P. I. Co. I have not yet finished paying out. The directory voted my salary $1818. which is certainly very poor pay for the labor required. There are a great many rumors about commissioners trying to settle the terms of a peace—also of Foreign recognition—The latter seem to me better founded than they have heretofore been—as for Peace it is yet a great way off—Hoods disasters in Tenn settled that question—the armies are concentrating in S. Carolina—Sherman moving up from Savannah[143]—a big battle will come off before Peace can be had—The Federal successes in Ga Tenn and capture of fort fisher have protracted the struggle[144]—It is rumored that Conf congress has passed a bill to seize the cotton & tobacco.[145] I hope it is untrue—Robbery & violence cannot produce peace and that is what we need. It has rained so much the roads are impassable—and it is still cloudy & threatening rain.

February 9. We rec'd yesterday in a telegram from Richmond of the 5th That President Lincoln and Mr Seward on the part of the U. States met Messrs Stephens[,] Hunter and Campbell commissioners sent by Davis and submitted as the terms of Peace the unconditional submission of the South—That the slavery question had already been settled by Amendments to the Constitution by Federal Congress—[146]The hopes for peace which some cherished have been disappointed—& it seems that the dreadful war will last still longer. May God help us—& give us

---

[143] Sherman moved his base of operations from Savannah, Georgia, toward Beaufort, South Carolina, in preparation for the march into South Carolina.

[144] Rear Admiral Porter's fleet began a bombardment of Fort Fisher on 13 Janury 1865. Union forces eventually captured the fort on 15 January.

[145] There had been an impressment of goods belonging to civilians—livestock, machinery, wagons, and foodstuff since 1863. Vouchers had been given in exchange for IOU receipts at fixed market prices.

[146] President Lincoln and Secretary of State Seward met with Confederate peace commissioners Alexander Stephens, Robert M. T. Hunter, and John A. Campbell at Hampton Roads, Virginia, on 3 February 1865. The Confederate commissioners insisted on an armistice before any talk of readmittance to the Union. Lincoln insisted on Confederate recognition of Federal authority as the first step toward peace.

strength to endure its terrible inflictions—[Benjamin] Cheat[h]am's wagon train passed thro town on yesterday—[147]

February 15. We have had the coldest rainiest time I ever saw and roads were never worse. The war still rages and constant insecurity and apprehension are felt of raids and ravages—Sherman is advancing in Ga towards Branchville and Augusta—with 40000 troops—there has been a fight about Petersburg—Confederate loss about 500 including Gen Pegram.[148] there really seems to be no end to the War. The federals are determined to admit no terms but submission—and the Confederates will not listen to that. Foreign recognition so rife some short time since has died away and the only alternative contemplated is a continuance of the war. In the meantime our husbandry is neglected and at Richmond they are on the eve of starvation. What further afflictions are in store for us God only knows. but he doeth all things well and we can only put our trust in him. for from man there is neither help or mercy to be expected.

February 17. There is still no light breaking thro the clouds that hang over our country—Sherman is advancing in S. Carolina and Gen Beauregard has command of Confederates: 17000 from Hoods army have gone to him[,] two divisions from Lees Army and Hamptons legion—oh that this horrid war would close—the talk is about putting negroes in the army.[149] Sent sows to Williamsons boar week before last say 4 Feby. Pigs due May 20 '65

February 22. The fine spell of moderate weather we have had for a week or more has wound up to day with a rain—there are no blossoms on the trees yet and the spring is backward. There is a rumor that Beauregard has whipped one column of Shermans army in S. Carolina—Affairs look very depressing—and no end is seen to the

---

[147] Benjamin Cheatham served in the Confederate forces for three years. He fought at Shiloh, Chattanooga, and Atlanta. During the Franklin and Nashville campaigns, he succeeded Hardee as corps commander. Cheatham was with Johnston in the last months of the war and surrendered with him in North Carolina.
[148] Confederate General John Pegram was killed on 6 February 1865 during a Confederate assault on Union troops near Dabney Mills, Virginia.
[149] Legislation passed the Confederate house of representatives on 20 February 1865 and the senate on 8 March to arm slaves in return for a promise of freedom.

war—provisions are scarce & goods high, brogan shoes difficult to procure and cost $50 a pair—common homespun woolen cloth $25.

By mid-February, there was no mail service so Benners was unable to keep up with military developments. He thought General Beauregard was in charge of the Confederate forces facing Sherman. Actually, it was Joseph Johnston who unsuccessfully tried to fend off Sherman's army. Rumors continued to abound, one of which had Lee defeating Sherman and taking his artillery. Of course, they never fought each other.

February 23. The news this morning is that the Confederates have evacuated Charl[e]ston and Sherman has flanked Beauregard and gone in the direction of Chester[150]—The rain continued all night and again to day it is pouring down. This will prove prejudicial to farming operations in fact it is difficult to imagine how we can possibly get our land ploughed in time. in the mean time the wheat is badly injured by the freezes—and prospects are bad—I dont think I ever saw so bad a spring for ploughing.

February 24. Friday—Still raining no mails—Sherman is advancing on Charlotte to take Lee in the rear—

February 25. Saturday—It rained nearly all day yesterday and last night—Thunder & lightning last night—and this morning and still raining. The flower pit at home has water 18 in of the top. Sherman is advancing on Charlotte. He appears to have eluded the Confederates & passed them and is probably marching thro N. Carolina to reinforce Grant. Charl[e]ston is evacuated & stores burnt.[151]

February 27. Monday—It stopped raining on saturday evening and yesterday sunday was a tolerably fair day but it is again raining to day and taking it all together more rain seems to me to have fallen than I ever knew. There is very little authentic intelligence from the operations

---

[150] Hardee evacuated Charleston moving his forces to Chester, South Carolina, on 17 February 1865.

[151] Sherman pushed northward cutting off communications to the interior. Charleston surrendered on 18 February 1865 and the first task of the Union troops was to put out fires set by the evacuating Confederates.

in S. Carolina—Sherman has outwitted the Confederates—it would seem tho there is some reason to suppose from yesterdays dispatch that Beauregard is in front of him above Columbia—Rainy gloomy times—the recognition of the Confederate States is again talked of by France to take effect it is said after 4th March—entitled to little confidence—the Foreign powers who heartily seem to desire the distruction of both North & South will not interfere until both or one lies powerless at their mercy and then their help must be paid for—God of Heaven send us reconciliation and peace—

February 28. no rain to day but dreadful accts are brought of the effects of the rains—Cahaba river 2 miles wide—Railroad submerged—from McDowells to Demopolis & this side injured.[152]

March 1. Wednesday—it rained again last night and there seems no end to the wet weather it is drizzly and lowering to day which is ash Wednesday All communications by mail from all quarters are suspended—and we shall get no mails for several days yet—bridges blown up and washed away—and water hig[h]er than before this winter.

March 2. It rained yesterday & last night & is cloudy & drizzly this morning. The corn planting must be very backward. When will Walker bottom be fit to plough—We have no mails from any where and are in great uneasiness not being able to hear.

March 4. Saturday it rained again yesterday & again last night and we can get no mails from any where—there is a rumor in town of a fight between federals & French at the Mouth of the Rio Grande—also of a raid coming down above Tuscaloosa—To day is the day for second inauguration of President Lincoln.

March 8. Tho cloudy it did not rain on Sunday 5th nor Monday nor yesterday but we had a rain again last night—this morning it is fairer and not raining. We have had no mails for a long time—and in the absence of them all sorts of rumors obtain—among them that Gen Lee has sent 3 corps from Petersburg and defeated Sherman and captured his artillery. The federals committed great depredations in Columbia it is said and burnt both sides of the main street and the old State house. great

---

[152] A. M. McDowell, civil engineer, Demopolis. Tharin, *Marengo County*, 24.

destitution and poverty prevail there—300 women and children were killed by the explosion of a parcel of shells—probably by accident—they were gathering up what provisons they could in the city after the federals left there. S. Carolina suffers much[,] Charl[e]ston evacuated and occupied by the federals and Columbia nearly destroyed—a force is said to have landed at Milton and it is feared threatens Montgomery—

March 9. It rained again this morning very hard. When can we plant the rivers are very full all the creeks d[itt]o—never such continued rain before. Gales Partridge has been with me since sunday—Mr J. I. Walton died on night before last—funeral to be at Methodist church to day.

March 10. It rained so hard yesterday the funeral was postponed till to day—Fast day by Proc[lamation]. It is said Mobile is on the eve of an attack 20000 troops having landed at Pascagoula. There is no reliable intelligence as to Shermans movements he is reported to have turned aside towards the Atlantic coast. The wind got north last night. Ther 32° this morning—Sun shining—Fast day.

March 11. We have a fair bright day but no mail—at least no papers—one only was rec'd—Singleton and Judge [space blank] have come from Lincoln again to treat of Peace it is said.[153] Exchange of prisoners is going on. Mobile is threatened.

March 13. Yesterday (sunday) was a bright day but to day is cloudy again—we are very backward in planting no corn yet—

March 16. It rained again on the 14th and again yesterday 15—last evening and night very hard—The ground is thoroughly sobbed—never so much rain little or no corn planted—Baby with measles—Ed stays home. have not got to plantation yet. Early whipped at Waynesboro by Sheridan. 1300 captured.[154] Sherman pressing for Atlantic from Pensacola threatening Mobile.

---

[153] James Singleton of Illinois led the delegates to explore the possibilities for peace. It was too late.

[154] On 2 March 1865, a Union cavalry force under the command of General George A. Custer completely routed the remains of General Early's army at Waynesboro, Virginia, taking prisoner more than 1,000 Confederate soldiers. This battle marked the end of the last campaign in the Shenandoah Valley.

Benners worried about a recent bill passed by the Confederate Congress authorizing the use of black soldiers. He was also concerned about the battles that the South continued to lose. His last wartime entry, on 30 March 1865, was about measures being taken by citizens to defend the Confederacy. There were no journal entries from 31 March until 5 May when he recorded the surrender of Robert E. Lee and his army. By that time, Confederate money had no purchasing power and there was little left in the way of food.

March 17. It faired off last night & this morning. we have a cool pleasant day—no important news from any where—recognition has subsided—Sherman not heard from supposed marching for Wilmington. Watts has called Militia—nigger bill said to have passed. President has called upon congress not to adjourn for a few days—great curiosity as to what it is—The institution of Slavery it seems has rec'd a severe blow by Nigger bill.[155]

March 18. Saturday—This is a lovely day—and after so much rain is particularly agreeable—no news.

March 21. It did not rain again till last night when we had a hard rain—no corn of consequence planted yet and the land not half ploughed. Shall we be able to make corn? I planted some garden corn yesterday.

March 22. It faired off yesterday evening & the sun is bright & welcome to day—but the afflictions of our country are increasing—Davis has written to congress a message indicating great misgiving & calling for men & corn—

March 27. We have had several bright days. to day it has clouded up. The peaches look a good deal injured. There was a battle at Bentonville in Johnston Cty between Sherman & Johnston—on the 19 & 20 March—report is that Confeds killed & captured 5000 took 3 guns.[156] a force is said to be approaching Montgomery from Pensacola—last accts were advancing on Greenville—much distress &

---

[155] Slaves were to be armed, but the states were given the final decision regarding the freedom of the black soldier.

[156] The Battle of Bentonville from 19–21 March 1865 was the Confederates' last major attempt to stop Sherman's advance.

perplexity—Oh God Father of our spirits—control these things for our spiritual good—in thy good time give us relief from our troubles and in thy mercy spare our bleeding Country for the sake of Jesus Christ our Lord.

March 29. Armstrongs brigade of Forrest's cavalry passed thro here yesterday and Starkes to day. Forrest is expected to pass thro with a division to morrow or next day[157]—Federal forces are reported to have been 3000 strong at Jasper Walker Cty on sunday 26th and uneasiness is felt—that they are moving on Tuscaloosa. Fighting is going on at Spanish fort near Mobile—many rumors are afloat the plot thickens—Starkes brigade left here to day in the rain and it is still raining very hard—(4 o clock).

March 30. The rain ceased yesterday it is cool and clear to day—news from Selma is exciting Citizens called to defend the city. fighting at Mobile not heard from. Gen Lee reports fighting about Petersburg. Sherman is said to have made junction with Schofield at Goldsboro[158]—Rumor that the raid above Montevallo has burned two of the iron works—1st Class ordered for six days to arrest deserters.

There were no entries during the month of April and the first days of May 1865. During April, the war ended and his four-year-old son, John, died. One can reasonably assume that these two losses made it impossible for him to write. John was the fourth son he had lost. Finally, on 5 May he began to write again.

May 5. Gen Lee's army of Northern Va surrendered to Gen Grant on [April] the 9th at Appomatox court house under an apple tree—this was followed by news of an armistice between Sherman and Johnston to

---

[157] On 2 April 1865, Northerners broke through strong defensive fortifications held by 5,000 Southerners under Nathan Bedford Forrest's command. Generals Forrest and Richard Taylor, both in the city of Selma, narrowly avoided capture but the Union troops captured 2,700 prisoners and a large store of enemy supplies. It was one of Forrest's few defeats in his many battles. John S. Bowman, *The Civil War Almanac* (New York: Gallery Books, div. of W. H. Smith Publishers, Inc., 1983) 259.

[158] On 23 March 1865, Sherman's army joined General Scofield's forces at Goldsborough, North Carolina.

settle difficulties.[159] There was then also an armistice between Gen Taylor and Canby in this dept and yesterday there was news recd that this dept had been surrendered & Bufords division are passing thro here to Gainesville to deliver up their arms. Our condition is a very sad one—the money of Confederacy has ceased to have any purchasing value and want of provisions is getting to be a very serious matter. What distresses are still in store for us God only knows. May he give us strength to endure whatever may befall—

---

[159] On 18 April 1865, Sherman and Johnston met at Durham Station, North Carolina, and signed a broad political peace agreement calling for a cessation of hostilities, general amnesty for Southerners, and recognition of all Southern state governments by the Federal government. This would go into effect when their officials took an oath of allegiance.

Chapter 3

The Reconstruction Years, May 1865–1877

May 1865

Reconstruction had begun and Benners felt considerable insecurity about the future. Fighting had ended, but no one was certain about how to treat the former slaves. Could they be kept on the plantations? Would they be paid? These were indeed unpredictable times.

May 8, 1865... There is still great uncertainty hanging over our fate[.] this department has been commanded by Taylor and it is said all are to be paroled from 16 to 60. It is also reported that all cotton is to be confiscated.[1] Sad are the prospects before us—The army of Johns[t]on is surrendered—and commissioners are said to be at work to adjust terms of settlement.

May 10. There has been issued a paper containing acct of surrender of Gen Taylor. also from Mobile an order of terms on which negroes in Mobile & vicinity can be hired. I do not think if those terms are inforced on plantations they can be worked. There must be great distress—

May 14. There is great gloom hanging over the people by reason of the destruction of the labor system of the Country—no one knows what to depend upon or what to do. I am afoot, Gen Chalmers having taken Sunbeam from me by an illegal impressment as I consider it. Mr Drake was here day before yesterday—he says none of the negroes have left as yet but many are leaving from the Plantations and going to

---

[1] On 4 May 1865, Confederate General Richard Taylor surrendered to General Edward Canby at Citronelle, Alabama, under the same terms that Grant gave Lee.

Selma—They are working very slowly—and with reduced stock and negroes demoralised a crop looks impossible.

May 17. George brot up a load of fodder yesterday. None of the negroes had left the plantation as yet—but they are leaving other plantations in squads. there is much excitement about it in the Country—a force of federal cavalry is expected through here to day. The sadness of these times can scarcely be described—

May 22. Mr Drake sent word by William yesterday that he could not make the negroes work—and the complaint is general—What will come of it God only knows—5 or 6000 Griersons cavalry passed thro here on last Wednesday—they did no mischief to me and while they rested in front of my home behaved themselves very well. My servants are greatly demoralised—…Lewis has left. There is great excitement and perplexity among the citizens.

May 27. Jeff Davis was captured at Erwinville in S.E. Ga on 13th and sent to Washington. A. B. Moore has been arrested and sent to Washington.[2] There is to be a garrison here. Fanny has been very sick but is better.

May 31. Mr Drake sent me word that negroes quit work on Saturday evening and wanting me to come down immediately. went on sunday evening Gave Wm & CA a good talk—told Mr Drake I did not want him any longer, May 30 , he could stay & try and get a place.

June 1. Just met a man who told me the Negroes said Mr Drake was carrying off my meat, went to plantation and found from his statement it was false.

June 14. Have been quite unwell for several days—and am still. There is great perplexity in the Country by reason of the President Johnsons amnesty proclamation excluding from pardon all whose property is estimated at over $20,000 and the other provisions[3]—The negroes are leaving constantly—and owners are required to hire them—

---

[2] President Davis was captured near Irwinville, Georgia, on 10 May 1865. He was brought to Fort Monroe, Virginia, on 22 May, where he was temporarily put in chains and locked in a cell. Davis was never brought to trial. Andrew B. Moore was governor of Alabama at the outbreak of the war.

[3] Under President Johnson's general amnesty proclamation, Southerners who owned more than $20,000 worth of property and those who held a high rank in the

The Freedmen's Bureau required that a labor contract be drawn up and signed by the plantation owner and the freedman. Between the planter's need for a disciplined labor force and the freedman's search for autonomy, conflict was inevitable. Benners did not know how to proceed and waited for further information, which came on 30 August when General Wager Swayne, assistant commissioner of the Freedmen's Bureau in Alabama, announced his labor policy. Freedmen and their employers would sign contracts, and the contracts required approval by the bureau. Food, shelter, and medical help were the employer's obligations, and the cost for the unemployed members of the family was to be deducted from the employee's pay. The freedman received a share of the crop according to how much of his expenses he paid.

June 28. The Labor regulations of the Freedmens bureau have disorganised the whole labor of the Country—owners are required to make a contract with their slaves and they not understanding it & considering that they are free dont have to work are very impracticable & difficult.[4] Virgil & Rhoda are anxious to leave and wont contract with me. Jenny dont know whether she will or not & Delia d[itt]o—We are having a bad time of it—an assistant to the bureau opened here in town yesterday—am very unwell—Matters are in a bad fix.

August 3. I employed Mr Herrin [Herran] to take charge of my plantations and superintend at both places until 1st Jany at the rate of $25 per month, am to find him & his family meat and bread. He set in under this contract on thursday July 13th 1865—I went to Demopolis and took the cars to Selma on friday 21 July. Got to Montgomery on Saturday evening—stopped with Mr Lyon at the exchange till Monday morning when I went to Col Powells and staid this tuesday

---

Confederate military or government would have to apply individually to the president for a pardon.

[4] The Freedmen's Bureau was established by Congress in March 1865. It was to distribute clothing, food, and fuel to former slaves and oversee "all subjects" relating to their condition in the South. It was seen as a temporary expedient for one year and was to draw its funds and staff from the war department. At the last moment, Congress included Southern white refugees as well as freedmen to counteract any impression of preferential treatment for blacks.

evening—came on the [steamer] Flirt to Selma and reached Demopolis on friday got home saturday—Saw Gov Parsons in Montgomery.[5] Forwarded my application for amnesty by Judge Walker to Washington.[6] I went to the plantation on Monday morning the 31 July and returned on tuesday the 1st August—Mr Herrin reported that A. H. Ravesies[7] had called for the govt cotton and taken from the Walker Place 59 Bales—one bale having bursted open was not taken—it was done July 21st 65—He had removed the cotton at Walker Place 26 Bales to the smoke house and overseer house and at Cheney Place 72 Bales to smoke house, old smoke house & potatoe shed to keep it safe from thieves who are stealing a great deal of cotton and in fact 5 Bales of mine had been stolen and was recovered and stored with Buck at Newbern. The whole country is excited about the cotton stealing. parties go at night to the plantation in most cases with Govt wagons and haul it off and it is heard of no more forever.

August 9. Went to plantation on monday 7th with Alfred and returned tuesday 8. Mr Herrin had got back the two bales cotton which had been stole—it was found in sugar cane patch near Barron's. He sent to Pollards where yankees had it hauled and brot it home. On monday night a raid on Mr Hatchs cotton at Henry's was threatened. I went over between midnight & day. The wagons &c had gone. Nine stack[s] fodder had been put up at Cheney place and 16 at W.P. The excitement of cotton stealing still continues—and there is no telling the extent to which the public seem demoralised.

---

[5] Lewis Parsons of Talladega was appointed provisional governor on 21 June 1865. He opposed secession but represented his county in the legislature in 1863. He had been a Union man and now assumed a very difficult job.

[6] Andrew Johnson issued a proclamation of amnesty on 29 May 1865, offering amnesty and restitution of property, except slaves, to all who took the oath of allegiance, with the exception of several categories. These categories included Confederate civil and diplomatic officials, army officers over the rank of colonel and naval officers above the rank of lieutenant, all who resigned their seat in Congress, those who mistreated prisoners of war, and all persons who owned taxable property with a value of $20,000 or more.

[7] A. H. Ravesies was a member of the Vine and Olive Colony, a failed attempt by Bonapartist exiles from France to grow grapes and olive trees in Marengo (now Hale) County, Alabama. Arcola, the home of Benners's father-in-law Alfred Hatch, was on their original land grant.

September 7. Last thursday was the day for the election of delegates to convention to bring the State back to the Union.[8] There was a great excitement in the town on that day—a federal soldier was killed with a pistol shot on the street by [William S.] Tood Cowin and one shot in the side by Tom Cowin.[9] The soldiers here were greatly excited and threatened to burn the town—they prepared matches. Col Green fortunately arrived just in the nick of time and allayed the excitement and saved the burning. the demand was then that [Tom] Cowin should be hung at 5 o clock—they were then persuaded to wait till morning that his mother might see him and he was two days afterwards taken to Tuscaloosa to be tried there—while the excitement was up they went to the houses and got the guns. I have not been able to recover mine nor Alfreds nor the little pistol.—I have had a sorrowful time in my family with sickness—Charlie died on sunday the 27th August. He had been sick from sores on his body—and not considered dangerous—when they continued & did not disappear we called in Dr Osborn—who called the disease Erysipelas. On saturday evening 26 Aug he assured us that there were no alarming symptons. On sunday at 11 o clock our dear little one had gone home to God. He was a sweet little fellow—always delicate—and I was always apprehensive we would not be able to raise him.[10] After his death—Fanny was taken sick with what the Dr called dyptheria and continued under his care 10 days—Ed was sick with

---

[8] On 31 August 1865, 56,000 Alabama voters elected delegates to the constitutional convention. Ninety-nine delegates were elected—thirty-three lawyers, forty-two farmers, six doctors, nine merchants, two teachers, and seven ministers.

[9] Sons of Samuel Cowin, planter, Hollow Square voting precinct, Greensboro. V. Gayle Snedecor, *A Directory of Greene County for 1855–6* (Mobile AL: Strickland & Co., 1856; ed. and indexed by Franklin Shackelford Moseley, Eutaw AL: *The Greene County Democrat*, 1957) 13. William "Tood" Cowin joined the Greensboro Guards on 13 April 1861 and served in the Confederate army. After the war, he was mistakenly struck by a Union soldier. In great pain, Tood chased after his assailant and shot him to death. His brother Tom also shot and wounded a nearby soldier. Tood was able to steal a nearby thoroughbred racehorse and escaped to Mississippi. Tom escaped from prison. Later the two returned to Greensboro. Yerby devotes a chapter to this incident. William Edward Yerby, *History of Greensboro, Alabama from its Earliest Settlement* (Montgomery AL: The Paragon Press, 1908) 52–59.

[10] Charles Benners was born on 15 March 1864 and died on 27 August 1865.

chills—Liz & Willie—and at this time my wife is sick. I feel as if I was sold to the Doctors for life.

September 9. Mr Herrin came up to day and reports that there are at

Cheney place packed	46 bales
at Walker place in seed–	12 "
at Cheney place in seed–	13 "
at Cheney place in pick room	10 "

September 12. This is the day for the meeting of the Convention called under proclamation of Lewis E. Parsons provisional Governor to adopt a Constitution and get back into the Union. W. P. Webb & A. S. Jeffries[11] are the delegates from this County. There is much violence and crime being committed in the Country—persons are robbed as they travel the roads. Cotton is stolen by raiders and mules and horses are taken—the effects of the war on morals is dreadful. My wife is in tolerable health—and my children have got better. I have been annoyed by the order of special cotton agents that private cotton must be given in—having been raised in Perry [county] it ought to be given in there—and I have sent a letter to A. L. Wilkinson by Mr Ramsay to give it in—and have written to Demopolis for information.[12]

Life had become more difficult. Although he was depressed by economic and political conditions, Benners managed to harvest his cotton and other crops and to practice law. He began to sharecrop some of his lands; it was an unpleasant but necessary experience.

October 25. I went to Eutaw to court on 16 Oct. 1st day of Court stopped with Judge Coleman one night[,] at Judge Pearces 1 night[,] rode on horseback. Judge Cobbs presided. By agreement no judgments were taken—came home Wednesday evening. Went with C. W. Hatch again Monday 23. Drove over in his buggy with my horse. Some 15 or

---

[11] William P. Webb, lawyer, Eutaw, A. S. Jeffries, planter, German Creek voting precinct, Greensboro. Snedecor, *Greene County*, 45, 24.

[12] There were agents of the US Treasury Department who seized Confederate property under the confiscation acts. Many planters were forced to pay five to ten dollars a bale on their cotton because of threats of seizure by these agents.

20 negroes were being arraigned when I entered the court house for divers offences, stealing mostly. Hatch's cases five in number, 2 for selling pistol to minor, 2 for retailing in Greensboro & 1 for selling Liquor to minor without consent of parent, were continued by the State—for absence of witnesses—and forfeitures taken vs C. A. Sheldon, Wm Christian, Andrew Johnson, Jesse Hamilton. I came home tuesday to dinner. the times are distressingly critical, the negroes are giving a good deal of uneasiness. It is certain they will not work—and the mischief they will do may be anticipated—...[13]

November 24. I have been afflicted with an eruption on the surface of the skin for the last two weeks which has been very disagreeable—and causes much loss of sleep. have not been to plantation in consequence. Edward and Want on Wednesday last hauled to Demopolis Eleven bales cotton—making 43 bales at AM. Mills Warehouse and with the 117 at Lyons makes 160 bales cotton at Demopolis and about four more to haul. This is a spell of lovely weather—but I am not in a fix to take advantage of it by reason of my sores. Mrs Willis and family are at my house and she is very desirous to get off to N. Carolina—has gone to Newbern to look for a chance of some one going—who can accompany her.

December 5. I went to the plantation in the buggy on yesterday Monday Dec 4th and returned same evening. The crop of cotton made the present year at the Cheney Place had been packed and made four light bales. This and two others which had been left over have been hauled to Demopolis to Mills (Breitlings) warehouse making 49 at that warehouse and with the 117 at Lyons making 166 bales.

December 14. I went to Arcola in the buggy on Monday evening and returned next morning. the road was very muddy. Dr Webb who had been sick at Arcola came at same time. I had expected a rise in the river and fall in freights but neither had taken place to do any good and I did not ship. Mrs Willis & her children left my house yesterday morning in

---

[13] It was difficult to negotiate contracts with the newly freed slaves who were worried that they would sign away their freedom. Landowners like Benners, on the other hand, needed reliable labor to work the land and harvest the crop.

my carriage for Newbern to go in Company with Mrs Maulds to N. Carolina.[14] The weather is very cold. Ther 26° this morning.

December 15. Friday—Mr Herrin killed 31 hogs on Wednesday 13.—16 at Walker Place and 15 at Cheney P. Edward brought up the fat yesterday—2 hams & 1 shoulder & sausage meat and spare ribs. The weather is still very cold—Ther 20°. Fanny & I were at Mr McClure's last night. Mr Herrin returned to me the weight of the hogs killed by him of 7214 pounds—

December 29. I went to plantation of friday Dec 22nd and returned on sunday 24th had five hogs killed while I was there weighing 830 pounds had them salted and put up at Walker place. Mr Herrin left me on the 22nd. Things looked desolate enough. Went down again on horseback on 27th ret on 28th divided the corn & eighth at both places with assistance of Burton J.P. Concluded to let Groce and Perry run plantation Walker Place in shares—see agreement—Trouble on trouble—may God help us.

1866

In the New Year, Benners was faced with the need to secure a reliable labor force to work the lands. This meant drawing up contracts that could be enforced—an increasingly difficult task. Also, he felt that the South should be readmitted to the Union as soon as possible—as states, not as territories. This was becoming more complicated as Congress and the president fought over the terms of readmission. Johnson felt they were ready for readmission, while Congress was uncertain, needing more time to develop a satisfactory answer.

January 3, 1866. I rode on horseback to the Cheney Place on 1st Jany '66 it rained every foot of the way and I got very wet Measured the corn in the pens and in the crib and we agreed that Jemison & Walker should take it at 2000 bushels at 75 cts per bu and fodder 3 stacks at 450 pounds making—1350—mill 150—[Lawrence W.] Walker & [Henry] Jemison staid till after dinner & Walkers son. I came home the next

---

[14] See entry of 5 May 1862.

morning—dreadful ride. They agreed to meet me in Greensboro on Thursday friday or saturday—next—to consummate the trade.

January 16.—Jemison & Walker came up on Thursday Jany 4th and consummated the trade for the cheney place. I have had much difficulty about servants. Rhoda and Virgil left me early in Jan'y, Delia d[itt]o, Jenny d[itt]o, Emline remained till day before yesterday—when she went to Mrs Tunstals.[15] I hired Salina from Ned Harper for a house girl at $5 a month, and Ned Pickens & his wife Maria and Daughter Abby & son Ronda at 16 a month. We have found so far that we have got along as well as usual. Kit is still holding on. I have made contracts with the others. I find there is much perplexity and difficulty with planters about hiring hands. They are so faithless to their promises—contract to day & leave to morrow. The Southern members are not yet admitted nor do I believe they are likely to be soon. The black republican party seem to be actuated by great animosity to the south and desire to retain the States as Territories. The President desires them re united as States.[16] The small pox is reported as scattered thro the Country—a negro died of it at Mrs Manasts. A case is reported at Jake Bush's[17]—Pestilence on the heels of war will fill up the measure of our afflictions.

February 22. Thursday. on Monday the 29 Jany I went with my wife and Ed in the carriage to Arcola to take the boat for Mobile. I got on board the admiral tuesday night—and reached Mobile friday morning February 2nd Went to Dr Longs boarding house and remained there until Saturday after Dinner Feby 17. took passage on the Lily and reached Eastport on tuesday night—and rode home in Ambulance Wednesday 21st Feby. The weather was very cold a portion of the time in Mobile and I suffered there & on the boat from Neuralgia and

---

[15] Eliza Croom Tunstal was Benners's next-door neighbor.

[16] Congress met in early December 1865 and refused to readmit the Southern states to the Union. A joint reconstruction committee was appointed to investigate conditions in the Southern states and report as to whether they were ready to be admitted. The committee's composition reflected a desire for accommodation, but Congress still believed that it alone had power to prescribe the terms and conditions of readmission. This alarmed many Southerners, including Augustus Benners who saw the committee as "actuated by great animosity to the south."

[17] Jacob J. Bush, planter, German Creek voting precinct, Greensboro. Snedecor, *Greene County*, 10.

derangement of the bowels, from which I have not yet entirely recovered. I sold 164 Bales cotton @ 41 cts. Charges were very high—and it netted only $29,586.98 cts in currency....

April 6.... The cotton market has drooped very much latterly and is now selling 34 to 35. perhaps I was fortunate in selling when I did. Gold is also drooping say [1]25 to [1]26 1/2. The questions most agitating the public mind at present are in reference to the admission of our members of Congress—the Pres has vetoed Civil rights bill so called—it is feared the two houses will pass it over his veto.[18] There was a total eclipse of the moon on the night of Good Friday March 30 & the acct appended below is from Mobile paper of 31 [March]

> Eclipse of the Moon. The Heavens presented a beautiful spectacle last night. The moon was in grand eclipse, and stood out like a bright diamond set in a circle of gorgeous colors. The groundwork was of a beautiful pea green, fringed by a rich purple rim, with a margin of light blue. The sky was very clear and spangled with twinkling stars, rendering the scene surpassingly beautiful. It was a heavenly tableau, and thousands of faces were turned upwards in holy admiration of the sublime scene.

April 12. Thursday. The president has vetoed the Civil rights bill and the Senate have passed it over his veto by a vote of 33 to 15. Dixon was sick and Stockton from New Jersey had been turned out.[19] This seems portentous of much trouble—and I cannot see how civil war will be averted. The provisions of the bill are very oppressive and if it goes into practical operation gives the management of the negroes entirely to the Dominant Majority party—We have had so much bloodshed war

---

[18] The Civil Rights Act of 1866, which President Johnson vetoed, was meant to give protection to the freedmen against state legislation that was discriminatory. Freedmen received protection of their fundamental civil rights as American citizens.

[19] For the first time in American history, Congress passed over a president's veto a major piece of legislation. It was supported by moderates and radicals. Senator Stockton was unseated before the vote, on the questionable grounds that the New Jersey legislature had illegally altered its rules in order to elect him.

and desolation It might have been hoped that on the close of the war we should have had peace. The President by Proclamation of April 3 has proclaimed it—but the radical party are apparently determined to carry on the war—Ned went yesterday with wagon to Marion for Mrs Huske's things—

April 21.... There is still much apprehension expressed as to civil commotion growing out of the purposes of the radicals in Congress. The Southern members are not yet admitted. Where we are drifting no one knows—

April 24. Tuesday—My wife was delivered of a daughter last night at 10-1/2 o clock.[20] Thanks to Almighty God for her safe deliverance I had gone to court at Eutaw on Sunday evening—had a hard trip over the river being very high and it having rained on the road. We had the night before being saturday night the 21st one of the hardest rains I ever saw. I remained in Eutaw till 3 1/2 on Monday & reached home on Monday night at 8 o clock. I found the river very high & rising.

May 3. May day was not celebrated here as far as I know was a dull day & rain in the evening and hard rains ever since—and it is still raining. Mr Wemyss reported on saturday last that he had sold my two bales cotton @ 32 and l bale Ins Co would pay for @ 200—he invested for me by purchasing $23,800 in gold at 126. Gold rose since and and went to 130.133. I wrote to him to day we are having a pretty dull time and serious apprehensions are felt as to the extreme radical measures in Congress & also of a foreign war between Austria and Prussia on the Schleswig Holstein question.[21] The Congress of U States are also threatening to tax cotton 5 cts a pound & with both[,] the prospects of cotton raises is blue—

May 8. my wife & baby are doing pretty well and Jane will be able to be out I trust in a few days. We are having a very rainy time—the

---

[20] Jane (Jenny) was born on 23 April 1866 and lived until January 1932.

[21] The Austro-Prussian War, or Seven Weeks War, was fought from 15 June to 23 August 1866. It was deliberately provoked by German Premier Otto von Bismarck. It ended quickly with Prussia overrunning the Austrians at Sadowa. The pretext for the conflict was over the administration of Schleswig-Holstein. It paved the way for the establishment of the German empire and the reorientation of Austria toward the East.

river is very high—and cannot be crossed. We yesterday held an election for circuit Judge and Probate & I acted as one of the inspectors to prevent its going by default. Cobbs, Morse & Dillard were candidates & Oliver for Probate had no opposition. It rained very hard about 1 o clock, and again this morning the rain is pouring down great damage to the crops.

May 10. The rainy weather still continues, and the river is reported rising and will soon be over the Low grounds.—The crops will be greatly injured. We are still unrepresented in Congress—and are awaiting What the Radical congress is going to do with us—There are cases of cholera reported at N. York and great apprehensions of its spreading are felt.

The situation continued to deteriorate as President Johnson and Congress fought over the Reconstruction committee report. Benners was beside himself with anger. These were "the most tyrannical and oppressive measures for Govt of the South."

May 21. Monday. We are having another fair day which is very acceptable after the long continued rains. The crops are reported very much injured by washing rains and some consider that the injury to the stand will be as much as 1/3. Cotton is dull in Mobile at 32 & gold 130. The President (Johnson) has vetoed the bill for admission of Colorado as a state on the ground of insufficient population—this bill was passed by the radicals to get two more radical votes in the Senate.[22] The contest for the admission of Southern Representatives still goes on. The Reconstruction committee so called have made their report—and prepared amendments to the Constitution in regard to rights of Negroes which when adopted by the states those adopting to be admitted. The

---

[22] President Johnson vetoed the admission of Colorado on 15 May 1866, expressing doubt as to the need for statehood for a region whose population was less than 40,000. The veto was sustained. Colorado was not admitted to the Union until August 1876.

plan is agreeable to no one, and it is supposed they never intended or expected it to be adopted.[23]

May 25. Friday. After a week of fine clear pleasant weather we had this morning before day a fine season of rain—quite acceptable in laying dust and fine for farms where the land had got too hard to plough. [F. E.] Stollenwerck writes to me that Mobile Mutual lost 100 bales in the late fire in Mobile. There is very little of interest transpiring at the present time. The radical Congress have in the House adopted the report of Com of Reconstruction without amendment.[24] In the Senate it will probably be amended—& passed. Cotton has advanced in Mobile to 34—Gold 130 1/4. The damage done to the crops by rains and overflow are the subject of very much inquiry—some say it will amount to 1/3 some as much as 1/2. My idea is that it will be at most 1/3—and my venture for the crop is that it will be at 1,500,000 bales—*nous verrons*—

June 1. Friday. Caroline came up on yesterday—her father & Mary [Hatch] having gone to Mobile. We have had several very cool days and this morning it is remarkably cool for 1st June.—There is every prospect of a foreign war[25] And cotton which had improved by reason of poor stands—to 36 & 7 has got a little weaker. Gold to 137. Public affairs at Home have not mended much. Congress is still in Session and pressing the most tyrannical and oppressive measures for Govt of the South. The complaints about the freed men are increasing—with floods & laziness the cotton crop will be very short. We are having fine vegetables from the gardens—Peas potatoes snaps onions, lettuce, parsnips—Potatoes are

---

[23] The joint committee on Reconstruction presented the Fourteenth Amendment to the House of Representatives. Benners was correct in writing that the plan was not satisfactory to six members of the committee. Still it was passed by Congress and sent to the individual states for their ratification. It was adopted on 28 July 1868.

[24] The report of the joint committee released in June provided an official explanation and defense of the Fourteenth Amendment. Republicans insisted that the freedmen would not be abandoned and defended the representation clause as a compromise that left voting requirements to the states.

[25] Benners may be referring to troubles along the Canadian border. The Irish-American organization known as the Fenian Brotherhood cooperated with the Phoenix Society in Ireland and did many provocative things inconsistent with American neutrality. On 6 June 1866, President Johnson issued a proclamation warning all citizens to desist from taking part in unlawful activities. The Fenian activities were effectively suppressed.

unusually fine—Bulger at McFaddin place was killed on 29th by a capt Black—Mr Badger of N. Caro is dead.[26]

June 12. I left home on sunday the 3rd of June for Newbern on my way to Selma it rained a great deal on sunday night & monday morning—and was raining when I left Parkers to go to depot. reached selma about 9 o clock. hard rains while there, dined at Sturdevants— remarkably good dinner—took St charles for Montgomery—reached there at 10 oclock tuesday—went to exchange. Attended District Co U States applied to practice—was admitted signed the roll of Attys, Judge Jones was indicted for treason & conspiracy bailed in $20,000—Judge decided pardon could be plead in bar where it had been rec'd before indictment found. Took Rail for Mobile on Wednesday night at 8. PM. to Mobile at 12 m. remained till Saturday at 5 & came up the river on the admiral to Eastport and got home Monday evening at 7 o clock. the river is higher than it has been this year & than it was ever before known in June.

The weather continued to be warm with a spell of ninety-degree heat in July and August. The crops suffered and there was considerable illness. Slowly, political efforts to resist Republican Reconstruction began to form.

July 30. I went to Walker Place in buggy with Alfred on last tuesday 24th Walked over the plantation. Corn is very poor cotton is a poor crop but is now blooming very well—on the whole the plantation will not repay the corn & fodder & meats and mules. Gen Perry has improved the home a good deal. Cattle are doing badly, hogs d[itt]o. Planting as a business with free negroes is neither profitable or pleasant. I had severe headache all the day. Went to Parker Hatches in the evening. Next morning Alfred & I went to Selma. Met W. R. Brown on the cars and agreed to take the stock $2500 belonging to Pleasants in the Perry Insurance & Trust Co. Found it very hot in Selma did not get my cert of stock in 1st National Bank—said secretary was not there. Alfred amused himself roving about town. It is improving very rapidly in buildings.

---

[26] George Edmund Badger, a senator from North Carolina, died in Raleigh on 11 May 1866.

Came to Newbern in the evening in the cars and drove home in buggy by 11 o clock. there has been a spell of very hot weather. Ther 90°—Ben Hatch is sick at Arcola and sent up for my wife on Friday she went down in my carriage on saturday with Alfred has not yet returned. There was a fire last tuesday morning in Richardson store. It broke out in the N.E. corner of store and was stopped before the flames had spread very far. Mr. Richardson had left the store a short time before it was discovered. there is much talk about the proposed Union Convention at Philadelphia—Aug. 17. The object is to form a party in opposition to the Radicals. The South has been invited to send delegates and in most parts people are moving to do so.[27]

August 15. Wednesday. I went in the Carriage with Mr Wemyss to Macon Station on Thursday Aug 2nd and took train for Mobile which we reached on friday Aug 3. I went to Pt Clear same evening—arrived about six o clock, remained till Thursday morning Aug 9th took cars at 4 o clock & got home friday evening Aug 10th went with Mr Wemyss to fish river. he is just starting his mill. Enjoyed the bathing at the Point very much. there was a very fashionable company and much gay dressing, music & Dancing. Mr Whitfield & family was there. I was very sorry on my arrival at home to find my wife & Alfred sick. They are not yet well & are very weak. While In Mobile I purchased from Joseph W. Field 25 shares in the Planters and Merchants Ins Company of which Mr Wemyss is president for a premium of 7 per cent—and after reaching home I bot of Pleasants 25 shares in Perry Ins & trust company for 2573.52 cts W. R. Brown of Marion President. We are having it very dry and dusty and there is a good deal of sickness. Cholera is in New Orleans and a few cases are reported in Mobile. The Phil convention is in Session and great things for the south are expected by some

---

[27] Supporters of Andrew Johnson sought a new organization to promote the conservative program of conciliatory reunification. The National Union convention appealed to moderate Republications, Democrats, and old Unionists in the Southern state governments. It had the support of President Johnson and tried to elect a Congress that would uphold his policies.

persons—not by me. The condition of affairs is very unpromising & more trouble is anticipated—[28]

September 11. another of our valued and estimable citizens is gone to his long home. Mr Richard Randolph[29] died last night at 12 o clock. It has cast a gloom over our Community—of him it may be truly said that no one could ever speak harshly or slightingly. I never heard any one say aught against him. Poor Dick—his earthly troubles are over Peace to his ashes—

Dr Groce came up this morning with Mr [blank space] I agreed to rent the Walker place next year to Kirksy and [blank space] and him for the sum of $1600—and to let him have the use of the stock there 15 mules & 1 horse for $320. The loss by natural wear and tear & use to be borne by me, but by any other cause to be borne by him—my wife has been quite sick & is still. Alfred has had a long spell of chills & fever and is still down. Ed is also down. it has been raining off and on for a week or more & the worms are said to have played sad havoc with the cotton. Groce says we may make 40 bales cotton—and not more than corn enough to do the place till Jany.

October 13. The Elections in Penn Ohio & indiana have gone against the conservatives—very great uneasiness is felt as to the situation of affairs.[30] Gold went to 153, but recedes to 150-1/2. Cotton is 36:37 in Mobile. I expect to leave on monday morning for Eutaw to attend Court. I would that it were well over with. Alfred after starting to college was taken sick again and not yet out I engaged Emma @ 6 a month as a cook for one month—hope she'll do, but I doubt it very much.

When the election of 1866 was completed in early November, Benners's "uneasiness" was confirmed. President Johnson's effort to build a new

---

[28] The National Union Convention failed to catch the imagination of the North. President Johnson hoped that the new party would draw many Republicans to his side. It was not to be.

[29] Richard Randolph, planter, Greensboro. Snedecor, *Greene County*, 36.

[30] The congressional election of 1866 was the first time the public was able to vote on Reconstruction. President Johnson gave notice that he would work to defeat all Republicans who opposed his policies, but Republicans continued to campaign on the strength of their reconstruction programs and policies.

Conservative Party had failed. Also his efforts to defeat the Republicans who opposed his policies was unsuccessful. The Republican Party won most of the governorships, gained control of the legislatures in every Northern state, and secured more than a two-thirds majority in Congress. Now they could override any presidential veto.

Benners made no mention of the election of 1866 or its impact on the South in the journal. Instead, he wrote about his legal business, his trips to Montgomery on political matters, and the loss of two dear friends.

October 27. Saturday evening—I went to Eutaw in McRarys [David F. McCrary] carriage (price 3.00) on Monday 15 Oct—Went to Hotel & staid there till tuesday. Went with Judge Coleman & staid till friday. Hotel till Saturday night. Went to Judge Pierces till Monday after Breakfast. Hotel cleavelands till friday after dinner. Came home in Atkins[31] carriage friday night 7 o.clock. Had very few judg'ts taken—and tho no very bad luck not much very good. There was a meeting of citizens on Monday to prevent judg'ts being taken. Capt Nott presided, but afterward told me he had no knowledge of what they intended to do—affairs look blue enough—our old citizens are dying off more rapidly than usual Mr Lem Hatch died at Blount Springs about the 5 oct & D. D. Stockton at Va Springs about 1st oct.[32] Mr Hatch and Mary came to my house to day and Mary was taken sick & Mr H. left after dinner carrying Alfred with him—Cotton is declining about 35.6 Gold about 1.45 [145] and declining. What new scenes will be enacted we know not.

I paid my bill to Cleaveland at Eutaw—the last one $16, having previously paid him $7 for 2 days 1st Octk. I returned J. B. Stickney claim on Averys to Richd Stickney this evening being unable to get any Blanks from Montgy. this was the order he gave in regard to it.

---

[31] John Atkins, planter, Newbern voting precinct, Greensboro. Snedecor, *Greene County*, 7.

[32] Lemuel Hatch was the brother of Alfred Hatch and the uncle of Jane Hatch Benners. He was seventy-one years of age. Daniel Stockton was a Greensboro merchant.

October 29. Troubles oh! how fast they come I have just received a letter from my Brother Edward from Jefferson Texas informing me that his only daughter Fanny had died on the 14th Oct. seven children of his have one after another been laid in the grave and only one remaining his son Henry—How my heart bleeds for his bereavement and how I wish I could comfort him—but a wounded spirit[,] who can heal? May God in his mercy and loving kindness lift upon him & my dear sister Helen and the afflicted brother the light of his Countenance and give them his peace which passeth all understanding—a lovelier child than Fanny was I never knew—Beautiful modest and winning in her deportment she seemed to attach every one to her—she died in the Communion of the church with a certain hope of everlasting happiness.

October 29. [second entry] Ned set in with me to day at 10 for a month to haul[,] drive the carriage &c 3-1/2 pounds meat & peck of meal a week.

November 5. Emmeline set in with me at $6 a month to cook and serve me for a month—

December 1. I went to Montgomery starting from Macon station on Wednesday Nov 21st & reaching Montgomery with Judge Coleman on the 22nd. The question of dividing Greene Cty was much canvassed in the Legislature and I thought in a good way when I left. Mr Waller & Huckabee favor Mr Pierce opposes. I returned home Monday night Nov 26th—all well. Pork had been killed by Weather at plantation and my half sent up—it was salted on tuesday and great fears were felt for it on acct of the weather, but it turned cool on thursday and continues so and we may have a good lot yet. it rained very hard on Wednesday night. Mr Harvey[33] returned from Montgomery on thursday morning.

December 18. on monday 3rd Dec I went to Eutaw Chancery Court. Rained very hard. Remained in attendance in the Court. Demurrer was filed by Jones' Lawyer, overruled by Chan[cellor] Loomis & leave given to amend generally. Answer was filed in Walton Case by John W. [Walton] Adm[inistrator] and Jas E. Webb appointed guardian *ad Litem.* I left Eutaw on Thursday & went by Gainesville to Mobile reached there

---

[33] John G. Harvey, editor and proprietor of the *Alabama Beacon*, Greensboro. Snedecor, *Greene County*, 21.

friday 7th very rainy—remained till monday evening 10th left at 7 15 P.M and reached home tuesday at 5 1/2. Had attack of Cholera morbus that night—While in Mobile recd transfer of stock from Wemyss & Stollenwerck to 25 shares each in Mobile Mutual ins Co. Mobile was dull, cotton 30 cts & drooping—

1867

January 1. Tuesday 25th Dec 1866 was a beautiful day. The church was handsomely decorated and we had a good dinner Mr A. P[arker] Hatch dined with us. The weather continued good till Saturday 28th [29] when it snowed and continued to sleet & snow all day—the ground was quite white and the cold continuing it has not melted much and on this 1st day of the new year it is quite white and on the walks & streets very sloppy—warm fires and closed door are the order of the day and the bad weather forbids the probability of many persons in Town to day. The colored people are not as numerous here since their freedom as in former days and little or no hilarity and joyousness is observable among them—care and perplexity comes with their boon of freedom—and a race of contented & happy & useful laborers has been changed into one of vagrants and moody dissatisfied and beggarly shiftless drones—

January 4. night before last before the old fall of sleet was melted we had a considerable fall of snow—the deepest I have seen in this State and there is still considerable on the houses. My gutter at the office which had just been made anew by Le[i]ser leaked badly, and he yesterday went up and threw the snow off. Edward and his wife have agreed to stay with me $10 for him and $5. for her—the two children who come with her are to be found by him and the girl is to go away as soon as practicable over the river. Emline agreed to stay with me at 7 a month to cook & milk the cow. Salina at $5—Kit at $10 and Amy a[t] 8.[34]

---

[34] Benners contracted with his former slaves. They were free, but many chose to work for him.

For many years, Benners worked to create a new county in western Alabama. When the Alabama legislature met in mid-January to discuss that matter, he attended and lobbied for its passage. His experience in the legislature during the 1850s and Civil War years was invaluable in securing the bill's passage.

February 2. I went to Montgomery by way of Selma on Wednesday 16th [Jan.] remained till 31 Feby [January]. Bill was passed for new County of Hale.[35] It was first introduced in the Senate to be called the County of King—and in order not to array the hostility of Pickens county—no part of that County was added to West Greene in the place of adding from Pickens a portion East of Warrior river was left in Greene Cty. In the Senate the Committee on County Boundaries refused to let any portion East of Warrior river remain in Greene but insisted that all east of the river should be in the new County & the river be the boundary—and to make up the deficiency on the West side they added to it that portion of Pickens South of the Sipsey river—and as so amended recommended its passage. It was then referred to Judiciary Committee to settle the questions whether the Legislature could Constitutionally pass a bill creating a new County and by same bill add to the County from which new County was taken. This Committee after we reached Montgomery reported that there was no Constitutional objection to the bill on that account—and upon Mr Huckabee in the Senate, moving to suspend in order to pass the bill, Mr Stansel from Pickens moved to postpone till Saturday at 12 o clock to enable him to hear from the People of Pickens Cty. Mr Stansel was very decided in his opposition to the bill, but consented to withdraw his opposition if we would call the County Hale County. Accordingly on Saturday at 12 o clock 26th Jany 1867 Mr Stansel moved to amend the bill by changing the name to the County of Hale—which was agreed to and the bill passed the Senate unanimously. It did not get to the house till Monday morning 28th Jany when it was reported as message from the Senate—and was referred to Committee on County boundaries. We

---

[35] Benners lobbied for the division of Greene County into two parts. He was no longer a legislator but was very experienced in the legislative process.

pressed them for an early consideration & they agreed to meet on tuesday morning 29 Jany. Accordingly we met the committee and Mr Pierce of Eutaw and Mr [Henry A.] Wolfe [Woolf] of Marengo also appeared before the Committee to oppose the bill—Stating that there was not the required number of whites for a county according to the Constitution—that they had examined census returns and there was not enough. I had also examined and footed up the numbers from the returns and assured the chairman that there was the requisite number. Messrs Pierce & Wolfe said they had taken their figures from the recapitulations of the returns—and on calling out their returns I discovered they had omitted four fractional Townships in Greene & one in Perry which they said they could not find. Whereupon I went to Sec of States office & brought up the returns and shewed the numbers in the Townships they had not found and the chairman decided that with those there was the constitutional requirement as to population. Mr Pierce made a speech to the committee against the bill and I replied to him after which we retired and the committee very soon adopted a report unanimously in favor of the new county—and so reported to the house. Mr Smith of Jackson the chairman of the Committee on County boundaries, thought it would be best to postpone the bill till next day Wednesday 30th on which day on motion of Mr [R. B.] Waller the rule was suspended and the bill taken up. When one or two immaterial amendments were adopted and the bill passed by a vote of 74 to 9, 67 being necessary to pass it. The clerk on order promptly Carried it to the Senate who concurred in the amendments and Capt Vick very soon after enrolled the bill and it was carried to the Speaker & President of the Senate and then to the Governor all of whom signed it—and it thus became a law. I apprehended an effort might be made to consider which they spoke of doing next day. So I remained over till thursday night—and came down to Selma on the *Joab Lawrence*. Mr Jeffries and Jones were in Selma on my arrival and we came on together and reached home on friday night Feb 1st 1867—

During the next few months, the Reconstruction Act of 1867 was passed and implemented. It divided the ten Confederate states into five military districts under commanders empowered to use the army to protect life and property. New state constitutions were to be written and recognized by Congress. Suffrage for all males regardless of color had to be part of any new constitution. It was called Sherman's bill because Senator John Sherman was chairman of the committee that drafted the bill.

February 28. There is much depression & anxiety from the recent passage in Congress of the bill for Southern States called Sherman's bill, placing them under military authority—dividing into 5 districts each to be under a Major General with military forces to carry out the Govt. It is said to require all persons before voting to take the oath, and all loyal persons can vote without regard to color.[36] It is expected the President will veto and Congress pass it over his head by 2/3rds. The tremendous fires recently in Mobile & burning of the Montgomery threw heavy losses on insurance co. in Mobile & of course I lost there smartly. Cotton has declined to 29-1/2 and I lose there some thousands. Gold N.Y. 138-1/2 last acctg. to day we have no mail—the more we want to hear the more it dont come—

March 7. Monday March 4th was the 1st election day in the County of Hale. There were a good many Candidates and much interest felt lest Greensboro should not be selected as the County site. There was a large vote polled here say 365 and the result is that Buckswort and 5 Mile are together beaten. Alfred H. Hutchinson was elected Judge of Probate and James E. Grig[g]s[37] Shff. The vote for judge was very close being only 8 votes between foremost man & next—The Territorial bill lately passed

---

[36] The Reconstruction Act of 1867 divided the ten Confederate states (Tennessee had already been readmitted to the Union) into five military districts under commanders empowered to employ the Army to protect life and property. New state governments were to be created and recognized by Congress. They had to write a new constitution providing for manhood suffrage, secure the approval of a majority of registered voters, and ratify the Fourteenth Amendment. It was called Sherman's bill because Senator John Sherman of Ohio chaired the seven-member committee that wrote the act.

[37] James E. Griggs, livery stable proprietor, Greensboro. Snedecor, *Greene County*, 19.

by Congress gives much uneasiness[38]—and civil commotion is not unlikely to grow out of it. Cotton is declining say dull at 29. I bot 50 shares of Stock in Mutual insurance Co of Selma. Keith Pres. Had a partial settlement with Clark of claim vs Robinson children, got $2270 in dft on Wemyss & Norris by Jno W. Walton. Sent to Mobile same day but mails are hindered by creeks. Many persons apprehend trouble from Washington.

March 19. We have had a cold snap commencing on on [repeated] 13 inst.—hard freeze sleet & vegetation killed. all the peas in joint killed. Peaches which were in full bloom killed and since the cold snap we have had very hard washing rains and altogether the start for a new crop is not good by any means. Alfred has had chills—but got out yesterday. Willie d[itt]o not out yet my wife d[itt]o. Mrs Brown & her child were brot to my house by Caroline from Arcola and left there she has now gone to Davis and prepares to go to S. Caro to see her mother—At Election for T[own] Council on Monday question was submitted. Tax or No tax & Tax carried by 63 to 18. This Tax is intended to procure a court house and Jail for Hale.[39]

March 29. We have had a great deal of rain and the rivers are still very high. The utter destruction of the peach crop is much to be regretted—the gardens have to contend as well with the continued washing rains as with the cold—and prospects are very poor. I had irish potatoes planted on Monday last 24 March—very little corn is up and it looks very badly—

March 30. Sunday morning—again this morning we have rain. The times are gloomy & depressing. Military Bill having passed over Pres veto.[40] The great question is what to do. It is clear we are for purposes of Govt held as conquered provinces and as such there is no questioning. Cotton is down to 27 1/2–28 in Mobile. Wemyss & Norris sold 16 bales on 28th at 27 1/2 nett $1663—Much less than I could have got & sold

---

[38] The term *territory* was not used in the Reconstruction act but it was understood that the Confederate states were under "territorial probation."

[39] The county seat where Benners lived was formerly in Eutaw, Alabama. When the new county Hale was created in 1867, Greensboro became the county seat.

[40] Andrew Johnson vetoed the Reconstruction act of 2 March 1867, which was quickly passed over his veto.

without my instruction, but thank God for his goodness that I have that much more than I deserve.

April 9. Rain more rain. We had it night before last we had it yesterday & oh we had it last night—nearly all night. Starvation and death seem all that are left to us. The Congress have imposed terms very bitter.[41] What can we do—Nothing—runaway where. We of course have sinned—and God is meting out justice to us. May he grant us patience & fortitude to do what we ought. My hay is hauled to Syd Nelsons[42] place. Nothing can be done right—

[newspaper clipping]
Old Folks.
Ah, don't be sorrowful, darling
And don't be sorrowful, pray
Taking the year together, my dear,
There isn't more night than day

The rainy weather, my darling,
Time's waves, they heavily run;
But taking the year together, my dear,
There isn't more clouds than sun.

We are old folks now, my darling,
Our heads are growing gray;
And taking the year together, my dear,
You will always find the May.

We've had our May, my darling,
And our roses long ago;

---

[41] On 23 March, Congress passed a supplemental Reconstruction act, again overriding Johnson's veto. This measure detailed the procedures by which federal military commanders in the South were to reconstruct civil governments. It directed a new registration of voters, an election of delegates to state conventions, and a ratification vote.

[42] A. Sidney Nelson, planter, German Creek, Greensboro. Snedecor, *Greene County*, 33.

And the time of the year is coming, my dear,
For the silent night and snow.

And God is God, my darling.
Of night as well as day;
And we feel and know that we can go
Wherever He leads the way.

Aye God of the night, my darling—
Of the night of death so grim;
The gate that leads out of life, good wife,
Is the gate that leads to him.

April 30. Cir Co Greene Co commenced April 15 I went over in my carriage with Pitman and remained till following Thursday week & came home on the Stage. The bogus order recd by judge Cobbs suspending him from his official duties from that date (5th April) produced considerable excitement and suspended Court two days. Goldthwaite was sent to Montgy to Gen Swayne to see if the order was genuine. he saw Swayne in Selma who sd it was a forgery. Court was resumed and many judg'ts taken. Many cases were moved to Hale Cty. Parkmans defalcation in 1st Natl Bank in Selma came to light during the week. He sd the Bank had been robbed and offered 20,000 for the thief. Was arrested him self and is in jail at Cahaba.

May 4. I attended the May celebration by the pupils of female academy last night at Dormans Hall. The exhibition was very handsome and creditable. The profusion of flowers was attractive and a large crowd in attendance. The presbyterian ladies had a supper in opposite rooms for benefit of the poor of the County. We got refreshments for Liz & Ed and I retreated early. Fanny remained and came home with Ed. I dont enjoy crowds—which is my fault. The children were much pleased, but it is no easy matter to be joyous when the heart is heavy. I sent Salina home yesterday, her condition preventing her from acting as a house girl any longer—regret the necessity as she had given in other respects satisfaction & the children & my wife like her & so did I. Cotton has again declined in Liverpool & on [May] 2nd was quoted 11 5/8 to 12d—have some unsold on which I fear I shall lose money—

From a poem entitled the burial of the Dead by Col Theodore O Hara a native of Frankfort Ky[:]

"The muffled Drums sad roll has beat
The soldiers last Tattoo
No more on life's parade shall meet
The brave and daring few

On Fame's Eternal Camping ground
Their silent tents are spread
And Glory guards with solemn round
The bivouac of the dead."

June 20. I rode to Eutaw Ch[ancer]y Co[urt] on Monday 10th June. Stayed till friday evening and came home in company with J. E. Webb & wife. Case of Carson vs Walton was submitted…Found great excitement in town among the negroes because Orrick who had killed Elliah Weller had escaped. they are reported to have threatened to burn the town—and James Green made a very inflammatory speech at night. They arrested Gewin and used him pretty rough—forced him to walk to town barefooted. they thought he knew where Orrick was. On Monday a company of U State soldiers came under command Lieut. Adams. quiet has been restored but it is only a lull in the storm.

July 10. My wife went to Bladen on 22 June and returned on 5th July 67 she did not get home in time for the Commencement at So University and to hear Alfreds maiden effort. She thought she was improved by her trip—and I only regretted she did not stay longer. We have had frequent and excessive rains damaging crops very much and she said making it not very pleasant to be at the Springs. Henry Benners[43] came in from Texas and reached my house on friday night the 5th day of July on a visit from Jefferson Texas. he is very thin and is seeking a

---

[43] Augustus Benners's nephew.

recreation & improvement of his health. They went to a picnic yesterday at Lem Hatchs. I dined yesterday at Mad[ison] Jones. We have Mrs Husk[e] & family at my home to Dinner to day.

[newspaper clipping of poem]

They Say.
They say—ah, well, suppose they do!
But can they prove the story true?
Suspicion may arise from naught
But malice, envy, want of thought;
Why count yourself among the "they"
Who whisper what they dare not say?

They say—but why the tale rehearse,
And help to make the matter worse?
No good can possibly accrue
From telling what may be untrue;
And is it not a nobler plan
To speak of all the best you can?

They say—well, if it should be so,
Why need you tell the tale of woe?
Will it the bitter wrong redress,
Or make one pang of sorrow less?
Will it the erring one restore,
Henceforth to "go and sin no more?"

They say—oh! pause and look within!
See how thy heart inclines to sin!
Watch, lest in dark temptation's hour,
Thou, too, shouldst sink beneath its power!
Pity the frail—weep o'er their fall,
But speak of good, or not at all!

Fall elections were held to begin the process of voter registration in Alabama. Three-man boards with one of them being a black member were established for the forty-four registration districts. This greatly disturbed Benners, especially the new role of black men in the process.

September 7. There appears to be no end to bad luck and misfortunes of our people. The order from head quarters requiring negroes to sit on juries it is true has been modified so as not to apply to this term of Court—but the future is dark & Lowering—the election takes place on October 1st or 23rd.[44] All the elections are to be held at County seats and the chances are we shall have a very disagreeable time of it—what the Convention will do no man can imagine. most likely they will make a constitution in accordance with the extreme radical views—and the confiscation scheme is likely to be a prominent feature. The negroes are in a majority and to retain hold on them they must be gratified with evidences of affection and to give them other peoples property is a cheap and sure way to do it. The cotton worm has come and is making havoc with the crops. What the next phase of misfortune who can tell. Alfred and Ed with Henry are still at Blount and will remain till I send for them last of Septr. Willie has very sore eyes and the baby is sick with teething. All discontented and no prospect of things improving. Well I hope God will give me peace to suffer patiently and without complaining. As suffering seems the badge of our times just now.

September 17. I start my carriage in the morning to Blount for Alfred Ed & Henry. Mr Hatch lends me a mule in lieu of Frank sent to Arcola. How the trip will turn out I dont know. Mr Hatch speaks of going in the morning & Fanny will go too. Court is coming on & I cant leave. We have no stirring matters of interest—there is a lull. Every one is waiting as to what will turn up on the registration question. Presidents

---

[44] On 31 August, Major General John Pope, now in command of the Third Military District, began the process of voter registration in Alabama. Three-man boards with one black member were established for the forty-four registration districts.

amnesty is variously interpreted. Some say it means all can vote who are pardoned. I dont see how they can in advance of a decision of Courts setting aside—Law of Congress—

September 18. Edward left with carriage this morning for Blount to bring home Alfred Ed & Henry. Mr Hatch started for Tuscaloosa. Ben Hatch went in his double buggy—and Caroline and Fanny in Mr Hatchs carriage with him for Tuscaloosa and a place—they dont know yet where they will go. We understand the election for Convention & delegates is postponed to 1st November.[45] The impeachment of the President Mr Johnson is much talked of.

October 19. the first Circuit Court ever had in the County of Hale commenced on Monday Sep 30 '67—Judge John W. Moore presiding. Dormans Hall was fitted up & used as a court room—and proved very convenient. It was a very satisfactory court and everyone seemed pleased with the Judge. He adjourned the court on Saturday of the second week. On last monday I rode over in Taylors hack to Eutaw Circuit Court—the judge (Cobbs) being sick no court was had till Thursday morning when orders were taken in plain cases. The juries & witnesses were dismissed and no jury trials will be had in civil cases. I took several Judgments & came home friday in hack. The docket there is very large & the judge promises an extra term.

December 9. I attended chy [chancery] court at Eutaw Nov 30. got decrees in cases of Randolph vs Jones & Carson vs Walton et al. Mr Garrett went & returned with me. The Convention to frame a Constitution has finished their constitution and it is published. Great tightness for many prevails and it is expected there will be a crash in Mobile & New Orleans. I carried Jane & Willie to Newbern and I went to Walker place last tuesday—Weathers turned over 8 more bales of cotton—

December 28. Christmas was a mild pleasant day. We all attended church and had Sacrament. Mrs Huske and daughters dined with us and Mr Hatch. This time of merriment & gladness to all others, brings

---

[45] This is not true. The elections were held from 1–4 October 1867. Of the hundred delegates, ninety-six were Republicans, including eighteen blacks. It was a major victory for the Republican Party.

trouble & vexation to me. Edward is persuaded by his wife Mary to go over the river & I shall greatly miss him.

At the end of his 1867 journal, Benners pasted the complete text of the Reconstruction bill, which was proposed in January and finally passed in March 1867. Clearly, it was important for him to have a copy of this "infamous bill" to refer to in the years ahead. Few things disturbed him more than this arbitrary legislation that meant that the South would be under Northern control for years to come. This may explain why he did less writing in his journal for the next few years. It is also possible that he had health problems that made it difficult for him to continue writing. On 9 January, he writes "I have a very unpleasant neuralgic headache and therefore abridge my entries."

1868

Benners made only six entries in the years 1868 and 1869. Finally, in 1870, he showed interest in the Democratic and Conservative convention in Montgomery and also in the beginning of the Franco-Prussian war in July 1870.

January 2, 1868. New Years day was cloudy & mild. I went in morning to see Isaac who sent for me. Mr Hatch came up. I have hired Emline & Edmond at $10 apiece per month. Fanny left in the carriage this evening to go to Arcola on her way to Mobile with her Grandpa—how anxious do I feel for her health & safety.

February 24. I started by Stage via Newbern to Mobile on Jany 15 reached Mobile on 17. Fanny was at Roper house. We went to N. Orleans on 24 left on 28 had a very stormy passage on the Louise[,] Capt Hopkins—24 hours over—staid in Mobile on account of severe cold weather till the 1st Feby came up with Fanny on Cherokee got off at Eastport rode home in Mays carriage. All well. Fanny enjoyed the trip very much. We visited theatre in Mobile saw the Black crook play and Jifferson perform in N. Orleans. Visited Levee[,] Market[,] Cemetery &c and rambled around generally. The Republican constitution was not ratified by a majority of all the registered voters by about 15000.[46] What Congress will do with it is still uncertain.[47] Taylor's stable was burnt up last night about 11 o clock. there was a high wind from SE but the fire did not extend—several horses were burned....

November 17. On 6th July I started with my family to Blount Springs. We geared up the old carriage, my buggy and the two horse wagon. carried tent for camping. first night we camped at church this side Carthage—next night stopped out of the rain at Hatters and used his room for sleeping—next night stopped at Vances. Next night at Smiths—next night at Jacks, and next night being Sunday at the [C. W.] Hatch houses. Next morning drove to my house at Valley hill. Livingston who was my tenant at will had cleaned up the house and moved out. We got some corn and fodder & provisions and I felt greatly delighted at my freedom from the old routine of cares & bothers at Home. We found that provisions were very plenty and not so high except corn as they were at home. Mutton 6 cts to 8 cts Venison do [ditto] chickens 15 Eggs 15 to 20 Butter 20 flour $6 per hundred [wt] lard 20 cts per pound. I amused myself with walking to Springs occasionally hunting & fishing & roving over the mountains. fine appetites and good fare made an improvement in appearance of nearly every one. My wife was sick for a week or so. With this exception none of the white folks were sick. Ed would ride in before breakfast and bring keg of water from Springs and whenever chance presented the keg went.

---

[46] The vote on the proposed constitution began on 4 February 1868. Because of poor weather, the voting time was extended until 8 February. The final vote was 70,812 in favor and 1,005 opposed—a total of 71,817 votes. This was 8,114 votes short of an absolute majority of eligible voters. Thus the constitution failed. General George G. Meade (who had replaced General Pope) made an unheeded recommendation that another convention be called to revise the constitution that had failed. William Warren Rogers et al., *Alabama: The History of a Deep South State* (Tuscaloosa: University of Alabama Press, 1994) 246–47.

[47] Congress decided to modify the requirement that a "majority of registered voters" vote in the election to a "majority of the actual votes cast." This change was put into law on 11 March 1868. On 25 June, Congress passed a law that paved the way for the readmission of six Southern states—North Carolina, South Carolina, Louisiana, Georgia, Alabama, and Florida. President Johnson vetoed the bill, which was immediately overridden by Congress. All the states but Georgia were seated by late July 1868. Ibid., 247.

Fanny Alfred & Ed went to parties at Springs and an occasional picnic relieved the monotony—thus the time wore on till 21 Septr when I left in Major Clarks ambulance with miss Kate Borden for Elyton & Montevallo—reached home on Monday 28 Septr. Maria had the yard swept up and seemed to be looking for me—my family got back on the 2nd November, all well—

1869

January 7, 1869. After heavy rains we have a fair day, but weather too mild for a long continuance. My wife & youngest children have gone in the country to see Mrs Tom Witherspoon & I have a very unpleasant neuralgic headache and therefore abridge my entries.[48]

September 23. I started from my house with my family on the 5th day of July for Arcola to take the S. Boat to Mobile on my way to Fish river. I took the Prairie State at Mr Hatchs landing on Wednesday night July 7th. The river was quite low and the weather hot. We reached Mobile on Saturday morning. I charted the Schooner Comet to carry my furniture Baggage & groceries to Mr Wemyss and with my family took the Planter on Saturday evening for Battles Wharf. I staid at Laniers all night and went on Sunday to Fish River in Mr Wemyss wagon which had been sent for us—We reached Fish river on sunday morning & took a skiff at Pease's Ldg & crossed over. I found the arrangements a little rough but very comfortable. We amused ourselves every day except sundays fishing or boating. The bathing too was pretty good and while there was a breeze it was very pleasant. I remained there till 15 Septr when I left for Mobile on my way home thinking it then too early for my family to return home—I reached home via Selma on Saturday 18th Septr. Kit & Maria had remained and taken care of the premises—My family came home by Rail Road to Van Dorn where Mr Hatchs carriage & my wagon met them on 4th October. We had no sickness of consequence at Fish river except Caroline Hatch who was quite sick having come down after a spell of sickness and exposed herself before

---

[48] Mrs. T. F. Witherspoon, wife of Benners's cotton factor.

recovering. Mary & Ben Hatch also staid with me. Mr Wills & Dr Batey spent some time with us. We found on our arrival at Home that there had been an unusual healthy season thro the summer very few persons having been sick—This was the case through out the Country—Tho at Arcola they had had some sickness and Mrs Dubois [child], Mr Hatch's grand daughter died as also Mr Strudwicks child.

November 30. I went in stage to Chancery Court at Eutaw Nov 25 and returned on 26 Got decree in Tinkers vs Wallers. Dismissed Ward against Mansfield and report was read in Lipscomb vs Carson.

1870

February 22, 1870. This day Alfred becomes of age and proposes to commence the practice of Law having obtained a license from Supreme Court of Ala.[49] Fanny and Ed went down to Arcola in the carriage to day thro rain and mud to attend Ben Hatchs marriage to Miss Tayloe at Macon Station on 23. I feel anxious to hear how they got along as the weather was very bad. Sam drove two mules in my old carriage. Alfred backed out on acct of the weather—

March 11. I started in the Stage to Mobile via Selma on 26th Feby took cars at Prairie Station reached Selma at 9-1/2 AM. Left 2-1/2 Saturday evening & reached Mobile Sunday morning at 10 oclock. Stopped at Gulf City—remained six days and came to Eastport on Cherokee. Times in Mobile were gloomy. Stewards failure cast a gloom on many. He had sold 5 B/C of mine and it was gone up. Cotton was running down to 21-1/2 gold 13-1/2. trip up the river was very pleasant but long—All well on my arrival at home—

April 19. The Two last weeks court has been in Session in Greensboro and the proceedings were uncommonly slow. The case vs A. C. Jones & Webb in which I was employed was settled by a judgt with stay of ex[ecution] until after next court—on Thursday of 2nd week the State vs Rossers was taken up and on Friday after dinner the argument

---

[49] Alfred Hatch Benners, born on 22 February 1849, was now twenty-one years of age and ready to practice law.

was commenced. Wm R. Smith opened for the state & Mr Fitts of Tuscaloosa followed for defense—these were the only speeches I heard as Mr Dubois reached my house at 2 oclock Saturday morning informing us of the dangerous illness of Mr Hatch at Arcola and that he had sent for Fanny & Alfred—they with my wife & myself went down in the carriage next morning & reached there by 12. We found Mr H very sick—pulse feeble & flickering, but after taking some quinine he recovered his pulse and continued to improve till we left on sunday morning Easter sunday—We came home by Prairieville & got home about 1 oclock. Rossers case had been continued to next court the jury failing to agree standing as I was told 8 for acquittal & 4 for conviction. On Sunday it turned quite cold and on Monday morning there was a white frost—the day was very bright and moderated towards night—this morning it was raining & is still rainy and cloudy at 3 oclock. It is supposed the frost will do not much damage as very little cotton is up and the corn too young to be killed. The peaches are past hope having been here to fore cut off and only the apples & pears in a condition to be hurt. the potatoes will no doubt be injured as the frost was a killing one and they were well up. We found the road by Harry Johnstons very rough & in returning by Prairieville not so bad but very tedious. Bridge being down we had to go round.

September 6. I started with Col Jones in his hack on 31 Aug 70 to attend Democratic & Conservative Convention at Montgomery. J. J. Garrett accompanied us. We missed the train at Newbern getting there just in time to see the cars leaving. We staid over all day at McCann's—and Mr Garrett & I left on the train next morning Sep 1. Col Jones had returned to Greensboro and did not go with us. We reached Selma 9-1/2 and laid over till 1, took cars for Montgomery and reached there at 4. I went straight way to the Capitol where the Convention was assembled, and was gratified to see so large and respectable an assemblage and especially to recognise so many old acquaintances. There were 6 or 700 delegates—and Hon E. W. Pettus was president, Micah Taul sec. the delegation from Hale were Coleman, Tayloe, Browder, Garret[t] & myself—Lindsay was nominated for Gov. Moren for Lt. Gov, McCoy for treas. Parker of Monroe for sec of State and Hodgson for Sup of Ed. and Sanford for Atty Gen. Mr Garret[t] and I stopped at European house and left on Saturday Sep 3 at 6 AM for Selma on our way home—reached Selma at 8 and Greensboro that night at 8-1/2 P.M.

The news from Europe is very startling the Prussians have achieved a great success having captured the French army under McMahon and taken the Emperor prisoner. McMahon is wounded & 20,000 French reported killed—Bazaine is reported to have been defeated also.[50] It is probable the statements are exaggerated. We are now having cool nights & mornings—and hot days—some sickness.

November 8. Tuesday. This is Election day for State officers and lower house of assembly & Congress. The misrule of radical party has caused immense discontent in Ala & very great efforts have been made to defeat Gov Smith Keffer &c who are radical nominees. Lindsay is the candidate of Gov of Dem & Conservative party.[51] The negroes have come in in very great numbers and the streets are thronged with them—and they are voting Radical Ticket nearly solid—the hopes of all good citizens it seems are that the party in power will be defeated but the appearances in this County are gloomy indeed. Fanny started with Annie for Gallatin on last tuesday & will remain at Mr Wemyss a few weeks.

The R. Road Reached the Greensboro depot on Friday Nov 4 and the to oos unusual sound of R. Road whistle & rumble is heard in our town it has animated the appearance of things very much—the road is

---

[50] The Franco-Prussian war began with France declaring war on 19 July 1870. The Prussians defeated the French and marched to Paris where they began a siege. Napoleon III was captured and the war ended with the Treaty of Frankfort, which was ratified on 21 May 1871. Marshal Marie Edmé Patrice de MacMahon who commanded the French army was wounded but lived to be president of France and died in 1893. William Bridgwater and Seymour Kurtz, eds., "MacMahon, Marie Edmé Patrice de," *The Columbia Encyclopedia*, 3rd ed. (New York/London: Columbia University Press, 1963) 1274.

[51] R. B. Lindsay was born in Scotland, educated at the University of St. Andrews, and lived in Alabama for fifteen years before the war. He was opposed to secession and gave weak support to the Confederacy. In 1870, he was elected governor by a vote of 76,977 to 75,568. Other Democrats were elected to state office, including E. H. Moren, lieutenant governor and Joseph Hodgson, superintendent of education. Walter L. Fleming, *Civil War and Reconstruction in Alabama* (New York: Columbia University Press, 1905; repr., Gloucester MA: Peter Smith, 1949) 752.

being pressed on to Eutaw—but the company is very low in funds and there is no telling when it will reach there—There has been no rain of consequence at this place for a long time and the streets are very dusty—the season has been fine for cotton picking and the crop will be larger than usual much depression is felt on acct of low price 14-1/2 for Middlings when 20 cts was anticipated. the European war is supposed to have caused it together with anticipated large crop—some estimating at 4,000,000.

November 17. First killing frost—several light ones heretofore, but none reliable before this morning. Mobile will be glad to hear it as the fever is still raging there and many absentees are waiting impatiently for a frost.

November 22. After 4 frosts it clouded up and on yesterday it rained nearly all day being the first general rain this fall. This morning when I waked and looked out of the window the snow had covered everything. It is still (10 oclock AM) snowing pretty hard—and it is rarely if ever we have had so heavy a snow certainly not so early. Fanny will see sights in Tenn. Graham who saw snow for the first time thought it was cotton. The absentees from Mobile left on Monday 21st for Mobile tho we have yet no news of decrease of mortality from epidemic—

December 14. Fanny reached home last night from Tennessee where she had been on a visit to Mrs Wemyss. I went down to Newbern on the engine at 4 o clock took supper at Parkers and on the arrival of the train found her on board and came on home with her. She came by herself and I consider it was quite an undertaking for her. The conductors were very civil and accommodating and she says she got along without the least difficulty; she is very much pleased with her trip and I have no doubt enjoyed herself very much. Mr Wemyss has written for Jane and myself to come and see them but at present I cannot give myself that pleasure. Miss Tunstals marriage to morrow night is engaging the attention of all the girls and somewhat engrossing their attention. Alfred has gone to Newbern on the train he expects to return this evening—

1871

Benners recorded the important points of his personal life with few references to his plantations, politics, or Reconstruction. He had little hope that the policies of Reconstruction could be changed and little apparent interest in being a part of such an effort. Instead, he wrote about the convention of the diocese of Alabama in Huntsville the second week in May. Then, after being elected a deputy to the general convention in Baltimore in October, he wrote about the convention and his impression of the delegates, their efforts to reduce the level of ritualism in the church, and his respect for the process by which the church made its decisions. Finally, he spent time in New England visiting his friend Henry Watson. Observing the New England culture, he wrote that the people were "immensely undemonstrative" and "their industry and frugality are very marked traits." He left with added respect for the North.

April 15. I carried Fanny & Willie to the Queen Sisters (Waldrons) exhibition last night at Dorman Hall, the audience was large and the performance entertaining. Alfred & wife & her sisters were there—the night was very dark when we came out at 11.15 oclock and it was not easy to grope our way home. where we arrived in time to escape a heavy storm of wind, rain & hail. The traces of the storm are visible every where—the leaves are strewn on the ground and many limbs and some fences & trees are prostrated—among the latter the beautiful elm at the church is blown down its prostrate trunk is saddening to many hearts who admired it as one of the loveliest trees in the country—I remember when it was planted nearly 30 yrs ago—and as I saw the men cutting it up as I passed to day I hurried from the scene sadly musing on events that have occurred since it was placed there. How many who were then actors on the stage of life have gone before—and how truly did it demonstrate that the fashion of this world passeth away.

April 27. The memorial association decorated graves of Confederate Soldiers yesterday evening—a storm of wind coming up and rain being imminent they adjourned to Court House to hear address from Mr T. R. Roulhac[52]—He delivered a very handsome speech under very

---

[52] T. R. Roulhac, lawyer, Greensboro.

unfavorable circumstances—the rain commenced to pour down the evening was dark and threatening....

May 26. The Convention of the Episcopal Church was this year held in Huntsville—Commencing May 10 1871. I went as a delegate from St Pauls Greensboro. We left on Monday May 8th Mr Cobbs & Miss Mary Avery[53], Mr C. E. Waller, Dr J D. Osborn, my daughter Fanny and myself comprised the party from here. We went on Selma M&M R.R. to Junction S&M to Selma—Selma R&D to Dalton [Georgia]. Western & Atlantic to Chattanooga. Chattanooga & Nashville to Stephenson [Stevenson]. M & Charleston to Huntsville which we reached tuesday 1 P.M. Col Beirne invited me to stay with him, and Mr Cobbs, Miss Avery my daughter and my self were very politely and hospitably entertained till Monday 15 May when we left at 11 oclock & reached home next evening at 7. ocl. I was elected a delegate to Gen Con[vention] at Baltimore. Fanny and I were very much pleased with our visit & admired Huntsville & its people very much.

June 7. Jane went to Newbern with Graham last Thursday & staid over until tuesday—they were both somewhat improved by the trip. Mr Hatch came up saturday—and Parker—who left sunday evening. Ben & wife came up on sunday & Mrs H. left this morning with her child & servant. We have had a great deal of rain and very high rivers & creeks. The spring & summer so far has been very wet and the bottom lands are ruined—cotton has gone to 19 cts in N. York and the prospects of a short crop is thought very probable—

June 9. Friday. The Greensboro fire company had a fine time yesterday. The Selma Protection Hook & Ladder Co No 1 of Selma and Tuscaloosa fire company were invited to a Picnic at Mears Grove—a good dinner & fine music and much dancing made it pass off very well. they returned this morning on the train. The engine had been beautifully ornamented and the truck was covered with wreaths. The behavior of the crowd was very good and the companies commended themselves to the good opinion of all.

---

[53] Mary Avery was a school teacher and sister of Fanny Cobbs, Mr. Cobbs' wife.

August 21. I went to Mobile by Montgomery July 15 arrived Sunday 16. took the Annie to Point Clear—had a pleasant stay till tuesday July 18. returned to Mobile collected Ins Divs and came home on 20th The bathing at the Point was very pleasant & the house well kept...fare $4 a day. On returning my trunk was by mistake transferred to Calera train and I was detained a day to get it. I afterwards attended a R. Road meeting in Selma on the [blank space]. Board resolved on the narrow gauge. I again visited Selma on the 14th Bot round table, $1400 Central City Ins Co Stock. The weather at this time is very dry and riding to the Spring is the only amusement of the people.

November 8. On Monday Oct 2 1871 I started in the cars with Fanny for Baltimore to attend the Gen Convention of P. E. Church in the N States as a deputy from Diocese of Alabama. We reached Selma at 9.15 and took the train immediately for Dalton which we reached about 10. 50 P.M. where we took the train for Bristol—which we reached at 11 oclock A.M. here we missed the connection and had to wait till the night train in consequence of our having been delayed before reaching Bristol by the removal of the train a head of us which had run off and smashed up killing the fire man. We reached Lynchburg [Va.] to breakfast and Washington City at 6 oclock Baltimore about 7.15. Went to Maltby house and staid till thursday evening when we removed to Mrs Lee's 118 St Pauls—Here we remained 5 days and on tuesday night at Oct 10th at 10.30 P.M started for N. York where we arrived at 7 A.M. on Wednesday. found Mr Henry Watson at the Irving House where we stopped and at his pressing instance we left at 1130 for Northampton on a visit to him We arrived at 6.30 and went in his carriage with him to his house. We remained till the following tuesday Oct 17 left for New York at 10.20 where we arrived at 6.20 P.M. remained in New York till monday night 23rd Oct left for Baltimore at 8.30 P.M. Reached Baltimore 5.40 AM Tuesday Oct 24. Remained till thursday 26 3.30 P.M. when we left for home but before reaching Cleaveland [Cleveland] Tenn. I found we would lie over Sunday & Monday in Selma and we went to see Mr Wemyss in Ten[n]. reaching his house on Saturday evening about 5 oclock—remained with him till Wednesday 1st Nov. I left Gallatin at 6.20 A.M. leaving Fanny to protract her visit 2 weeks longer. I reached home on thursday night Nov 2nd 1871 8 P.M. Found all well tho my wife had been sick & Alfred had a chill & raining. I was very much gratified with my visit to Baltimore for tho I did not make many ackquaintances the assembly of the whole church in Council was a very interesting body and impressed me very favorably. We boarded the greater part of the time at Mrs Lees No 118 St Paul Street—and were satisfied with our accommodations—it was only two blocks from Emanuel church where the Convention sat—and the boarders were unexceptionable people. Baltimore as a city pleased me very much and the extension and growth of it were very obvious and impressive. We found the street cars very convenient and used them frequently—our boarding house was a long way from the heart of the city and as the cars ran close by our house we went in them when we wanted to go there. We very much admired the Druid Hill park—which I visited twice. The sessions of the convention interfered somewhat with my getting about. I considered the Lord Bishop of Litchfields visit to the Convention one of the most interesting occurrences of the occasion—he is a very fine looking man and of earnest piety and enthusiasm. The bishop of Nassau and other English ministers were also present. The Convention dispatched much routine business—and very extensively discussed the question of Ritual. No decisive canon was enacted. The two presented by the Bishops failed in the House of Deputies—which adopted a resolution deprecating all ritualism which symbolised false doctrine—The house of Deputies which consisted of over 400 members was a very respectable body and I never was more impressed with the unity of purpose of any assembly. Very little was said as I considered for display—and every one who spoke seemed to have something to say worth saying.

    The House of Bishops always sit with closed doors and no persons are admitted to their midst—of them as a House I could form no opinion—They were however a very grave and dignified looking set of men.

    With our visit to Mr Henry Watson at Northampton we were very much pleased—and never was I received and entertained with more consideration and politeness. Mr Watson had his equipage for us everyday and went with us everywhere. Thro the city, thro the Connecticut valley among the meadow grounds, to East Hampton, Mount Holyoke, Florence, Amherst where the college is, Hadley where the town is apparently unfrequented by its inhabitants as we saw none in passing thro. We took long rides visiting the factories &c and on Sunday I went to church with him. The ministers theme was the Chicago fire—which is considered the largest that ever happened in ancient or modern times—60 miles of Street were burned 2500 acres of houses 100,000 persons were destitute and the whole North was aroused to the exercise of charity & contribution. The appearance of the congregation and church did not impress me with a idea of growth or progression. They are I presume what are called low church. Fanny was invited to a dance & went with Miss Julia and Fred. Mr Watsons establishment is a very handsome one—and very complete in all its arrangements. Order and system prevail in every department. There is a furnace in the basement for warming the house, by means of which warm air is conveyed at will to any room, dispensing thereby with other fires for that purpose. There is a cistern on the top of the house into which water is forced by a self acting ram and from the cistern by means of pipes his kitchen and Laundry are supplied. Our visit to Mount Holyoke was very interesting. We ascended to the top of the mountain by a railway—the cars one going up as the other comes down being raised by horse & windlass at the foot. the ascent at first makes one feel dizzy at the possibility of breaking loose and being precipitated so far, but I suppose as the proprietor told me he had lived on the mountain 23 years & had worked his rail Road 17 years—that it is perfectly safe. the road is covered over and in the roof at intervals there are dormer windows to give light. From the top when we looked out the view is extremely bewitching—several villages & towns are in sight and the Connecticut river and valley thereof made a landscape of rare beauty & novelty. The Country is mostly cleared & cultivated or meadow ground—the only forest being the trees on some of the mountain sides. The frost had colored all the foliage and some of the leaves were of deepest crimson while others were of golden hues—and these features with the various shades of color caused by the difference of crops or stubble which checquered it something like a bed quilt made a prospect very pleasing and not soon to be forgotten. It is said in clear weather west rock in New Haven can be seen from the top—and it is also said that points 40 miles distant can be seen. our atmosphere while there was somewhat smoky caused by the extensive fires in Wisconsin & Western N.Y so we did not get the most extensive view. We here enjoyed a very fine Lunch and rambled to some extent on the mountain. After descending we went thro Hadley to Amherst. The college is here—I was interested in seeing a very large collection of Meteorites—said to be finest in the U. States. Some weighed 1200 pounds. We were told a specimen or specimens were in the fire proof iron safe—considered so valuable that they must be thus protected from possibility of destruction by fire. We visited the Hall of Icknology which being interpreted means the science of tracks. Large slabs of stone with indentations supposed to have been made by birds feet are adjusted on pivots, to enable both sides to be examineded. these fossil tracks prove that at the time they were made the rock was soft. What that proves I dont know—here also we saw tables of stone from Nineveh—older than the Christian Era. There was an air of quietness almost amounting to Sombreness about this place and the surroundings—which in fact seemed to characterise all New England as far as I saw it. The people are eminently undemonstrative—and if they have any feelings or passions they are carefully kept concealed. Their industry & frugality are very marked traits. I saw no loafers or vagabonds here. In New York we visited Central Park which we greatly admired. The entire park is said to contain 843 acres, much of which is covered by the Croton Reservoir and the lakes, and the walks and drives being very wide and sinuous occupy a large portion of the remainder of the surface.

November 20. On friday the 17th day of Nov I took the train with Liz & Ed to attend the fair in Selma—leaving at 6 oclock we arrived at the fair grounds at 10, having had a very pleasant tho a very crowded ride. The Seminary Scholars of Marion got on there and took one car. The fair as an exhibition was no great things—no cattle, few hogs and poultry and not much machinery. The day was very pleasant and John T.

Morgan[54] made a long speech which very few people heard. We returned on the cars in the evening and reached home at 10 oclock pm. There was a very white frost on the ground on morning of 17th and had been also on 16th which I consider the first killing frost we had. There was a rain night before last & yesterday sunday was an unpleasant raw drizzly day. Mr Cobbs preached in morning I did not go at night.

December 9. I went to Selma on the 27th Nov. and from there to Mobile by Meridian R.R fare being 9.75 remained in Mobile till Wednesday evening 29 and reached home via Montgy R. R on thursday. the evening of my return was very rainy & forbidding. While in Mobile I bought a Herrings safe from Moser & co which he was to ship to Eastport by the Hale. My groceries I bot from Mr Vail to be shipped by the Hale 18 Dec.

December 26. Tuesday. Christmas on yesterday was a delightful day—as mild as May and very bright—we had a very interesting service at our church and a capital christmas sermon from Mr Cobbs. Mr Watson who is out on a visit dined with me. Alfred and Margaret were at Col Jones. Miss Lizzie Batie and Parker Hatch were the only other guests we had. It rained last night—but is mild and promises to be a bright fair day—

1872

Early in the year there was snow—then in the spring considerable rain and thunder. Benners's mood, matching the weather, was one of gloom. He even included a newspaper clipping of a Longfellow poem—"The Rainy Day." However, in May the political situation heated up, and Benners began to sense the possibility of Grant not being reelected. Southern states were anxious for Horace Greeley, a Democrat, to be elected.

---

[54] John Tyler Morgan served in the Confederate cavalry during the Civil War rising to the rank of Brigadier General. After the war, he practiced law and was involved in politics until 1876 when he was elected as a Democrat to the US Senate and served consecutive terms until his death 11 June 1907. *Biographical Directory of the American Congress 1774–1949* (Washington, DC: US Government Printing Office, 1950) 1587.

January 3. The Christmas week was unusually mild & pleasant. New years day was cloudy but mild, yesterday was mild tho cloudy, last night it rained & to day it is wet underfoot but the wind has got north and the sun shined out prettily—and we are having a good evening.

January 25. We are having a pretty fall of Snow the first of the season, the ground now at 2-1/2 oclock is white and snow still falling, we hear by telegraph it is snowing in Tuscaloosa.

January 26. Friday—Sure enough we have a nice snow—it commenced falling about 1 oclock yesterday and continued to fall till after night. This morning is beautifully white and boys & girls are enjoying the sport—Snow balling is the order of the day and much fun is the result—

March 1. we had a fall of snow which would have lain heavy & deep on the ground but that it had rained a good deal just before—the flakes were unusually large and there was lightning and rolling thunder several times whilst it snowed.

March 23. Yesterday was one of the gloomiest days I ever saw—after several cold days it commenced raining on Thursday night and continued all day yesterday—at times being uncommonly dark—and once in a while thunder & lightening—this morning the rain has ceased—river reported high & rising. My wifes health bad—

[*Newspaper clipping of poem*]
The Rainy Day
By Longfellow

The day is cold, and dark and dreary;
It rains, and the wind is never weary;
The vine still clings to the mouldering wall,
But at every gust the dead leaves fall,
And the day is dark and dreary.

My life is cold, and dark and dreary
It rains and the wind is never weary;

My thoughts still cling to the mouldering past;
But the thoughts of youth fall thick in the blast,
And the day is dark and dreary.

Be still, sad heart, and cease repining;
Behind the cloud is the sun still shining;
Thy fate is the common fate of all—
Into each life some rain must fall;
Some days must be dark and dreary.

May 3. Up to 1st May we had had no rain for 3 weeks on that day we had a light shower and hoped the much desired season had come, but after a very light shower the wind whipped round north and it turned cool and clear and has remained so up to this time—no signs of rain yet. The cotton corn & gardens need it badly—my wifes health continues very poor—and I am somewhat troubled myself with neuralgic headache—skating rink inaugurated 1st May—and Selma fair is the talk. We have been consulting about adding to the church—one and another cause has delayed commencement. Now [Hugh] Watt is sick. much interest is felt in the Cincinnati Convention of Liberal republicans—The object being to defeat General Grant—Trumbull, Davis, Adams, Cox and Greeley are spoken of.[55]

May 12. Sunday morning. on the 8th May I left home to attend Episcopal convention at Montgomery. Mr Stickney & I being the only delegates who went from here. Mr Jeffries coming to hand from Mobile. We had a very pleasant trip—arriving in Selma at 10 1/2 dined at St James and took the train at 3 for Montgy where we arrived about sundown—Mr Cobbs brought us an invitation to go to Mr Stringfellows—which Mr Stickney accepted and I declined—and went to the exchange Hotel where I staid until Saturday morning at 10 & left for Selma—we were promised a return in full fare paid—but conductor

---

[55] As the nomination of Grant became a near certainty, disaffected Republicans formed a third party, the Liberal Republican Party. They met in Cincinnati in May and nominated Horace Greeley as its presidential candidate. He was the well-known editor of the influential *New York Tribune*.

declined to take our certificates & Mr Pollards[56] assurance was of no avail, on his road—the Central & S M&M accepted the certificates. The weather was very pleasant but dry & dusty—There were no incidents of special Interest in the Convention—There was a little jarring on the part of Christs church Mobile on acct of assessment $880 dollars which they desired reduced to $715 which convention declined to do—and delegation protested—We had a lunch so called on Thursday at Hamner Hall[57] to which convention was invited. I took breakfast on friday morning at Mr Pollards—we reached home Saturday night May 11th and found my folks all well. I think a little want of interest on the part of Montgomery was discernible—the convention had been changed from Tuscaloosa to that place—The next convention meets in Trinity church Mobile—

May 17. The drought still lasts. We had a little sprinkle this morning but not enough to lay the dust. My first grandchild—son of A. H. & Margaret Benners was born on 13 inst. We were very much distressed by the possibilities of a fatal issue, but in Gods good providence the mother & child were reported as doing well—the baby was born at 12.30 on 13 May 1872. Three Doctors were in attendance and they represented the case as a very critical one. Since which the mother has done very well but the baby dont nurse satisfactorily. He is not yet named and I object to his being named for me as I want him to be lucky—...[58]

May 24. We had rain all last night and this morning. Bill Wyatt died in Marion yesterday and the train leaves at 1 to carry employees to his funeral. More rain will be prejudicial to cotton & corn as the heavy fall prevents the working of crops. The amnesty bill has passed and politics are waxing warmer & warmer.[59] Greeley is in ascendancy in this Section so far as the talk of the Whites is concerned.

---

[56] Charles Teed Pollard, a leader in the Episcopal church in early Alabama.
[57] An Episcopal school.
[58] Later he was named after his grandfather Augustus.
[59] The Republican Congress acted to defuse the potential appeal of the liberal Republicans. They offered an amnesty plank that removed the office-holding disqualifications from all but a handful of ex-Confederates. It was a very attractive proposal.

June 7. went to U S Dis Co at Montgy on 1st June—Got judgt pro con in Breene's case set said and filed answer. Staid till Thursday got home that night—there was much talk about Judge Busteeds modes of proceeding, there were soldiers in Montgomery and it was said in Court room. Sup Co was also in session—Mr Pittman was with me at Exchange—Greeley's nomination was much discussed and his adoption as the man to vote for to beat Grant was generally approved. The elections for State affairs was much canvassed—Grant has been nominated at Philadelphia and Democratic con[vention] meets in Baltimore in July.[60]

June 24. The Democratic & conservative convention met at Montgomery on 19 and nominated the old officers except Lindsay & Reynolds. T.H. Herndon of Mobile was named for Governor and T.J. Burnett of Butler for Auditor.[61] I did not attend—there is no little complaint about the Gov. he is regarded by many as having been too ultra to be popular. Saturday last we had a hard rain Sunday it rained very hard again last night and the crops must be injured if the rain continues—

Severe weather in mid-July caused considerable trouble. Rains damaged the crops and even the railroads. For a time, mail could not be delivered.

July 12. Left on Saturday 8th July for Memphis to attend convention of Directors S M & M RR via Meridian—where we arrived at 5.40 reached Jackson at night—slept till 3.50 and reached Memphis via Canton & Grenada on Sunday at 4. put up at Overton. Met [Gen] For[r]est on Monday. no quorum—met tuesday no quorum. left at 12.40 via Memphis & Charleston got to Chattanooga to Breakfast Birmingham to supper, left 120 [1.20] PM Selma 5 A.M. left at 4 reached Newbern. Cars stopped by train run off [the track] and slept on cars all

---

[60] In July 1872, the Democratic convention endorsed the Liberal Republican's candidate, Horace Greeley, and accepted his platform as its own.

[61] Democrats nominated Thomas H. Herndon who was in favor of conducting a more aggressive political campaign.

night—breakfast at McCanns Dinner at McCanns—Hand car home friday evening 4 o clock.

July 16. We have had almost incessant rains since Thursday July 11. The water courses are said to be very high and river rose 60 ft at Tuscaloosa. The effects on crops must be very damaging—much of the cotton was not laid by and now cannot be ploughed to advantage—and some of corn will fire from wet, it is still rainy and the R. R. track near Cahaba river being under water we have no mail—Mr Waller & family started yesterday to Virginia and had to come back—river at Cahaba bridge not being practicable.

July 20. Ed Started in wagon with Messrs Haefner, Atkins & Nance to go to Blount Springs via Akron on Wednesday the 17 July—The road being washed up and the train stopped we were informed by the young man who drove the wagon that they concluded to go across 5 Mile in a skiff and get a conveyance to Tuscaloosa since when we have not heard from them. It was fair yesterday but rained again last night & we are still without mails, the river is over the low ground and much cotton & corn is doubtless ruined. I never heard of such rivers in July—The new bridge on the Warrior N&S road was washed away, Cahaba river bridge is impassable by trains and accounts are gloomy enough as far as we hear from—The grandson was christened Augustus on the 18th at Col Jones by Mr Cobbs.

July 22. It rained very hard again on Saturday evening 20 inst, and the ground was very wet on Sunday Morning—to day it is not raining yet but the weather is warm & sultry. We are still without any mails and are cut off as it were from the outside world. The damage on the river lands is expected to be very serious—Ala & Warrior are both out of banks and it is too late to replant.

August 7. Having business in Mobile I left home via Selma & Montgomery on Monday 29 July and reached Mobile on tuesday 30 at 5 AM. Took breakfast and dinner at Battle house and at 5 PM left for Miss City reached there at 8 PM and left on friday at 10.50 arriving in Mobile at 1.20—took dinner at Battle house and left at 11.25 PM reaching home Saturday night Aug 3 at 8-1/2. I was much pleased with my short respite on the Gulf, enjoyed the salt bathing and had some very good fishing—Salt water trout was the main catch. The N.O. Mobile & Texas R R is very well constructed. Cars run very smoothly and very rapidly making it was said a part of the way 60 miles per hour. On monday I went to Marion to settle my dividends with Perry Ins & T[rust] Co—carried Willie with me and returned at night. The cry of cotton worm is increasing—and some plantations are said to be ruined—weather is not oppressively hot nor is there much sickness.

Politics began to heat up in late August and continued until mid-November. Benners's hopes for the election of a Democratic president began to fade. On November 5, he observed that "a throng of negroes came in and like a dark cloud settled on the town." Once again the future looked gloomy. Efforts of the Democrats and Conservatives were not enough. But Benners was now engaged in following the political process. He clipped out the election return for governor of Alabama and pasted it in his journal.

August 22. Alfred has had a chill & several fevers but is up to day. Ed is still at Blount and we get no letters. North Carolina Election resulted in anti Grant legislature majority of 20. 5 out of 8 Congressmen and the Lieutenant Governor. Caldwell (Grantite) is said to be elected by about 2000.[62] Merriman will contest on ground of fraudulent voting. The worms did not do as much damage as was anticipated to cotton—but a new crop of worms is reported in many places—and the cotton is failing very much—in consequence of dry weather—It is not yet very sickly but fears are expressed that it will be. We have had pleasant weather for the season. Ther 90 to day nights are pleasant—

August 24. Saturday. We have had several days of Warm weather Ther 92—it has been very dry for weeks and the cotton has given way under it very much—It was very much stimulated by the frequent rains, and suffers more from heat & drought in consequence. There is a huge outcry about cotton worms and the chances are a great reduction in the

---

[62] Tod R. Caldwell was elected governor, receiving 98,132 votes to 96,234 for Augustus S. Merriman. There was a cry of fraud, but the conservative state executive committee decided not to contest the election.

crop. Alfred is again complaining having had a fever last night—There is a lull in matters and great dulness.

September 3. We have had several very pleasant days—Ther from 76 to 86—nights very cool. The cotton worms have finished their work in this section having stripped every vestige of foliage from the plant. Where the cotton was early the matured bolls will make a 1/2 crop but where the cotton was late this cannot be reached. The drought is said to be very severe in Texas—and in Ark crop is poorest ever made. South Ga is said to be stripped by worms and in Tenn & N. Ala drought has prevailed. The prospects now are that crop will not exceed last year say 3,000,000. Ed is still at Blount and I have heard nothing from him—it is said that N & S road will be finished thro on 7th Septr.

September 8. Sunday Evening. Mr Cobbs being absent in V[irgini]a I was lay reader for the Congregation in church to day. There was no music and number small. The dry spell still continues and dust is abundant. Ed is still at Blount & we got letters yesterday saying he would return on 15 Sep—The road is finished past my house and will be thro by the 10th. Crops of cotton in this County will be very short—the worms having stripped the leaves & small bolls and many of those left being immature & insignificant. Politics are quite rife—and Blanton Duncans convention of Straight outs has met & nominated Mr O Connor of N. York & J. Q. Adams The move is called Grants side show—as being only in his interests—Vermont has again gone Radical by a very large majority—25,000—

October 15. I went to Selma yesterday got home at 9 oclock P.M. Found people I met much depressed by short cotton crops and radical success in elections. The opinion is very general that the present out look is very unpromising and that this cotton section is getting poorer every year. The hope of defeating Grant is very faint since the heavy majority for [John F.] Hartranft [Pennsylvania] radical candidate for governor—it being over 35000.

We had a frost this morning first general one this season tho there have been several partial ones in low places last week—There is no cotton to be hurt by it & everyone is glad of its appearance. The season which was feared [to] be so sickly has proved in our town to have been unusually Healthy & none of our town folks had died except Mr Hugh W. Watt—of yellow disease. The country and some of the neighboring towns have been quite sickly. Alfred has made a very poor crop of cotton and is much perplexed what to do with his plantation next year.

November 5. This is election day for Pres & Vice President of U. States—Grant & Wilson Radical Candidates Greeley & Brown Liberal Republican & Democratic & Conservative.[63] [Thomas H.] Herndon is candidate for Gov on Greeley side. D. Lewis on Radical—there is an immense concourse of Negroes in Town and the vote here will be a large one—W B Young is candidate for county Solicitor & Spann Contr[oller]. It has drizzled a very little this morning and the weather is very uncertain at present being very cloudy. There are two polling places one at the courthouse and one at Sam Briggs office on the corner. There are no county candidates nominated. Trice is running independent. Duskin the Radical nominee for State Senate—no opposition.[64] On 27 October I took the train for Junction there to Meridian there to Okolona, where there was a meeting of the Directors of SM&M R.R. Left tuesday night 12 o clock went to Corinth—from there to Decatur there to Blount Springs—there to Birmingham there to Calera where we were detained in consequence of accident on SR&D. Road—two men killed & many wounded by the collision—left at 12 & reached Selma at 4 A.M. Saturday & home Saturday night Nov 3 1872.

November 6. Yesterday the election was held for Pres & Vice Pres of U.S. A throng of negroes came in and like a dark cloud settled on the town.[65] The day was cloudy without rain and the election passed off very quietly—the vote of the County not yet ascertained—but enough known to shew the Rads have carried the County by a very large majority.

---

[63] Henry Wilson, a senator from Massachusetts, was vice presidential candidate of the Republican Party. Benjamin Gratz Brown, senator and governor of Missouri, was vice presidential candidate for the Liberal Republican Party and Democratic Party.

[64] George M. Duskin, Republican, was elected district attorney, Southern District of Alabama, 1873, 1875, and 1879. He was elected to the Alabama House in 1870 and Alabama Senate in 1879. Sarah W. Wiggins, *The Scalawag in Alabama Politics, 1865–1881* (Tuscaloosa: University of Alabama Press, 1977) 140–41, 148–49.

[65] Black Americans overwhelmingly cast Republican votes.

Rumors from other elections are also coming in—which shew that if they are true, Grant is again elected—Louisiana is said to have gone for Greeley—Ala doubtful.[66] it is raining very hard and the political prospects and the weather are in unison. I have not been able to get to dinner & write this as a memorandum.

November 11. The Presidential election came off on the 5 and has resulted in the defeat of Greeley and election of Grant by a very large majority.[67] Hale County went for him by about 2800 majority the colored people voting solidly for him. Great hopes were entertained of a change in the Government by his defeat—but it has been otherwise ordered and the almost certain loss of the State ticket adds to the disappointment of Democrats & Conservatives. The future looks gloomy. Jim Green colored & R L Bennett are elected from Hale to the House and George M Duskin to senate. Hays reelected over Billy Smith to Congress—Lewis Governor.[68]

November 13. Alfred has been quite sick several days—better to day—a great fire has occurred in Boston—commencing about 7 oclock P.M. on 9th Saturday—it has destroyed 5 miles of Streets & 70 acres of Houses—loss estimated at $200,000,000. Cotton still declines and estimates of crop are being enlarged. 3,600,000 bales are now taken as the probable crop.

November 14. Yesterday was comparatively pleasant. last night we had a thunderstorm & to day cool & windy tho clear—we have had an unusual amt of rainy cloudy weather for the last week or 10 days—and its effect on the feelings & health of the people is perceptible—many are desponding—and there are many complaining of colds. Alfred is better. The Selma fair is progressing & our folks were some of them disappointed in not being able to go to it—the excursion was given out.

December 26. yesterday was a very gloomy drizzly disagreeable day for christmas—the more so because by reason of the accident on R. Road

---

[66] The outcome reflected the loyalty of the black electorate, a stabilization of the scalawag support, and a number of Democrats who chose not to vote.

[67] Grant received 3,597,000 votes, and Greeley received 2,834,000 votes.

[68] David P. Lewis, a native Southern white Republican, was elected governor, defeating Thomas H. Herndon. The full Republican ticket was elected in Alabama.

on friday 20 Dec we were without mails & almost without groceries. I worked hard to try & please all with presents—poor business and thankless—Smaw had party last night went with Fanny[,] DuBoses & Miss Ellerby went also. very dark cold & Rainy night—To day very cold & rainy.[69] Alfred & wife & child & servant are going to dine at her fathers. We are having bad time for working on church freezing & rain, foundation is laid—suspended work till after christmas.

1873

Benners spent much of his time practicing law and allowed his son Alfred to run the plantation. Alfred wanted to be successful, but the severe weather, low prices for cotton, and growing problems with cotton worms made it difficult. In May, a family quarrel between Augustus Benners's father-in-law, Alfred Hatch, and Hatch's brother, Lemuel, over a Civil War cotton produce loan caused bad feelings in the family. There was little that Benners could do.

January 3. New Years day was a very sloppy cloudy disagreeable day few people in Town. There having been since Christmas the coldest & most disagreeable weather experienced here for many years. Thermometer at 8-1/2 on 27 getting in our passage at home as low as 20° Never before in my recollection have R. Road accidents been so numerous—there was no arrival on SM&M RR till 1st Jany—on which day I got a portion of groceries ordered for Christmas. We had hard rain again yesterday morning—Alfred came from plantation. He has concluded to carry on planting himself not being able to rent to advantage. I very much fear he will be very sick of it....

January 29. We have this morning a very low Ther (24°) and a light snow on the ground. There has been more excessive cold and fewer fine days this month than I ever remember for the same time. While the accts of cold at the North are distressing, Mr Watson who reached here a few days ago says that the Ther ranged below zero at his house

---

[69] William R. Smaw, planter, Hollow Square voting precinct, Greensboro. Snedecor, *Greene County*, 39.

[Northampton, Mass.] half the time and in coming out Knoxville was the first place he reached where it was not below zero....

February 5. On Sunday 2nd Mr Watson & Mr Randolph dined with me—it was the 2nd anniversary of Alfreds marriage and Col Hatch & wife & Mrs McRee came in and dined with us. Monday & tuesday were fine bright days but again to day the murky clouds are overhanging & it having rained last night threatens to rain again to day.

February 17. Mr Watson left for Selma on his route home Saturday 15 Feb 1873.

February 24. We have had with exception of a few open days a cold & rainy February. On Thursday night last a deluging rain—The weather had been most unpropitious for our church extension—and again & again has the rain poured in thro the open uncovered roof. Yesterday morning there was frost & ice & this morning there was a little ice. I have had Fanny's flower pitt bailed out Two or three times & there is still water in it. Mr Hatch & Ben were to dinner at my house to day. Alfred went on train to plantation—his baby has two teeth and has been quite unwell cutting two more and he also had symptoms of croup. Colds are very prevalent and I have come in for my share.

March 4. The spring is very backward Ther this morning 24° Ice & frost, a few peach blooms have made their appearance which were only born to die—Alfred went on train to Plantation this morning has about 50 acres bedded and seems much interested in his operations on farm. Election came off yesterday for Mayor and aldermen. [Lewis] Lawson elected Mayor—Col Jones has gone to RR meeting at Memphis—I am to read service for Mr Cobbs who has gone to Tuscaloosa this evening. Cotton is 19-1/4 in Selma. The excessive receipts are disappointing our people very much and they are living on hopes of better crop in 73—corn is 1.00 Fodder Do [ditto]—To day is the day for Grant's reinauguration. May he do better next 4 years than last.

March 20. I went to Montgomery on 15th with Pittman to attend case Bailey vs Breene. Case was heard before Worel Reg in Bankruptcy on Saturday 16. We staid over to prepare briefs. on Monday rec'd telegram that Cochran would be examined for comp on tuesday—Breen who had started home ret[urned] from Selma. Cochran was examined on

18. Breen reexamined in case.[70] Paper could not be found in files and case adjourned till Wednesday 26 & we returned home—stopped while there at Mrs Pickets—good quarters & entertainment—Legislature was still in Session—did not see them in session. Saw Bethea, Anderson, Hamilton, Manning and others—Have little hope of Breens case before the court which has it.

March 28. Friday. I went to Montgy on tuesday with Mr Pittman on Breens matter before Worel Register. Left Thursday 10-1/2 and got home last night. My wife and Fanny have gone with Mary & Hatty Daves to Kornegays in the wagon.[71] it is raining and roads are very disagreeable—visited Capitol and was not at all pleased with appearance of things. Black spirits & white commingled.[72] Boarded at Mrs Picketts @ 2. a day—Mr Clay came to the house while I was there—

April 26. There is no rain yet and the weather continues quite cool. The cotton that is up is looking very badly and much apprehension is felt that unless it rains very soon the cotton will be irreparably damaged. Parker & wife & 3 children came up yesterday evening and spent the night with us. Ed & Willie went to the river fishing yesterday—memorial services for Confederate dead are to take place this evening. It is very dusty and a shower much needed. Alfred went to plantation this morning....

April 29. We had a good rain last night accompanied with thunder lightning and wind. It is very acceptable as the stand of cotton was very inadequate and drought prevented seed coming up. The clouds have been dispersed and the sun is shining beautifully this morning 11 A.M. Alfred did not get from plantation last night.

---

[70] Robert F. Breen, tinner, Greensboro. Ibid., 9. Breen was a colorful character in Greensboro. His store was on Main Street. He wore a Prince Albert coat, top hat, and had long hair. His tombstone with two carved eyes in Stokes Cemetery reads: "Remember man when you pass by, as you are now so once was I. As I am now so you must be. Prepare for death and follow me."

[71] Mary and Hatty Daves were Fanny's cousins, and the Kornegays were her aunt and uncle.

[72] Benners appeared to be unhappy with mixing of blacks and whites in Montgomery. He believed there should always be a separation between the races.

May 1. We had another hard rain this morning commencing at 5 AM and continuing 5 hours—in fact it has been raining or threatening all day and now looks like it would pour down—the most unlike a May day imaginable. Alfred went to plantation this morning. The papers are full of the fights with Modoc indians.[73] A reconnoitering party of 60 went over the Lava beds to find out where they were hid—and they did not find the Modocs but the Modocs found them firing upon them from ambush. they killed or wounded the most of them and that without any of them being seen much less killed. An Indian war is thought to be imminent—[74]

May 13. Went to Selma yesterday & returned last night—bot 23 bu corn from Hardie & Robinson @ 82 cts, 28 bu oat @ 57 cts, 56 lbs hams @ 15 cts. Selma was very dull middling cotton 18. Messrs Cobbs, Jones & Hatch were along going to Mobile as also Mrs Avery, Mrs Cobbs & two of her children. The corn on the road not more than 5 in—cotton backward but little chopped out. Mr Harvey who had his leg broken by a kick from a mule last tuesday is reported not doing so well to day the splinters are working out and causes great pain and he got no sleep last night. Alfred went to Plantation yesterday morning & returns to night—

May 29. We had rain yesterday last night and again to day. There was confirmation in the church of 8 persons last night. Mr Snedecor, Eddie Bell, Misses Poe, Hill, Harris, Mrs W. White Jones & two others were candidates. There is to be service this morning & to night—Mr Banister has preached for us 3 times. Bishop Wilmer is to preach this morning—church is to be reopened—chandeliers which were ordered have not arrived.[75] Mr & Mrs Willie Pickens spent the night with us. On Saturday last Mr A. Hatch came up and told me while here, that he had settled with Lem Hatch in order to buy his peace for the claim his

---

[73] Near Medford, Oregon.

[74] The Modocs led by Chief Kintpuash (called Captain Jack by the military) refused to return to a reservation in Oregon in 1872. The attempt to bring them back brought on the Modoc War. Captain Jack and his men retreated to the lava beds on the northern California border where they stayed for four months.

[75] There was a major expansion of St. Paul's that started in 1872. The slave balcony was removed and the architectural design of the church was changed from Greek Revival to Gothic Revival.

mother thro him was making for cotton of hers sold after surrender. The terms exacted were $200 cash note due 1 Jany 73 for 2600 and the surrender of the claims he had against them. This claim as made & insisted upon was not only to all appearance from Mr Hatchs acct of unjust but really cruel. Mr Hatch denied that he owed a cent on that account. His case as he states it is that Lemuel Hatch, his brother, shortly after the commencement of the war subscribed 50 bales of cotton to Confederate States, Produce Loan—by the terms of subscription the cotton was to be consigned on acct of Confederate Govt to factors in Mobile—sold on acct of said Govt & the price it brought to be paid to the Govt which was to give Confederate Bonds for the amt.[76] In 1862 or 3 Confederate Government proposed to let subscribers to the Loans pay out their cotton in Confederate money at its then value—and retain the cotton or in other words pay confederate money in lieu of cotton and receive bonds of said Government for the amt. Confederate money was at this time valuable & not the worthless commodity it afterwards became. Mr Thomas H. Daves has given Mr Hatch his verified certificate that at Mr L D Hatchs request Mr Alfred Hatch paid out the 50 Bales of Cotton he (Rev L D Hatch) had subscribed and at the same time paid out the 50 bales of cotton which A P Hatch had subscribed. He (Mr A Hatch) states further that after the surrender Rev L D Hatch sent him 33 bales of cotton to sell and repay himself what he had paid out on acct of the 50 B/C—he sold it & Martin Lyon (who is dead) made out the acct deducting from proceeds pd amt which A Hatch had paid to release the cotton and gave him the statement & in the paper contg [containing] the statement the amt of proceeds minus what had been paid. That he gave this to his Brother Statement & money without himself looking at it—his brother insisting he should take something for his trouble & handing him a $500 bill (Greenbacks) that he took this and subsequently when he visited his brother—he having no corn he gave

---

[76] Under the Produce Loan Act of 16 May 1861, the Confederate Congress authorized the issue of $50 million in 8 percent bonds, later increased to $100 million in bonds, which could be paid for in specie: military supplies, manufactured goods, or agricultural products. Lemuel Hatch subscribed 50 bales of cotton to the Confederate states. This act allowed citizens to avoid the use of money in the purchase of government bonds if they so desired.

him back this five hundred Dollar bill—no complaint or claim has ever been made up to Col L D Hatchs discovery that Alfred Hatch owed for cotton—There is no way of getting at the precise time when sale was made to Lyon. Mr Hatch claims that he owed his brother nothing that having paid him the balance due the matter was settled—and that it was impossible he should have had this amt or any amt of his brother's in his hands and his brother not only never have called for it but never have said anything about it.

June 6. Friday We have had and are having a great many rains very much damaging the prospects of a large cotton crop. The trouble is the grass is taking possession and the rains prevent ploughing It has caused July futures to advance a fraction and they are quoted @ 19 3/16. Alfred is low spirited about his crop and is not very well. Jenny also is puny and there is much complaint of Bowel disease the cholera is in New Orleans & Memphis. The forces of U States have captured Capt Jack & the Modoc war is over.[77] The question is what will be done with them. Ferguson Bank failure has caused much loss in Selma and only $4320 found in vault he fails for 200,000—

June 9. Monday. At Mr Cobbs request I read the service & a sermon yesterday morning in church. He has gone to Forkland. I am suffering inconvenience from cholerine—it is very weakening—chandeliers have been put up and look tolerably well—1st pew collection in New church was taken yesterday & amounted to only $28. outside col 85 cts. Money is very scarce and the continued rains make planters look gloomy. Alfred was to go to plantation to day but it having rained again yesterday & threatening now he deferred his trip. Grass is thought to be master of the situation. The exposure of the Henry Ward Beecher scandal in Brooklyn is in the papers—& causes quite a buzzing in the Plymouth church hive.[78] Mrs H Beecher Stowe if she chooses can make

---

[77] An attempt to mediate peace between the US government and the Modocs failed when a peace commissioner and a US Army officer were killed by the Indians. Then the US Army conducted a siege that eventually ended the war in June 1873. Captain Jack and five other leaders were hanged, and the Modoc tribe were dispersed to Oklahoma and Oregon.

[78] Henry Ward Beecher—a preacher, orator, and lecturer—was a leader in the antislavery movement, later a proponent of women's suffrage and a convert to

a supplement to her Byron scandal—here are choice materials at any rate.

June 10. Tuesday. The cry is Still it Comes—and nearly all night we had rain. The rains of this season are unlike last season in this that they are more extensive. Texas Arkansas Georgia & Tennessee are washed this season by excessive rains as well as Ala. There is quite a lull in business matters—and much dread of another failure of crops which in our staggering condition will be highly prejudicial. Dulness characterizes every department and perhaps it is best that it should be so—so far as trading is concerned.

June 13. It rained again yesterday but the sun is shining to day which has been a rare occurrence for some time. The accounts of cholera in Memphis & Nashville continue—tho a very severe rainstorm in Memphis on the 10th is said to have had the good effect of checking it. Alfred has gone to the plantation to day by rail. The list of depositions in Fergusons Bank is published and fills two columns & a half in Selma times. The aggregate indebtedness of his bank is said to be $250,000—the blow is a severe one & comes at a time when hopes are very hard to repair. Marion Savings Bk loses $11,000 Mobile deposite savings $13,000. A. Stollenwerck unknown Selma Sunday School $304—...

June 18. Jane returned from Ben Hatchs yesterday evening—having staid there with Jenny Sunday & Monday night prevented from coming monday by the rain. Fanny went down the country to Mr Seldens and has had a rainy time since she left. 11 AM it is not raining but is clouding up. The chances are bad for good crops of cotton & corn on acct of grass by reason of so much rain. The cholera at Nashville & Memphis still continues.

June 20. Went to see Wash Haywood[79] yesterday morning found him in a pretty low way and John Haywood[80] very infirm. Wash

---

evolution. In 1875, a sensational lawsuit brought against him ended after a long trial. The jury acquitted him by a nine to three vote and his friends acclaimed him the victor.

[79] W. D. Haywood, physician, Newbern, Greensboro. Snedecor, *Greene County*, 21.

[80] John S. Haywood, planter, Newbern, Greensboro. Ibid., 21.

Haywood is tormented with imaginary fears & unwilling to eat from fear of poison—his condition is pitiable. I came home to dinner. It did not rain yesterday & only a light drizzle to day Alfred has gone to Arcola—...

June 23. Monday. yesterday was a bright hot day and the appearances this morning are that we shall have a fair bright warm day. Ther yesterday in my hall 86°—great complaints of grass & ruined corn & cotton from blacklands. The cholera is still bad at Nashville & Memphis. Carson goods are being sold by assignee S. W. Chadwick. Alfred took cars for plantation this morning.

June 25.... T. K. Carson & Co Bankrupts are being sold out by Chadwick assignee. Charley Waller was to have been married last night—will have party at Wallers tomorrow night—

June 28. Exhibition of Mr Cabells school at Dormans Hall last night. Music, conferring distinctions and an address by Principal on Education. Liz read a composition and her diploma as a graduate should have been given to her, but principal had not procured them. Her voice was distinct in reading & it was much admired. It was a pleasant occasion not unmingled with sadness at the thought that her school days are over & real life now opens up before her.

5:50 [P.M.] we have a good hard rain and the fall in town is acceptable to lay the dust—if it is on the Walker Bottom it will destroy the last chance to come out.

July 3. The college commencement is over and the students and visitors are dispersing to their respective homes. Alfred made an address before the Alumni on tuesday July 1st. Gen Morgan who was to have made the address before the graduating class before his was made failed to arrive and therefore Alfred had to speak without a forerunner. His address was a very pretty one and was well received—Morgan got in on the train last evening and made his address last night—The party afterward came off and we did not get home until after 1 o.clock. The weather here during the week has been warm but pleasant very little dust.

July 10. I went to Montgomery on 7 and returned home last night I went to argue demurrers in case Tindel et al vs W. B. Drake et al—Drake having died, C. E. Waller adms & the heirs of Drake were made parties by Seifa. I thought if I did not go it would look like indifference because he was dead. [Thomas] Seay[81] argued it on same side and [William P.] Webb on the other side. The court intimated they should reverse the decree of Chancellor sustaining Demurrer. There was some excitement in the town on the question of cholera. W. A. Sorsby from Birmingham died of Cholera at Blount Springs and the company there all but 5 stampeded—75 coming to Montgomery—of course it produced some excitement. I procured a bottle of cholera mixture as did nearly everybody in Montgy—I felt very unwell on my return trip & had fever last night.

Cholera appeared in many parts of the South. Benners contracted it in July and recovered quickly with the help of a calomel pill and quinine. The cotton worm continued to frighten the public. Benners believed that it "amounts almost to a panic."

July 24. I had a fever several days after my getting home. Dr Osborn gave me a calomel pill & quinine. The sickness I think proceeded from derangement of the liver—and was complicated with bowel disease—I have not got strong yet but feel very feeble & my head aches every morning when I awake. The cry of worms in the cotton is getting very rife—It is in many plantations but is not yet doing much mischief—Paris green is all the talk as a remedy and upwards of 1000 pounds has been ordered from the North to poison worms with. The weather is very favorable to their appearance & increased having been rainy cool & cloudy for several days—night before last a very hard rain, to day cloudy—

July 28. Monday Morning. Mr Cobbs having been absent yesterday at Uniontown—at his request I read the service and a sermon in the church yesterday. The day was very pleasant and the Congregation large—many outsiders being present. Alfred reported on his return from Walker Place that the caterpillar is all about in the cotton tho not in

---

[81] Thomas Seay was governor of Alabama from 1886–1890.

large numbers yet. The worm killer Paris Green is all the talk and instalments came by the train Saturday night. The dread of the cotton worm amounts almost to a panic and the popular mind is greatly engrossed by the subject. Henry Stollenwercks experiment is reported successful—he is said to have applied it with Siflux-15 sprinkling 70 acres per day.[82] The figs are now ripe & plentiful—Peaches poor and hard & wormy—Tomatoes abundant, quite healthy—

August 9. I went to Mobile Aug 2 by Mobile & Ohio R. R. being unable to have payts of my dividends on that day Saturday. I went to Miss City, got there to dinner and came to Mobile tuesday Aug 5 to dinner collected my several amts & went to Battles Wharf on the Annie had spell of vomiting after getting there and came next morning to Mobile by 9 oclock stopped at Gulf City & left for home by M&O RR on the 6th at 6 P.M. reached home friday night at 7 o clock Aug 8 found Alfreds baby sick and several of family had been complaining—Jane had had chills—& things at low tide generally—The bathing was fine at Barnes Hotel & I enjoyed my little respite there very much—there was preaching on sunday in a little Episcopal church & I attended—subject of sermon was angels. Got acquainted with a Mr McRea from N. Orleans found him pleasant company Spanish Mackerel were caught at the Wharf. I hooked a very large one but he dropped off. Saw a pompano the first I ever saw—admired the appearance very much. Saw some fields of cotton above Macon station which had been ruined by worms—also some cotton on which the poison had been scattered apparently saved by the process. Alfred reports myriads of cotton millers in his crop on this day 9th and has scattered the solution of Paris Green in water over some of his cotton—

August 11. Alfred went down this morning to plantation. The caterpillar is increasing and appearing on more northerly plantations. Several worms have been caught in my field by Willie & Ed. The cotton in the field is very rank in places and I apprehend some of the bolls will rot in consequence having frequent showers—which is unfavorable to

---

[82] Henry Stollenwerck, a planter, and his brother, Alf, operated a drugstore in Greensboro for many years. Snedecor, *Greene County,* 41.

the poisoning as it supposed to wash off the stuff. Mr Hatchs crop is reported badly damaged by the worm—

August 27. My wife went to Newbern on Saturday 23 and returned last night on the cars. Alfred coming from plantation came with her. He reports the cotton eaten up by the worms—and opening very fast. Thinks the poisoning prolonged the duration of leaves 10 days—but they finally were destroyed. The field back of my house has been entirely stripped and Ed is very blue in consequence. He is having fever to day & I much fear he is going to be quite sick. The Town at present is quite healthy there up to now having been no sickness in it of a serious character—at Mr Cobbs requested [request] I read the service in church on Sunday and a sermon—

August 29. Ed had a slight fever last night—looks quite badly his mouth being covered with blisters. He sat at the table at dinner. The worm destruction of the cotton leaves is very great and said to be very extensive. Florida and West Miss are reported to have had them very bad. Mr Hatch came up to day & reports his probable crop at 50 bales in place of 150 which he ought to have made. The RR excursion for the Negroes came off to day. I went to Depot to see them off and never before saw so big a crowd so brim full of anticipated enjoyment—there were 3 Passenger cars and eight flats arranged with Benches. The number leaving here was about 400.

We have had this afternoon a thunder squall & quite a good rain. Alfred will have a hard time pulling up from the plantation to which he went this morning in the buggy. My wife was complaining to day of severe headache and Jenny is looking very badly—

September 19. On tuesday evening Sep 9 after dinner I went with Willie, Jenny & Graham to fish in the branch. Coming back the latter trod on the fin of a catfish he let drop from his hand and made a painful puncture in the ball of his foot—it bled a good deal and I carried him home—it was promptly washed and bathed in Spts Turpentine and very soon he ceased to complain of it & seemed as lively as ever—but the next morning was strangely afflicted. His pulse was very low—his skin bathed in perspiration—pupils of his eyes dilated and he complained by pointing to the pit of his stomach of great pain—very soon he shewed symptoms of a spasm coming on—he was put in a mustard bath & asefetida administered—And the Doctor sent for—before his arrival the worst symptoms were ameliorated. The Dr was much alarmed, thinking he was threatened with Lockjaw prescribed an emetic and an enema which emptied his stomach & bowels—and gave a prescription from drug store he got steadily better and is again quite well. Mr Al. Stollenwercks infant son Gus died on Monday night of dip[h]theria and three other children of his are still sick supposed with the same. The accounts of the yellow fever at Shreveport are very distressing—there are said to be six Hundred cases and great fatality. Two telegraph operators have died—and communication is difficult. 1st frost in N. York is reported on night of 15th. We have had a spell of cool dry dusty weather now there is a slight drizzle and we hope for a rain on acct of the dust—

The Panic of 1873 began in September. Jay Cooke & Co., a pillar of the nation's banking establishment, collapsed after being unable to market millions of dollars in bonds of the North Pacific Railroad. Within days, a financial panic engulfed the credit system. Banks and brokerage houses failed, the stock market temporarily suspended operation, and factories began laying off workers. It was a painful time for Benners. He had little cash and only certified checks were accepted by the banks. Financial matters preoccupied him for the rest of the year and beyond.

September 21.... There is a great panic in financial circles N. York. Jay Cook[e] & Co and other celebrities having suspended payt. Great crash is thought to be at hand—
September 29. The Banks in Selma & Mobile have suspended and the condition of affairs is very embarrassing. I have about $1000 locked up in Southern Bank on deposite. What is to be the issue of all this yet remains uncertain—No cotton is selling and until money is procured from that source, folks must do without money—The Selma Savings is thought to be unable to come through without a loss to the Stockholders—City National is suspended but believed to be all right—The yellow fever is in Mobile & Montgomery—and there is

some sickness about here—but the season is considered to be a healthy one....

October 3. H. A. Haralson has been appointed Receiver by the Chancery Ct of Dallas Cty Receiver—and has called on all the debtors of the Bk to come in & settle. The step of a receiver is said to be to prevent being thrown into the Bkrupt Court. The City National makes an exhibit of a very satisfactory character if the Bills recvble are good. Mr Hatch came up yesterday & was reexamined by Dr Young for the N.A.L. Ins Co—he is to borrow the money for 3 m[onth]s from them to pay his prem. Jane went with her father to Arcola on yesterday to stay till Monday. Have a letter from C. A Lathrop who gives a cheering acct of matters on Mobile business owing to his co not affected &c.

October 10. The Selma Times reports that the Savings Bk has resumed business. What the statement really means I am at a loss to conjecture but hope their condition may be better than we were led to believe. The National Trust is said to have resumed business. Cotton is reported advancing being quoted Mid 17-1/2 to mid 16-1/4 to 1/2 S.G.O 15-3/4 G.O 15 cts in Selma In N. Y Decs are quoted 17-1/2. There is great scarcity of currency and none is to be had in Mobile except certified checks and Deposite association bills—which are not a satisfactory substitute up the Country. Alfred ret from Walker Place last night reports 12 B/C gathered will get another—has been mowing hay—with Patent mower of Nelson & Jones—it is very quick in its work—doing it perfectly. Cuts 6 acres per day. Ed has gone with John Nelson to day to Walker Place—for Alfred to finish mowing—

October 16. Thursday. Mrs Hobson was buried yesterday evening having died suddenly on Monday night of congestive chill. James E Griggs died on Saturday morning—buried on 11th had been long time in very bad health.[83] His good nature & kindness of feelings made him many friends. The yellow fever tho frost has fallen at Memphis is still very fatal there—1200 are reported to have died there since the 15 Sept, 900 of whom died of Yellow fever. There are 2 deaths last 24 hours of this disease in Mobile & one in Montgy. The stringency in money

---

[83] James E. Griggs, livery stable proprietor.

matters still continues—the Banks are not yet paying out. currency—certified checks are all they give—cotton is quoted 17 mid in Mobile.

October 18. It is still excessively dry & dusty—days warm nights comfortable—no satisfactory clearing up of financial complications yet. Certified checks are the only means of paying for cotton in Mobile—and the Northern Bks have not yet resumed currency payts. gold is 7-7/8 [*sic*]. Fanny is at Arcola. Liz went yesterday to Kornegays. Alfred went this morning to plantation. Yellow fever in Monty is pronounced epidemic by Board of Health. Still very bad in Memphis, abating at Shreveport. There is a convention of Negroes in Town to day—many a one is here. Price for cotton unsatisfactory—Selma 14-1/2.

October 19. Sunday morning. There was a good rain last night & there is this morning a cool wind & no dust & we anticipate a frost for tonight. Two more yellow fever deaths in Montgy and a large no. in Memphis. St Louis Bks resumed....

November 2. Heavy frosts on last Wednesday Thursday & friday mornings. Weather lovely. Liz went to Arcola with Mr Hatch on Wednesday who came up to bring Fanny. The Lock in money matters still continues and the failure of Sprague's of R. Island has caused much anxiety & embarrassment. A & W Sprague of Providence were protested on 31 Oct. Cotton is very depressed and Low Middlings are not worth in Selma over 12 cts. The truth is it really seems as if the bottom had dropped out and we had not yet got to the bottom. Stocks & bonds have gone down with a run and not stopped yet....

November 12. We have had several brilliantly beautiful days and cloudless skies. Temperature delightful. last night the wind rose and to day it is bright & blustering but not cold. The election for State Senator was held on yesterday. Snedecor was nominee of Radicals, C. W. Hatch independent radical and W. B. Young was voted for by democrats & conservatives. Report is that Hatch leads[,] Young next & nominee behind—The charges of stealing which were openly made in public speeches against Hatch did not seem to damage him at all with the nigs and his election is a sad commentary on their morals. I have directed Kit to patch the kitchen roof and want to have the shed rooms fixed.

Financial matters are still very depressing. Boggs in Selma has made an assignment and panic in England is reported—when shall we touch bottom—Thousands of operatives are out of employment—

November 17. An election for Senator was held last tuesday Nov 11 to fill vacancy in State Senate caused by resignation of George M Duskin. V. G. Snedecor was nominee of Rad. party—C W Hatch independent Rad. and democrats voted for W B Young. Hatch was elected by 130 majority over Snedecor and Young behind both. Hatch was openly charged with stealing money from letters while P. Master and with forgery, for which last he had been indicted & escaped by a quibble it was said. The Stealing was not denied—the negroes went for him with a relish. He is seen in trouble from a U. S. claim of $1000 for money due as post master.... The execution of the crew of Virginius in Cuba has caused much excitement in the north & New Orleans, and a speck of war with Spain is visible—much distress about money—operatives continue to be discharged and the winter out look is gloomy enough—Mobile Banks have not yet resumed.

November 19. The weather this morning is clear & windy—quite cold—no paper from Montgy the cars failing to make connection—there were very few telegrams in Selma paper the storm of sunday night having broken the line. What messages came were by St Louis, Texas, N. Orleans—a very circuitous route. Alfred & Ed returned from their hunting yesterday 3 petrels & 3 partridges—no local events. Mrs Pickens is still very low.

November 26. We are having a beautiful mild day, Sunday 23 was cloudy & at night threatened rain some wind. The previous sunday nights storm was very extensive in the north rain & snow storms. Mr Watson came to hand on Saturday 22nd [from Northampton, Mass.] dined with us Sunday. The Spanish difficulty is still threatening—great activity in the Navy yards, & recruiting offices are opened at different places, one in N. Orleans. To go to war with Spain at this time looks like very stupid madness—the defense of Cuba if we had it would cost more than it would yield to the Govt. and an uncongenial race of Mongrels & Negroes would be an accession to the ranks of radicals but of advantage to [n]one but the Radical party—while the cost of the war piled on to present debt would be a burden for posterity for many years. Alfred is at the plantation—comes up to night. Selma fair is going on—

December 3. Mr Watson & Col Jones dined with me on Monday 1st and in the evening Ed & Jane went to Mr Kornegays. They have not yet returned it having been a rainy day on yesterday. Gen Forrest came to see me last night & left on train this morning.[84] The municipal elections in Montgomery came off on Monday 1. There was a considerable row between negroes & white folks and several negroes were killed and some whites wounded. Radical candidate elected. Miss [Virginia] Inge is to be married to Mr Selden tonight. The bell of Episcopal church is ringing for Missionary praying. The weather is so rainy there will be a small gathering. Alfred returned on train last night having been to Selma & Union Town—Bot 100 bu corn @ 55 cts. Sold a Bale cotton in Selma @ 14. There is some improvement in prices—but all the gain has not been sustained. The Department estimate crop at 3,700,000. Spanish complication settled—

December 4. Thursday. Miss [Virginia] Inge was married last night to Mr [Armistead] Selden. Fanny waited on her and Maggie & Alfred went to wedding about midnight we had a very severe storm of wind & Rain some hail & Lightning & Thunder. The weather had been very mild & moist. The wind veered to the North and to day it is clear & colder. Mellown owns up that he cant pay me and I have had to advertise the land mortgaged to me, to be sold on 27 Dec 1873.[85] As there is no money in the Country I shall have to buy it—I would like to be excused but see no alternative.

December 5. Friday. We had another hard rain last night—some thunder & lightning—was very unexpected as the day had been bright &

---

[84] Nathan B. Forrest, Confederate general, was building a railroad with immigrant Chinese labor from Selma, Marion, and to Memphis during the years from 1869 to 1874. There was no record of their conversation. For more information, see Daniel Liestman, "Chinese Laborers in Reconstruction Alabama," *Alabama Heritage*, no. 8 (Spring 1988): 2–13.

[85] David [Ewing] Mellown, listed in the 1870 census as a farmer, age twenty-eight, and his wife Julia [Hagins] had real estate value of $800 and a personal estate of $500. Although Benners was reluctant to buy this property, in the hard times of the 1880s he bought a number of properties whose owners could no longer pay the mortgages.

pleasant—to day it is very wet & rainy. Ed Scott came to the house last evening & asked permission to drive in and stay all night—he was moving his brother Tom & family over the river 12 miles from Eutaw. Toms family consists of wife 7 children & 1 grandchild and as poor as he can be. Edwards caring for him & coming to shoulder the whole concern is a most creditable exhibition of fraternal feeling. The more as he himself is poor—and Tom & family are no earthly account—they had a dreadful day for travelling but Ed felt obliged to go lest the river might be up. Several R. Road disasters have occurred—Central, SR&DR & others—none reported from our SM&M RR.

December 10. We have had a spell of foggy drizzly & disagreeable weather for a number of days. Not yet cleared off but the air is more elastic and some promise of a clearing off. Chancery Court Monday closed tuesday. Award in Atkins vs Stollenwerck established. Sickles minister to Spain has resigned, Underwood of Va is dead—Bishop Cummins has seceded & wants to establish a reformed Episcopal church. Legislature is a failure no reduction in per diem & mileage. Meantime money is very scarce & times difficult. Mellown land is adv to be sold 27 Dec. Ed wants me to buy it for him.[86] Smith & Jones from Mobile have been here in attendance on the Chy Co. No clearing up yet in the financial pressure—

December 22. After several days of warm mild weather it commenced raining last night and to day we are having a moist day and our wintry weather seems to have commenced. [C. W.] Hatchs seat in the Senate was declared vacant the last night of the session on the ground of ineligibility—he having failed as P. Master to acct for monies in his hands—a parcel of folks gave him a mock serenade night before last. The ladies to day are to commence dressing the church for Christmas & to morrow night there is to be a fancy masquerade party at the Dubose house. Cotton has declined a 1/2 cent and low middling in Selma is worth about 14 cts—

December 26. Christmas was a cloudy day but without rain. The children had a good time emptying presents brought to them by Santa

---

[86] Edward Graham Benners, his third son

Claus. The monkey cost 10 cts pleased Graham more than any thing. Jennys ring with emerald sets gave her very great pleasure. Ed made me a present of a handsome cup & saucer. Liz made me a vest. Maggie gave me a picture frame. We had a large congregation at church. The dressing of the church was much lighter than heretofore. Col [Allen] Jones & John Nelson dined with us and Miss Lizzie Beattie.[87] The usual ham & turkey was on hand and a fine dessert. To day it is still cloudy & sunshine has been a scarce article for a long time—it is moderately cold.

1874

The economic downturn continued. Money was scarce and many Southerners sold their land for taxes. A number of Alabama banks even reduced the salaries of their employees. Cotton had done poorly for several years. Fortunately, Benners continued to do well as a lawyer. He remained active but was particularly unhappy with the number of Negroes now demanding attention. The freedman was now part of the judicial system, and Benners would have to get used to it.

January 1.... This New Years day is cloudy & cool, and a rain or snow would not surprise us. The So Bk informed me they had resumed full currency payts. Money is very scarce and much land will be sold for taxes. The Virginius[88] sank near Frying Pan Shoals south of Cape fear. The Mellown place was sold by me on the 27 dec & bid in for me at 1200 dollars. I shall let Ed try his hand out there—He has to do something and wants to farm.

January 2. We are having a pleasant spell of weather mild & sunshining. Ed moved his furniture out to Mellown place yesterday—and has gone him self to day. The emigrations of nigs to Miss still continues—

---

[87] She is listed as Lizzie Beatty in the 1870 census, sixteen years old, and living with the James M. Hobson household in Greensboro. Hobson was a lawyer.

[88] A Civil War blockade runner. The wreck lies in forty feet of water six miles offshore of the Cape Fear River sea buoy #FP6.

January 6.... The Steamer Virginius which was threatening at one time to be a "belli teturima causa" was sunk by stress of weather on coast near Frying pan Shoals. There is a talk of Spain's demanding indemnity as it appears she was not entitled to carry U.S. Flag. Congress was to have convened on Monday 5th....

January 7.—... Castellas was defeated in Spanish Cortez and Pavia coup d'état Threatens compli[c]ation with U.S....

January 23. we have had a long spell of mild cloudy weather without rain—till last night when we had a good hard rain. I went to Selma yesterday & returned same day. Bot of Meiss & Kahn a wardrobe for Liz & a mattrass $50. Selma Savings Bk had elected Ed Fowlkes cashier of same place of White resigned. H. S. Stollenwerck Pres. who is also pres of Central City. Woodruff is pres of Central City & Cross sec. Salaries were reduced. Savings Bk has 40,000 bad 10,000 doubtful—City National is all right 12-1/2 per ct Surplus—Bot 2 bbls land plaster fr[om] Geo W. Baker to use in rolling cotton seed for planting at home & for Ed. When I reached home last night it was raining very hard, rode home from depot in Potters Hack. To day is bright & beautiful Ed has sown oats—...

February 3.... The preliminary trial of Harris & Wedgworth for assault on McArdle is progressing at Court house. Alfred is employed to take testimony down—a great cock & bull story about the finding of a large amt of gold bullion on the Marshal[l] place has been food for the quidnuncs.[89] I think it turns out instead of the treasure being found—a negro dreamed he had found it. This & nothing more....

February 4.... Alfred is still engaged taking testimony in the case vs Wedgworths. No Adv[er]tiser to day.

February 9. The hearing in State vs Harris & the Wedgworths was concluded on Saturday night. Harris & Middleton Wedgworth being required to give bail in $1000—and John discharged....

February 14. We had a hard rain yesterday & to day fair & cooler. Willie went to Ed's to day—Saturday. There is a seeming calm on the face of matters now. Cotton still low & receipts continue largely in

---

[89] Quidnunc—One who is curious to know everything that is going on: a gossip.

excess of last year. The season for preparing has been a good one—and much more grain sown than in former years.

February 19. Tuesday we had rain—yesterday ash wednesday cloudy & cool—to day threatening—with wind from the East. Cabell goes to Louisville & I am at a loss what to do with Willie—he is at Eds since tuesday. The cotton continues to come in—largely in Excess of last year—and price 14-1/4 Selma. The greatest possible anxiety is expressed as to the results of next planting—as our people are impoverished by the bad crops of the two bad years.

February 23. Yesterday was a very mild pleasant sunday—and of course was not kept as an anniversary of Washingtons birth.[90] Last night it rained & the wind whipped round to the North and it is quite cool this morning. Alfred has gone to P. and Ed who spent the day with us yesterday goes out this morning. Cotton is down a 1/4 and is 7-7/8. We have had several cases sore eyes. Mr Hatch & Parker were up on Saturday & the latter left yesterday evening.

February 25. It rained yesterday and nearly all last night. To day windy & cold and clearing off. The question of taxes is a very troublesome one and the Tax collector is proposing to levy on Personal Property—not more than 1/2 have paid as yet & money is tight. Mr Cabell who has resigned the Academy leaves for Louisville tomorrow.

March 3. at municipal election yesterday Roulhac was elected Mayor—Beck, Chadwick, Powers & Tucker were elected Councilmen & Jesse D Hamilton,[91] Marshall [marshal]—R Atkins for marshal was defeated. Alfred has gone to plantation. The morning has been brilliant this evening cloudy. Had some fruit trees bot from Burge[92] planted in orchard. There is considerable perplexity with many about the town. Sales are to be advertised this week.

March 10. We have had a spell of fine weather since the rain of Friday (6th) night which was very hard—Morning cool and moderating

---

[90] There was no celebration of George Washington's birthday in the South after the Civil War began.

[91] Jesse Hamilton, boot and shoemaker, Greensboro. Snedecor, *Greene County*, 20.

[92] Either C. F. Burge or Thomas. E. Burge, planters, Hollow Square, Greensboro. Ibid., 9.

& warmer at noon. I planted yesterday (9) a few grains of very large corn given by Mr Hicks[93], said to be very prolific. Mrs M[adison] Jones gave a reception on last thursday (5) on arrival of NBJ[ones] & wife from Miss—large company and general invitation. Alfred went down yesterday morning expected to night—fine time for corn planting. Liz flower seed from Vicks arrived to day.

March 11. It commenced raining last evening and thro the night rained very hard—this morning cool & cloudy. Jane is suffering from Neuralgia & Jenny from very bad cold. Alfred came on train last night. Papers announce the death of Millard Fillmore[94] aged 74. one of the best men of the Country beyond all question. Corn planting will be suspended by hard rain. Ed was planting yesterday—

March 16. It rained Saturday night and yesterday was one of the rainiest sundays we have had—to day it still rains and high rivers & overflows are looked for—Mr Sumner died last week and remains have been carried to Mass.[95] Mrs Willie Pickens has been on a visit being unable to go back as yet by reason of the rain. Ed came in Saturday evening went out this morning. Irish potatoes are up & looking well....

March 23. Yesterday sunday was not a very pleasant day in consequence of rain and cloudiness—No service in the evening by reason of bad weather—To day the clouds look heavy & threatening and it is much cooler. Judge Saffold has come to hand and we are to have court this week the Docket is distressingly insignificant and the crim Doc crowded with negroes claiming attention—Ed came in Saturday night & leaves for home this morning—he is put out by the rains—expects to be ready to commence planting cotton by 1 April—

April 6. Court has been in session two weeks, and continues this week, there were three capital cases last week. State vs Hendon & Hendon acquitted.—vs Wilson, Genia, manslaughter 5 yrs. Henry Par.

---

[93] Tilman Hicks, planter, Clinton. Ibid., 22.

[94] Millard Fillmore, thirteenth president of the United States, opposed Lincoln's election and supported Johnson's opposition to Republican Reconstruction measures. He took no active part in politics after the Civil War.

[95] Charles Sumner, US senator from Massachusetts, 1851–1874, helped organize the Liberal Republican Party in 1872. He served in the Senate until his death in 1874.

Rape mistrial—the trial of Bob Murray for arson & murder and of the negroes who killed Tisdale the pedlar is set for this week—there were two light frosts on the full moon before Easter but very little harm done—Yesterday Easter was a lovely morning and the church services were extremely interesting & impressive—the childrens festival came off at night and $304 was collected. The tax sale of delinquents is advertised for to day. Alfred started yesterday for Mobile via Eastport. The Firemans procession comes off Thursday and Boats carry passengers at a round fare....

April 9. I had a fever again yesterday morning—and am not feeling first rate to day. We had hard rain last night & much thunder & lightning—Ed got in before the rain. There was a conviction for rape yesterday & confession on part of one of the Tisdale murderers with sentence to Penitentiary for life. I have just had another jaw tooth pulled out. Friend after friend departs—there is some stir around among colored folks. I think they take unusual interest in rapes—

In spring 1874, Senator John Sherman of Ohio introduced the currency bill of 1874, which was designed to stabilize the economy. However, a number of amendments were tacked on by Southern and Western senators and it was transformed into an inflation bill. The bill proposed to add $64 million to the circulation of greenback and national bank notes. Deeply opposed to the measure, Benners watched uneasily as it was passed by congress and sent to President Grant for his signature. At the same time, the Mississippi River overflowed its banks causing great damage.

April 13.... the weather has become cloudy & threatening rain—Miss River is out of its Banks...Financial bill passed Cong—Folks wonder if Pres will veto[96]—Court is over & we are in a collapse—

---

[96] Senator John Sherman presented the Currency Bill of 1874 designed to stabilize the currency. However, a number of amendments pressed by Westerners and Southerners of both parties transformed the measure into an inflation bill by proposing to add $64 million to the circulation of greenbacks and national bank notes. Eric Foner, *Reconstruction: America's Unfinished Revolution, 1863–1877* (New York: Harper & Row, 1990) 522.

April 14.—We had rain this morning which will make it unpleasant for Alfred who has gone to Plantation this morning—I don't yet feel quite well my head aches & I fear seeds of my disease are not all eradicated....

April 15. 1-1/2. [a.m. or p.m.] We have just had a hard rain with thunder & lightning—will retard farming operations—Alfred came home last night, back water has been all over his low grounds—reports his work 10 days in advance of last year. There is great dulness in the town & not a ripple on the surface of affairs.

April 17. Hard rains all day yesterday felt unwell & staid at home—to day is cloudy and threatening—Miss River is out of its banks and M&NO RR is under water. Currency bill gone to Grant[97]....

April 30. at last we have a mail—there having been none before since last thursday. The Pres vetoed the inflation bill and there not being 2/3rds vote it is defeated.[98] Great sensation in the west about it while the north is rejoicing. The Miss is falling at places and our rivers are also—

May 1. Yesterday was a bright cool day there having been a slight frost in places. To day is lovely, Ed came in last night & returned this morning. Cotton is said to be improving in looks. Altogether the outlook is gloomy for crops. There is great distress in the overflowed country—and congress has sent them 20,000 tons of rations—for 25 days—...

May 7. Thursday yesterday & the day before were cold & fires comfortable. to day is a bright day & the sunshine very pleasant—the cotton improves very slowly and it really looks as if it ought all to have been ploughed up and replanted—the corn looks pretty well—My wife and Alfred & wife went in Potters Hack to Mrs Withers to the marriage of Col Jones to Miss Eliza J Withers which takes place at 4-1/2 this

---

[97] The inflation bill was sent to President Grant for his signature. Grant had expressed interest in such a measure and many believed he would sign it. J. G. Randall and David Donald, *Civil War and Reconstruction* (Lexington MA: D.C. Heath, 1969) 670.

[98] At the end of April, he vetoed the bill and Congress failed to muster the necessary two-thirds needed to make it law. Grant had prepared a message to justify the approval of the bill but changed his mind at the last minute. Ibid. 670; Foner, *Reconstruction*, 522.

evening. Did not go, not feeling well and not in company mood by a great deal. Mrs Wemyss left with her children on Monday morning for Tennessee. The skaters are at their sport and the rolling on the floor can be heard from my office by listening—The National Savings Bank for freedmen is reported broke—and Cuffee is victimised as he thought in the house of his friends. Adage says Save me from my friends & I will take care of my enemies—[99]....

May 12. Ed came in last night & reported a shoat stolen from him. Thieving is one of the greatest curses with which we are afflicted.

May 14.... The suspension of the mails is a very great inconvenience—3 times a week is unsatisfactory having had none since Monday night. Took off my flannel for the first time to day. Mr Stickney went with Mr Cobbs to Eufaula to Episcopal Convention....

In late May, the Civil Rights Bill, a memorial to the death of Charles Sumner, passed the senate. It had been held up in the house for nine months before its passage. Benners disapproved of the measure and the effects it would have on black participation at the local level and party conventions.

May 28.... The civil rights bill has passed the senate and is very stringent in its provisions. Fines & imprisonment besides damages are strewed pretty thick for violation. It is hinted that Grant would veto it. Carpenter voted agt it because its requirements as to jurors in State Courts infringed upon the Constitution—mischief & only mischief continually seems the mission of Radicalism—[100]....

---

[99] The Freedman's Savings and Trust Company was chartered in 1865. It was a private corporation that actively sought deposits from freedmen while instructing them on the importance of thrift. Most accounts were under $50 and some only a few pennies. The company invested in Washington DC real estate and made unsecured loans to railroads and other companies. The company went bankrupt and only a half of the depositors received any of their money, usually about 60 percent of the value of their accounts. Foner, *Reconstruction*, 531–32.

[100] Matthew Hale Carpenter, senator from Wisconsin 1869–1875, was best known for his work representing the federal government in the celebrated McCardle case, which tested the validity of the Reconstruction Act of 7 March 1867. There was a possibility that the Supreme Court might declare the Reconstruction Act unconstitutional. Instead, the Court bowed to the Legislature allowing that Congress

June 10. No rain yesterday—weather hot & pleasant. Alfred & family came from Arcola yesterday—reports very violent storm of rain at Arcola on Monday—crop report favorable—he has gone to plantation to day. Ed came in last night & went out this morning—has carried out the Nelly cow—speaks favorably of his prospects of corn & cotton. House refused to take up civil rights bill—which is supposed to have killed it for the present—[101]....

June 14. yesterday was a lovely bright day & a fine air stirring made it pleasant this morning too there is a pleasant breeze & the morning delightful. Beat meeting yesterday to send delegates to County Convention in July—to elect delegates to State convention in Montgy. The race issue was sprung & I opposed it—It is a mistake in my opinion.[102] Ed arrived to Supper and spends the day with us....

June 27. We had a good hard rain yesterday evening—very acceptable where crops are clean. The cotton is growing very fast—corn do [ditto] Willies corn patch looks not so good—not having been well ploughed—not broke near enough to corn & not thrown back sufficiently. Congress has adjourned—currency bill is signed by Pres—Permits free banking & redistributes amt of banking capital & dispenses with reserves—[103]....

The Benners family vacationed at Blount Springs from 2 July to 14 October. It was their longest vacation in many years. They were refreshed by mild weather and cool waters. Jane had been growing weaker in recent years

---

had the right to define matters of jurisdiction. *American Congress*, 951; Randall and Donald, *Civil War and Reconstruction*, 645.

[101] The House of Representatives passed the civil rights bill in February 1875. They cut the school provision making discrimination against blacks illegal in schools from the measure before passing it. James M. McPherson, *Ordeal by Fire: The Civil War and Reconstruction* (New York: McGraw-Hill, 2001) 570.

[102] Benners was opposed to sending black delegates to county political conventions.

[103] A bill fixing greenback circulation at $382 million was passed and signed by President Grant on 20 June 1874. Later in the year, Senator John Sherman proposed a law that satisfied the South and West on the matter of banknote currency. The law also changed the number of national banks and the extent of banknote circulation. Randall and Donald, *Civil War and Reconstruction*, 670.

and thoroughly enjoyed the change. Each day, Benners visited the springs and felt refreshed: "I begin to feel reluctant to leave this white mans mountain country and if I could have all my family and all satisfied should be tempted to stay here." In September, he received news of the political conflicts in Louisiana with the Republican Reconstruction government fighting for its life.

September 18. We recd on 16th Sep news of the conflict in N. Orleans—Penn Lieut Gov of McEnery party with citizens driving out Kellog[g] & Co.—Grants proc[lamation] of 15 is recd and the situation is perplexing and critical—they claim to have peac[e]able possession and that by Grants own programme he cannot interfere except to keep the peace. ...[104] Dr Robertson's son is reported killed by negroes at Rowe place near Demopolis—

September 19.... affairs in N. Orleans are said to be compromised by turning over the Govt to the military under Gen Emory—[105]

September 21.... Grant has reinstated Kellog[g] in N. Orleans.[106] No news from the negro riot in Sumter. There are not many persons at the B[ount]/S[prings]....

Benners took a farewell draught of spring water before leaving for home with seven trunks and two bundles of bedding. He arrived in Greensboro on 16 October to a city with an unsettled mood. There had been a murder.

---

[104] An Illinois carpetbagger, William P. Kellogg, defeated John McEnery for governor of Louisiana. There was considerable violence in the campaigning prior to the election. On 14 September 1874, 3,500 mostly Civil War veterans overwhelmed the black militia and the metropolitan police commanded by General James Longstreet. They withdrew with the arrival of Federal troops that Grant had ordered. Foner, *Reconstruction*, 551.

[105] General Emory suppressed the insurrection on 17 September by a general war order. Carrying out the order, General Brooks demanded the surrender of all arms and state property and took command until the government could be reorganized. Ella Lonn, *Reconstruction in Louisiana after 1868* (New York: G. P. Putnam's Sons, 1918; repr., New York: Russell & Russell, 1967) 275.

[106] On 19 September, Kellogg returned to the statehouse and the metropolitan police resumed their regular duties. Ibid., 275.

October 17. There is a considerable excitement in Town to day caused by the killing of [M. C.] Knight—John T. Walker & John Atkins Jr were in a *rencontre* and the deceased who was a night patrol stepped between them to make them desist when he was killed by a shot from one of their pistols. The Jury of inquest is now sitting on the case in the sheriffs office the killing was not far from Burges on the main street at 2 oclock this morning.

October 19. Yesterday was a beautiful day—Mr Stickney read a sermon in the morning and Jane & Graham & I went to Ed's after dinner. He was not at home and we had a pleasant walk home—Col Jones took tea with us and after supper Cicero brought the carriage from Arcola reporting Mr Hatch sick and wanting Jane & Alfred to come down. They left after breakfast for Arcola—

October 20. No news from Arcola—one of the soldiers died yesterday—to be buried to day—Billy Erwin is dead—yellow disease. Walker and Atkins are to stand preliminary trial for killing Knight before Charley Waller J.P. The weather is as fine as possible—and but for the deranged condition of society and the hard times everything would be favorable enough. Corn is reported as selling at 50 cts a bushel. I have just returned from burial of one of the Cavalry, a Romish priest officiated and the ceremonies were military—

October 21. Wednesday. My wife and Alfred got back from Arcola yesterday to Dinner—report Mr Hatch very sick—kidney disease—and threatened with yellow disease. I feel very uneasy about his condition as his age renders his sickness very dangerous. The preliminary examination of Walker & Atkins was commenced yesterday before Charley Waller N[otary] Public actg as justice of the Peace and it is still in progress. The reports rec'd from Ohio Indiana & West Virginia are favorable to the Democratic & Conservative party.[107] Tom Wetmore has been arrested in Sumter by U.S. Dep Marshal—Intimidation seems to be the object & purpose of the Rads. There is some diptheria in town among children. McGee has lost two. The weather is very pleasant but warm & dusty. All well except childrens colds.

---

[107] Democrats won the governorship of Massachusetts and swept to victory in New Hampshire, Illinois, Indiana, and Ohio. Foner, *Reconstruction*, 523.

October 23. Friday. Weather pleasant and mild—there was a slight sprinkle of rain yesterday evening & last night—a good rain would be very acceptable. Ed carried out the mule horse & wagon to haul & gin his cotton at Martins Gin house—Alfred & Inge & Ward tried the pistols used in Walker Atkins affray to test relative penetrating power—at courts appointment.[108]

In late October, Jenny, his eight-year-old daughter, became ill.

October 28. Jenny was reported to me sick with a very bad sore throat on the morning of the 25 and we sent for Dr Peterson—who pronounced it diptheria and a bad case—she has been sick ever since & to day has fever and sorethroat.... Peterson called this morning—and his suggestions were not reassuring—[109]

October 30. On yesterday evening Dr Peterson considered Jenny better and symptoms favorable—and it being the 5th day was more significant as a turn is common on that day. this morning she still complains of her throat but we hope & believe she is better. Liz & Ed went out on the train to Sophy Sawyers wedding staid all night & came home this morning. They had a very pleasant time. Ed has packed out his cotton at Martins Screw and reports 4 Bales—a better turn out than he expected and better than his neighbors. It is highly probable that he lost the benefit of his manuring by reason of the drought.

October 31. Jenny is still improving tho very weak. I went to supper last night to Mr NR Jones and saw Mr Watt & his bride who had just arrived—returned about 10-1/2. The weather is quite cool and there would have been frost but for the wind—

The election of 1874 was looked to with newfound confidence by many Southerners, including Benners. He spent some time electioneering and made a speech. The election was held on 3 October. The Democratic Party won two-thirds of the Southern house seats, reclaimed Arkansas, and gained control in

---

[108] Both Walker and Atkins were acquitted since it could not be determined which one fired the shot. Yerby, *History of Greensboro*, 188.

[109] F. M. Peterson, physician, Greensboro. Snedecor, *Greene County*, 35.

Florida and Alabama. Benners was pleased and hoped that Reconstruction would soon end.

November 2. At Col Harveys solicitation I went with him to Newbern on Saturday evening—we each made an address on the political situation—there were about 80 persons present & returned home to supper. John Atkins was there and Jim Green.[110] Yesterday morning we had frost. I read a sermon in absence of rector—there was another frost this morning—quite white in places after breakfast & ice—Ther in hall 36 breakfast time—Jenny is still improving but Doctor visits her twice a day. Tomorrow is election day & matters are likely to be lively.

November 3. This is Election day and there is in Town the biggest crowd of negroes I have ever seen here—the race issue has not diminished the black voters—and there will be very few blacks voting democratic ticket. So far it has progressed very quietly, it is exceedingly dusty & the third frost was seen this morning. Jennie is considered better and I hope is recovering but mends very slowly.

November 6. The Elections have resulted it is thought in the overthrow of the Rad party.[111] Ala has elected Dem over Lewis Rad by about 13 thousand[112]—and all the Dem candidates for Congress except Hays & there is a talk of contesting his seat—[113]The white people are jubilant & there is to be a demonstration next Wednesday night—Mr Hatch was in town yesterday—said they had jollification in Demopolis—Selma Jollified last night.

---

[110] John Atkins, planter, Newbern, Greensboro. Ibid., 7.

[111] George Smith, a former Alabama senator, was elected governor by a decisive margin—107,118 to 93,934. It was a convincing victory for the Democratic Party. The margin was provided by new white voters who voted in large numbers. Sarah W. Wiggins, *The Scalawag in Alabama Politics, 1865–1881* (Tuscaloosa: University of Alabama Press, 1977) 98.

[112] George S. Houston, Democrat, from North Alabama, was governor from 1874–1878.

[113] Charles Hays, a scalawag and one of the largest planters in Alabama, supported secession and fought in the Confederate army. After the war, he joined the Republican Party and served in the House of Representatives from 1869 to 1877. Foner, *Reconstruction*, 297.

November 9. Mr Cobbs preached yesterday having returned from the General Convention at NY on Nov 2. We have had a very dry time and dust has been very uncomfortable. It drizzled a little yesterday and is cloudy to day—the Democratic majorities in Ala are still increasing—Houstons 13,000 perhaps more.[114] Jenny is getting well. There is to be a jollification on Wednesday 11th.

November 11. The dry weather still continues—Alfred went to plantation last evening—to Union Town to day. Ed came in last evening we went together to depot after supper—Charley Hatch came in on the train. There is very little demonstration as yet for the jubilation. We shall see what we shall see—

November 13. The Democratic & Conservative Jubilation came off and folks I suppose enjoyed the occasion very much—There were houses illuminated and tar barrels burnt and transparencies and speeches—the appearance of rain forced the speaking from the front of Dugger Hotel house to the courthouse My wife and I came down to the show for a little while James T. Jones was speaking—we left to get ahead of the rain and got wet a little in going home. Parker & two children & Mr Hatch and Mr & Mrs Kornegay came in and spent the night with us—my wife prepared supper for company expected to come from Marion—and waited for them but they did not come—Last night we had a light rain and to day weather is clear & cool.

November 20. The prospect of rain has been flattering for several days but except an occasional Drizzly misty rain none has fallen for a long time—and the ground is too hard to break to sow grain. The excitement of the last few days has been whether county officers elected by the Rads would make bonds. It is said that Mr Atkins who was elected Judge of Probate has filed his it having been approved and endorsed by Radical Judge Craig at Centerville. The offices of the others were vacated on yesterday by Judge Hobson for want of sufficient bonds—except WW Jones whose bond was held for further consideration....votes for Gov are to be counted in Montgy to day—

---

[114] It was 13,184, a significant victory. Wiggins, *Scalawag in Alabama Politics*, 98.

November 23.... Alfred has gone to plantation to rent to negroes—having Texas in view—Ed was in yesterday and went home this morning. we had a hard wind last night & some rain—it cleared off without giving the much desired root soaker. Gov Houstons inauguration takes place tomorrow—

November 27. The storm of sunday night was very terrible in north Ala—12 persons killed at Tuscumbia and several at Montevallo and many houses in Town & country blown down. We have not yet a good rain. Weather cool & clear. Alfred has rented to his hands. Inauguration of Gov Houston on tuesday 24 a grand affair 25000 persons present. Thanksgiving day yesterday. Went to church.

November 30. There was a very white frost this morning and we have had a beautiful day. The question of county officials bonds is still an engrossing one, and much discussed. Ed came in yesterday evening & left this morning. There has been great backwardness in Sowing grain for want of rain. Ed sowed oats Saturday 28th Nov.

December 2. Capt Wemyss took dinner & tea and stayed with us last night—he is on his way to Florida to look for a convenient winter resort. Alfred talks about going to Texas next week. I shall miss him sadly but there is so poor a prospect of business here I cannot find it in my heart to dissuade him, his trip is one of observation & experiment. Ed killed two of his hogs yesterday one weighed 250. I fear the weather is a little too warm.

Then, in early December, Alfred, Benners's eldest son, left for Texas to seek his future.

December 8. yesterday was one of the sad days of my life. My son Alfred left us to look out a place of residence far away from home.[115] How it cuts my heart strings to part with him can be known only to God and myself—of the pleasure of his company we are deprived—and what griefs & trials await him in his battle of life who can imagine? My little

---

[115] He went to Texas to practice law and settled in Dallas. However, he returned to Alabama after his father's death, practiced law in Birmingham, and later became a judge.

family has heretofore been unbroken now its chief member is lost to our society, we went together to Selma walked together & dined together I felt as if I were having my last day with him. We parted on our return at the Junction he for Mobile and I to my home now no longer lighted by his presence. My deprivation hangs over me like a pall of gloom and I find it hard to rally. It may be for his good, but it looks to me & feels to me as if he was mine no longer & I have lost my son—ever affectionate ever dutiful—henceforth our way in life is separated and as years advance upon me I know not how to spare him—

December 21. We heard from Alfred at Galveston last Wednesday—expected to leave for Dallas. I wrote to him to day—the weather for a day or two has been rainy till to day. Ed came in yesterday. Mr Nelson dined with us to day. The ground is wet & weather unsettled. We have no news. Legislature has adjourned to Christmas & after to 13 Jany. Cotton is low 13-1/2 in Selma.

December 23. We got two letters & a postal last night from Alfred at Dallas. He was staying at Ben Ward's, and had not come to any decision as to his location. We have had a fine day & Town is putting on its Christmas look. Mr Borden & Mr Hatch dined with me to day—

1875

Benners, despite the cold weather, continued his regular round of activities in the first months of the new year. He enjoyed playing whist, went sleigh riding, entertained guests, and often dined with friends. At the same time, he continued to follow politics. The Democratic Party was making a comeback as Republican rule in the South weakened and the federal government became reluctant to use force to maintain Reconstruction. Benners hoped that the Civil Rights Bill passed by the Senate would die a natural death, but instead it was passed by the House of Representatives and signed into law by the president.

March 4. The Civil Rights bill has passed Congress and is approved by the president.[116] Two Hotels in Alexander & one in Baltimore are closed on acct of it. Great uneasiness is felt lest the force bill has also passed. There have been great floods of rain at Chattanooga Huntsville, Knoxsville & Moulton [Ala] & Hurricanes....

March 6. Congress adjourned on the 4th and the force bill was not reached[.] there is great rejoicing at this as the Habeas Corpus is much prized by the People.[117] The Senate met in Executive Session & Grant is to send his message to them on Monday—

March 8. After a damp cloudy day yesterday, the clouds last evening were blown away & we have this morning a very white frost, and a clear beautiful day.... There are no events of consequence transpiring. Civil rights bill is being tried by colored persons at different places. Court in Wilmington decides Bar rooms not to be included in it—...

March 10. another lovely morning. Letter from Alfred last night—reports spring opening and country beautiful. Says he is making a living, I wish I could help him more, but expenses increase upon me as revenues diminish. There is no stirring news by the paper....

March 13. We had rain yesterday & day before. to day has been a warm growing day—& Peach Trees are in bloom. There is no event of stirring importance—garden corn is peeking up and Spring has opened. Mag & Gus went yesterday to Lem H[atch]s and come in to morrow—Grange speech by Gen Johnston at court house to day.[118] Sent

---

[116] The civil rights bill was passed but seldom enforced. Some railroads, streetcar lines, restaurants, and theaters in the South as well as in the North served blacks on a non-segregated basis after the passage of the law. Most, however, in the South did not honor the law. Finally in 1883, the Supreme Court ruled that it was unconstitutional on the basis that it violated the Fourteenth Amendment. One clause of the act regarding juries was held to be constitutional.

[117] The force bill, an effort to protect black voters from intimidation, was never passed. There was little enthusiasm for it in the North and even less in the South.

[118] The Patrons of Husbandry, or the Grange, was founded in 1867. Responding to the need to fight railroads and their ever increasing freight rates, farmers joined into cooperatives and then into politics where they secured the passage of many Granger laws. In 1877, in *Munn vs. Illinois*, the Supreme Court ruled that states could regulate businesses clothed with a public interest—railroads and other common carriers. It was a landmark decision. Joseph Johnston, former general of the Southern armies, was an active member of the Grange.

Wash Grant rations of meat & tobacco this morning by train to Newbern for Alfred.

An accident that happened to Jane's father caused distress to the family. Jane went to his bedside to help. Several weeks later, Alfred returned from Texas to take his family back home from their visit. Needless to say, Benners hated to see them leave.

March 20. on Tuesday evening my wife got note from Mary at Arcola informing her that her father had been thrown from buggy & badly hurt and asking her to come down she left on Wednesday 17 with Ed on the train—to go to Van Dorn where carriage would meet her. Wednesday night got telegram from her at 6 oclock from Arcola via Demopolis that he was worse—since then I have had no news from him. The weather has been very rainy & wheels impossible.

March 22. Ed came on a mule last night from Arcola and I got a note from Jane saying her father was better—had no fever tho still very low—we are greatly in hopes the crisis is passed. She will come when her father gets better—Ed is going to send mule back to day. We had white frost this mg and I suppose in places the fruit is killed—garden corn is bitten again.

March 27. Saturday. I went to Arcola on Wednesday to see Mr Hatch. took the train & went to Van Dorn Wednesday—walked to Arcola 4 oclock PM. Mr Hatch was very weak—but I supposed was better—he had no fever and some appetite. Jane concluded to remain with him till to day and as we have a rainy morning she may conclude to stay over. I hurt my leg getting on train at Union Town coming home and it gives me considerable inconvenience....

April 14—Alfred arrived from Texas last night—looking very well and much delighted with his news—will remain a week or so. It was quite cold last night and there was frost in spots. Clouding up to day—and quite cool—

April 17. It keeps quite cool & dry and the streets are getting very dusty. Cold winds on cotton up make it look very bad. Corn is yellowed but not hurt much. Jane, Mag & Fanny took tea at Col Jones last night with Alfred. I was too hoarse to go. Alfred has rode to the plantation to day & a disagreeable ride he will have of it he expects to leave on Wednesday Ap 21. Annie Withers & Mary Avery dined with us to day. Parker Hatch came up here to day to get money to pay the tax on land. I gave him to pay with $80 State money & 5 Greenbacks. I am in for a big Job running non paying plantations. Alfreds is on my hands & now his.

April 18. Alfred got home from W. P. [Walker Place] last night & with his wife took tea at Col Harveys—he goes to Arcola this afternoon—The weather is still cool & dry—& cotton up looks sickly.

April 19. Ed & Alfred went down to Arcola with Dr Hoyle yesterday after dinner by the long way. expect to be home to day. It was very cool again last night but no frost about my place. Mr Stollenwerck & Lee had vegetables killed by frost on 17th (night) corn looks very yellow—my head is heavy at the prospect of my children leaving Wednesday for Texas.

April 20. Alfred & Ed got back from Arcola last evening. Mr Hatch mending. Weather warmer and to day cloudy. Thursday is the day now named for starting to Texas. The drain on diminished resources is heavy. Letter from Liz last night they had snow 14 in[ches] deep in Mass.[119]

April 21. Alfred got his furniture on cars for Dallas yester evening—and with Mag Gus & Fanny leaves to morrow. we are in trouble about the breaking up. Light shower of rain last night—cloudy to day.

April 22. My children are gone—Alfred & his wife & son & my daughter Fanny left this morning for Texas—I have often wondered how so much happy concretion as all my family together could last and now it is broken and a divided household is all that is left. Jones came round at 3 am & with Ed, Willie & myself accompanied to Depot—a little running about a getting of checks a buying of tickets a hurried embrace—and the train moves off carrying my pride my pleasure my companionship away from me—Poor little Gus was in high spirits—and the idea of riding filled his little heart—there was no room for grief. May he never have any....

---

[119] Liz left on 6 February for a trip to Northampton, Massachusetts, to visit the Henry Watson family.

In May and June, Democrats won local elections in several cities, including Selma. At the national level, Grant continued to talk about a third term, much to the displeasure of Benners.

May 26. Having just reached the office with Graham now comes Willie after the Dr to go to see Jane. She was feeling a little unwell when I left, and I am going up to see. Weather still very dry. Letter last night but one from Alfred going next day 20 to housekeeping. Ed came in last night returned this morning. Woodruff independent democrat has beat Woolsey Democratic nominee for Mayor of Selma by 107 votes—nine out of 10 Democratic councilmen elected. Democrats are sore—my wife came down after dinner and was feeling much better.…

June 11. We are having still a warm & fine spell of weather—rain much desired. Jane returned home from Carries [Kornegay] yesterday morning. Ed in last night. the crop accts continue good—but corn on sandy land needs rain. Grants message on the 3rd Term written to the Pres of Pen[nsylvania] Rep[ublican]convention—saying he did not desire it any more than 1st is much ridiculed—and the general opinion is it would have been more commendable if he had said straight out that he desired it greatly—…

Dissatisfaction with Republican rule brought the Democratic and Conservative parties together to hold a convention. They put together a slate of delegates to a convention for the purpose of revising the Alabama constitution. Benners attended this meeting with high hopes for its success.

June 26. Nice shower yesterday evening—heavier at Eds. he is gone to Plantation this morning. Convention to nominate delegates to the Convention meets to day.

June 28. Mr Tutwiler & myself on Saturday June 26 were nominated candidates to the Constitutional Convention by the Democratic & Conservative party—I accepted the nomination and made a short speech to the Convention acknowledging the honor. We had a fine shower yesterday evening and clouds are overhanging this morning.

Cotton and corn prospects are improved by the rain. Ed went to WP on Saturday reports the crop very promising—...

July 1.... The nominations for the Convention will impress on me the duty of canvassing to a certain extent and we are to have speaking on Saturday July 3....

July 3. 4 oclock. I addressed the People this morning at 11 oclock at the Courthouse on the Constitutional Convention. There was a very fair crowd & some colored folks. The weather was warm & hour & a half talking made my shirt very wet. My principal aim was to impress on them the importance of registering & voting for convention. Mr Hatch was up to day and dined with us. We had no rain here on yesterday—...

July 8.... We argued Tindel vs Drake before Chan[cellor] Turner yesterday—court is still holding—opinions of Chancellor are very favorable.

July 9.... Mr Stickney dined with me yesterday and Mr Pittman to day. Letter from Liz night before last. Alfreds postal card came to hand this morning. Mrs Roulhac left for NC to day....

July 14. I went to Selma on Monday 12 and returned in the evening. The crops on the road are the best promising I have ever seen between Greensboro & Selma.... This morning by invitation of Colored people I addressed them at colored school house on Convention question—no rains lately—

July 16. Yesterday was warm & dry. Ben Hatch and wife came to our house on Wednesday evening and on yesterday 15, went to Picnic at Keiths Spring given by the Grangers on yesterday. Jane went with them. I went with Mr Rich'd Stickney. Had a very pleasant day and after Grange exercises & speeches by Gen Chambers & Gen Law were over, had a very beautiful repast characterized by good behavior & no ill breeding. After Dinner Grangers installed their officers and then Mr Alex Davidson of Perry [county] candidate for const[itutional] Con[vention] made a speech and I followed him....

July 17. We are having a very hot spell of weather and need rain—last night & night before even at my house I found the night uncomfortably warm & to day opens for a hot one. There have been as yet no opposition nominations made—and there is to be a meeting to day. I had figs for dinner for the first time and the grapes are turning—The vines are very full and if nothing happens we shall have abundance. The success of the convention question is by no means assured. The scarecrows which are used to frighten the people are having their effect & radicals generally are opposing [constitutional] convention....[120]

July 20.... My wife is quite unwell having been taken with Cholera Morbus last night. The papers are barren of interest & the dull season is here. Probabilities are rads will run a candidate or candidates for Convention. The colored people are not disposed to do so but act under orders from others—... Stone in Montgy will be beaten and Judge Coleman thinks he will also. Mr Tutwiler has not arrived—is expected daily—...

July 22.... The convention question creates no real excitement. My idea has been to keep as quiet as possible, unless the opposition stir up. The vote has fallen off very much—some 600 will probably have to register on election day—if they vote I now think there will be nominees and I shall be defeated.[121]

July 24.... Republicans meet to day to nominate candidates to Convention. We are looking for Liz to night. Jenny, Graham & old Liddy are happy. We are wanting rain again cotton is shedding. Willie & Ed went to Kornegays yesterday and from there to the plantation—weather pleasant....

August 2. on tuesday July 27 I went to Greene Springs and spent the night there. Mr P. Tutwiler went with me in Hack hired from Potter on 28 we spoke on the Convention question to the People at Havana next day at Carthage—next day at Flinn's Mill [at Five Mile]—next day at Greensboro where we had a large audience. The rads having

---

[120] With the state government firmly in their hands, the Democrats began to change and dismantle Republican policies and political mechanisms. They reduced state lotteries from $30 million to just under $13 million. And they wanted to change the hated 1868 Republican constitution. Republicans feared that it would take away the right of blacks to vote. Rogers, *Alabama*, 265–66.

[121] Benners's worst fears came to pass. He lost the election. Still, most of those who were elected across the state agreed with his views. He kept a clipping of the final vote in Hale County and the advertisement of his candidacy.

recommended Dr Foster & Baird Johnson our chance of election is slim. I had a very pleasant visit to G[reene] Spgs and old memories were revived. Mr Tutwiler dined with me on Saturday 31. We had a rain on my way home from Flinns Mill & stepped out of it at Latimers. Last evening there was another very hard rain here & a rain again last night & it is very cloudy to day. Tomorrow is the election day.

August 4. I went to Newbern on the day of election and returned on the train. The vote at Newbern was 292 for to 436 against Convention. The Convention question and candidates are beaten about 1000 in the County—throwing out Macon vote because the election was not held at the place of holding the election. the maj[ority] vs convention is 500. Foster & Johnson are elected. I am trying to get ready to go to Blount. I visited Willies place yesterday & crops are good—corn some what blown down—

August 5. yesterday was a mild day—& no rain.... Majority ag[ains]t us is about 1000—if Macon box is thrown out it will be only 540. Convention news is very meagre and only 15000 is claimed as the majority for Convention. further returns may vary it.

August 6. The convention is reported carried by 20000 majority—20 only of Rads & independents being elected—The weather is pleasant and cloudy this morning. Judge Coleman from Greene is reported elected by 500 majority....

Benners lost the election by 573 votes. Though hoping for victory, he was not surprised by defeat. Immediately, he took his family to Blount Springs for seven weeks' vacation, from early August through September. The weather was warm and moist at first but became rainy for the rest of the vacation. Still there was much to do. They saw friends at the local hotel, shooting gallery, and bowling alley. Weddings, hunting, and riding provided pleasurable entertainment. Benners enjoyed the springs and the mineral water. During these weeks, there was no reference to the past election or any political matters with exception of two clippings he put in the journal. One was the vote of Hale County on the constitutional convention on 3 August 1875, and the other, a reference to his candidacy for a position in the constitutional convention.

Benners returned to Greensboro in early October to his plantation and family business. The constitutional convention released its revised constitution and submitted it to the Alabama voters for a vote on 16 November. He was asked to speak in favor of it, but the weather was so threatening that he decided to back out of this obligation.

November 15. I read a sermon on Sunday 15 in the church. The day was cloudy having had rain the night before. Again this morning it is warm and cloudy. The election comes off tomorrow on the question of the new Constitution. Geo M Duskin has appeared here just in time—he is opposed to the new Constitution of course. The negroes not being able to procure the tickets "against" sent to Selma on Sunday & got a supply. They go solidly against. The first time their rights have been guaranteed by conservatives they have no more sense than to vote against it—

November 16. The election for Constitution is progressing very quietly—up to now 12 M there are 285 votes polled. The negroes are generally voting against the new constitution, but many of them are at a loss and seem disturbed and dont know what to do. The voting in precinct of residences is a great improvement and renders it quiet & unobstructed.

November 19. Weather warm and moist—rain drizzly yesterday evening—the election day here was very quiet and the new Const rec'd a maj at this box 86—in the County 743 in the State about 40000....

The voters ratified the new Constitution by a vote of 85,662 to 29,217 on 16 November 1875. It was an overwhelming victory, which pleased the Democrats and disheartened the Republicans. There was no doubt that Alabama was once again a white man's state. Benners also noted the corruption in the Grant administration, particularly the Whiskey Ring in St. Louis.

December 7. Yesterday morning the land reports heard early reminded us that the new Constitution had gone into operation—the 6th day of December having by Proclamation of Gov Houston appointed as the day for that purpose. The cloudy weather holds on and again last night we had a hard rain. Messrs Roulhac & Waller came round last evening to see Mr Watson and we amused ourselves till 1 oclock playing whist at which Charlie & I beat Watson & Roulhac 2 games (ahead). The weather this morning is cooler & wind from NW and we hope for a clear off.

December 8. The US house of Representatives have elected [Michael] Kerr of Indiana Speaker, [Henry] Wilson [Massachusetts] vice pres having died, [Thomas White] Ferry of Michigan the president of the Senate—[Orville E.] Babcock the private Secretary of the Pres of the U States for defrauding the revenue in connection with the Whiskey ring at St Louis....[122]

December 26. Christmas was a warm cloudy day without rain. To day warm & threatening. We have had a remarkable spell of weather very warm for the season—

December 27. Monday morning—yesterday was warm & cloudy but no rain till last night when we had a wind some thunder & heavy rain for short time—and this morning it is much cooler and still very cloudy. Mr Fred [Watson] left this morning on the train for Selma—he & Miss Mary Cocke & Mr Watson were our Christmas company. The children got many presents and I got a pair gloves from Ed a shaving brush from Willie and a [illegible] from Lizzie. Mr Watson gave each one a pretty present and they enjoyed them very much.

1876

During the early months of 1876, Benners continued to raise crops and practice law. He lost one of his favorite servants, Gus Hall—"He gave as much satisfaction as any servant I have had in a long time." In February, he and Jane visited Montgomery, where they heard Edwin Booth, famed Shakespearean actor, in Hamlet. *Benners felt that "his representation of the character was perfect and his elocution & expression marvelous." The next*

---

[122] Robert A. Divine, et al. *America Past and Present* (New York: Longman, 1999) 504.

month a terrible storm struck Greensboro. Soon thereafter there was a major fire in the city.

March 16. Thursday The most terrifying storm I ever heard broke over us last night about 11-1/2 oclock. I was waked by the thunder and perhaps that fact made it more impressive. The flashing of the lightning was incessant and thunder almost continuous. These were accompanied by a very violent wind—and at its height the hail came rattling down making altogether such a commotion of the elements as I never before experienced. I struck a light and went down stairs to the childrens room until it had subsided—the morning disclosed the face of the earth washed by torrents of rain—many fences and trees blown down. The wild cherry tree in the garden was blown across the fence breaking it very badly. Eds fences were badly blown—and his well [damaged]—at the Stickney place a large tree was blown across the house crushing it in and breaking thro the floor. A negro was killed at the Isaac Smith Place & 3 or 4 others in different places are reported. Dunlap died last night of Pneumonia having been sick only 2 days—he had attended the funeral of Wm T. Trice his nearest neighbor the day before he was taken sick—[123]

March 17. The weather after the storm was yesterday bright & cool, the same to day. I went to Eds yesterday evening—he was replacing his fences. Last night Liz & Miss Morgan came on the train from Newbern having gone there from Kornegays where they were on a visit. They attended the reading last night at Mr Cobbs. Webster is reported as having failed and the Bank of the State of New York suspended—Storms are evidently brewing in financial circles—many failures reported in London—

March 18. Yesterday was cool bright & windy Ther 42° to day bright gusty & quite cold. Ther 32 at 8. The financial outlook is very bad. The news of suspension of State Bk of N York and the many failures in London & N York may produce a panic. Congress occupied principally with Rascalities....

---

[123] William T. Trice, overseer, German Creek, Greensboro; A. J. Dunlap, warehouse clerk, German Creek, Greensboro. Snedecor, *Greene County*, 43, 16.

March 24. The houses on Main street known as Potters shop with mill house blacksmith shop and cotton press were destroyed by fire this morning about 4 oclock. I was waked by the bells and light which shined in my room and hurried to the spot. Fortunately there was very little wind and houses were damp from a slight drizzle. The houses were nearly burnt up when I got there and a big fire it was. Boardmans home was in great danger from falling fire as the drift was in that direction. Jeffries is said to have rented it yesterday & did not pay in consequence of Mr Stickneys not being at the store to receive the money draft as agt for John E Love who had not [illegible] before bought the property under a mortgage he held ag[ains]t Potter—a number of vehicles were burned, among them two new trotting sulkys of Dr Blackford.[124] The remarkable brightness of the fire was owing to so large a mass of wood. A noticeable feature of the occasion was the number of birds attracted by the light. They would circle around and round and some are said to have plunged into the fire—had the wind been high more terrible results would have followed—fortunately it set away from Mrs Brands house which tho nearer than any other escaped. This morning is very cloudy and wind from S.E. chilly & unpleasant....

In late May, the Conservative and Democratic parties met in Greensboro and nominated delegates to the state convention that was to meet the first week in June. Benners went as a delegate.

---

[124] William T. Blackford practiced medicine in Greensboro before the Civil War. When the war broke out, he served as a doctor with the 5th Alabama Regiment. In 1868 he was elected judge of the county probate as a Republican and served until 1 March 1871. He testified before a US congressional committee that he had been harassed by the Ku Klux Klan and resigned from his office. A. S. Jeffries, a grocer in Greensboro, testified that there was some violence in Greensboro but there was no organized Klan in Hale County. Jeffries helped buy Blackford's property for $5500, $1200 less than it was worth, so Blackford could leave Greensboro in 1871. United States, Luke P. Poland, and John Scott. 1872. *Report of the Joint Select Committee to inquire into the condition of affairs in the late insurrection states, so far as regards the execution of the laws, and safety of the lives and property of the citizens of the United States and Testimony taken.* Washington, D.C.: US Government Printing Office, 42nd Congress, 2nd session, H.R. doc. no. 22, pt. 9: Alabama, v. 2 [contained within serial set 1536] 1271–1302, 1491–1504. (In succeeding years, Blackford visited his family in Greensboro as Benners noted in his journal.)

June 5. On 30 of May I went to Montgy as a delegate from the Dem & Conservative party of Hale to State Convention at Montgomery. Jet Jones, Tramil, T L May, CC Huckabee and JHY Webb were the others. Conservatives nominated Houston for Governor.

Boyd for Sec of State
Crawford for treasurer
Brewer for Auditor
Boyd Sup of Education
Sanford for Atty General
Pugh
Morgan   Electors for State at large
L. R. Waller

C. C. Langdon
John T. Morgan   Delegates for State at Large
Shorter

1st Dist S. T. Prince of Choctaw   Alternate   G. B. Clark
2nd   J. T. Hollyclan, Montgomery   J. R. Hubbard, Pike
3rd   J. F. Waddel, Russell [1}   J. W. Foster, Henry
4th   J. Y. Kilpatrick, Wilcox   A. Benners, Hale
5th   W. H. Northing, Autauga   J. M. Richard, Charleston
       W. G. Little, Sumter   J. B. Sanford, Fayette
       S. H. McSpadden, Cherokee   M. H. Cruikshank, Tal[ladega]
       H. C. Juno, Lauderdale   Dan Coleman, Madison

...The meeting was large & harmonious. there were said to be over 500 delegates and all its proceedings were characterized by unusual freedom from ill feelings & rancour. I staid at the exchange. Met more old acquaintances—was one of the vice Presidents and was tendered the positions first of Delegate from 4th District to St Louis—then Elector[,] both of which I declined and was placed on the state Ex Committee which I also declined and had Mr PA Tutwiler put in my place. I left Montgy on friday morning June 2 and reached home same night....

June 6.... Blaine is thought to be damaged by his connection with Northern Pac R. R Boards and refusing to produce letter he wrote—and Gen Hancock on Democratic side is apparently gaining power at the South....[125]

June 15. Thursday. We had a shower on yesterday evening and it is raining again this morning. Had the field ploughed day before yesterday & Sol is setting out potatoes to day. Republican Convention to nominate a president met yesterday at Cincinnati. Pomeroy of NY chairman. great int is felt in proceedings. Blaine is supposed to be the strongest man. He had a sun stroke on sunday but is reported improving. The cloud under which he rests about Bonds & Stock falling dont seem to damage him with the party of great moral ideas a cent.

June 19. on the 16th I went to the depot to get election news—while I was there about 7 PM there was a very unusual appearance in the heavens from the west to the east leaving southerly towards the west there was a very sharply defined arc of a cloudy white color—and south of it and parallel at a distance of 20° degrees after a little while another exactly similar appeared. I was curious to know what they bode. there were clouds in the west beautifully fringed by the setting sun—and there were some clouds opposite—shortly after sunset there was a cloud seen rising in N.W. and about 9 oclock a very hard rainfall. It was partial or local—not extending to Mr Kornegays. Ed had his oats cut & they turned out he says very well he brought me a load. Mr Hatch came up on Saturday & returned after dinner. The news of nomination of Hayes of Ohio was rec'd here on friday night & of

---

[125] James G. Blaine, a congressman since 1862 and a speaker of the House of Representatives from 1869–1875. While Speaker, he purchased securities which sold for a price above their market value. Accused of impropriety, he protested innocence, but the damage to his reputation had been done. Winfield Hancock, a Union general in the Civil War and hero at the Battle of Gettysburg, was a popular politician in Pennsylvania in the post-war years.

Wheeler of N. York for vice the next day.[126] It is regarded as a very formidable ticket—because he is said not to be obnoxious to charges of corruption like the other strong names—He beat Blaine in the last ballot 7 votes—[B. H.] Bristow getting 213.[127] The anti Spencer wing were admitted in Convention. Mr Cobbs went to Marion Saturday and I had to read yesterday. I have been feeling a little unwell for a day or two. Pain in my head in the early morning—the mornings are quite cool—crops promising weather fine—...

Nine days later, the Republican Party met in Cincinnati to choose its platform and candidates for the November election. The Democratic Party met in St. Louis to choose its candidates. It was a great opportunity for the Democratic Party to recapture the presidency. Benners hoped they would nominate a ticket that could win.

June 26. Ther was 90° in the passage yesterday fine local shower after dinner the three last days have been very calm & hot. Ed came in and spent the day & night I went to church morning & evening—congregations very small by reason of the heat. Dem & Cons Convention meets to morrow in St Louis. Tilden is the most spoken of as probable nominee for Pres. If the 2/3rds rule is abolished he will be nominated—If it is retained I think he will not be but that Gen Hancock will—and perhaps Hendricks Vice Pres.

June 29. Thursday.... We get news from St Louis to day that Tilden is nominated on second Ballot....

June 30. We had a continuation of the very hot weather yesterday. Boys speaking at college at night. I was on the committee. The Supper for Miss May Avery was last night Jane Willie & Graham [went].

On my return from College last night it threatened a storm but blew off—without rain. Tilden was nominated on 2 Ballot vote. Tilden

---

[126] Rutherford B. Hayes, a three-time governor of Ohio, graduate of Harvard Law School, and supporter of hard money, was popular among reformers. William A. Wheeler was a congressman from New York.

[127] Benjamin H. Bristow of Kentucky, secretary of the treasury, pushed through investigation of the Whiskey Ring during Grant's administration. Randall and Donald, *Civil War and Reconstruction,* 657.

535 Hendrick 60 Allen 54 Parker 18 Hanco[c]k 59 Bayard 11 Thurman 2 Whole vote 738 necessary to a choice 535....

July 1.... Tilden & Hendrix [Hendricks] nomination is enthusiastically rec'd. Politics are ripe and speakings numerous....[128]

Several nonpolitical events captured Benners's attention in the next ten days. There had been an effort to include Northerners and Southerners in celebrating the 100th anniversary of the American union. A number of ideas submitted by Southerners were not accepted. This made Benners unhappy.

July 4. This is the centennial 4th of July and at the North extensive arrangements have been made for its celebration—Philadelphia goes crazy—we of the South can scarce repress our feelings of sadness that in the first Hundred years of our experiment the Yankees should have so clearly demonstrated that written constitutions are violated with sanctimonious hypocrisy—and nothing is too sacred to stand in the way of their lust of power and money. We had a good rain last evening—very local. Ed's place got it and I think the corn crop is safe—...

July 9.... We have accts of a very disastrous fight with the indians at Little [Big]Horn Creek in Black hills. Gen Custer & 2 brothers killed—with nearly the whole of the command engaged. Congress is calling for volunteers....[129]

The political season was now heating up. State elections in Alabama were held on August 7. Benners was on vacation at Blount Springs from mid-July until August 3, when he went home to vote, returning to Blount Springs on 7 August, and staying until 2 October.

---

[128] Samuel J. Tilden, governor of New York with impeccable reform credentials, led the attacks on the Tweed Ring. Thomas A. Hendricks, a senator and former governor of Indiana, was the vice presidential candidate.

[129] George Armstrong Custer was assigned to the 7th Cavalry as lieutenant colonel. He served in the Dakota Territory and commanded an expedition into the Black Hills. He attacked an Indian encampment on 25 June 1876, in what was called the Battle of Little Bighorn and died the same day.

August 4.... I am thinking of going home to vote. Dont value the vote so much as the manifestation of interest I feel in election....

August 7. Greensboro. This is the day for the State elections and I came home to vote. Left Blount Springs Friday evening at 7 oclock, got to Calera at 10 P.M. staid there till 6 AM reached Selma at 10 and home at 7. Went to church yesterday—came to town to day and voted Democratic ticket and want to leave in the morning for Blount.

[*newspaper clipping*]

THE PEOPLE'S TICKET.
For Governor,
GEORGE S. HOUSTON
For Secretary of State,
RUFUS K. BOYD.
For Attorney General,
JOHN W. A. SANFORD.
For State Treasurer,
DANIEL CRAWFORD.
For State Auditor,
WILLIS BREWER.
For Superintendent of Education,
LEROY F. BOX

HALE COUNTY
For State Senator—32d District,
THOMAS SEAY.
For Representatives in General Assembly,
JAMES M. HOBSON
JAMES M. JACK.

August 11. at Blount again. I left Greensboro Aug 8—and reached Blount Spgs on 9th at 12 1/2 AM.... Got dispatch from C. E. Waller that Hale had gone democratic by 738 majority....

August 13.... Houstons majority is over 40,000.

August 15.... I got a Beacon and [A]dvertiser at P. office saw Col Powel[l] & Dr. Sykes—all hands are in high gratification over the result of the election....

August 25. yesterday was the day for the Democratic Jollification at Blount Spgs and Excursion trains from North & south brought passengers. [John T.] Morgan, O'Neal & [James L.] Pugh spoke & at night they had a ball—we picnicked at the Spring and rode home in hack. Fanny Liz & Willie staid to the ball & got home 230.

The early appearance of worms, first in June and then in August and September, was very troubling. Benners was not worried until late August. This development combined with extreme heat meant considerable loss.

August 29.... The news from Selma about worms in cotton is bad. Ed reports them in his—and J. H. Y. Webb will not make over 25 Bales—in the mean time the co[un]try goes on and no stop to that....

September 3.... Ed writes that worms have eat up all the cotton in his neighborhood & probably at Walker Place. The news is very bad from South Ala about them. Ex Gov Lewis has declared for Tilden & Hendricks.[130] The govt are for sending troops to help the negroes to vote right.

September 12.... Crop news from home continues very gloomy—and fields are reported stript by worms....

Benners was enthusiastic about the coming election. He supported Tilden and on several occasions spoke in his behalf.

September 26.... There are riots near Hamburg S. C and much trouble from negroes. Election matters are getting exciting and it is thought if Indiana can be carried for Tilden then his election is sure. Frauds in colonizing negroes from Ky are much apprehended—and a determination to prevent is expressed....

---

[130] David Lewis explained his decision by saying that the Republican policy of Reconstruction had been a "disgraceful failure" and he saw no future for Republicans in Alabama.

October 10. To day the States of Ohio & Indiana elect Gov's & much interest is felt in the election and much excitement. one or both are necessary to Dem Success....

October 13. The dry dusty weather still continues—some clouds to day for the first time and we are all hoping for a rain to lay the dust. First news from Ohio Indiana & West Virginia was favorable to Dems in all three—various & conflicting news has come by wires—but the last opinion now is that Ohio has gone Radical. Indiana & West Va Democratic. Guns were fired at Selma last night and here by Democrats and the anxiety about results has been very intense....

October 16. Court commences to day. I went to Newbern on Saturday. and made a speech in fav Tilden & Hendricks. Colored folks seemed very reluctant to listen—a mulatto named Tom Walker spoke after me and Coleman after him. Went to Parkers to dinner and got home 6 1/2 oclock. the meeting was not large or enthusiastic some good may have been done....

October 21.... the Pres has issued his proclamation for So Carolina, and troops are ordered there.[131] Cotton is still low and Ed only got 9 7/16 for his bale sold yesterday to Mr Shackelford it was a very pretty sample.

October 29. There were a great many negroes in town on friday and yesterday—and they are being stirred up about politics as the Presidential election draws near. [James T.] Rapier negro is radical nominee. Jere Haralson negro is also running as a Radical. Gen [Charles M.] Shelley of Selma is the Democratic nominee. The negroes hereabouts are for Rapier, Dallas [county] for Haralson.[132] Gov Houston is to speak here Thursday....

---

[131] President Grant sent additional troops to trouble spots in the South—to South Carolina—and also placed several thousand deputy marshals and election supervisors on duty in the South. This show of force reduced violence at the polls.

[132] James Rapier, a free black before the war, was a cotton planter after the war. He served in Congress from 1873–1875. He supported the emigration of blacks to the West. Jeremiah Haralson, 1846–1916, former slave and minister of the gospel, served in the Alabama legislature in 1870 and US Congress as Republican in 1875–1877. Charles M. Shelley, 1833–1907, of Selma, Alabama, Confederate general, elected as Democrat to US Congress, served 1877 to January 1885.

November 7. The long looked for day has at length arrived for election of President of U States—and the hearts of all people are beating high with hopes of relief from Radical misgovernment by success of Tilden & Hendricks, their defeat will cast a deep gloom over the land and presage the worst evils we can imagine from bad men & bad government.

[newspaper clipping]

TILDEN AND HENDRICKS
REFORM TICKET
For Electors of President and Vice
President of the United States:
JOHN T. MORGAN
JAMES L. PUGH
JAMES T. HOLTZCLAW
JAMES F. WADDELL
JOHN Y. KILPATRICK
WILLIAM H. NORTHINGTON
WILLIAM G. LITTLE, JR
SAMUEL K. McSPADDEN
HENRY C. JONES
For Member of Congress.—Fourth District,
CHARLES M. SHELLEY.

November 8. the election passed off very quietly here. The US. Dep Marshall from Montgomery who took his seat on the railing over the polling place in the court house was asked out as he had no business there. The Rads have probably carried the counts by 150. News from abroad is very encouraging. New York is said to have given—as far as heard from—16000 gain over last election—in counties outside of City. Indiana is reported democratic Louisiana d[itt]o.[133]

---

[133] Early returns appeared to foretell a Democratic victory. Tilden carried New York, New Jersey, Connecticut, and Indiana. Victories were also expected on the West Coast and in the South.

Ed sold his cotton to day for 10 1/16 to Mr Shackelford.[134] He has sold 4 B/C and has about 200 lbs over which I agreed to buy—
November 10. We have rejoiced at Tildens reported success. Then came news that it was doubtful and then Hay[e]s was elected and now it is believed Florida has added 4 to Democratic line making 188, 185 being necessary. Louisiana is not reported—it is believed they will Doctor the returns to elect Hayes if possible the state of anxious suspense is indescribable. Abe brought a B/C & got 11 1/8 for it—no recpts from plantation yet—
November 13.... The election uncertainty still continues. Tilden has 184 votes certain—one more necessary to elect—Oregon S Carolina Louisiana & Florida are the chances they are all reported to have gone democratic—but are not conceded. Cotton is off 3/8. Jim Chiles brought up 2 Bales rent cotton for Alfred to day & Henry Chapman 2/B/C. sold to Stollenwerck for 9 7/8—classed poor.
November 18.... The public mind is much disturbed by the probability of fraudulent count in S. Carolina Florida and Louisiana—all of which are necessary to elect Hay[e]s.
November 20.... The agony of suspense as to Presidential election still continues—S Caro canvasses have been ordered by Sup Co of State to proceed to count ministerially—Five of each party being present at the count. Louisiana Board exclude everybody & claim judicial authority to purge the returns of frauds. Kellog[g] Packard & co are at their old tricks on a large scale. Great indignation is felt and expressed at their behavior....[135]

The election appeared to be over. Tilden had 184 electoral votes. Benners was elated, but then the tide began to change. Tilden was one vote away from final victory; Hayes still had a chance but he needed all twenty of the remaining electoral votes. Benners worried that fraud might decide the election. It was a time of great suspense.

---

[134] Robert Shackelford, merchant, Greensboro. Snedecor, *Greene County*, 28.
[135] The Louisiana Returning Board converted a Tilden victory of 7,500 votes into a Hayes majority of 4,500 votes. To Benners, it was dishonest and illegal.

[newspaper clipping pasted in journal]

Tilden, Hendricks & Reform
TICKET
For Electors of President and Vice-President
of the United States.
JOHN T. MORGAN,
Of Dallas county.
JAMES L. PUGH,
Of Barbour county.
SIDNEY T. PRINCE,
Of Choctaw county.
JAMES F. WADDELL,
Of Russell county.
JOHN Y. KILPATRICK,
Of Wilcox county.
WILLIAM H. NORTHINGTON,
Of Autauga county.
WILLIAM G. LITTLE, JR.,
Of Sumter county.
HENRY C. JONES,
Of Lauderdale county.
For Representative in Congress from the Fourth
Congressional District,
CHARLES M. SHELLEY.

[newspaper clipping pasted into Journal]

The election in Hale, so far as we are advised, passed off quietly. Here, there was not only no disturbance or disorder,—but, so far as we saw, not the slightest effort at intimidation, or to control, by any means, the vote of others. Every one, it seemed to us, voted as he pleased.

Though unable to give the official vote, the following figures will be found very nearly correct:

Aggregate vote,—4,568,—of which the Hayes and Wheeler ticket received 2,396,—for Tilden and Hendricks, 2,182,—showing a Republican majority of 224.

Congressional Vote.—For Rapier, 2,349; Haralson, 47; Shelley, 2,172. The different Precincts voted about as follows:

Precincts	Rapier	Haralson	Shelley
Greensboro	464	1	363
Hollow Square	268	0	270
Newbern	203	1	319
New Prospect	133	0	81
Macon	464	2	119
Cedarville	395	0	148
Warren's	31	0	113
Laneville	141	43	288
Five Mile	17	0	47
Havana	150	0	169
Carthage	42	0	134
Harrison	40	0	80
Phipps	1	0	41
Total	2349	47	2172

The Tilden and Hendricks vote, we learn, is the same as the vote of Gen. Shelley.

The impression prevails here as we now write—Thursday forenoon—that Gen. Shelley is elected. The contest is between him and Haralson,—with the chances believed to be in favor of the former.

The country was in an unprecedented situation. Congress was deadlocked over Grant's successor. Twenty electoral votes had yet to be counted. Each of the four remaining states—South Carolina, Florida, Louisiana, and Oregon—had contesting sets of delegates. Which delegates should be accepted? For the next few months, there would be no solution. Benners was very angry and believed that the *"country is much disturbed by the possibilities of Civil War."* The country was collectively holding its breath.

November 22.... The public affairs are in a very threatening attitude for the Peace of the Country—it is said all three Florida S. Ca & La have been counted for Hayes & Wheeler.

November 24.... News to day is revolutionary & alarming. S. Ca Board of Canvassers have disobeyed order of Supreme Co. To count votes from Edg[e]field & Laurens & in secret session have given the cert's of election to Republican electors & adjourned sine die. rumor is they have been arrested for contempt by the court....

November 27.... The State of the country is threatening. South Carolina Radical Board of Canvassers disregarded order of their Supreme Co to count Edg[e]field and Laurens and gave certificates to Radical Electors & officials and adjourned *sine die.* The Court it is said have put the board in jail. Grant has massed troops at Washington & a crisis seems impending—Louisiana & Florida have not yet finished counting—what the end will be no one can guess—...

November 28.... The court in S. Car has arrested canvassers & put them in Jail. No definite action in Florida & Louisiana. The Country holds its breath at the possibility of the future. Troops are gathering at Wash'ton. And the purposes of Pres Grant are as solemn and veiled as those of any usurper in history.

November 30.... So Ca State house occupied by Grants troops under Chamberlain.... Two Legislatures in S.C. Rads & Dems Civil War imminent. Peter brought up a B/C weighs 516 lbs. Went to church this morning—good sermon fr Mr Cobbs. After service ret to my office & here I am. Letter from Mag. Alfred has been sick but is better or well.

December 1. Friday.... There is yet no solution to Presidential difficulty—two houses have organised in So Ca. and one Senate. Soldiers have possession of State house....

December 5. Tuesday.... We have nothing as yet definite from Canvassing Boards in La & Fla. The country is much disturbed by possibilities of civil war—Florida may decide it. So Ca has two Rep's bodies in one Hall both act the senate. Ruger is in charge of soldiers seems disposed to hold off & is apparently expected to move us.

December 6. This is the day Electors cast their votes for President. It is not known how Louisiana & Florida have gone. S. Ca. was declared by board of canvassers carried for Hayes but it is claimed their actions were illegal as they were in contempt of court at the time. What will come no one knows many think Grant wants to make such a mess that he can hold over.[136] The weather continues freezing cold, this morning cloudy & prospect of a change. The Methodists are having Conference here in the court house.

The electoral votes had been cast but still there was no ending. Benners believed that Congress had to go behind the certification to examine the process.

December 7.... Florida & Louisiana have been given to Hayes by Boards of Canvassers. Much anxiety is felt and committees to come South and examine into the election have been appointed one by the senate and one by the House—Grants message is silent about Southern states.

December 8.... Grants message has been rec'd—he says nothing about Southern States or Boards of Canvassers—Talks about St Domingo, Naturalization & Education and any thing except the all absorbing subject.... Oregon is peculiar 2 votes are said to be for Tilden and one for Hayes. The 3 are necessary to elect Hayes giving him all claimed. To get the other Oregon Electors vote counted for Hayes—Congress must go behind certification which will let in examination of Louisiana Florida & South Carolina....

December 13.... The crisis in national affairs is still threatening—what is to come of it no one can tell—Committees are sent to Florida S Ca & Fla to report on elections and I believe to report on

---

[136] All the electoral votes were cast by the various states in Washington DC on 6 December 1876. The vote was 184 for Tilden, 165 for Hayes, and twenty electoral votes yet to be decided. There were disputes about which slate of candidates from four states—South Carolina, Florida, Louisiana, and Oregon—Democratic or Republican, would be accepted.

Oregon. The newspapers report Grant as very intemperate & reckless his impeachment is spoken of—

December 14. There is no relief to anxiety about Presidential election. Committees from Senate & House have come South to investigate and the feeling is intensifying. Oregon voted two for Hay[e]s and 1 for Tilden which with other states is said to make the required 185. The gov of Oregon considered the Post Master ineligible & gave certificate to next highest who was [a] Democrat.[137] Mr Lane took tea with us last night. Jane & children went to Arcola with Mr Hatch...

December 16.... The political situation is very threatening. Both sides are obstinate & Grant is said to be determined....

December 19. My wife came from Arcola yesterday to Dinner. Mary came with her—the weather is very cold Ther 18—am having grates placed in dining room & upstairs. The situation is politically unchanged. Ed is pleased with his horse and I have let Paul Moore [sharecropper] have the mule. He took him down to day.

December 20.... No light yet in Political matters—Marines ordered to Washington & troops from fort Sill—armistice to May is said to be agreed on in Turkey. Miss Jackson staid with Fanny last night. Killed hog on yesterday weighed 200.

December 22. Yesterday it drizzled & rained all day and last night was damp and cloudy tho not very cold. There have been violent storms at the north and very cold weather. Ice formed in NY 3 Inches. There was no mail to day—Route agent not being on hand to receive the mail. There is no change in the political situation. Chamberlain has threatened to prosecute Hampton for treason. Violence is feared. Foreign affairs less belligerent—...

December 25. This christmas is a very gloomy one. The weather is damp & drizzly not very cold. the streets are very muddy. Political affairs threatening and outlook not good—war in Europe likely. Pauperism at

---

[137] John Watts, postmaster of Lafayette, Oregon, was ineligible to be an elector. He resigned as postmaster but was not allowed to be a Republican elector. Democrats tried to have E. A. Cronin take his place but Republicans accepted Watts's resignation as an elector and then appointed him as the third elector. Keith Ian Polakoff, *The Politics of Inertia, The Election of 1876 and the End of Reconstruction* (Baton Rouge LA: Louisiana State University Press, 1973) 227–28.

the north increasing 50000 men are reported to be without employment in N.Y. Wade Hampton is trying to be Gov of So Carolina. Chamberlain is backed by Grant.[138] Florida Louisiana & So Caro are being investigated by Coms of Congress—and amidst it all I have drawn 1 yr near to the close of my mortal career. Graham & Jenny got their stockings this morning. Ed stayed with us. Liz gave me a cup. Ed some hdkfs [handkerchiefs].

December 28. The sun shone a little while yesterday except this. We have had a drizzly cloudy sloppy rainy time since christmas. The weather is not very cold but is unpleasant. There is no change in the political situation....

December 29.... Florida Rads on Canvassing board have refused to comply with order of Sup Co & recanvass the vote. Gen Cocke Atty Genl alone complies—Louisiana State house barricaded by Rads....

1877

In the first weeks of 1877, there was no change in the political situation. Benners hoped that "honest Republicans" would aid Tilden since it was obvious that he had won both the popular and electoral votes. Still, both parties were preparing for the inaugural ball. There was no end in sight.

January 2, 1877.... S Caro has been decided by Cong committees to have voted for Hayes. [George Franklin] Drew,[139] Dem Gov of Florida is conceded to be elected. Presidential question still undecided—Louisiana is unsolved—Kellog[g] has had troops around State house and makes a show of fight. It is said Blaine as well as Congling [Conkling] will not

---

[138] The contest for governor of South Carolina was fought between D. H. Chamberlain, incumbent Republican governor, and Wade Hampton, Democrat, a former Confederate general. The legislature, controlled by Radical Republicans, declared that Chamberlain was elected despite the action of the board of canvassers, which certified the election of Hampton. Hampton refused to concede the election to Chamberlain, which produced a dangerous situation. Randall and Donald, *Civil War and Reconstruction,* 690.

[139] George Franklin Drew served as governor from 1877–1881.

support Hayes inauguration if count is not fair. Terrible snow storms are reported all over the Country & Fires are frequent....

January 6.... No change in the Political situation. The impression is that honest Republicans will aid Tilden.

January 11.... In New Orleans Democrats have driven out radical Supreme Court and put theirs in and taken possession of all the police stations. Matters are very threatening. No change in the Presidential look out—both parties are making arrangements for inauguration ball—

January 12. The weather after a very cold spell was yesterday moderate Ther 56° to day mild & cloudy—no change in political situation. Grant wont recognize in & or either side if he can help it till com[ittee]s report. Rads have State House, Dems balance.

January 13. Rain last night. Moderate & cloudy this morning—Central City Ins Co dec 10 pr ct—$280 [or $2.80] rec'd dft this AM. Mr Watson and I played Bezique last night.

January 16. yesterday was a mild drizzly day and to day is no better. Mrs Coleman died this morning—the Judge is overwhelmed with grief—and how deeply do I sympathize with him. A negro was killed on Col Jones place by Gus Oliver who is said to have fled. We went to church yesterday except Fanny. The situation is unchanged politically and reported threatening.

January 17. I went to Mrs Colemans burial yesterday—the Methodist church was full. Dr Lewis & Br Smith made addresses. a very large concourse went to grave yard. It rained again early this AM. and is now raining 11-1/2 AM the roads are getting very bad. Maggie C. Steamboat sunk in Tombigby river. Mr Watson & daughter are having a spell of very bad weather for their visit.

January 19. Yesterday was a cloudy foggy drizzly day—and this morning is the same—the long protracted cloudy rainy weather following the snow has made the earth in the roads very spongy & soft—and wagon & vehicles produce slush & bad roads. We play Bezique of an evening and night visiting for the few past day[s] has been impracticable. Young ladies & Ed are invited to night to Mrs Avery's party. Eastern affairs are as incomprehensible & threatening as ever and it looks to day as if war was inevitable—... Situation unchanged at New

Orleans. Committees of Congress at Washington have agreed on a Method of counting Electoral vote but it does not yet appear what the plan is. It is said to have been adopted unanimously except Morton & one Democrat.[140]

January 20. I rec'd telegram last night to appear before the Senate Committee on privileges & elections and am preparing to leave on train Monday. I regret the call but must go. Weather drizzly & warm roads very bad—the two houses in Washington have agreed on mode of deciding disputed electoral votes—

Washington Imperial Hotel No 69.

Friday morning Jan 26 at my room

I left home on monday morning Jan 22 laid over in Selma till 5-1/2 took SR&D road at 5-1/2 PM reached dalton had a good sleep on the sleeper reached Dalton at 10-1/2. I was on the road…and had to lay over at Lynchburg missing connection—left Lynchburg 4-1/2 P.M. reached washington 12-1/2 AM. Took omnibus to Imperial Hotel, got room 69 and slept very soundly till morning.

February 2. Washington DC. On tuesday I dined at Dr Beales and on wednesday he called in his Buggy & gave me a ride to Georgetown where I called on the Marbury's. Mrs M is a fine looking lady and very polite. Dr A. M. is an old batchelor [sic] and a very wise specimen of an old school gentleman. The views about Georgetown are lovely here we see many fine trees of Forest Growth—all of them about Washington have been cut down. From here we see the Arlington Estate of Gen Lee's family it is a burial ground for federal soldiers and is taken by the Govt. I afterwards visited the Agricultural Department the Corcoran Gallery and Smithsonian Institute and went on the top of the Capital this view is by far the finest I ever saw. The pictures on the dome are seen to great advantage from here. On Thursday Feby 1 I witnessed in the Hall of the house the opening & counting of Electoral votes for Tilden & Hendricks & Hayes & Wheeler. The certificates were opened

---

[140] The Electoral Commission law established a body of fifteen members—five senators, five representatives, and five Supreme Court justices. They were to determine which electors were to be counted. An excellent description of the politics of the Electoral Comission can be found in Polakoff, *The Politics of Inertia*, 269–313.

by Mr [Thomas White] Ferry of Michigan Pres of Senate & read by the teller and on being read the President of the senate asks if there is any objection to the vote as read being counted—when no objection was made the vote was counted & recorded—when the state of Florida was reached the President of S[enate]. handed a certificate from there certified by Gov [Marcellus Lovejoy] Stearns giving the 4 votes to Hayes & Wheeler—he then opened and handed another certified by atty Genl of Florida giving votes to Tilden. He then opened and handed another certified by Drew the new Democratic Governor giving vote to Tilden. The counting of the Dem returns being objected to by Reps and of Rep ret[urns] by Democrats—the papers were all referred to the High commission of 15 to be passed upon by them—after which the counting was suspended until they report when it will be resumed. This A.M. I visited Treas Dep and White House and think I will go up there this afternoon to Mrs Grants reception.

February 7. Washington. I attended the session of the Commission on Electoral vote.... I dont think their efforts were extraordinary. The room was very crowded and that was the last time I was able to get in.... I spent a part of the morning in the Senate and [H]ouse and then went with Judge Wood to Navy yard. visited the Man of War Wyoming....—then went with him to Georgetown and visited the Cemetery—...

February 8. Thursday—accidentally found that the com were carrying on examination yesterday morning in com room of Naval affairs—on going there found them examining George Harris[141]—he testified that he had been ostracised—that he had been hit. That he had been serenaded with tin horns, that he had been offered to have his bond made & money besides in 1874 if he would let a democrat have the boxes on the night before counting out. I crossed him lightly—did not know of any intimidation did not leave his associates & keep bad company when he turned radical—his acquaintances quit him—said greater efforts were made to carry the Aug & Nov elections in 1876 than ever before—did not know many democratic negroes were only 7 or 8 white rads in the

---

[141] George W. Harris, planter, Union. Snedecor, *Greene County*, 20. He was sheriff in 1876.

county—did not think the change of the white leaders carried many col[ored] voters.

[William E.] Cockrel[l] was then examined—he swore to intimidation generally. 1 white man with a revolver could stampede 500 nigs—was very full on intimidation—and on not getting leave of absence—[142]

Marshal[l] Thornton was examined next.[143] he testified that on counting votes the Three inspectors were present and would turn the ticket partly over and call out Democratic ticket & the other inspector would put it in another box and so he would call republican tickets same way—they were afterwards counted according to the score kept—said Capt Young in counting came to a [Joe] Haralson ticket & threw it down saying—here is one Haralson ticket (with an oath) and it was passed to box as others—

Crossed said he knew of no intimidation at any time—except by negroes who were thought very badly of if they voted the Democratic ticket. Women thought hard of men in the same way.[144]

February 11. yesterday was a cold bright day. The Com met at room of naval affairs Judge Wood of Opelika was examined. Com then adjourned to attend the joint sitting of the two houses to report the decisions of Comp Com on Electoral vote as to Florida.[145] It was read

---

[142] William E. Cockrell was a twenty-three-year-old Republican member of the lower house of the Alabama legislature elected in 1874 and 1876 from Eutaw, Greene County. He testified that hundreds of black voters were not allowed to vote, that it had been difficult to open the polls, and that he was an election officer in 1876. *Report of Committee of the Senate of the United States for Second Session of the Forty-fourth Congress, 1876–1877* (Washington, DC: US Government Printing Office, 1877) 203–23.

[143] Marshall Thornton was a tenant farmer on Benners's land. He was active in politics and attended a Republican convention in Montgomery in May 1876 along with George Harris and others. Thornton maintained that Republicans had great difficulty registering and voting in the election of 1876., Ibid., 257–59.

[144] Benners testified that Thornton's testimony was "absolutely and utterly false." Ibid., 281.

[145] The first preliminary vote of the commission was announced on 6 February. It concerned accepting F. C. Humphreys as a Florida elector. The vote was eight to seven with Republicans prevailing. Judge Bradley voted with fellow Republicans on all of the votes on Louisiana, South Carolina, Florida, and Oregon. Polakoff, *The Politics of Inertia*, 287.

deciding that the Hayes' Electors were entitled to be counted—as they could not go behind the returns. Objections to counting them were interposed by [David Dudley] Field of N York [Dem.] signed by 5 members of the House and 5 of Senate. The Houses then separated to deliberate separately—and the house after discussion as to whether they could rightly take recess on the point of order—The chair decided that the motion for recess was in order and an appeal from decision was taken & ruling of the chair sustained—Great anxiety is felt and excitement of a smothered kind intense. It is considered that the decision of the tribunal is purely a partisan one—and that all the other rulings will be of the same character and that Hayes will come in. To morrow will be 3 weeks since I left home and I dont yet know when I shall get off. I want to leave to morrow.

This morning I went to St Pauls Church. Ritualistic & heard a sermon on Charity. Surpliced quires,[146] candles on the altar & more Carvings than I have usually seen was among noticeable things. Music good and a great deal of it.

February 13 tuesday. I was examined to day before sub Com of Senate on Elections in Ala. The questions put were many of a general character as to the votes in 75 & two elections in 1876—and the reasons of the democratic success in those elections. I was also questioned as to the fairness of each & if there was any intimidation—also about the ostracism of white republicans. My answer was in effect that when a man came out of the Dem Party and joined the Republicans he was not cultivated by his old acquaintances much—and I believed the same thing was true in churches. When members left & joined other bodies, I knew of no intimidation but the relations were not as cordial as before. I was questioned about the Newbern box where Stroback had testified he thought 400 votes had been given and a much smaller No. counted. I stated Mr Lanzen by telegram had stated that Harris's statement about bribery was absolutely false—and he would come in if they wanted him—I have had delay on getting my pass and have only a certificate for

---

[146] Quire, var. of choir.

pas[sage] which is not cash. am trying to get ready to leave in the morning—by midland route at 10 A M.

February 22 Greensboro. I left Washington at 2.10 AM on Wednesday Feby 14 by Midland route by way of Danville Charlotte & Atlanta reaching Montgy Thursday night 5-1/2 P.M. The Supreme Court was in Session & I went there on friday morning, finding my case of Tindel vs Drake would not be reached before tuesday I left Montgy at 1 oclock on friday and reached home that night at 7-1/2 found all well & enjoyed my return very much. I again left on tuesday morning at 4-1/2 and reached Montgomery at 11. Put up at Dr Rambos and went straight way to Supreme Co Mr J. E. Webb was arguing his side on my arrival. Mr Seay followed him and I followed Mr Seay and next morning Mr Webb closed. We thought we had the last of the argument. I left at 1 and reached home on last night.

February 27. Yesterday was cool & cloudy wind north. Mrs Baird, Mr W[atson] and the girls visited Mrs Randolph. Mr W spent the evening at Mr J.H.Y Webbs and the young ladies spent the evening & night at Mrs Averys.

Political matters are not yet quieted. Oregon by reports of returning Board has been counted for Hayes. Pennsylvania next has been objected to on ground of ineligibility of an elector. What will be done further is not known—

March 2. Yesterday the first day of spring was cool & rainy. I remained at home after dinner & Mr W & I amused ourselves with Bezique. Last night the young ladies & my wife & Mr Watson went to Mr NB Jones. My cold was my excuse for not going. South Carolina has been counted for Hayes & it now seems pretty certain he will be inaugurated. The excitement about it has lulled and his promises to conciliate the South will prevent further opposition from that quarter.

March 3. Yesterday was a bright pleasantly cool day. Mr Watson & Miss Ella went to his plantation in a buggy & returned at 6 oclock PM Last night Miss Mary Cocke took tea with us and after went to the college to Clar[iosophic] exhibition. Mr Watson & I played Bezique and retired about 12. Band serenaded Miss Ella. This morning Mr W &

daughter left for Selma—he comes back to his plant'n to night to remain a week or two she remaining in Selma.

The news came by wire at noon yesterday that the count was finished and Hayes declared elected at 4 AM The action of the Electoral Commission is severely criticized—especially the judges. The vote in the commission was a party one from first to last & was disgraceful to them & the Country.[147]

March 5. The weather yesterday was bright & mild. Ed & I in the evening walked up to Smaws & the Greene yard. The Japonicas are in bloom and where not injured by cold look very pretty. Last night was first meal at my house in two months at which we have not had company to sit down with us. Mr Jones came to see Liz last night. Mr Hatch came up on 3rd and ret same evening—reports Tom Daves Better—He is evidently failing in mind & body. I paid him the balance of his money after paying his taxes—affairs are very gloomy with me. My children are not doing or likely to do any thing. I have no aid in getting along—what will become of us God knows. Hayes has been declared Pres and was to have taken the oath of office yesterday.

March 6. Yesterday was cool & rainy last night cleared off cold & whiter frost to day clear & cold. Letter from EB Haywood requesting me to go to see Wash. Hayes was to swear Sunday every body is gloomy—hands are teasing nothing is promising well—am on the eve of some great trouble. George Jones came to get meat. Eating only business fully carried on and with great punctuality.

March 7. Yesterday was a cool bright day. Night bright and lovely—to day as fine as possible Ther 60° Hayes took the oath Saturday March 3rd and delivered his inaugural on Monday from North Portico of Capitol. His speech is a very poor affair—a bone is flung all around—to the North a commendation of their glorious achievement turning loose the nigger—to the South promise of impartiality in his favors—to the nig universal Education and to all hands a hope of office because offices are not to be rewards to partisans. Poor Hayes—if he had any of the sensibilities of a man of Honor how terrible would be his fix.

---

[147] Augustus Benners was a bitter man. He believed that Tilden deserved the presidency and was the victim of an unjust process.

But it is would be a violent presumption to suppose that any qualms of conscience could afflict or disturb a man who could so readily accept what was stolen from another—Poor Hayes his little day will be flaunted out in stolen finery and if not forgotten he will be censured by posterity for his crime.

March 8. Yesterday was very bright & spring like. Clouded up last night & rained very hard this morning and is still threatening. Ed came in last night & returned after Breakfast. We heard by Telegram that Mr Hayes had appointed

Wm M Evarts	NY	Sec of State
John Sherman	Ohio	" Treasury
McRary	Iowa	" War
Thompson	Ind	" Navy
Carl Schurz	Md	" Interior
D M Key	Tenn	PM General
Gen Chas Devins	Mass	Atty Gen

No action as far as heard from as to Nichols & Hampton. Blaine threw down the gauntlet in Senate that Hayes could not recognise Nichols—cause why—same folks made him President—[Lucius Quintus Cincinnatus] Lamar of Miss was seated—[George E.] Spencer objected to him & [John Tyler] Morgan—which last was not seated at last accts.

March 9. After the hard rain yesterday during which there was thunder & lightning the wind rose after supper & blew very hard—turning much colder. this morning it is bright & cold. Some of the early blooms are doub[t]less killed by the cold. Mr Lamar has been seated in Senate and Blaine has thrown down the gauntlet to Hayes & Co on the SC & La questions—do it if you dare—acknowledge [Francis T.] Nichol[l]s or {Wade] Hampton and you declare yourself a usurper. Hayes seems to have a hard road to travel. Morgan not yet seated.

March 10. Ther this morning 30° & Ice plenty—it is feared much of the fruit is killed. Weather to day beautiful and cold. Gen Morgan was sworn in to Senate on Thursday—Spencer not being present and only one Quigley[148] voting No—So the great Ala investigation proved a failure. I bot from Kornegay Lard & hams @ 15 cts to day. There is no local matter of int[erest].

March 13. Yesterday was a beautiful mild bright day—attended church in the morning—and funeral of Mr Seldens child in afternoon. Ed came in and spent the day & night with us. It clouded up last night and is raining this morning—having recd letter from Dr EBH[aywood] of Raleigh asking me to visit his brother Wash. I sent for him to come and see me. Bob came in with note that he was too unwell to come unless very necessary—replied it was not—raining to day & I cant go—

March 14. Yesterday was a very rainy day. Morning & evening quite mild. The President had interview with Judge Wright,[149] Cardozo [?] & others of Rad party—and promised to maintain Status quo which Gen Grant left—considered in some measure a compromise Inaugural promise. The cabinet are all of them confirmed on reports of Committees—no minority reports—

March 15—Yesterday was a chilly damp day—last night it turned off cold to day bright & cool. The Peach trees still look as if some blooms survived. Tho how they did it no one can see. No change in Washington matters. A new election in LA & So Ca is talked of. Jim Chiles & Wash Grant came up to plough to day at 11.10. I want my field broke up and planted in cotton.

March 17. Yesterday was a mild bright day—It clouded up last night and before day we had thunder lightning wind & rain. To day cold damp & cloudy, it is feared the fruit left will be killed to night. Wash & Jim ploughed up the field and got through last evening. Wash was sick & he & Jim stayed over till to day.... No settlement yet of La & So Ca. [George M.] Duskin is nominated for Dist Aty for Southern Ala—...

March 20. yesterday bright & mild—had a slight neuralgic headache all day. My wife complained of the same—to day the weather is mild & growing but has clouded up this evening. Hayes has made the nigger

---

[148] Quigley—Benners means "Radical"—the origin of "Quigley" is not known.

[149] George Grover Wright of Iowa, justice, state supreme court 1854–1870, Republican senator, 1871–1877. *American Congress*, 2047.

[Frederick] Douglas[s] Marshal of D.C.[150] Morgan sustained the nomination as did [John Brown] Gordon....

March 23. Continued fine weather. Ther this morning 46°. Stollenwerck failure is much talked of. To day it is reported that Capt Wemyss had $5000 with them and that they owe savings Bk Selma $35,000 both of which may be untrue. There are many unfounded rumors & these may be of that sort. Hayes sends a commission to La to examine & report—very poor performance on very fine promises. Gen Morgan sent me a copy of Report by Cameron Chmn of Wisconsin of the sub committee of Privileges & elections who investigated Alabama.

March 24.... It is now reported that Mr Wemyss had $4000 with Stollenwercks—and the break is a very bad one....

March 25. It rained Saturday night a little, and yesterday was a cold cloudy day. Mr W. dined at JE Webb on yesterday. Willie got his arm out of joint at the elbow, fell down wrestling with Inge. Dr Peterson was sent for & pulled it to its place. He Willie reports it better to day. Mr W & I are invited to A[llen] C. Jones to tea to night. There is a little ice. Ice in exposed places this morning. if the fruit escapes it must be tough. Richard Davis died on Saturday 24 was buried on 25 by Masons[151]—he left his property to Henry Smith for life & then to two illegitimate colored children & if they died without issue to the Lodge at Greensboro.

March 27. The chilly cloudy weather of sunday was succeeded yesterday by a fine bright day. Afternoon W & I walked to Smaws at night. Went to A. C. Jones to tea—got home about 12 and this morning he left for Plantation. Willies arm is reported better. My wife is comp[lainin]g of sore eyes, and I am looking for an instalment of company as soon as they leave. I have expected to commence ploughing at home to day. George & Nick came up this A.M. Kit has got up 3 panels of the fence by Tunstals.

---

[150] Frederick Douglass was appointed US Marshal, District of Columbia, by President Hayes and served from 1877–1881. His nomination was supported by John Tyler Morgan, senator from Alabama, and John Brown Gordon, senator from Georgia.

[151] Richard Davis, broker, Greensboro. Snedecor, *Greene County*, 14.

March 28. We are having a few bright spring like days—the mild hazy pleasant days suggestive of summer and fishing—yesterday George and Nick planted cotton in the field—on monday Fanny gave us Lettuce and radishes from her garden. An unusual dulness pervades the town. Politics are become nauseating. Hayes sends for Hampton. Commission is to go to Louisiana. It is said Hayes has ignored Nichols Supreme Co in La.[152]

March 30. This is good friday—and a very pleasant bright day only a little cool—yesterday was bright & beautiful as was also the day before in the afternoon of the 28. I walked to Eds with Graham and he fished a little in Caldwell on way home. Ed came in and spent night with us & went home this morning. George Jones and Nick came up on 27 and planted cotton for me in field on 27 & 28 March and went down on 29. The dreaded full moon in Easter has not been accompanied with frost this year—and we hope the earth will be warm enough by next full moon to prevent a frost. Messrs Jeffries, Castleman and Jeffries are inspecting accts CL & RH Stickney $11000 more cash has been paid out than is entered as received....

April 3. Mr Watson came up on Easter sunday went to church with us in the morning & at the festival and left for Selma via Plantation on yesterday after dinner. The weather was very threatening on sunday—in the evening there was a shower of rain about 5 & having slacked up many persons ventured to go to festival. We had barely reached home after it was over before the rain commenced again and we had a nice rain—yesterday was a nice day & to day cloudy—the receipts from the collection sunday morning were $50, and at night $200. the sunday school applied $72 to church debt and balance to a window. Letter from Pittman promising to make the payt $700 in all this year no bill due.

April 4. The weather yesterday was mild & cloudy and drizzle towards night—last night light rain, and drizzly rain this morning. The

---

[152] President Hayes decided to end Reconstruction by recognizing two Democrats—Wade Hampton as governor of South Carolina and Francis Nicholls as governor of Louisiana. The federal government lost interest in continuing the policies of Reconstruction. Soon Hayes would remove Federal troops from these two states. Foner, *Reconstruction*, 581–82.

La Commission is to sit to day. Hampton is to be Gov. by troops being withdrawn from State house. It is said a quo warranto has been issued to Hayes fav of Tilden as to his right to hold the office of President of the U States.

April 5. Fine spring weather yesterday. Liz went to Ball at Cowins last night. Louis Brought mule to Ed yesterday evening—he came in & spent night. The gardens are improving very much. Peas long as a finger—order has been issued for removal of troops from State House S. C. Commission has gone to Louisiana—I expect trouble to grow out of it. Nichols will not compromise & Hayes cant recognise Nichols—[153]

April 6. The fine mild weather continues. Yesterday I planted a few choice melon seed in the orchard field. Corn is coming up in the garden, and is reported doing well in the Canebrake. Vegetation has been backward but is now hurrying forward very rapidly. Willies sow having lost one of her pigs has now 8 little fellows that seem to be doing well. Last night the clothes ordered for self and Willie arrived by Express. I have had neuralgic headache at night & bad taste in my mouth in the evening. Watson leaves Selma next monday for Ten[nessee] on his way home.

April 7. I[t] commenced raining last night and the ground is quite wet this morning—and clouds are still heavy & threatening. Mr Haywood called this morning. The order for withdrawal of troops from State House at Columbia has been published—to be executed next tuesday. Jim came up to day for meat. The day is dull & compromising.

April 9. Monday. I went home saturday in good time to escape the rain which came down very heavy in the afternoon and continued with little intermission till 12 oclock. The train was delayed and mail did not get here till Sunday 10 AM. It was quite cloudy yesterday P.M. & I did not go to church. Beautiful rainbow yesterday evening and stars were

---

[153] Benners did not know that President Hayes had agreed to recognize the Democratic claimants to office in Louisiana, Florida, and South Carolina in order to become president. Thus Hayes recognized Francis T. Nicholls, a conservative, one-armed former Confederate, as governor of Louisiana. US military troops were removed from New Orleans and Reconstruction was over. Joe Gray Taylor, *Louisiana Reconstructed, 1863–1877* (Baton Rouge: Louisiana State University Press, 1974) 499.

shining last night—this AM clouds again look heavy & threatening. Latimers wagon was carried down Caldwell creek and Ed Pasteur got in the creek where he tried to cross going home. Roads are reported to be washed up. Train started out on new schedule at 6 A.M. this day.

April 10. It was cool & cloudy yesterday with very low barometer. the negroes had their emancipation celebration yesterday. There were a great many in town, the cool & threatening weather was not favorable. no Advertiser last night. road at Benton washed up. Sel R&D & SM&M are the only ones not failing.

April 11. Train now arrives at 5.25 PM leaves same time A.M. The news of high water continues to reach us. Capt Robertson was drowned in French creek on Monday—(I believe) It was cool & cloudy yesterday & cool & brighter to day. Eastern question still unsettled Protocol presented to the Porte—who is thought will give evasive answer. Troops were to have been removed on yesterday from Columbia.

April 12. Yesterday was pleasant & bright last night there was a drizzle this morning cool & cloudy. The troops were removed from State House Columbia S. C. yesterday at 12 M & Chamberlain agreed to turn over everything.[154] La still unsettled. Com is there but make no progress. Tried to settle Stickney matter—try again to day. Jane is quite unwell as this time last year & called in Peterson.

April 13. Friday.... Settled award between Stickneys yesterday. RHS pd 100 a year for 5 years as a reduction of salary with int and 2/3 of rent of shop for self & Waddel for 1 y 7 m 20 d. CLS pd note for int in Tanyard purchase with 100 day 6 int $1840.40 cts—handed money & statement to RHS yesterday evening ($1099 2 ac[c]ts) in presence of Wooten. Their affair reflects very little credit—and to reduce salary paid for 5 years is queer to say the least of it. Southern Hotel in St. Louis burned & many lives lost....

April 15. Yesterday was bright & sunny & very acceptable to farmers—the night was cool but no frost. Mr Parker Hatch came up and

---

[154] President Hayes issued orders for the removal of troops on 3 April. The troops were to be removed on 10 April. Governor Chamberlain turned over his office to Wade Hampton at noon on 11 April.

leaves after dinner to day. La commission have as yet done nothing Nichols wont trade worth a cent—

April 16. Court begins to day if Judge is here. Yesterday was a beautiful day—and this morning promising. Ed spent the day & night. Jenny came up with me and got a calico dress for a birthday present being 11 yrs old yesterday. Sadness predominates—outlook cheerless—my children give me great anxiety—if I could see qualities developing I could take hope. Nichols La question still unsettled....

April 20. Friday—The weather yesterday was fair. wind high—court took up crim. doc. in the afternoon. Ed is filling out his week as juror. Mr R. B. Waller died to day at 10 oclock will be buried on Sunday at 11 oclock[155]—Having had a stroke of Paralysis several years ago & been an invalid ever since his death might have been expected at any time—But it is sad to lose ones old friends when the number left is so small—he was a man of excellent traits. More uniform equanimity no man ever displayed—and it may be truly said we have lost a good man—

April 23. The funeral of Col Robt B Waller took place yesterday. The corpse was taken to the church which was densely crowded the funeral procession was the largest I have ever seen here. the church services being finished, Masonic ceremonies were had. The Bar on Saturday passed resolutions of respect & also did the vestry of the church. Oh how sad to lose a friend so much beloved & respected—so long and intimately known & loved....

April 25. Yesterday the weather was warm and streets dusty. Last night there was a dance at Mr Cowins and Fanny & Liz went—The troops by order of the President were to have been removed from the State House (so called) at N Orleans & Nichols Legislature will have a governor.[156] The Eastern War is imminent and Russia is expected to publish a declaration of War on 29.[157] Grain & provisions have advanced and cotton drags but a slight advance in Liverpool is reported 6-1/4 pence.

---

[155] Waller was one of Benners's lawyer friends.
[156] On 24 April, in accordance with the order of the secretary of war, the military troops withdrew from New Orleans to barracks in the vicinity.
[157] Russia declared war on Turkey on 26 April 1877.

April 26. the troops were removed from N.O. on tuesday 24 ap. Judge Spofford was elected US Senator. The Czar has declared war and given orders for army to cross the frontier. Cotton is down to 6 pence. Yesterday was a fine day warm & cloudy last night a nice shower which was very acceptable to lay the dust. Recd invitation from Moore to stay with him at Convention.

April 27. The day yesterday was very threatening with a good shower about 3. oclock. at 4 the procession started from Pres[byterian] church to decorate the graves of Confederates. It sprinkled on the way & then a beautiful rainbow spanned the eastern sky and it rained no more. WC Garrett delivered a handsome speech—flowers were strewn and company dispersed....

Chapter 4

The Later Years, 1878–1885

1878

Benners's greatest concern in the early months of 1878 was the depressed price of cotton and the war in Europe. Each day, he watched the progress of war between Turkey and Russia, which he referred to as the "eastern question." His greater concern was the possibility that Great Britain might be involved, which would have serious consequences for the cotton market. He also worried about providing for his family because so much of his wealth was tied up in cotton.

January 1. The new year opens with a bright cool morning Ther 34° before breakfast. Mr W & I took tea last night at Mr Snedecors—and got back about 10 PM. The frost this AM is very white and air bracing. European news is discouraging for continuance of Peace. England has been getting ready for war and it seems imminent. rented Pool Place to Frank Moore (colored) for 80 dols saving the little house on the road and the garden which I rented to Hannah Garner for $2 per mo....

January 3. Yesterday was lovely. Bright sunshine and pleasant temperature. We took tea Mr W[atson] & I at Mr Cobbs. Mr W started for the train this morning but reached depot too late. The eastern question is still threatening and chances are England will go to war. France is comparatively quiet. Cotton 10 1/2 LM....

January 12. Yesterday the sky was clear and weather moderate & pleasant—a large ring around the moon last night gave token of a change and this AM it was cloudy & wind from SE & cool and disagreeable. Foreign news is still unsatisfactory tho there is a probability of an armistice. England is in a very feverish condition and her politicians are much divided on the war question. The queen and Beaconsfield are said to favor a war. The Nation seems to desire peace....

January 22.... Another fire in Mobile my co's lost about $3500. It seems to be an unlucky streak just now. Bankruptcy & ruin everywhere. Kit is no better. Ed is at Home. Willie is going to college. Children—Draughts on me increase as means diminish—& who cares?

January 28.... I felt very sad all day and cannot shake it off. I know not what to do. I called to see Watson in the evening at Mc[C]Rary's. he is under the weather a little, unwell. I have made no conclude for Ed or Willie—Oh Lord. The news from the Eastern question presages a close of the war. But it is not settled whether England will be implicated. The queens Government has asked 6,000,000 pounds to prepare for war and there is great excitement. Cotton is very Low say 10 LM Dull.

January 29. Fine weather yesterday & bright night. Venus was so bright she cast a shadow about 7 1/2 oclock.... The crisis is about reached in Eastern affairs and we were looking for Peace or War & up or down in cotton. I slept very badly last night. Ed is working in the field. Willie is at the college. Watt called for Fanny to go to theatre and Willie & Liz went. There are more than common of these strolling fellows....

For some time, his favorite servant, Kit Jones, had been sick, but he usually recovered. Then, on 4 February, he died. It was a tragic loss for Benners.

February 4. Kit Jones col[ored] died on yesterday PM at 5 oclock—he suffered a great deal & thought his time was come. I feel very deeply for the loss of my trusted humble old servant & friend. He was to me obedient and useful, and his place cannot be supplied. Poor old Kit, together we have been fighting lifes battle for over 20 years, and he has gone ahead of me. May he rest in Peace and may the change to him be great gain. The Doctor pronounced his disease heart disease—he appeared to me to have the dropsy. On going in to see him yesterday morning, he raised his eyes and recognized me but could not speak—one of his hands was very cold and I could feel no pulse in either wrist. Archie Peck has agreed to superintend the burial.

February 5. My Poor humble friend & servant Kit was buried yesterday afternoon in the Town graveyard. It was very cold and raw but I attended at the church & grave. He was a good man and never did any harm that I know of. He was valuable help to me and his place cannot be filled. Mr Watson is better this morning, and as the morning is bright will come up town. Ther 34 morning bright.

February 6. The loveliest day possible we had yesterday. Ther 46° at 2 PM. I paid Wesley Jones for coffin for Kit....[1]

February 9.... European affairs are very threatening. Russians are said to have occupied Constantinople. It is suggested that Turkey failing to get aid from England has allied with Russia and there is great excitement in Europe. No change in cotton LM 10 Selma.

February 10.... The war news is bad. Russians are said to occupy Constantinople and English fleet has been sent there—great excitement in England $6,000,000 [*sic*] pounds voted by Parliament. Cotton will go down. Affairs are sadly out of joint all over this world and a gloomy period is on us....

February 18.... The news from East has a spice of possible peace in the telegrams. Emperor may halt outside Constantinople & English fleet at Princes Island. Cotton was quoted 1/8 higher in Selma. The loveliness of the weather suggests gardening & farming.

February 19. Another lovely day yesterday bright & spring like. Gardening is in order & David [house servant] has been fixing grape arbor.... The news from Europe is more pacific. It is thought Germany has interfaced with the Czar & Grand Duke gone to Constantinople as an invited visitor it is said....

February 22. Washingtons birthday to be nominally a holiday, would that the integrity of his character could be more studied and produce an improvement in this generation....

---

[1] Wesley Jones, a respected black wagonmaker, owned the property across the street from St. Paul's Episcopal Church. His wife was custodian of the keys to the church for decades.

The Bland-Allison act required the Treasury to buy two to four million dollars of silver each month and turn it into coin. It was passed over President Hayes's veto. It was an inflationary measure that Benners opposed.

February 26.... Silver bill as amended by the senate passed by the house and gone to the president. Free coinage stricken out and coinage limited—gold contracts shall still be payable in gold. We killed Christmas Turkey yesterday and have him for supper to night. Col Harvey & wife & Mr Cobbs family are invited to supper.

February 27. It clouded up yesterday but no rain yet. Mr & Mrs Cobbs & Mr & Mrs Harvey & Miss Mary Avery took supper with us last night. Miss Timberlake could not come.[2] The Eastern news is very discouraging & English complication is very likely. The time for conference not fixed....

March 3.... Cotton is 10 1/8 LM tho the war seems imminent. The coinage of Silver has commenced the act having passed over Presidential veto....

March 7.... Cotton is a little better 10 1/4 Selma L.M. probably affected favorably by the news of Peace between Russia & Turkey—advance is 1/8 all around. I ordered sale of 26 B/C by C[arlisle] and J[ones] yesterday.

When Russia won the war, it negotiated the Treaty of San Stefano on 3 March 1878, a treaty that provided Russia an outlet to the Mediterranean and bypassed Constantinople. This change in the power structure in southeastern Europe sent shockwaves throughout all of Europe. Bismarck convened a conference in Berlin to revise the treaty, and with the cooperation of Benjamin Disraeli, this was done. Austria and Great Britain benefited from the new treaty, which diminished the Ottoman Empire. Benners was pleased since it stabilized the price of cotton and insured that England would continue to buy large amounts of cotton for its factories.

---

[2]Mary Avery, sister of Fanny Avery Cobbs, Mr. Cobb's wife, was a church organist and school teacher who taught the Benners's children.

March 8. It was a pleasant day yesterday and sun rose bright this AM but it has clouded up and looks like rain. The cotton report last night from Selma LM 10 1/4. Peace news helped it up 1/8. I directed 26 B/C sold—afraid to hold any longer in Selma. The prospect is not wholly serene. Austria is dissatisfied, and the conference is to meet. some apprehension still exists and preparations are warlike—...

March 15. Another fine day yesterday and a clear night.... I read the service yesterday—Mr Cobbs being at Marion. Ther at 8 AM 56°. The time for Congress at Berlin has not yet been agreed upon. Russia is objecting to a general discussion—of the whole treaty.

March 16. Fine weather continued thro yesterday & last night. David took mortal offence on yesterday because after he cut up without orders honeysuckle back in the garden. Fanny told him when he had a lot belonged to him he could cut what he pleased. He called at the office and demanded to know how much he owed me having pd his fine $9.75 he owed 3.50. He is a smart boy and I dislike to lose him but he evidently has been unsettled since he forgot to pay Miller the money I sent to pay for Herrings and had the 60 cts chd to me....

March 20.... Treaty is talked of between England & Austria—Russia nears Constantinople and is much disposed to take the bit between her teeth. Gold 1 1/4. Congress news unimportant at present. Supreme Court of La Discharge Woll & Anderson the members of the Louisiana returning board who had been indicted for forgery in altering the Returns from Vernon parrish in the presidential election which forgery defeated Tilden and elected Hayes. Supreme Court say the return altered was not such a public Document as comes within the Statute—and parties are discharged....

March 24.... Cotton is not quite so sick as before 10 1/8 LM Selma. Markt quiet. Failures are so frequent as not to attract attention—and now National Bk of Tarrytown New York has failed. The passage of the Silver bill has not produced any great effect any way. Gold 1 1/8 Bonds steady....

April 5. It pushed a frost pretty close last night but except in very low places there was none.... The news from Europe is a little more hopeful. Russia has not finally shut the door and may consent to a reassembling of the Congress. Cotton is no better but no worse, LM 10, Selma.

April 6. Beautiful day & bright night Ther 50° Ed and I took a walk thro the woods along the branch yesterday evening, poor luck fishing caught only 2 little ones. There is some sickness about. No new light on the war. Cotton firmer, L.M Selma 9 7/8. Strawberries are very promising more blooming than usual. Maryland wants to try Hay[e]s title in Supreme Court. Better let it alone. Least said about disturbing the title the better—...

April 10. Yesterday was a very pleasant day altho the ground was wet from previous rain. The negroes had their anniversary celebration of their Emancipation. Not as many in procession as last year tho the crowd was large. They behaved very well as far as I could see. Jenny and Graham came a part of the way to my office with me this morning and we counted quite a number of the newly planted water oaks on the streets that were putting out. Eastern news no change. Cotton firm 5 15/16 at Liverpool....

April 13. Fine weather continued yesterday. I read service in the afternoon. Letter last night from Alfred about wanting to build a house wants $1500. I fear his views are not judicious—entails too much expense besides the house. Ed & Willie went fishing and staid all night not back yet. Graham & Jenny came down with me this AM. Jenny to get pair of shoes. Vegetation progresses finely. Cotton unchanged.

April 14. Sunday.... Foreign news last night is a shade better. Russia relaxes a little & Germany is more demonstrative. Cotton is firmer L.M. Selma 9 7/8. Jim Chiles was up yesterday to get his shoes changed. Cotton has come up finely in the field & is almost a stand. We had fine strawberries from Mrs Jones day before yesterday and ours are doing very well. The trees planted on the street many of them are putting out and will give shady walks when they are big enough....

April 19.... Huge strike among cotton operatives in England. Reduction of wages resisted. Tweed is dead & buried. Repeal of resumption act is before congress. Eastern question no better a shade worse. Cotton Liv 5 15/16 very dull. Parker stayed with me last night....

April 25. After the terrible rain storm of the previous night yesterday was fair & lovely and stars shone brightly last night. Court still trying criminal docket. Mitchel[l] is to be tried to day for killing another negro. Jury were empanelled yesterday not sworn and kept together last night & the others summoned were discharged. Mr Ed Pasteur took tea and spent the night with me....

April 26. It was a lovely day yesterday and opens clear & cool this AM. The case of the State vs Mitchell for killing a negro named George, the verdict was guilty of murder in 2nd degree and sentence 15 yrs in the Penitentiary. He killed the deceased with a slat of a bedstead by a blow over the head. it occurred on Bob Drakes place. The storm of tuesday seems to have been very extensive and disastrous and the track of the Tornado was from S.E. to N.W. Mr Tutwilers house was damaged and Powers houses blown down. it was severe in West Va—an engine on Central Ala went thro a trestle 8 miles East of Meridian & killed engineer and fireman. Wash came up yesterday Creek had got out over an acre in corner of Walker field. The Strike in Manchester & other towns among cotton operatives is very formidable....

May 11.... Great things were expected from Shuvaloff Russian ambassador going to St Petersburg[3] but now it is said he cant be gone on this business as that would be for England to make terms direct with Russia without the Powers which is not likely she would try to do. Cotton is seemingly a shade better.

Augustus Benners's interest in politics was as strong as ever, but for health reasons he was unable to do more than help nominate delegates to the state Democratic convention.

May 12. The weather yesterday was very fine. Burke ploughed the orchard and Pauldo came up to get money to buy corn & get his cow out of the pound. crop prospects are reported very good—there has been a great deal of rain in latter part of April & this month which it is considered is not so good for crops. The Democratic Beat meeting was

---

[3] Count Pietr Andreyevish Shuvalov, ambassador to England (1874–1879), sought to smooth over difficulties caused by Anglo-Russian rivalry in Asia.

held yesterday to select delegates to County Convention to nominate delegates to State Convention. I was one of the delegates to the County. Eastern news no better its vibrations are marvellous. Fanny & Liz have not yet come back from Arcola & Demopolis. Cotton bad off LM 9 7/8 Selma, [Thomas] Seay is named for senate and there are several aspirants to the house among them Coleman and C. E. Waller....

May 16.... There is much canvassing of the candidate question. Coleman & Charley Waller want to go to Montgy and the county ought to have one at least....

May 20. Saturday was cloudy & hot—at night about 12 a severe wind storm blew up and before day there was a very good rain. Yesterday morning was very threatening but it did not rain. Mr Banister took tea with us Saturday night & Misses Cobbs, Stickney, A. C. Jones & Mrs Stickney. They left just after supper to go to the reading of a Miss Barrow. Liz went with them. on Saturday 18th we had the County Convention. Seay was nominated for the Senate and Waller & James for the Lower house. The nominations do not give universal satisfaction and I am of opinion it was not judicious for the young men to want to go—Judge Coleman would have made a good member but could not get the nomination—a resolution was adopted instructing delegates to support Mr Tutwiler for Sup of Education. The proceedings were quiet enough but not very flattering for fair success. I was one of delegates to Montgy. Mr Banister preached twice on Sunday. In the morning from text, Blessed are the dead who die in the Lord &c It was a very appropriate, being a quasi funeral sermon for those of his old parishioners who had died since he left here—Mrs Avery Jackson, Withers, Mr Waller & others....

May 22.... The weather was very warm and I found my change to thin shirts very comfortable. The Potter resolution so called to investigate the frauds of returning boards in La & Florida has passed the house and is causing much discussion as to its propriety. it is asserted that it is not intended to assail Hayes title to the Presidency....

Names of Delegates & Alternates to Montgomery
1878 May 29

Delegates	Alternates
John S. Jones	L. J. Dawson
W. C. Christian	Mat Moore
Jno H. Turpin	T. T. May
J. H. Y. Webb	C. L. Stickney
T. R. Roulhac	Dr S. T. Henley
W. C. Tunstal[l]	G. R. Johnson
A. Benners	J. W. Locke
Chas W. Whelan	B. J. Knox
T. G. Hilton	Jacob Huggins
W. B. Young	S. Stollenwerck
G. C. Trammel	S. S. Coleman

...*June 1.* I left home on tuesday 28th May as delegate to Democratic & conservative convention of State of Ala to nominate State officers reached Selma 9 1/2 left at 3 reached Montgomery 5 1/2 took a room at Exchge 2nd Morning then had a slight attack of cholic Monday. Got the convention thursday night, took cars Friday morning May 31. got to Selma at 10 1/2 left at 3 got home 6.30 PM found all well. Convention nominated R. W. Cobb of Shelby for Gov, Vincent Sec of State, Screws Treas, Brewer Auditor, Tomkins Atty Genl, LeRoy Box Supt of Education. We were very anxious to have Mr Tutwiler of Hale nominated for this last office—taken on the 1st Ballot he only got 196 votes to Box 300. We concluded there was no chance and Mr [Francis Strother]Lyon who nominated him withdrew his name. our delegation was John S Jones, W C Christian, W B Young, Hylton, W C Tunstal[l], T R Roulhac, Turpin, Trammel, JHY Webb [blank space] & myself. I was honored with the place of chairman. Our Delegation was not as harmonious as on former occasions. Our highest interest was election of Mr Tutwiler. It seemed as if one (or two perhaps) subordinated to Cobb. S. S. Coleman had been elected an alternate and Trammel not attending he went in his place. We had a very hard rain in Montgomery the night of 30th and I found on reaching home there had been no rain here....

June 5.... I have been feeling quite unwell & despondent. Thinking of the future of my children causes a real solicitude. Congress is called in Europe at Berlin. Cotton 10 7/8 Selma....

June 7. Yesterday was a very pleasant and bright warm day a growing day and cotton goes forward very rapidly. Jenny went in the evening to Mrs Stickneys. The emperor of Germany has been again fired at by a Dr Nibling—he the informer was riding in his carriage when he was struck with shot from a room where Nibling was. the shot from two barrels struck him in his face neck & shoulders. his condition is said to be satisfactory, but his arm is swelling.

June 8. Saturday. We had a fine rain yesterday evening and last night—It is very acceptable. The Potter investigation is being carried on in regard to Frauds in Pres Election in La & Fla in 76. It is not intended to invalidate Hayes title but to see who were the guilty parties—Emperor William was shot at by Dr Nibling is doing well so said. The war cloud is dissipated for the present. Cotton is stiff—prices unchanged....

June 18.... Potter committee progresses. Matthews & Sherman are considerably compromised. House passed resolution that Hayes Title is good....

June 20. I went to Selma yesterday to see about selling some 34 B/C with Carlisle & Jones...got home at 5 1/2 near Coleman's plantation the train ran over and killed two colored boys who were lying fast asleep in the middle of the track. The train had got to top of an up grade when for first time the engineer (Chadwick) saw something on the track he blew the whistle violently to scare them up and downed brakes but it being a down grade the car could not be stopped and ran over the boys and was not stopped for about 100 yds beyond. train was locked to them and the sight was a very ghastly one. the head of one was cut off & holding by the skin and the other was knocked on the head the life was not quite extinct in him. a crowd of negroes gathered around their lamentations were distressing—a wagon to put them in to be hauled off was sent for and our train came on....

June 22. Yesterday was a fine day without rain. John Edwards came up and ploughed the field and goes down this morning. Mrs McCulloch was buried at 10 oclock. got no cotton retns fr Selma. Mary & Hatty are with us. I have made no arrangement about Blount. [illegible] from Marion came over last evening—he reports excitement among the negroes near the accident—he wanted my vision of the thing. Mr Cobbs came on train from Marion reported many negroes gathered on the road as he passed but they may have expected an inquest....

In early July, worms were reported to be moving toward Benners's plantation. This alarmed him, but there was little he could do. At same time, news of a final settlement of conflict between Russia and Turkey eased his concerns about the price of cotton. It meant that prices would be more stable.

July 10. There was a shower of rain yesterday 6 P.M. Ther 88° 1 PM in the hall and last night quite warm. We are trying to get ready for Blount trip. The worms are reported at Tunstals and other places in canebrake. Conditions seem favorable for them. Butterflies June Bugs and Katydids are more abundant than usual. European congress approaches finality. England gets Cyprus, Austria, Bosnia & Hers[e]govina. Cotton is 6 5/16 Liv....

July 16. yesterday Ther 92° at 1 PM then there came up a shower & breeze and it fell to 82° Capt Tayloe & Bea Hatch were at our house and dined with us & waited before starting till the shower was over.... Congress in Berlin have finished the treaty and signed it not yet published—60 articles and is the longest ever made. I am trying to get ready to start to Blount to morrow.

July 17. Ther 90° yesterday.... Worms are much talked about. The particulars of the treaty are published. Prospect of our having Indian war increases. Miles had a fight with them killed 13, he says.

June 18. ... Potter committee progresses. Matthews & Sherman are considerably compromised. House passed resolution that Hayes Title is good....

His summer vacation began on 18 July and lasted until 10 October. The family had been under the weather and needed a change of environment. In Blount Springs, the family enjoyed nice breezes, more moderate weather, cooler mornings, lots of ice cream, and many games of ten-pins—as well as rides in carriages and dinners with friends. But everywhere they went, there was talk about yellow fever moving toward Mississippi and Alabama. From mid-August until the end of their vacation, the stories grew in intensity, becoming more alarming. It scared Alfred Hatch, Benners's father-in-law, who decided to go home to Arcola. He had fallen down and felt very weak.

August 21.... Yellow fever is increasing in N. Orleans, Memphis, Vicksburg & Grenada and some travellers were turned off at Blount Spgs yesterday from Vicksburg. The times are not as pleasant as usual at our house—

August 22.... Yellow fever accts from N Orleans Vicksburg Memphis and Grenada are very bad.

August 23.... Mr Hatch had a very bad spell after breakfast and alarmed us very much. He got better about 10 and went in the Piazza to lie down. He got up to go in the yard & fell down near the chimney. very luckily he did not fall on a rock. I supposed it would be impossible for him to leave as he intended, but the carriage came out at 1 and he insisted on riding...

August 25.... Many persons have left and yellow fever is spreading in Miss and Willies letter says there are 1 case in Union Town Ala.

August 26.... There are reported two deaths from yellow fever in Tuscaloosa, and Liz Batie [Beatty] writes Liz one reported in Union town. Company has thinned out very much....

August 28.... yellow fever rages in Vicksburg, Grenada, Canton [Miss.] N. Orleans, Greensboro they say is quarantined. Postal from Mr CL Stickney says worms are ruining his cotton....

September 3. Fanny & Liz & Willie & I went to town yesterday morning and rode home in Browns carriage. Pains at the Springs about yellow fever had abated but Gen Walker told me there were two cases at Huntsville and had stopped his leaving for home. Liz walked on Robinsons Mountain Fanny rolled ten pins....

September 5. Warm yesterday—went to Town played backgammon with Garret[t] & Coleman the former beat me the latter was beat by me. Montgy dont rescind quarantine. It is reported at Holly spgs but said not to be yellow fever....

September 7.... Yellow fever accts are horrible from Grenada Vicksburg N. Orleans & Holley Spgs....

September 11.... Letter from Wash says worms have ruined crop and he may make 25 bales—weather this morning cloudy windy fall like....

September 19. Liz & I went in. Rolled ten pins Willie returned from picnic at Bret Randolphs. Walked with Graham toward Kelsers. Met Fanny & Jenny. Yellow fever is reported at Huntsville & Decatur—Weather bright and warmer.

September 23.... Considerable talk about yellow fever in Decatur & Chattanooga talk of trains stopping. Expected to leave 26. what now....

September 27. Greatly flustrated by trains stopping. Ala Central is stopped. Weather yesterday bright warm. after dinner went to Town. Mr Mad[ison] Jones & family visited us yesterday eve going home uncertain on acct of stoppage of trains....

October 1. No frost yet. this tuesday morning opens lovely & cool. Liz & I went in yesterday—she rolled ten pins I played backgammon with Mr Garrett of St Joseph La. Saw Mr Reid who informed me Mr Cobb would be here today. Railroads still upset & irregular by quarantines....

October 10. We reached home from Blount County last night at 7 oclock having left on Tuesday Oct 8th at 2.40 PM and travelled by way of Selma we made due connection at Calera at 5.30 PM and got to Selma at 11 P.M.and took rooms at Tilmans and started on Ala central at 3.15 P.M. We found there was considerable excitement at Birmingham about increase of yellow fever at Decatur and we hear trains are stopped above Birmingham. Our trip home was a pleasant one but we found the night much warmer in Selma than Valley Hill. There is great uneasiness about yellow fever and cars are boarded by Health officers to inquire where passengers came from. We found our house lighted and Mrs Harvey & Miss Lizzie Beattie each had sent some nice tea & warm supper for us and happy were we to lay down to rest in our own home.

Yellow fever and quarantines continued into early November. Benners wrote on 30 October: "Panic in England is affecting price of cotton—Crop estimated at $5 million." There were few reports of yellow fever after mid-November. The midyear elections were held in Alabama on 6 November; Democrats were ahead from the first counts.

November 6. The election passed off so far very quietly, tho Democratic ticket here is reported 231 ahead. Henry got 82 votes. Mr Pittman dined with me yesterday. he is here attending to the settlement of CW Hills estate. Mobile & Montgomery have removed quarantine but there are still cases reported in Memphis, Mobile, Vicksburg & New Orleans. The weather has been and is perfectly delightful—mild and clear—

November 8. Indian Summer yesterday.... Election returns indicate a solid south & Alabama all democrats, but Lowe Ind[ependent] demo who beats Garth. Cotton quoted at 1/8 better in Selma LM 8 3/4.

November 9. Fine mild weather yesterday. Election returns show democratic Losses in New York, Penn, Connecticut and New Jersey it is believed that the House of Reps will be Democratic and a majority in the Senate is claimed. The Greenback & National labor party damaged the Democrats very badly. In Ala the Congressional delegation is solidly Democratic. Lowe who beat Garth in the 8th being independent Dem. the other candidates elected are Forney, Williams, Lewis, Herndon, Shell[e]y and Samford & Herbert. Cotton LM 8 5/8 S[elma]....

November 28. Thursday. This is Thanksgiving day and for what unnumbered mercies should we thank God. Pestilence has in many places prevailed we have been spared. distress & gaunt want has dogged the steps of oh how many. We have fed bountifully and Gods goodness has given us a place to live and all the comforts we have had. Praise the Lord oh my soul and forget not all his benefits—who saveth thy life from destruction & crowneth thee with mercy & Lovingkindness. Mr Hatch came up yesterday—he is failing—memory failing—mind enfeebled. Poor old man he asked for the collaterals he gave me (negro mule notes) as security to his debt to me, and I let him have them. he went to Carries in the afternoon....

Murders were unusual in Greensboro, but one happened on 9 December.

December 9. It rained yesterday & we did not go to church in the morning. In the afternoon we went to the church to the funeral service of Jim Williamson who was killed in Atkins drug store on saturday evening about 3 oclock by Willie Dorman. I heard 3 shots and when I went to the door there was a great excitement and a running to the drug store and in a few minutes I heard that he had been killed by Dorman—it appears that he was in the store with his mother. Williamson came in with a pistol in his hand & not seeing him passed him when Dorman shot in the back & on his turning round shot him in the throat & he fell dead. Dr. Parrish, Messrs Harvey, Isaac Benners & AP Hatch took supper with us saturday night & 'Doc—The Doctor is looking well and I was much gratified to see him Isaac & Parker stayed all night till after dinner yesterday. Cotton still declines—LM 8 3/8—

December 12.... Cotton lost an 1/8. LM 8 1/8, receipts at ports are very heavy and matters in England are very complicated.

December 13. Another fine day yesterday. I had tho to stay out of my office to have the fire place fixed. Prophet Christian laid the hearth and fixed the back putting a piece of iron in the back. The preliminary trial of Dorman for killing Williamson came off in the courthouse before Roulhac....

December 14.... Dorman on his preliminary examination which lasted two days & 1/2 was discharged on plea self defence....

December 15. It rained nearly all day yesterday my wife had a bad time to go to Arcola—Her father sent for her and she and Willie got off at 1 oclock. It rained very hard after they started. He is very feeble & failing. It was a very disagreeable day all the turns of it were uncanny. I dreamed about Mr H the night before & told my wife of it. Troubles come all along lifes journey—The sickening disappointment by the fall of cotton is truly discouraging—an[d] many are at a loss what to be at—...

December 31. I got a telegram from Ben Hatch at Demopolis on friday 27th that Mr Hatch was worse to come immediately. I went on train to junction on 28 waited till 11.48 & went on Ala central to Vandorn [Van Dorn] and rode Kornegays horse to Arcola met Ben Hatch going home his child being sick. he said his father was better. I found him still very low—two Doctors there & Rev Mr [blank space] of Demopolis. He was considered a little better—but next morning worse again and better in the evening & again not so well on Monday morning. My wife is quite well and still remains there.

1879

For Augustus Benners, it was a year of anguish because of the death of his father-in-law, Alfred Hatch, and the deteriorating mental health of his son, Ed.

January 31, 1879. The sad event has happened. I rec'd a dispatch from my wife this morning that her father died yesterday at 2 PM and asking me to have the hearse at the depot this friday evening—long expected this heavy blow comes with crushing weight on his family—He was their all and his affection for them endeared him as few fathers are loved. We expect the funeral to be from my house at 11 tomorrow—the burial will be at my lot.

February 2. yesterday was one of the sad days of my life. My father in Law Mr Alfred Hatch was buried. Funeral took place from my house at 11 oclock AM. services were conducted by Rev Mr Cobbs—the weather was cold windy & very disagreeable—the procession of Carriages was quite large considering the short notice and bad weather. The corpse had been brought on the R. Road & reached here the night before. Poor old man, his journey of life is finished—he was a good man and a valuable one and lucky will we be if in a final reckoning so much good and so little harm can be said of us as of him—he was a fond father a good citizen a very temperate conscientious moral man. To do good was his delight, always disposed to befriend he had many warm attached friends, and community has lost one of its best allies.

He continued to worry about his sons Willie and Ed. Willie was enrolled in Southern University in Greensboro but lacked a clear sense of direction despite his father's many efforts to help. This distressed Benners and caused many quarrels. But the greater concern preoccupied him every day, which was what to do with Ed. Ed had tried to raise cotton at Mellown Place, participated as a juryman on three occasions, and continued to look for other forms of employment. Now 27, Ed was at loose ends and his health began to deteriorate.

May 22.... Willie hurt his face with harnessing horses in stable lot. It is badly swelled and continues his failure at recitations. Ed is very wandering. Have mercy on me....

May 26.... Ed is very unwell...very dissatisfied & unhappy—what to do I dont know. God give me grace & strength to suffer if I cannot remedy....

May 31.... Sent for [Dr.] Peterson to see Ed last night, gave him prescription and it was operative and he thinks he feels better this morning tho very weak.

The situation with Ed remained the same until late November. Then it got considerably worse.

November 20.... Ed was more out of the way than usual yesterday distressing us very much....

November 27.... Ed came to my office first time in 6 mos. When I went home he wanted to come down the country and to Mr Dubose's either to ride or walk which I objected to....

November 29.... Ed went on foot as far as Randolph's plantation. Isaac went and got him to come back. He is I think in a bad way & what to do I don't know—may God give us grace & patience. I went to depot but he had left before I got there....

December 2.... Ed was about the same. his timidity is distressing. He wants Graham to sleep with him—he dont want to—my wife is surely troubled and it tells on her....

December 4.... Ed is not appreciably better and our affliction is heavy especially when his mother who is about and has to be constantly in sight....

December 5.... Ed helped very little [with] Paul about compost heap. I am much afflicted with him. he is wholly unreasonable and melancholy. has no pleasure that I know but making himself & others wretched.

December 8.... Ed is deviling us again about going to DuBose's. God forgive me I am almost for giving up. how very shortsighted we are.

December 9.... Ed started afoot to go to Mrs D. Mr Cobbs persuaded him to come back. this morning he was much excited. Mr Inge & Fanny have gone with him and his carriage to Isaacs....

December 10.... I was sent for after getting to the office by my wife to please come home. Ed had a very bad turn—raved & thought Mr Cobbs was trying to kill him. Mr Inge & Mr Jones came over before I got there. Mr Inge very kindly brought his carriage & went to Isaac's carrying Ed & Fanny. They came back to dinner & Isaac came with them and remained last night. He is melancholy but quiet this morning. I pray God give me strength.

The family met, and after much anguish, decided that Ed should go to an asylum in Tuscaloosa. They could no longer take care of him.

December 11.... My wife went with Ed & Isaac to his house about 1 P.M. remained last night. Mr Cobbs rec'd dispatch yesterday evening late from Dr Bryce in reply to telegram—"Yes." and he came to our house last night & we tried to get ready to start with Ed from Isaacs this morning for Tuscaloosa but it rained hard last night and turned cold & is now 10 am cold & raining with wind from the north & we postponed the start.[4] I hope I am not making a mistake and pray forgiveness if I am.

---

[4] Dr. Peter Bryce was the first medical superintendent at the Alabama State Hospital for the Insane when Ed was admitted. Alabama was the first state to appropriate sufficient funds for the construction of a mental hospital designed for humane care, non-restraint, and occupational therapy, which in later years would become basic practices of modern psychiatry. See Robert O. Mellown, "Mental Health and Moral Architecture." *Alabama Heritage*, no. 32 (Spring 1994): 5–17.

My heart bleeds but I take comfort in the hope & belief that Gods Grace will be sufficient for me.

December 12.... It was a day sad to me my poor boys fate weighing heavily upon my heart. Mr Cobbs called by in the Hack this AM before 7 oclock on his way to Isaacs to go with Ed & Isaac to Tuscaloosa. God give me grace & strength to stand it—the weather is very cold & ground frozen. May God bless my poor child—Jane is at Isaacs & I must send out for her.

December 13.... Mr C got to Isaacs about 7 oclock. Isaac advised Ed after Breakfast that Mr C was going to T & I wanted him to go there & be treated by the Doctor—he was willing to go if I said so—and they got off about 7 1/2—must have had a very cold ride. I have heard nothing from him since. It almost breaks my heart. God forgive me if I have done wrong and give me strength. My wife came in with Mrs Stickney.

December 14.... Mr Cobbs stopped at the house on his way from Tuscaloosa. He & Isaac got Ed up there as he said without the least difficulty. The day they went up was very cold & coming back very rainy but not so cold. He thinks we have done the best possible for Ed. When they started to leave next morning he wanted to come but they did not leave till he consented to stay. I owe many thanks to Mr Cobbs & Isaac for their kind and self sacrificing sympathy & substantial kind[ness]. No two could have been kinder & certainly none more proper for the occasion. Ed rambled with them all about and seemed satisfied—their leaving was of course a great trial to him. My heart still bleeds when I think of my poor son. and his saying at Isaacs—If Pa wants me to go I will go—has made a deep impression and makes me feel more than ever for my poor boy. Oh God save him & bless him for Christs sake. Oh Heavenly father have mercy upon him, and strengthen us in this heavy sorrow with thy Heavenly Grace.

For the next week and for the rest of their lives, Augustus and Jane Benners thought about Ed. They never saw him again.

December 23.... We have no news from Ed. Christmas is a time to remember him....

December 24.... I got a letter from Dr Bryce for the first time. he reports favorably of Ed & says he manifests some interest in his surroundings.... Thank God for his goodness. I also got a letter from Alfred. He has made $1150 this year. his affliction is very great by reason of Ed. May God give us a grace to patiently suffer his Holy will with thankfulness—for why he knows what is best for us.

December 25.... Christmas day! oh how different a few more only remain to me. Sad not merry is Christmas for me. Disappointments are my lot. I got a letter from Dr Bryce he reports favorably of Ed. My poor child....

1881

Jane Benners had wanted to visit her eldest son, Alfred, in Dallas, Texas. Her younger son Willie also wanted to go to Texas. However, Augustus dreaded the trip and worried about Jane's health. It was a long trip, but she would not change her mind. He decided not to go with her.

January 28, 1881.... Jane speaks of going to Dallas next week with Willie I dread it but I cant help it. of course they will have to pay for their experience....

January 30. Ther 50° at 7 PM 46 at 8 AM—a pretty day—... My mind is much depressed & distressed about Jane & Willie going to Texas—I tremble—God help me....

January 31.... I am much exercised about my wifes departure with Willie. No one to take care of them....

February 1. Ther 66° at 9 PM 64° at 8 AM. it rained last night & drizzles yet Jane still speaks of going to morrow. I am not a little upset. Cotton has declined 1/8 in Selma LM 10 3/8. I try to have faith & patience—but the weakness & infirmities of mind & body almost give up. I have not yet heard of Willies getting home from Batey's—be still my heart. oh how I would fold my children to my heart but they wont let me—

February 2. Ther 50° at 5 P.M. 44° at 9 PM and 34 this 9 AM. Jane and Willie left on the train for Dallas via Selma. I feel very sad. I cannot see how my wife can encounter such a rough travel without getting sick. I hope for the best, but it will be a great trial to her & my poor son Willie. May God help him. My heart bleeds for him, and he dont know it....

February 3. I felt very sad & gloomy yesterday—the leaving of my wife & son left me very blue—I was persuaded to accept Snedecors invitation to dinner....

February 9.... I got a letter from Jane & Willie at Little Rock of 4 Inst. they reached there at 11 AM missing the connection and had to wait for next train at 11 P.M. they got on without any accident and had their baggage checked from there to Dallas....

February 12.... I got a letter from Alfred. Jane & Willie got to Dallas Sunday evening Feby 6 at 3 PM. They were well and not as tired as expected. All were well & great joy. Thinks he can get a place for Willie....

February 15. A cold bright day yesterday Ther this morning 38° Mr W & I last evening took tea at Col Jones with Mr Jacob Thomison of Memphis. Roulhac was there & we had a game of whist. The night was beautifully bright & I enjoyed the walk home very much. Found on getting home a letter from Jane & Gus & card from Alfred. They are all well and much pleased. Gus writes like an old fellow. Card fr Selma quotes steady LM 10 1/8....

February 23. Ther 40° 7AM. yesterday was a lovely day not a spec of cloud in the sky but blue all over. Mr Stickney came up and dined with us and Mr Roulhac & Cad[wallader] Jones came after supper. We got letters from Dallas late as 18th. Weather has been cold and rainy. They are all well & Jane & Willie say they are pleased. Mr Watson and Miss Julia are on their way to Marion having left this morning. Graham & I went in the hack with them to the Depot....

James Garfield was inaugurated as president on 4 March 1881. Benners opposed his candidacy in the fall election, voting for Winfield Hancock. He never warmed up to the new administration.

March 4.... Garfield is to be inaugurated to day. Mortifying....

March 5. The world moves. Yesterday was the day for inauguration of Garfield in the office once held by Washington what a fall was there—There was a very heavy snow storm in N.W. at Chicago & Milwaukie heaviest of the season—it was threatening at Washington—...

March 6.... There are no pleasant or promising things in sight for us. We are down good & matters get no better socially or politically. Perhaps my spectacles—

March 8.... There is little interest felt in the new administration—Garfield is held to be an unscrupulous partisan & smart as contradistinguished from great—

March 9.... We have the Garfield Cabinet [James G.] Blaine State, [William] Windom Treas. [Wayne] MacVeigh Atty Gen. [Robert Todd] Lincoln, War. [William H.] Hunt of N.C. Sec of Navy. [Thomas L.] James PM Gen [Postmaster General], [Samuel J.] Kirkwood of Iowa Interior—...

March 10.... Pauldo [Moore] came up for $6.00 for clothes. I set him to work in the fields to opening cotton furrows for planting—I rolled some in ashes planted nearest the Withers fence & there stopped fearing the ashes might injure the seed. Mr Watson came on the train last night. I was very glad to see him. His views of affairs in Canebrake are very discouraging....

March 11. Ther 56 8 PM 52 8 AM. a lovely day. Math ploughed in the field covering cotton—which Pauldo had opened and planted. The prospect is very blue. Hungry lazy negroes in my hands to supply and no probability of repayment. Mr W & I played Bezique in afternoon. I am glad to hear Jane is pleased in Dallas—her letter shews she is enjoying herself very much....

Considerable rain began falling on 12 March and continued for two weeks with frequent thunder and lightning.

March 12. Saturday. Ther 62° 8 PM 56° 8 AM. a fine day quite warm at midday. I went to the church to read service for Mr Cobbs at his request he being in Selma. There came up a rain with thunder lightning

& rain about church time.... It continued to rain a good part of the night—and was very acceptable....

March 13.... The rain the night before was reported to have been a very hard one about Newbern. Several of the creeks were swimming. There is no reaction in cotton yet—receipts continue very heavy in excess of last year and the crop reported nearly 400,000 in excess of last....

March 14.... Mc Rary [McCrary] who was bitten by a cat a few days since has a very painful sore on his leg from it. Dr Avery was also bitten by a cat. There is much talk of mad animals. Starving dogs increase mad dogs I think. The rain of Friday night was a very hard one—beating ploughed ground....

March 16. Ther 60 7P.M. 60° 8AM. It was a partly cloudy day yesterday. I read service at 5 oclock The cloudiness increased and it rained last night. there was also some wind thunder and lightning and is raining this AM. The Czar of Russia Alexander II was murdered on Sunday last March 13 about 12.30 PM by explosion of a bomb thrown at his feet. the discharge broke both his legs & destroyed one eye & lacerated lower part of his body. Alexander III has become Czar. cotton quiet LM 9 1/2 Selma.

March 17.... It was cloudy & threatening and last night we had a hard storm of thunder lightning wind and rain. the ground this morning is very badly washed—it is still cloudy 9 AM. It is supposed the R Road must be washed up in places. I read service yesterday afternoon—Bishop Wilmer was to be here to night, but it is more than probable the train will be delayed by washing....

Hard Rain!

March 19. a cloudy day. Ther 66 7 PM 64 8 AM. Bishop Wilmer was to have preached last night but it rained in the afternoon and a very severe storm of rain Thunder & lightning came up again after supper. It lasted till after 11 oclock The rain poured down and the streets are very badly washed—opening of spring is unfavorable the rains are prodigious.... Cotton LM 9 1/2 Selma Steady....

March 22. Ther 48 at 7 PM 38 at 8 1/2 AM. The day opened promising but began to cloud up and at 5 oclock was very threatening with high wind and a little rain. I did not read the service in afternoon because of bad weather—no mail last night, road being impassable by Cahaba bridge on acct of high water—62 foot rise reported at Tuskaloosa—derangement of trains everywhere. Bishop & Mr Cobbs have to return. Mr W could not start to plantation, no train.

March 23. Ther 48 7 PM 36 8 AM. Bright cool day yesterday. The train returned about 10 AM being unable to get along at Valley creek. Bishop went to Union Town. Mr Cobbs returned here. of course we had no mail last night. Train started to Junction this morning at 7 to go to junction to await orders. There was frost this morning and Mr W stated Ice. The fruit is gone I fear....

March 24. Brilliant day.... Letters from my wife & my brother in Texas. the latter inviting me very cordially to come and see him. Jane & the family are well ... Mr Watson left this morning for his plantation—he has been a great deal of company for me and I enjoyed his visit very much. I shall miss him greatly...

[Clipping]

WATCHMAN
EXTRA

Greensboro, Ala., March 23, 1881.

High Waters Receding!

After going to press, we received the following dispatch:

Selma, March 23.

The Alabama river is three inches below the high water mark of last year. The water twenty-four inches over Rail at Valley Creek. Fell six inches at Montgomery last night. We look for it to commence falling here to-day, and hope to get the train through in a short time. Say to our patrons I will get freights through at the earliest moment possible. Will run in connection with the Alabama Central Road at the Junction for the mail and passengers. The track will be repaired between Elizabeth and Valley Creek by to-morrow evening.

A. M. Fowlkes,
Superintendent.

March 26.... Letter from Major Banks at Tuskaloosa—my poor boy [Ed] has had a slight attack of Pneumonia but is well again. Letter discouraging for improvement. Cotton very low LM 9 1/2 quiet. The fact is the afflictions & perplexities of life are very distressing & I pray God to give me patience—without sympathy or aid & raided upon from all quarters. There was no Montg'y paper last night trains are not connecting yet by reason of wash ups.

March 27. Sunday.... The night was bright starlight. Venus especially brilliant in the west. Fred Black came for meat. 100 lbs given him. It was a blue day to me. outlook bad. Mr C. L. Stickney reported that damage from rain on Friday 18 exceeded anything he had ever seen—and reports are that rivers have been higher than ever since 1833. We got no Montg'y papers last night—there are 3 due. Cotton quiet LM 9 1/2 our trains dont run thro yet....

March 29.... Letter from Alfred asking for $200 on his rent notes. Willie has not procured a situation.... God help me. and he will or give me strength. I need it....

March 30.... Cotton 9 1/2 Selma quiet. The lookout for it now is very gloomy indeed—daily recpts reported are excessive and there dont seem to be any thing to cause a reaction—Estimated crop 6,000,000 and over. Consumption is very large—...

March 31. Thursday.... It looks as if Spring would never come in earnest. There never was so threatening a start. in the meantime cotton is going down....

April 3. Ther 56° @ 7 PM 52° 8 AM. a pleasant day clear & cool. I went with Fanny to church last night Mr Patterson preached. "Thou fool this night thy soul shall be required of thee." His manner is excentrick & peculiar. his business here is in the interest of Suwannee [Sewannee]. The memorial window to Mrs Avery has been placed but is covered by a cloth to be taken off at Easter. There are great fears that fruit is killed. If cold could kill it I should think it was gone. Selma card repts cotton quiet LM 9 1/2 no demand for low grades—all head winds—...

April 6.... The ground is very hard and my cotton cant come up. I will have to plant over again. Things with me are working horribly crop ways—

April 7.... The sadness of current affairs is unprecedented. The negroes are ragged & pinched, white folks drained & disheartened. Cotton declined 1/4 LM Selma 9 1/4 quiet. Liv firm @ 6d. The calls for meat & corn from Walker place continue. Got receipt from Tuskaloosa for dft for 70 sent for Eds board. It is generally considered all the corn will have to be planted over, having rotted in the ground....

April 8.... Cotton advcd 1/16 in Liv 9 1/2 LM Selma. CJ & co write they think the bottom has been reached and prices will improve. hope so. letter from Watson in Selma. he will remain a season. Letter from Major Banks [at Tuskaloosa]. Ed is no better. Enclosed letter from Jack Dubois who went to see him. he does not think he will recover. he answered questions was satisfied and in very good health. God help me & bless all who have done me or mine any good & forgive who have done or wished me evil. There is a heaven on high which is all I have to look forward to and that only by Gods infinite mercy—

April 25. Ther 74° 8 PM 70° 6 AM a cloudy day with shower of rain in the morning. I read the service and a sermon Mr Cobbs having gone to Macon. The rain came just at church time & cong was very small. I wrote to Jane in Dallas in afternoon. The state of affairs looks very discouraging not to say alarming. Provisions going up Cotton going down Having to advance knowing that it is money thrown away. Vegetation is coming forward with great rapidity. Mr Jones sent me a saucer of strawberries....

April 29.... The dull times now set in. Jeffries has reopened with a handfull of goods[5] & Dominick Brothers have bought out Hafner, and are keeping store at the same place. Money never was scarcer, and I should think very little selling but bread & meat—

---

[5] A. S. Jeffries, merchant and farmer. In the 1870 US Census, his real estate is valued at $211,500 and personal property, $24,000.

April 30. Ther 70° at 7 A.M. a fine bright warm day summery & beautiful. Roses in full blast but not so fine a blooming as usual by reason, no doubt, of the very cold winter. The tide still runs strong dead against me. Cotton drooping—provisions at starvation prices and I having to furnish. Alfred writes business quiet—and if there is a cheerful ray around my horison anywhere I dont see it—...

May 5. I went to Selma yesterday & ret in the evening. Cotton was so low I concluded not to sell at present and ordered my cotton insured—Williams said there would not be any additional storage. Selma was dull & things blue—the cotton on the road seemed to be a good stand and in some places was chopped out. Corn looked better than cotton—the day was warm & streets dusty. The excursion was almost a failure & the excursion came back in car hitched on to our train. Cotton LM 9 cts—...

May 8.... Letter from Dallas from my wife, she speaks of going to Jefferson and then returning home. Willie is gardening for Alfred. Mag has no cook....

May 9.... The sky is dark & times are blue. Cotton 9 1/4 LM. Money is oh so scarce. I never saw as tight a time. I got letter from Jane she has not been to my brothers. speaks of coming home this month....

May 13.... Jeffries auction was continued & there was an exhibition of the screw pulveriser. It is very ingenious and will do well for level dry lands in breaking for grains or grass. I went with Post & looked at McCrary's grass. It is very fine & shews what manuring & ploughing will do....

May 14.... auction going on. sacrifice great. Marshal Hamilton has levied on a portion of the good[s] claiming to have a lien on them for Town Taxes.... Screw pulveriser exhibited as a cultivator at Powers in corn and did good work. it is claimed it can go over 20 acres Letter from Alfred. Jane will come home on last of May. Sent NY dft to get a ticket for her—

May 17.... Auction continues. Jerry is chopping out cotton in the fields. We had a big scare last night—the soot in the kitchen stove pipe caught afire and the weather being so dry the flying sparks alarmed me very much. Wind from Northwest. Letter card from Alfred he says they are all well. I expect them [them crossed out] to leave for Jefferson the 17. I am very sorry I cant go for my wife, but my affairs are are [repeated word] so unthrifty I cant make the trip. I had neuralgia in my head this morning. Selma card LM 9 quiet....

May 19.... Auction continued. Liddy[6] very low. Mr Cobbs & Stickney home from Huntsville. Mr C saw my poor son in Asylum—his health is very good & he seemed to be happy, is fond of dancing & plays billiards....

May 21.... Liddy died yesterday afternoon at 6 PM. she had lived to about 85 years of age and a good woman is gone. she was remarkable for her fidelity & friendliness and was a great favorite with all who knew her. Her disease was paralysis. I spoke to Wesley Jones to make the Coffin and Ness Williams to dig the grave along side of old Kit. she had a very loving disposition and having no children she always lavished her fondness on some pet. Peace be with her, poor old woman. I got a letter from my wife last night—she was to go from Alfreds in Dallas to Jefferson to visit my brother & his wife on 18th and spend a week with them before coming home....

Benners had hoped to go to Texas to see Jane, Willie, and Alfred's family, but he waited too long. On 23 May, his wife of thirty-five years died. At first, the message was that she was sick, and he made plans to go quickly to Dallas. Then the message came that she had died. Now Benners could only wait for her body to be returned for its burial in Greensboro. It was a very sad time.

May 30. My dear wife died in Jefferson Texas at my brothers on 23 Inst. after a sickness with dysentery of two days. She and Willie left here on 1st Feby '81 to visit Alfred & Maggie and my brother. She left Dallas for Jefferson on 18th was sick two days and died on Monday night May 23 on that afternoon Mr Sam Criswell was sitting in my office with me, when the little boy Landy handed me a telegram from my brother Edward Jefferson Texas, saying "Jane is quite sick come on" My heart sank in me. I felt it meant death, and I could scarcely see. I had to tell my

---

[6] Liddy was the long-time cook for the Benners family and accompanied them to Blount Springs on their vacations.

children. They thought it would prove a temporary sickness. My heart said no. I put a few clothes in satchell and next morning went to depot to go to her—before leaving I dispatched that I was about starting for Jefferson. Got to Selma at 9 1/2. went with Mr Carlisle to depot of SR & Dalton Road to see about Ticket—the agent had not the tickets there & I was to come for it at 3 Oclock. on returning from the depot, I suggested to Mr Carlisle that I would inquire at telegraph office if any message might have passed over the wires for me. He told Carlisle he would look and bring word to Carlisle's office [Carlisle & Jones] and we went there to await his answer. Mr Carlisle went back to the office & in a few minutes returned & handed me a dispatch which had been sent from my brother that my wife died on Monday night May 23, 81. The news crushed me to the earth. I went with Mr Carlisle & Williams to his room & waited in untold agony till 3 when Mr Carlisle placed me in his carriage with Mr Parrish went with me to depot to return home. My friends Mr Harvey & Reed & Cobbs had a carriage at depot in which I rode home Alfred arrived with remains on friday night and my beloved wife was buried on Saturday morning from Episcopal church at 9 A.M. and desolation has brooded over my heart. oh what goodness was buried. oh what a world of fond devotion & affection have I lost and my poor motherless children. God of Mercy comfort and sustain and defend them. From my wife during our thirty five years of married life I rec'd nothing but affectionate consideration—and never did she ever have for me one single word of reproach or fault finding. My heart sinks as I think of my loss—God help.

May 31. I went to my wife's grave early yesterday morning and the new grave and withered flowers on it told the sad truth my dear Jane was buried. I cannot realise the awful truth—a monstrous void seems around me and if my mind gets off & dwells on another thought it soon returns & my desolation is awfully present. I received great kindness & sympathy from friends. I have received messages of sympathy from several friends—Mr Haywood, Mr Borden, sister Helen have sent me words of condolence. I begin to recognise the goodness of Gods providence—it was his wisdom & goodness. How poorly could my poor dear wife have scuffled at my death with the cold cruel world, and only a few short years would at farthest have rolled around before the dread event must have happened. That she must have left me or I have been taken from her and my poor motherless children have been called to mourn their sad bereavement—God doeth all things well, & may he comfort my aching heart with a sense of his goodness tho he has taken to himself my Dear wife—

May 31. Ther 72° at 8 P.M. a light rain yesterday at 2 P.M. not sufficient. Alfred is looking very badly. Dr Peterson prescribed for him last evening. Poor fellow. My poor heart is so distracted it bleeds for him & my poor bereaved children. Jenny was taken with measles yesterday evening and Fanny sent for Dr Peterson. he says it is very trivial Mary is still with us. Graham poor little fellow looks lost & knows not what to be at....

June 2. Ther 74° 8 PM 72° 7 AM. It rained very hard yest. about 1 PM and again last night. It is hoped we shall have no more for the present. Mary[7] is staying a few days with us and Alfred also is still with us. His health is not good and he is looking very thin. Got Letter last night from Mr Watson. My wife was a great friend of his. Her death leaves a great void in my life which recurs to my mind continuously. I can scarcely yet realise that she is dead. Quicksands represent my footing around all is dark & dreary. But God is my refuge. He will help & comfort me. Mrs [Victoria Jones Walker] Hatch has filed bill to sell Arcola to pay debts about $23,000 including her anti nuptial note for $10,000 with Int. from date....[8]

June 4.... Alfred is improving—tho quite thin. He is a great deal of company for me and I need him. Head neuralgia in morning & evening—The void continues—May God help me—no trunk arrived yet. Alfred took check [for trunk] at Little Rock to Selma via Meridian. I fear it is lost. Alfred is at Probate office rummaging over the records. No card from Selma—

---

[7] Jane's sister, Mary Hatch, married Seneca Hatch, not related.
[8] Victoria Hatch, the second wife of Alfred Hatch, was thirty-four years younger than he. The children of the first marriage were older than Victoria and were unhappy with the disposition of the will since most of the estate was left to her.

June 5.... Fair day & warm Mr Stickney walked up with Alfred & me to dinner In afternoon Alfred & I walked over to the woods lot. I count the short precious moments he has to stay with me. Mary is with us. The void continues. God is helping me to bear my load....

June 6.... Went to church with Alfred. sad enough I felt. His return cannot be delayed many days & parting with him adds to my grief. We walked in afternoon in the woods back of the pasture. Graham went with us—all things are tinged with sadness. his appearance has improved in point of health but is very thin—we have yet no news from the trunk....

Trial Day

June 9.... Alfred had arranged to leave this morning for Dallas. I waked before day & on opening the shutter found the sky cloudy & threatening. On going out in the yard I saw the dark clouds gathering in the north with considerable lightning. They were all astir and Alfred tried to get off before the rain but did not quite make it—the rain came down very hard & he waited till it slacked a little when he told us good bye and Jerry carried his satchel and he went to the depot. My Heart be still! Jef[f] Blount [Blunt] & Capt Reed & his wife & her sister called over last night....

June 10.... Telegram from Alfred Selma he found the trunk at central Depot, and sent it by train. It was delvd at the house this morning. Oh Lord. Help me. Card from Alfred he got ticket by Mobile & NO for 23.55 cts 2nd class limited. Letter from sister Helen with PO order for $2.50 for crochet shawl kept as a remembrance of my poor dear wife. God is helping me. Perplexities abound but I suffer them better I hope. Henry Chapman again calls for meat & bread—which I can barely give him but I will. The truth is it approaches a famine with the negroes. The card from Selma reports LM 9 1/2.

June 11.... We had a fair day & quite warm night bright moonlight. Fanny & Liz opened the the [repeated word] trunk. There were mementos for all her friends nearly. Oh how it tore open my heart afresh—Old Liddy's present was too late, she was buried the saturday before my wife—I got a very kind letter from Mr Wemyss last night—He had a similar trouble—his then whole family died—I got no further news from Alfred yesterday....

Benners continued to watch the skies and think about his wife and family.

June 12.... Day fair Liz & I took evening walk.... The very walk I so often took with my wife. she called it Our Walk. The clouds were feathery, bright, pretty. I wrote to Mr Wemyss. his kind heart prompted a letter to me of sympathy—Desolation once overtook him.... There was total eclipse of moon last night. I waked Graham at 11.20. It had just commenced. At 1.20 I called him & Fanny & Liz & Jenny to see it—was total. I called Fanny at 4 to look at Venus ...

June 14..... Got letter from Willie last night dated 10th Inst he reports all well and had heard of Alfred from Montgomery by Telegraph same time we heard from him by postal. Liz & I walked through the field to Jones wood last evening. Feathery clouds in West & North West very pretty....

June 17.... At last we got letter from Alfred. he got home Sat night at 11 P.M. family were not expecting him. found all well. The letter was a great relief to me. I feared he was sick....

June 21.... waked up Liz to look at moon & venus & saturn this morning they were very pretty—Card fr Selma LM 9 1/4

June 22.... I called up the children this morning to see the beautiful appearance of the sky in the west. The strip of a moon Saturn & Venus were in a line in Eastern sky at 4 1/2 AM and presented a very beautiful sight. The weather is very warm and days & nights short. Earth not cooling off good before another hot day begins....

June 26.... I came down about 3 1/2 AM to see the comet—it is very conspicuous—33° above Horizon in N East—Head large, tail about 2 yds—turned from the sun.[9] gardens are suffering very much for rain and so is the field. South of here the rain on Sat 18th relieved them. Liv Mid 6 3/16 quiet.

June 27.... I called out Fanny Liz & Graham this AM at 4 to look at the Comet. Venus & Saturn were still very bright and beautiful but it

---

[9] C/1881 K1 (Great Comet) passed closest to Earth on 20 June. Gary W. Kronk, *Cometography, A Catalog of Comets*, 3 vols. (Cambridge: Cambridge University Press UK, 2004) 2:472-83.

was too light to see the Comet to advantage—it looked rather dim. Liz & I took a walk yesterday evening thru my woodland to Jno Harvey's fence. It was quite warm but cloudy & we enjoyed the walk. Marshal Thornton came this morning to finish out my cotton—it begins to suffer for rain and the corn is badly suffering. Marshal is putting 3 furrows. Fanny went last evening to Jeffries.

June 28. Ther 86° 7 PM 82 8 AM very dry & hot. Ther 94 1/2 Liz & I walked in Jones wood back of the pasture—a threatening cloud very rapidly developed last night—and Graham & I went down stairs. Saw a comet due north from back Piazza. Went out 3 times before day but saw no comet—it was cloudy in south. The amt of rain that fell was very small not enough to run on the ground. rain is very badly needed by the gardens. cotton begins to give way in places in the field—corn is firing badly—no cotton card from Selma. Liv & NY are easier.

June 29. Ther 82° 7 PM 76° 7 AM. Hot & dry clouds & promise of rain in evening—but none fell—it turned cooler and perhaps hailed in the neighborhood. I took a look for the comet before retiring, but clouds prevented its being seen at that time, about 11 PM I waked up Graham and showed it to him thro the trees & went down & waked Liz & showed it to her from the corner of the kitchen. Letter from Willie last night. he has been sick, now well again. Ther down town there 102 in shade—96° is highest I have seen it at my house.

June 30.... Had a view of the Comet last night & saw it from the Barn at the orchard and Liz Graham Jenny & I saw it at 9 oclock from the street near the corner of Mr Harveys front yard. I came down stairs at 1.20 AM and saw it from the corner of the bathing house. The tail was reversed, being to right last night it was on left side. Card says LM 9 1/2 quiet. wrote answer to cousin Betty Haywood's letter—

President James Garfield was shot by Charles Guiteau, a disgruntled government clerk who had lost his job under the new administration. The assassination gave the final push needed for the passage of civil service reform. Garfield lingered for two months between life and death and then died on 19 September. It was a terrible time for the country and for Benners. He wrote, "The long agony is over & I think he is to be considered fortunate."

July 3.... a pleasant cloudy day. Comet again in sight after Supper in NW. City National sent me Div Dft for $100. After supper I came up to P. office after supper & meeting Dr Ward. he informed me that President Garfield had been shot twice at the RR depot in Washington. one ball in his arm and one between hip & kidneys, bad wounds but not necessarily fatal, it caused considerable interest & excitement. and every body hoped he would recover. Arthur vice president would be a very unacceptable president.... The rain we had has made our people more hopeful of the corn crop. it is said the Cotton worm has made its app in several places—I do not think the cotton in the field is doing anything extra in the way of fruiting....

July 5. Ther 80° 7 P.M. 76° 7 AM. a lovely day. Not a cloud. College exercises came off as usual—not as much stir as usual in Town. I walked to Depot after trains & Evans told me he just rec'd a message that Garfield was better with every hope of his recovery. Bessie Hatch came up on the train. I got letter from Dr Parrish. No card from Selma. crops are doing very well since the rain. very dry in Dallas Tex. No rain 4 weeks. Comet was visible last night about 8 1/2 PM not very bright by reason of the moonlight. Mrs Stickney called and carried Graham out with her to stay all night. I missed him very much.

July 6.... Garfield is reported improving at 4 PM yest. It is not easy to describe the excitement his shooting caused. I think Gitteau was a crazy man. He is in prison. His father who was a very respectable man in Freeport Illinois, characterised him as a crazy desperado as far back as 1879. I do not think he or any like him ought to be turned loose on society—He should be put out of harms way, society cant afford to be exposed to the murders of its citizens because the man is crazy. The expressions of sympathy for Garfield & family and indignation are universal at home & abroad....

July 8.... Garfield still said to be improving. Mr Hall called on crutches to see me, and Mr C L Stickney dropped in from Tuskaloosa much pleased. Ed was looking very well. no mental improvement reported. Jenny came home yest evening. a crazy man went to

Washington he said to kill Blaine. He was arrested and put in jail. I think the two last nights the hottest of the season....

July 9.... Garfields condition still reported improving. It is thought now Gitteau had no accomplices but was a crazy fool. $250,000 has been tendered to Mrs Garfield by the N.Y merchants to relieve the Pres mind on the subject of his family....

July 12. Ther 90 at 7 PM 80 at 7 AM. very hot. Clouds towards night and a light drizzle of rain in night. Corn is very badly damaged and cotton is small, but fruiting well—worm talk very strong—...

July 16.... Drought continues very hot and dry yesterday cloudy a part of the day. Garfield improves.... Cotton worms are heard from everywhere. CLS reports he has them. Sandy land corn cut off.

July 17.... Crop outlook on sandy land especially is poor. Corn is being cut to save it as fodder & in my field the forms are many of them literally burning up. Liv is 6 9/16 Selma LM 9 1/2. Garfield is still reported improving. Trying time. God only knows what the Country will do....

July 22.... There seems to be a good deal of sickness about. mostly from the country—The weather has been exceptionally hot. I walked out very early to stable lot morning was warm—Venus shining very brightly and Mars & Saturn in close proximity....

July 26.... The President had a bad turn night before last—fever rose & symptoms threatening, had a chill—last account he was improving....

August 12.... The condition of the President has caused great anxiety. his fever continues to rise in the evening and after the 2nd operation febrile symptoms & weakness increased. his condition is precarious I think tho the Doctors are reassuring....

August 17.... The condition of President causes great fluctuation in Stocks, and things are very sadly out of joint....

August 18.... Stocks vibrated in New York and will run down very heavily. It is a great strain to transfer a government from one faction to another. Arthur to be Pres of United States will be a very great strain. No one wanted him for anythin[g]; he was nominated simply to pacify [Sen. Roscoe] Conkling after Grant failed to get the nomination—and after that crowd was beat to come in to power will be a trial to the patience of our people and strength of our institutions. Garfields chance of recovery looks to me very poor. his extreme debility after 6 weeks Confinement—his weak stomach—and high pulse look to me to indicate approaching dissolution....

August 19.... The danger now seems to be not so much the wounds as his physical condition—extremely debilitated and his stomach so weak nourishment has to be administered by anema, and when attempt was made to give him a little beef juice, he was again threatened with nausea and it was discontinued. The papers are some of them claiming that by reason of his inability Arthur is now president, and the reasons are plausible....

August 23.... The worms are in full force in my field and cotton considerably fringed in places. It was very sudden. We had smelt them before but had not seen them....

August 24.... The worms are very destructive made rags of my cotton....

August 28.... My cotton in the field is nearly finished by worms. one half I think is gathered if not more....

August 31.... I got a terrible letter from Alfred. Willie has procured no situation—is moody and dissatisfied & wants to come home. Oh Father of mercies spare me.... Oh how sad I feel. I looked out for comet last night but brightness of moon prevented its being seen. It is a little to N of W. to west of & below the last star in handle of dipper.[10] cotton news from abroad indicates weakness—Tho the crop reports are of much damage by drought....

September 8.... The Pres was moved to Long Branch on special Train stood trip very well. left 3.30 arrived 1.30 was pleased at the change. Pulse got up to 124 receded to 106....

September 9.... The President is reported to have stood the trip to Long Branch very well—the weather very hot 94° in his room, but there is a pleasant breeze....

---

[10] This comet could have been the Great Comet that Benners noted in his 26 June entry, as it was still visible to the naked eye, or it could have been C/1881 N1 (Schaeberle). Ibid., 483–88.

September 18.... News from the President is bad. Lung complication very distressing & feebleness increasing....

*September 20....*Graham went to Depot...heard the telegram that the President had died last night at 10.30. The long agony is over & I think he is to be considered fortunate.

September 21.... The death of the President is the theme of conversation. In my opinion he died at a fortunate time for him. The sympathy & kindly feeling for him is universal. Gov [Rufus W.] Cobb has issued a proclamation calling on the people every where to assemble and pass resolutions expressive of their sympathy & appreciation. We got no news last night from Arthur the vice President. Cotton is down a little LM. 10 in Selma. quiet.

September 22.... Arthur took the oath as president of U States at his private room in N. York. Brady of N.Y Supreme Co administered it. Cotton is drooping. I got no card. Garfield will be carried to Washington & lie in State in the Rotunda till Saturday & be carried to Ohio for burial. Great meetings on subject of his death.

September 23.... The papers are full of the funeral obsequies of the President. he lies in State in the rotunda at Washington Wednesday, Thursday & Friday to be carried to Cleaveland via Pittsburg on Saturday. Cotton has stiffened. LM 10 1/4. The autopsy of the President discovered the ball to be in the rear of the heart and not in the abdomen above the groin. Science has been greatly at fault and the cuttings he was subjected were great mistakes—Drs [illegible] & Agnew and Hamilton no doubt feel very badly. Arthur the new President is going with the funeral procession to Cleaveland. Grant comes to the front & so far seems to stick to him very closely. shall the country never be clear of his vulgarity and self conceit, not the least of the dreaded consequences of Presidents death is restoration to public notice of the man Grant. Got telegram from Alfred of birth of daughter[11] on 22nd about daylight mother & child doing well.

September 24.... The papers are full of the funeral obsequies of Garfield. 80000 persons are said to have viewed the remains in the

---

[11] Margaret Erwin Benners.

Rotunda. Arthur swore again in the Marble room. Waite swearing him this time. He will not call the senate. He appointed monday 26th for religious exercises in U States—for Garfield....

Times were difficult for Benners since little money was coming in while expenses continued to mount. He wrote: "My burden seems heavier than ever. I pray constantly for strength and wisdom to know what to do and bear what comes."

September 27.... I employed Loyd Grigg to Gin & Pack the cotton at Birdsong place left by my runaway renter Cornelius LeVert. I am to pay him for hauling ginning & packing & delivering the cotton & seed at rate $4.25 for 500 lbs.

September 28.... Jim Chiles came up and reported 2 Bales of his packed & hauled two Bales Wash 3 B/C John 1 small Bale 360 lbs Henry. I bot 1 B/C from WW Jones 11.15 and went to Depot in afternoon & got B/L—Loyd brought in cotton he packed in his Gin weighed 404 lbs—poor sample. Cornelius left me with the bag to hold—and I am glad to get anything....

September 30. Friday.... a warm day, no dust. Liz is well again and Carrie[12] about the same. I got draft from City National on NY for $300 and mailed to Alfred as advance of so much on his rent cotton for 1881....

October 1.... I got letter from Willie. he had rec'd the $60 dft & said he was much obliged. Mag & children doing well. Brown finished front grove fence and I paid him off. I shall never get thro fixing....

Benners watched national and international events on a regular basis. Change in the world could affect the price he received for cotton.

October 2.... There is no change yet in Arthurs Cabinet. Senate is called for 10th Oct. It is said Democrats will elect Pres of senate. Steps are in progress to indict Guiteau in Washington....

---

[12]Carrie (Caroline) Kornegay was Jane's sister and had been staying with the Benners family while she was ill.

October 11.... Democrats in canvas[s] at Washington selected Mr [Thomas Francis] Bayard their candidate for Pres of Senate. The senate was to meet yesterday. The nomination is regarded very important. the Pres of the Senate will be Pres of U States if a vacancy occurs by death of Arthur—cotton is still dull 10 1/8 for L M Selma.

October 12.... I have no easement of the perplexity of disposing of Walker Place. Cotton has declined 1/4 LM 10. I suppose the probability of increased receipts from the fine picking season & high rate of int in Bank of England has produced it. It will probably recover more or less. It is very discouraging. There is no corn brought from country to sell....

October 13.... Guiteau has been indicted for murder of Garfield in Dis of Columbia. Cotton is drooping no card from Selma last night....

October 15.... David Davis [Sen., Ill.]has been elected pres of Senate to turn out Bayard.[13] He voted with rads and they seem to have made very prompt payment—in his speech he says he was honored in this way because he was an independent.

October 19.... There have been heavy storms in England & continent with great damage to shipping & loss of life also on our coast at & about Savannah. The upper Mississippi is rising rapidly. Cloudy & fall like this morning here—acct from Tuscaloosa recd. cotton is off an eighth in Selma L.M. 10 1/8. Yorktown centennial commenced yesterday. Atlantic cotton Expo is going on....

October 21.... Irish affairs are very threatening, a rebellion seems imminent. The land league refuses to pay rent till Parnell who was arrested is released—and more troops are sent to Ireland. It is bad for Cotton and the French are on the eve of a Financial crisis. Yorktown celebration closes to morrow. It has been a grand affair—...

He was involved in an interesting legal case, Jeffries vs. Roulhac. *This case had been delayed until late October.*

---

[13] David Davis, former associate justice of the US Supreme Court, was elected US senator from Illinois and served 1877–1883, was elected president pro tempore of the Senate on 30 October 1881, and served for two years.

October 25.... Jeffries vs Roulhac was called and put off till this morning. Mr Stickney took dinner with me. call last afternoon at office from Judge Brooks. (Jeffries Lawyer)....

October 26. Jeffries case vs Roulhac on trial. Stickney took dinner with me. There are many witnesses, all under the rule—Coleman cross examined Jeffries very persistently not thro yet—

October 27.... Stickney took dinner with me being in attendance as a witness in Jeffries vs Roulhac & et al. I was called last evening—he was not but has to come in again to day. The scaffold fell at the College in which some men were working in taking down one of the towers & falling on a scaffold below it on which Lieser & a boy named Woodruff and a colored man named McSpaddin were working—threw it down & carried them to the floor. Mr Lieser had both legs broken & one arm & badly bruised—and each of the two others were badly hurt. Liz & I called at Liesers last night....

October 28.... Jeffries vs Roulhac et al was dragging its slow length along. Mr Stickney came up to dinner. The argument begins to day. I visited Mr Lieser last night. he is suffering a good deal with his broken legs and arm but says there is no internal injury. How he fell the distance he did without being crushed is a mystery. The little boy is getting along pretty well but Mack the negro was reported to be dying....

October 29.... Mr Lieser is said to be doing tolerably well. Jeffries vs Roulhac went to the jury last night and they are hung this 8 AM.... The Jeffries case consumed the whole week & not yet decided. Judge Moore wants to leave here to day to go to Lowndes.

October 30.... In Jeffries vs Roulhac verdict for Plff after breakfast $1754.48. Moore finished court & went off—Lieser was reported as well as could be expected....

November 2.... I went to the college building at 9 1/2 AM with Derrick & Snedecor to look at the place where scaffolds fell with Lieser and others and it looks like a miracle that they were not all instantly mashed to death by a fall of 50 ft....

November 6.... called to see Mr Lieser last evening on return from P. office—he is suffering greatly. Knitting of bones has set in & is very painful. The other wounded ones are reported doing well....

In the last months of 1881, Benners tried to collect from his renters. While a few paid full rent, most paid little or nothing. He had no one else to take their place, so they stayed on the land. He saw no choice but to continue in this unfortunate situation.

November 29.... a fine day yest I settled with John Edwards & Pauldo, Eli promised to go to Pascagoula & make the money & pay me. Mr Ervin who bought the mortgaged mule said he had sold him to Judge King but would pay what I required, but he would pursue Eli & I agreed to look to Eli. Mr N B Jones is very sick. Carrie is better. very little cotton in Town yesterday. Burke having failed to pay anything on his acct I told him I should not be able to advance to him again. Rhodes brought me this morning a 1/4 of Beef weighing 73 pounds. I sent Tom Lee to put it up.

November 30.... a cloudy day & to me a very unpleasant one. Henry Chapman came up & what to do with him is my difficulty. he makes no impression on the large debt he owes. I got 1 B/C from A T Cook on his debt to me & bought two from I. E. Stringfellow . Orren Adams has badly disappointed me in his treatment and so have others—The experience is right hard....

December 1.... a rainy disagreeable day yesterday. Buck Taylor came up again. My kindness results in his not paying a cent on his advances which he owes for 76, 7, 8, 9, 01 & 42 lbs rent unpaid....

December 2.... I had a very busy day. Henry, Jim, Wash & Pauldo had to be attended to and each rented and gave mortgages for "wances" next year. of course it is a poor business but that is Walker Place lay out. I have no offer from any one else to rent or purchase....

December 3. Saturday.... I had a very busy & very troublesome day. Math a failure was on me to know what I was going to do about it. Burke before I got seated. Abe worried me into a renewal of his contract. I sold him Burkes mule & Eli's wagon for $135 & agreed to advance him 35 on the next year. Ed Wallace paid me 2 B/C on his debt, & has 3 more B/C....

December 4. Ther 64° 7 PM 60 7 AM. Pleasant day very cloudy in evening. Mr Stickney dined with me. we went to Depot after dinner. Round ticket by Either road to Atlanta $6.85 good for 8 days—a large company from here leave in the morning—he one of them. I cant go being obliged to stay & enjoy myself with ungrateful negroes & reluctant debtors—... Letter from Alfred last night. says his practice is better this year than last. Health poor. Could have been worth $1000 if he had sold Walker place 4 years ago. I wish he had. He got the proceeds of the Bale from Burke on the rent of last year. Burke has paid me nothing for 2 yrs & never will—he owe[s] between 2 & 300 Dols A. T. Cook delivered on 30th 1 B/C on his debt & came in and gave me B/L yesterday—Abes Bale sold for 10 5/8s—Town was very full of idle negroes yesterday....

December 7.... The Guiteau trial for Garfields murder still progresses and he is as conceited and impudent as ever & says it was the Lords doing. To turn such a creature loose upon society would be as great craziness as his—...

December 10.... There was not much cotton in Town. I got 1 Bale. There is a depression in the market all around. The meeting of congress creates not much interest. Arthurs message is rather a commonplace affair a sort of omnium gatherum[14]—indicating no special policy—the composition is good & there are no minatory utterances. He is a mere figure head in my opinion. Grant & Conkling in power—...

There was good news—Willie had a job at an insurance office for $35 a month. Alfred was successful in Dallas. However, Ed remained in an asylum; showing little evidence of progress. It saddened Benners. The holidays were no longer happy times, with his wife gone, Alfred in Dallas, and Ed in an asylum.

December 25.... a fair day till evening. There were a great many negroes in Town, and all the stores seemed to be crowded. a sad reminiscence of my loss, no wife to help me fill the childrens stockings. My poor Jane is no more. God help me it is very bitter. I had Jimmy Tunstals will proved and recorded yesterday. There were no persons to

---

[14] A miscellaneous collection.

dine with us yesterday. Isaacs children are there. Joe had a chill and fever. The presents were under the plates this morning....

December 26.... I went to church in the morning. My sadness almost overpowered me. My thoughts would run on my poor wife. It was oh so sad a Christmas to me—my poor little children. We had Isaac's children & Mary Walker to dinner. Mr Kit DuBose came in after dinner & Jef Blount last night. The weather was cloudy & uncomfortable with drizzle in afternoon & it rained last night a good deal—and is threatening rain a[nd] snow this morning.

December 31.... Liz went visiting and spent the night at Jeffries. Graham & I played Bezique. The cotton card shows an 1/8 decline LM 10 1/2 quiet. Package of christmas presents came from Alfred. Liz Fanny & I rec'd a pair of gloves. Jenny Silk Hdkf & Graham a neck tie—all were delighted—and presents highly prized—Graham went hunting killed only one bird. We are looking for Mr Watson—and so goes out the year 1881. To me it has been loaded with distress and perplexity, but God knows what is best for us—and even those bitter afflictions and bereavements may be for our future welfare—what the coming year will disclose fortunately we are not allowed to know. May God grant that be it what it may I may receive it with thankfulness to him knowing it is the dispensation of a kind & loving father.

1884

The cotton market remained disappointing throughout the early months of 1884. Receipts continued to fall as heavy failures in businesses affected the market. Some of Benners's properties were without renters. The Mellown Place was a special concern; it went without a renter for almost two months. He finally found a buyer in late February. Many who owed him money wanted to extend the time for paying their debts. This bothered him.

January 6.... I have not rented Mellown place yet. No news from Ross Grist—Played Bezique. I beat 4 out of six. No card from Selma. The falling off last week was 90.000 Bales....

January 8.... No news from cotton last night. No montgy paper. Mails are strangely deranged. I am much worried about not hearing from Jenny & Willie.

January 9.... Fitzhugh wrote me a letter about renting Blount Place. Answered letter & would take 25 dollars—to 1st December 84, reserving right to occupy houses. Mellown Place is still on my hands unrented....

January 10.... Parker Hatch[15] & Wash came up on the freight train. The former paid me $41 on his rent note 83 and the latter fixed up to run me again for 84. Parker stayed last night—I got no card from Selma—and by newspaper cotton is unchanged in Liv 5 15/16 NY 10 5/8. falling off 1 day 10,348 bales....

January 11.... I have Mellown place still on my hands—and have heard nothing from Ross Grist—Defaults in payment are numerous & prospects not good.

January 17. Ther 40° 36° a very cloudy day with rain after supper. Ross Grist came up from Buckridge. Holcroft came to say he ginned the cotton and put 106 pounds of his own cotton in the bale with mine—which was very unsatisfactory to me—as I have no certainty how much he put in nor that the quality was equal to mine—cotton is off a little in Selma 10 1/2. I wrote to Baker Lawler & Co to turn the Bale over to Ross and to Ross to sell it. Graham has a very bad cold & stays home.

January 22. Ther 34° 28° Another very cold day & night. Ice everywhere & a very white frost this morning. The Scarff corner property was sold at auction yesterday.[16] Tom Cowin bought it for $1325—it is said he is going to put up a hotel there—The property was sold for division among the 8 children of Allen C Jones & his wife Catharine Jones legacy to them by Mrs Erwins will. There is no change in the cotton market. The card from Selma reports Mid 10 1/8 nominal.

---

[15] Parker Hatch was son of Alfred Hatch, Benners's father-in-law. He lost his lands and began renting from Benners.

[16] W. D. C. Scarff, cabinetmaker, Greensboro. V. Gayle Snedecor, *A Directory of Greene County for 1855–6* (Mobile AL: Strickland & Co., 1856; ed. and indexed by Franklin Shackelford Moseley, Eutaw AL: *The Greene County Democrat*, 1957) 38.

The receipts continue to fall off but heavy failures in business are affecting the market.

January 26.... Graham went to Debate at college—Question is this world growing better—decided in negative.... Mellown place is still on my hands & I do not know what to do with it. The negroes are burning it up. It annoys me no little....

January 27. Ther 34. 40 A very fine day clouding up before morning—there were many negroes in Town and a bad day for me—John E. Harris came & paid the mortgage of J.H. Hany—L.H. Smith came to bother me with his requests....

January 29.... The pressure for money is very tight—Randal Pickens was in on me in the morning—he borrowed 12 dols. I agreed to let him board the house & put new sills where needed and to allow him 12 & pay for the nails—the indifference of persons who have got money from me in their necessities is great—Mellown place is still on my hands—but God is good....

January 31.... Mellown Place is still on my hands. No bidders—I am very tired of it—and would sell if I could—The sale of Public Lands in Ala at Montgomery & Huntsville has been suspended pending legislation—very proper action I expect. Syndicates were ready to gobble them all up—and coal mining would certainly not be expedited by the sale....

February 1.... A very cloudy moist warm day. After supper a few stars shone out and in the night it turned colder and was clear & bright at sunrise. A Mr Townsend agent for Appleton & Co called and delivered the Cyclopedias I had subscribed for and I sent him the old Americana 14 vols and paid him $114 for the 24 vols of Appleton Cyclopedia—Graham is very much delighted with the purchase.... Graham had holiday examination going on—I am sorely puzzled to know what to do with him. The amount of learning he can acquire at this concern is not very great & I hate to send him off by himself. We have no late news from Willie—he was undecided to go back to Trezivants.

February 2.... Had a call from J.D. Cook—wanted his debt extended and to borrow more money—Every body is distressingly short....

February 3. Ther 60° 56° A pleasant mild day clouding up after supper and very cloudy this AM. L.H. Smith besieged me again & I loaned him a little to get rid of him. Wm Chadwick paid 6.50 on his long delayed loan. Jenny Vail came to dinner brought Willie Pickens with her—There were a good many people in Town. Cotton is nom 10 1/4 Selma Liv Dull 5 15/16. NY D.10 3/4. Got a letter last night from Watson from the Plantation. He was going to Henry Stollenwercks, said he had been nursing the fire very closely and took first fair day to go to Stollenwercks—

February 4.... No call for Mellown place yet—it bothers me no little as the place without a tenant will be pillaged & ruined....

February 7.... I am annoyed by destruction at Mellown place—no tenant yet nor likely to get one. To farm it is to spend money without any return—& no one wants it....

The winter remained severe. Benners seldom went out unless absolutely necessary, preferring instead to play Bezique with his friends and to entertain company. He also worried about storms and the rivers that were overflowing, causing considerable damage.

February 14. Ther 72° 36° A very cloudy threatening day. Thunder storm after supper. wind shifting to the north and turning cold. Very cloudy and cool this morning—Manuel came yesterday & I was persuaded to try him again. he failed to pay what he owed by $46. It was such an ugly evening I did not come to office after dinner played Bezique with Watson. Cotton outlook is not good owing to strikes &c in the north. Liv is off 1/16 6 3/4 Selma quiet 10 1/8—Graham has finished his examination & commenced a new term at college—

February 15.... The river is reported as having risen 38 feet and an overflow is looked for. There are great floods in the Ohio & Kentucky & Mississippi rivers and much loss & distress. Cotton advcd 1/16 in Liv. Selma 10 1/8 easy—...

February 16.... Ben Vail came to tea. Henry Chapman writes for meat. We played Bezique. Mr W beat me 3 to 1.... The floods on the Ohio river were very disastrous & Congress has made an appropriation for their relief—...

February 20.... A very remarkable day. I went to depot to see Mr Watson off on the train, he leaving for Selma. I returned to my office and on looking out of my window about 12 1/2 oclock I saw a very black threatening cloud in the North West—to get ahead of the rain I shut up and went home—the wind commenced to blow furiously. I laid on the sofa & took a nap & on waking discovered we had had a very hard wind, & rain. It stopped and faired off and I went to my office after dinner. The wind continued high. I went to depot in afternoon. Mr Evans told me they had a severe storm at Marion, Hamburg & Scotts—that several persons were reported killed. The wind continued high and blew very hard last night. Ther fell 32 degrees in the night and there was ice and a very cold morning—the wind blew off the top of the mulberry tree at the corner of the Piazza in the backyard. it was very old, being there when I moved to the house....

February 22.... Mr Watson returned on the train last night. He said he had a good time in Selma. We played Bezique last night. He beat me 2 to 1. I rec'd no card from Selma—I hear the demand is good—at 10 1/8 for Mid. The decrease in recpts continues very heavy—Strikes & general derangement in business prevents advance. The cyclones of 19th were very extensive & destructive.

February 23.... The accounts from the tornado of 19th February are awful—it extended from N. Carolina to Miss. Number of persons killed large. Played Bezique last night. I beat 4 to 1.

February 24.... I rented Mellown place to Charles Wynne Sr for $70. It was a great relief to me. As soon as it was rented another man came in to rent it, and I had still another call for it yesterday morning. Card from Selma rep's 10 1/4 good demand. Mr Tutwiler paid me the balance of Mrs Grigg's debt. We played Bezique. I was beaten 2 to 1. Mr W is talking of going home next week....

His good friend Watson had remained in Greensboro for many months but decided to return to his home in Massachusetts. This bothered Benners, who needed the companionship of his best friend—"I missed Mr Watson very much. He will be shocked at his Northern climate leaving a mild pleasant bright & getting into snow and arctic conditions." With his wife gone, Benners depended more heavily upon his friends. Mary Avery, a good friend, had a fire that destroyed most of her house. Benners, with the help of friends, raised enough money to restore the house.

April 3.... Th e residence & kitchen at Miss Mary Avery's place was burned yesterday morning about 10 o'clock. I walked out there on hearing the news with Mr Snedecor. A sadder sight I never saw. The fire caught on the roof from a burning chimney and the wind being very high and the house built of cedar logs burned very rapidly. Everything Miss Mary had including all her papers trinkets & 40 in gold & silver was burned. The clothes of all the family was burned. Johns gold watch & chain & Mr Cobbs gun were burned. Oh it was a pitiful scene—The old homestead where all the children were born & raised a smoking ruin. I invited Mary Avery & the two girls to come & stay with us—she went last night to Mr Bayols.[17] We have started a subscription for their relief and have 7 or 800 dollars subscribed. The sympathy for them is very strong—I read acct for Ed's Board yesterday $150.40 cts for which I sent by mail to W.C. Perkins dft on City National Bank of Selma. Mitchel ploughed in the field yesterday and continues to day. Cotton advc'd in N York to 11 1/2 for min. I got no card. got the news from R H. Stickney.

April 4.... A beautiful day—bright and breezy—I was engaged nearly all day with subscription to Mr Cobbs & family—the response from the community was very liberal about $980 was subscribed before night. I wrote a long letter to Mr Watson & sent him a partial list of subscribers—Liz got a letter from Ella & a present of a beautiful apron.... Liz is sewing for Mary Avery—...

April 5.... The subscription for Mr Cobbs & family reaches $1200 & over. I never saw a finer exhibition of sympathy & liberality—Letter from Willie states he has gone to Denton [Texas] to run an insurance agency. The confinement was too great for him where he was. God bless him & keep him. He represents Liverpool & London Globe, Fire Association of Phil., Continental of N.Y., Niagara Fire Insurance of N.Y. & several others secured since his card was printed. Letter from Dr

---

[17] Edward Bayol, planter, Hollow Square, Greensboro. Ibid., 8.

Bryce & recpt for $150.40. Eds health is good—sleeps well—attends the discussions & enjoys himself.... The subscription for Mr Cobbs & the family reached 1300....

April 7.... Gen Bocock is reported to have sent $50 for Mr Cobbs & family—It has now passed $1300....

April 10.... Miss Mary Avery and two of the Cobbs children are staying with us. Yesterday was emancipation day was not observed as usual. Negroes had a supper at Eborns old store. Isaac & I came uptown after supper and saw the Babel in there from the Street....

Mary and the Cobbs children stayed with the Benners family for many weeks. She also stayed with other friends until she was able to make arrangements for a permanent residence. During the same time, a skating rink opened in Greensboro. Everyone wanted to skate or watch the skaters, and Benners enjoyed going down to the rink and watching. It was a special experience for many in town who had never gone skating or even seen a rink. Graham tested the rink and was very satisfied.

May 4.... Mr C.L.S went with me to dinner. Miss Mary Avery & Willie Cobbs came to supper & spent the night. We all went to skating rink. John Cobbs came in to supper. Graham was one of the skaters & got along very well. They were all tired enough when they got home. Cloudy this morning....

May 6.... Liz & I went to the skating rink last night at Dorman's hall. Mrs Harvey & her children went with us. It was entertaining. We were much amused with the perseverance of a little Miss Shivers who fell very frequently—she would jump up & go it again. Bycicling was also introduced....

May 7.... There was skating again last night and I went with Liz. Fanny & Mary Walker went with Graham. Exhibition was quite entertaining. Mr Knight caused much amusement by his falls & good naturedly taking them. Mrs Erwin skated very gracefully. Grahams skates did not suit him & he soon quit....

May 8.... I went to rink last night with Liz—was much amused....

The political season began early. Both parties decided to meet in Chicago to choose their candidates for the fall. The Republicans met in early June and the Democrats one month later. Benners could sense a chance for a Democratic victory, the first in twenty-eight years. He became very excited and watched the campaign closely.

June 2.... The Republican convention at Chicago meets on the 3rd. Blaine seems to be ahead. Arthur next. Sherman next. No changes in price of cotton....

June 4.... Chicago Republican convention met yest in Chicago. No news yet. Ala State convention meets to day....

June 5.... The news from Rep. Con. at Chicago is looked for with much interest. Lynch negro from Miss. was elected temporary chairman beating Clayton Scallawag from Arkansas....[18]

June 6. Friday.... Chicago news is indefinite. No one knows how it will result. Gen Sherman declined to run—In Montgomery Jim Webb was appointed a delegate to Dem Con at Chicago & Syd Moore....

June 7.... Republican Con at Chicago nominated Blaine & Logan for President & Vice President. The grand agony is over & result—no one had put together beforehand. I think Blaine if elected will try to signalise himself by some great thing & do mischief. I would rather have had Arthur—he would have made less trouble. Col Harvey came over last night to say that Mrs Harvey & children would like to go to the Cantata of Jep[h]thas daughter with us and Fanny & I went & they went with us. The performance was very creditable for amateurs. The Miss Lavenders did very well....

June 12. Thursday.... Blaines nomination is very unacceptable in all New England except Maine—a number of papers and prominent men of Rep party say they will not support him. The Times of N. York one [of]

---

[18] John Lynch, served in Congress from 1873–1877. Member of the Republican national committee for the state of Mississippi 1884–1889 and temporary chairman of the Republican National Convention at Chicago in 1884. He defeated Powell Clayton, former senator from Arkansas, for the position of chairman of the convention. *Biographical Directory*, 1485.

them. [Henry Ward] Beecher says he will never vote for him while he lives. Cotton 6 7/16 Liv, NY 11 5/8 firm—it rises mighty slow....

June 14.... Blaine & Logan are filling the papers. There is much disaffection among decent republicans....

June 15. Sunday.... Got papers New York Worlds from Mr Watson. Independents pretend to be organising against Blaine in Boston & New York. Tildens letter declining to run leaves everything at sea as to the dem nom'n. Mr Bayard is spoken of & Mr Cleaveland & Field & Thurman. No one can guess who it will be. Cotton is unchanged. The stringency in money prevents its rising....

Jenny was at a boarding school in Montgomery. She was ill during the winter. Liz made dresses for her, and Benners sent money regularly. On 15 June, he sent a ticket and $5, asking her to come home for a while. She arrived on the eighteenth and stayed until the end of September.

June 16.... I sent $5 and my 1000 mile ticket to Jennie to come home Wednesday 18th....

June 18. Wednesday.... We look for Jenny from school to night. It will be a happy time for her and us all. I have not heard her report....

June 19. Thursday.... Graham & I went to the depot to meet Jenny who got here last evening from Montg'y. Lula Stickney and Annie Cobbs came same time. Jenny rode home in Stickneys carriage. Mrs Stickney was sick & did not go to meet them. Jenny looks quite thin. Got 2nd prize for good behavior....

June 20. Friday.... Jenny was perfectly delighted to get home.... Mary Walker called to see Jenny—and in the evening Mrs Harvey & Mrs Inge. We took a short walk before supper & after supper Fanny & Jenny & I went to Methodist church to hear a service of Song. Prof Irvings class sang very well. It was a bright night & stars shone brightly....

June 21.... Jenny is getting over her fatigue & is happy. Mary Avery's school[19] closed yesterday. Graham finished his examination & last night went to the skating rink....

June 24. Tuesday. Ther 80° 76° A fine bright warm growing day. The prize declamation came off at the College & as Graham was one of the speakers we were all much interested. He spoke very well—Lord Chat[h]ams speech in parliament. Henry Beattie & Rich Hobson[20] also spoke very well & I think the Prize will go to one of them. I went with Graham & Liz & Jenny again last night—Major Ivey Lewis dined with us—it was very pleasant....

June 27. Friday.... Jenny had Mary Walker, Sally Pasteur, Bland & Maria Randolph to dinner with her. Last night Jenny Liz & I went to skating rink but there being no one there but a few boys skating we did not go in but returned home. Graham joined the singing class at Pres church....

Benners supported Grover Cleveland, the Democratic nominee. He worried about splits in New York and Ohio over the tariff. Cleveland had not been his choice, however, Benners began to recognize that he was a strong candidate, one who could unite the party and reach out for Republican votes.

July 8. Tuesday.... To day dem Con meets at Chicago—a very hot time anticipated. P&M Ins Co report 10 pr ct div payable on 14 Inst. We have no late news from cotton—the weed is fruiting very poorly. My big cow has no calf & dont look like she was going to shortly. I am still in perplexity about what to do with my family & myself.

July 9.... Convention met yesterday. Hubbard of Texas selected as temporary chairman. Arthur vetoed Fitz John Porter bill. Senate loaded down Mexican Bill with arrears of pensions for Union solders to amt 200,000,000 & killed it—its original friends voted against it....

---

[19] Mary Avery's school was Oak Grove Academy. Her father was John Avery, rector of St. Paul's 1835–1837.

[20] Richmond Pearson Hobson was Graham Benners's closest friend. He fought in the Spanish American War and became a hero at the harbor of Santiago de Cuba. He served as U. S. Representative from Alabama 1907–1915. He was a crusader for alcohol prohibition and introduced the first national alcohol prohbition bill in 1911.

July 12. Saturday.... The nomination of Cleaveland was rec'd by telegraph. It was a disappointment to our people who wanted a bigger man. Thurman or Bayard or Hendricks or McDonald or Field. To day I hear Hendricks has accepted nom for vice President....

July 13. Sunday.... The nomination of Cleaveland was a little disappointing to our people who wanted Thurman or Bayard.[21] They are much pleased at nomination of Hendricks.[22] Tammany was defied & went off very sore headed. Price of cotton is very weak. N.Y. 11 1/8 Liv 6 3/16....

July 14. Monday.... Cleavelands nom is well rec'd by all but Tammany—Their trade is Politics & Cleaveland was not the man for their Jobs & swindling.... The contest for Presidency will be very bitter. Dem prospects now are good—

July 15.... Tom Seay & Wiley Tunstal[l][23] returned from Chicago yesterday, the latter was alternate for J.E. Webb who did not attend. Seay regards success of dem ticket much endangered by splits in NY & Ohio & on the tariff. I was very uncomfortable & perplexed about what to do. I have packed my trunk & am nearly ready to leave for Washington & the North. I cant carry all—& I dont know what to do....

Mr. Watson invited Benners to visit him in Northampton, Massachusetts. He had done this numerous times, but Benners had always refused. He did not like to travel, but this time he accepted the offer because he needed the help of a good dentist. Also, he enjoyed Watson's companionship and wanted to see the changes in Northampton. So he left Greensboro on 15 July and arrived in Northampton on 21 July. The family was pleased to welcome him, but the daughters—Harriet, Ella, and Rosa—"were much put out that Liz did not come with me. I had to make my peace the best I could." His first days in Northampton were spent in sightseeing.

---

[21] Allen G. Thurman, former senator from Ohio from 1869 to 1881 and delegate to the Democratic National Convention in 1884. Snedecor, *Greene County*, 1919.

[22] Thomas A. Hendricks, senator from Indiana, 1863–1869. He was unsuccessful as the nominee for vice president on the Democratic ticket with Tilden in 1876. Ibid., 1298.

[23] Wiley Tunstall was the first president of the Alabama Railroad Commission.

July 21.... After breakfast Mr Watson gave me a ride in the buggy around horse mountain. It was very beautiful. We also rode along mill river. On Sunday I went to church morning & afternoon. Was pleased with the Peal of bells in the morning—had the service in afternoon. I called yesterday to see Dr Jones the dentist and in the afternoon I rode to town with Miss Harriet & she drove around the town considerably—it was a beautiful ride—on reaching home we took tea & Mr Watson & I squared for a game of Bezique. I beat 5 games straight along—after which we went to bed about 11 oclock. My trouble now is the pain & expense and discomfort ahead of me in having my teeth fixed. I dont know how I shall stand it. Mr Watsons place is perfectly lovely—and grounds are kept in style. The city has grown very much since I was here.

July 23.... I called in the morning to see Dr Jones—& he was engaged—again in the afternoon Mr Watson hitched up for a drive. I called again at Dr Jones. He pulled out three teeth and an old stump and filed the front teeth. I have to wait till next week to have in impression of the jaw taken to have some new teeth made. I was much pleased with expertness & quickness with which he operated—after he was through. Northampton is a beautiful place—and the trimness and neatness of the city & streets is a perfect wonder—I visited the cemetery with Mr Watson—the same neatness and order prevails here. There are some handsome monuments—but plainness & solidity are characteristics. The weather has been very cool—and overcoats have been very comfortable. Mr W has fires every night & morning—they say it has been very hot this summer—& will be again. I feel very much improved by high living and the bracing air. We played Bezique last night. I got beaten twice. I played a game with Miss Harriet & beat her. I shall be gratefull at the completion of my teeth. I was surprised & pleased at quickness & expertness of his filing my teeth and pulling them out—he certainly is very expert at his business—the filing was done by a small emory wheel revolving by motion of his foot—it was very cute & creditable. I am impatient of the delay necessary. I was unwilling to have my front teeth pulled out as they seemed so solid....

July 24. Thursday.... I went to town in the morning after Breakfast—and then Mr Watson drove to East Hampton and round by the foot of Mount Holyoke—the mist in the air seemed to magnify & elevate the mountain very much. I passed along by the bend in Conn river. There were a very huge amt of logs brot down the Connecticut river. I had a magnificent drive. I am still so much impressed with the neatness of the houses & grounds around here. The fountains and flowers are very pretty—I begin to like the idea of no fences. I think it will be extensively adopted....

July 27. Sunday.... Yesterday was perfectly lovely. I looked out on rising to see Mount Holyoke. The outline was very sharp & distinct. After breakfast Mr W. invited me to take a ride with him to Holyoke. We had a delightful ride stopping in Town to get the mail. There were quite a number of persons visiting Mt. Holyoke. We mounted on the inclined R Road to the top. The sensation of ascending & descending is not pleasant, but the views from the top are very pretty. The meadow looks like patchwork a striped—& was very pretty. We saw by the clock in N Hampton that it was 11.15. There is a large Claude Lorraine [Lorrain] glass[24] and spectacles of a color to produce a similar effect. Mr French the proprietor gave us some music on the Autophone. It is a wonderful instrument. Perforated papers are inserted & music is made by blowing the instrument....

July 29. Tuesday.... A nice pretty day. I called on Dr Jones and he said he could not fix my teeth till Aug 20 at 1/2 past 2. This is disappointing. Mr W. gave me a splended drive to top of Mt Tom. It is higher & the view larger than Holyoke. I took a walk with Ella in the afternoon which I enjoyed very much. Played Bezique with Mr W last night. Beat 2 out of 3 games. Got a letter from Liz. She reports all well and pretty warm—we have a cool time here. It rained last night and is raining this morning....

August 1.... It was a mixed day sunshine & shade and a little rain in the evening. I walked to P. office in the morning and got nothing. I played Bezique with Miss Ella and beat her twice—and with Mr W. who

---

[24] Lorrain glass—A smoked convex lens used for viewing landscapes, its name deriving from the artist Claude Lorrain who used one.

won 3 out of 4 & Miss Harriet I beat 1 game. We took a ride in the spring wagon to Town. Miss Ella & Miss Harriet went along—we went around on two sides the grounds of Mr Lyman, a tea merchant of N. York. They were terraced & very handsome. I am very sorry Dr Jones could not fix my teeth & be done with it....

August 3. Sunday.... I received a letter from Dr Sereno Watson[25] inviting me to visit him in Cambridge—and wishing Mr W. to come with me—which he agreed to do and we expect to go over there next week. This will be novel experiences for me. I shall be very glad to see Dr Sereno whom I admire & like very much....

August 5. Tuesday. Mr Watson & I rode to Depot in Northampton and took the train at 11.30 yesterday for Boston. We missed a train at Springfield leaving at 12.49 & had to wait for next one at 1.35 and reached Boston 4.00 and came out here in the Street cars—I got a smell of salt water as I came out. I was much impressed with the city as I saw it. It is very pretty. Dr Sereno Watson is keeping house in Cambridge & we are his guests—I am sorry to say it is raining this morning. I write from my little room in 3rd Story. The windows have gauze to keep out mosquitos—rain seems very unfortunate. Boston is a big Town 300,000.

August 7. Thursday. Cambridge Massachusetts. It was a pleasant day Wednesday. It rained on tuesday morning. Mr H Watson went over to Manchester to see his cousin Mrs Dance & Dr Sereno carried me all over the colleges—Austin Hall, Memorial Hall &c &c. Library is very large & well kept. in that afternoon he drove me around every where in a buggy & it was a glorious drive—at night we played Bezique—he beat me 2 to 1. Mr H Watson returned at 8 oclock P.M. yesterday. after breakfast we visited the Old South, Faneuil Hall, Market house &c &c and at 12.30 took boat for Nantucket Beach—it was a splendid day & we had a delightful ride over—took dinner at Nantucket house—enjoyed the walk on the Beach & seeing the bathers—and at 5 returned for Boston. Rode out in omnibus & Street cars—got tea and about 9.30

---

[25] Sereno Watson, Henry Watson's brother, was secretary of the Planters Insurance Company, a bank in Greensboro before the war. He was an abolitionist and left the South when war broke out.

went to bed in little room in the attic where I am now writing before breakfast. It is very quiet here....

August 8. Friday.... We went on Street cars to Boston. Mr H Watson felt unwell and returned. Mr Sereno & I went to Common, State House, Art Museum and Trinity Church. It was raining when we got thro and we took a cab for street cars & in them we came home. it rained all the way. We had no umbrella. I changed my clothes—Dr Sereno lent me his coat. He is a splendid fellow. Trinity is the finest church I ever saw....

August 10. Sunday. Fine day. Pleasantly warm. I left Mr Sereno Watson in Cambridge and Mr Watson & I and he went to corner of Shepard Street & North Avenue where we bid Mr Sereno good bye & took North Avenue cars for Boston and then took cars to Union Depot where we took 11 AM train for Northhampton. Had a very pleasant trip—had to wait in Springfield nearly an hour for Connecticut River RR train at 3.15 P.M. which we took and got home at 4.10. Had a very pleasant visit. got mail from home—letters from Fanny, Liz, Graham & Jenny & they reported terrible rains on Thursday Aug [blank space]. Crops badly damaged....

August 21. Thursday.... I read & played Bezique in the morning—and after dinner Mr W. drove me in buggy to Dr Jones office to get my teeth fixed. I dreaded it very much but the discomfort was not as great as I expected. I took my seat after he got thro with a little boy whose tooth pained badly—In a short time he had his composition ready and took an impression of under jaw—and then of upper—There was very little inconvenience or discomfort. I am to go there this morning at 10 oclock ...

August 22. Friday.... After breakfast I went with Mr W. down to Dr Jones and he worked on my teeth about an hour—after which we returned home. I amused myself reading Hudibras....[26] Miss Julia gave Miss Dagget a small party last evening from 4 1/2 to 6 oclock. 2 Misses Cook, Mrs Cooper, Miss Maultby & 3 Mr Clarks were there. It passed off very well. They amused themselves chatting and looking at the

---

[26] Poem by Samuel Butler, 1612–1680, a satire aimed at the Puritans.

flowers—among others at the moon flower which spread 4 or 5 of its flowers but not till the company had all gone. They were treated to ice tea & chocolate Peaches & milk and buttered bread. At 6 1/2 company had all left and we had our usual tea—after tea we talked and played whist. Mr Arthur Watson & Miss Mary Dugget played against Rosa & me. They beat us two games. I got a card from Graham yesterday. Jim Chiles says crop is good....

August 26.... We had a magnificent drive—went to Hadley where we saw Bishop Huntingtons farm and his Jersey cattle. I did not think the latter as fine as I expected from what I had heard. We saw the Bishop himself chatting with a Butcher who had driven his wagon into the yard. It looked like a very extensive river farm. The views & scenery on road to here were especially beautiful as we frequently got a look at Con river. We drove by Mass Agricultual College and drove to Amherst—saw the beautiful Episcopal & Congregational churches & many pretty neat places in Amherst—did not go to the college buildings. Came home to dinner having ridden upwards of Twenty miles. After dinner went to Florence to get horse shoe....

August 28. Thursday Ther 66° The sun rose very bright and it was a fair day. I walked to P. office with Mr Arthur Watson, found Dr Jones in his office looking for him to send me a message—he asked me to give him a sitting which I did for over 2 hours. The lower teeth he said fit very nicely—he had to make upper ones over on account of their not matching lower ones. Gave me the lower ones to wear which I did—wore them yesterday—glands under my throat are swollen. Rode with Miss Julia & Rosa—played whist last night. Ella & I vs Mr W & Miss Harriet. They beat 2 to 1.

August 29.... A very pleasant day. I went to P.O. with Arthur. Mr Watson drove down in carriage and we took a nice drive to South Hadley falls. They are very pretty and the ride was a very pleasant one. I saw the Holyoke Seminary for young ladies which is a very large & handsome affair—the observatory a very pretty little structure for astronomical purposes. I got home 12.45 and after dinner went to Dr Jones—he fitted the uppers and I came off with the teeth in my mouth. The sensation is not pleasant and the risk of falling out makes it disagreeable. I hope I shall get used to wearing them when they will feel more natural. I got a long letter from Liz—she reports them all well, Carrie was going to Livingston. Mr Cobbs had gone to New York & Mr C.L.S. had to send for them. Charles had picked 100 pounds of cotton. There is 1/16 advance reported in N.Y. 10 13/16—and now I must think about going home. I dread the trip no little.

August 30. Saturday.... We rode down thro the rain after breakfast. I went to see Dr Jones to see how he thought of my new teeth—he liked them very well and eased them in one or two places. I got him to reduce again one of my large front teeth. They of course feel strangely in my mouth but are not as uncomfortable as I should have expected. I got letter from Alfred—he said all were well and Willie had gone to the book business in partnership with Mr J.R. Burton—they will carry on a bookstore in connection with Insurance. Gus sent specimens of his work at printing. It rained so much yesterday I did not get out of the house after riding home in a hard rain. We played cards—and again last night. I am to see Dr Jones again to day. My mind is occupied now with thoughts of getting home—I dread the Journey very much....

September 5. Friday Ther 78° 67° A very bright lovely day. The sun rose bright but a fog soon rose and hid the mountains—but was gradually dispersed. Mr W. fixed up a picnic for Whatelys Glen about [blank] miles from here and it is certainly one of the prettiest places I ever saw. Company was Misses Harriet & Julia Watson, Miss Mary Avery, Mr Henry & Arthur Watson & myself.[27] The sun was warm & we carried umbrellas but had a pleasant ride out there, mailed our letters at Whately—and drove on to the Glen. We found the road obstructed when we got there with a gate & it locked. Mr W. went back to the house for the key and brought it—the woman telling him that it was against the rule for horses to stay inside but his might for a dollar... We opened the gate & proceeded to the Glen—and explored up the brook a quarter of a mile. It was a mountain brook in a deep gorge of the rocks making a succession of lovely falls & cascades & most melodious music.

---

[27] Miss Mary Avery and Mr. Cobbs went to New York for him to get his ear worked on and for her to visit friends. She continued on to Northampton for a visit with the Watsons.

Mr Sanderson the proprietor had arrived in our absence and gave Mike permission to make a fire for cooking—and it was made & corn & potatoes & beef steak under way. He was greatly mollified in finding who we were—said he had lived in the South and knew on seeing me that I was from there—The greenness of the wood prevented the fire from burning as fast as we desired. It was finally done to a turn. Mr W. gave Sanderson a toddy—and he left apparently well pleased—and we had on the rude planks which were there for a table, a most delightful repast. Irish potatoes roasted, corn ditto, Beefsteak, buttered bread, crackers, cider, cakes mangoes &c. After the repast was over Mr Arthur & I went to top of the mountain and got a very extensive and lovely view—then returned to the glen where folks were resting—Mr W. taking a nap. I laid down on plank seat but did not go to sleep. I especially enjoyed the music of the waterfall. We hitched up locked the gate behind us & leaving the key at Mr Sandersons we had a very pleasant ride home which we reached in an hour and thirty five minutes. Miss Avery went to depot to go to Williamsburg. Miss H & Ella & Rosa & Arthur going down with her. I played Bezique with Mr W. last night & he beat me 3 out of 4 drawing double Bezique nearly every time....

September 7. Sunday. Ther 76° 66° Day was bright & warm. I walked to Town. Got letter from Jenny, went to Depot to see Miss Mary Avery off, she left for Orange N.J. on the 10.15 train. I returned in spring wagon with Mr W., Mr Arthur & Miss Harriet to town. Went to see Dr Jones and paid him $25 for his plate & dentistry service. I got him to take an impression of mouth so that if one of my teeth is broken out I can send on & get him to replace it. Mr W. drove Rose, Lula Bates & myself to Hatfield. The ride was very pleasant. Played Bezique last night—had a run of bad luck....

September 15. Monday.... My vacation is closing and I feel sad at leaving my friends of Northampton from whom I recd so much kindness.

Benners thoroughly enjoyed his time in the North but was anxious to return home. Mr. Watson had asked him to stay longer than expected, and the dentist had taken longer to fix his teeth than he expected. He was ready to go home. He returned, stopping in New York for five days with friends who showed him around. He saw Coney Island, Brighton, Manhattan, Staten Island, and much more. From there, he went on to Augusta and then home to Greensboro. When he arrived, all was well. He had considerable fears that his absence might hurt the running of his property, but fortunately, there were no major problems except for the illness of his daughter Jenny, who quickly recovered.

The presidential campaign was now in full swing. Benners did not participate in the campaign. He was no longer interested in the day-to-day political combat but preferred to give advice and watch the campaign unfold. He hoped that Ohio would go Democratic, but it went Republican by a 17,000 vote margin. West Virginia, however, did go Democratic, though by a smaller than usual margin. Still, it was hard for Democrats to feel confident that Cleveland would win. Benners was uncertain but hopeful.

November 1. Saturday.... There is a sense of failure in the election which is very perceptible. We dont chirp as loud as we did....

November 2. Sunday.... The coming election absorbs all other subjects. There is more misgiving about result than heretofore. The last opinion seems to be that Cleveland will carry N.Y. & Blaine will be elected....

November 4. Tuesday.... Election progresses very quietly here.... I feel nervous about the election. Louisiana is considered doubtful. There is a slight decline of 1/8 in cotton M 9 1/8....

November 5. Wednesday.... New York is said to have gone for Cleaveland by 60,000 majority—very little news is yet rec'd—we are all cross and uncomfortable—

November 6. Thursday.... News is very discouraging. New York is said to have gone for Blaine.... The first news was very flattering—but soon began to look squally. We are doomed to disappointment....

November 7. Friday. Ther 46° 36° A fine bright day yest turning colder at night. White frost this morning. There was great uncertainty about the news yesterday. Telegrams came first one way then another. Last night came that Cleavelands election in New York was conceded by every side and they were firing guns in N.Y. about it—and this morning

Dawson sends from NY that N. York is conceded and Cleaveland is elected....

November 8. Saturday Ther 41° 40° A very fine day. News was coming in all the morning—first Democratic then Radical—towards evening it preponderated for Cleaveland & opinion settled that he was elected—but it was very close and the interval of suspense was very unsatisfactory. It is said New York, New Jersey, Connecticut, Indiana & Illinois must be added to solid south 153 electoral votes making 241. There was a great jubilation last night—cowbells, tin pans, guns, anvils &c....

November 9. Sunday.... Democratic news continues to arrive. Seay telegraphed that the Chairman of Rep Ex committee concedes Cleavelands election—Fanny & I played Eucre. I one ahead....

November 10. Monday.... Rad's still claim New York and signs are unsatisfactory. They claim Election by 218, Democats are swearing Cleaveland is elected—and everywhere firing guns & fireworks. Our folks postponed to Wednesday night. Harvey came over last night, he is very unsatisfied about the election....

November 11. Tuesday.... The anxiety about the election is intense. New York is to be counted to day....

November 13. Ther 60° 50° Another fine day. We had no company. The interest still continues in the count in New York. We got nothing final and great feeling to know positively prevails. There was a jollification last night. Procession and torch light procession and transparencies & speaking—Charley Waller, Turpin, Hill and others spoke. They had fireworks & gun firing and rockets and at the close burnt the transparencies and Bloody shirt—and were generally happy. Fanny & Graham went with Mr Harvey & I afterwards.

November 14. Friday.... No decisive news about N.Y. election—majority estimated about 1274.

November 15. Saturday.... The count in New York absorbs public attention and all the Counties but four are reported. It has not materially changed the figures and democrats are believed to have carried the State....

November 16. Sunday.... News came by wire yesterday evening that the count was completed in New York & Cleaveland & Hendricks are elected by majority of 1265. Glorious result....

November 17. Monday.... Great gratification as news of count closed in N.York. Cleaveland & Hendricks 1265 ahead and Blaine giving it up. Cotton is a little back.

Finally, after twenty-eight years, the Democratic Party had won the presidency. New York was a key state and it barely went for Cleveland. In fact, it took a week to be certain since the vote was so close. Then, there was great rejoicing in the South, and Benners was overjoyed by the great victory.

[*poem glued in journal*]

Life's Sunny Side

What—you are dull to-day?
In a sad mull to-day?
Up and be social and stirring, I pray.
Why so lugubrious?
Take a salubrious
Walk, and we'll talk for I've something to say.

Verily, verily,
Things will go merrily
When you are merry and busy and brave.
But if not cheerfully
Tempered, but tearfully,
Life is a tyrant, and you are its slave.

If you go wilfully,
However, skilfully,
Nursing your moods and your delicate whims,
Life will be dumb to you,

All things will come to you
Touched by a shadow that saddens and dims.

Life has two sides to it,
Take the best guides to it,
Look at the best and the brightest, my friend.
Be a philosopher,
Dont look so cross over
Matters you never can alter or mend.

Look not so dismally
Down the abysmally
Dark—hanging over the precipice brink.
Worst of all bias is
Hypochondriasis-
Sunshine is healthier than shadow, I think.

If you would drive away
Gloom, and would hive away
Honey-like peace in your innermost cell,
Work—like the bumble bee,
Soft let your grumble be;
Burn your own smoke and the world will go well.
C. P. Cranch in the Youth's Companion.

1885

Augustus Benners was busy balancing his account books, collecting rents from his tenants for the previous year, and renting lands for the new year. On 3 January, he wrote, "Worked hard on my books—not up yet." And they would not be "up" for several more weeks. But he did collect some money and continued to lend money to those who were in need.

January 1.... There were a good many people in town. RHS[tickney] paid his debt and Hooten a payment & D. G. Stevens a payment. I loaned W. Jones 905....

January 3.... Worked hard on my books—not up yet....

January 4. Sunday. Ther 40° 34° A cold bright day—and a very busy one. Wash & John came up & rented again. Pd Eds acct to 1 April. Loaned B. F. Chapman 100. Made a loan to D. G. Stevens. Acct sales from Keeble for cotton, Don, Win & Sheldon. There were a great many people in town. Mr G. W. Haywood came up—sold 2 B/C deposited $25....

January 7. Wednesday.... Liz & I played Backgammon. No cotton news. Jim Chiles, Wm. Jones & Henry Chapman were all on me. I rented again to all three. It was very disagreeable and disgusting but I did not know what to do. I had a disagreeable day certain....

January 10. Saturday.... Manuel came up and settled yesterday & I again consented to give him a credit of $300—and I ordered 500 lbs of meat for him. Cotton dull 10 1/4 for Mids Selma....

January 21. Wednesday.... I had a troublesome day yest & day before. Wash & Henry Chapman Monday & Ross Grist yesterday—he wanted a mule. His son was with him. I gave him money to buy a wagon & an ox $47. Stokes paid his note & Rhodes pd. his. We have heard nothing from Mr Watson. I fear he is sick. The weather is very cold & cloudy....

January 29. Thursday.... I wrote to several who are owing me yesterday. I had my usual quantity of annoyance from needy negroes. Last night I played Eucre with Fanny. I won 9 to 3. I walked to depot yesterday evening—train whistled as I got back. Heard no cotton news....

February 7. Saturday.... The Town was a little excited over the passage of the Coleman bill—forbid the sale or giving away of any liquor for any purpose except on a physicians prescription. News was also rec'd of capture of K[h]artoum by the Arabs....[28]

---

[28] The Siege of Khartoum in central Sudan is one of the most famous sieges in world history. It lasted from 12 March 1884 to 26 January 1885—a total of 320 days.

His friend Henry Watson came to see him. The weather had turned cold and it began to snow. It became difficult to get around, but it was fun to have his good friend in Greensboro again. There was much they could do together.

February 11. Wednesday.... I walked to depot last evening and met Mr Watson on the train. I was very glad to see him. He brought cold weather with him. I thought last night was the coldest I ever felt. I got up several times to warm my feet at the fire. There have been terrible snow storms in the N.West. Miss Ella Watson is in Marion and is coming over in a day or two.

February 12. Thursday..... This morning when I opened the window it was snowing & in a short time the ground was covered with snow. Mr Watson complained very much of his head. Put a hot brick to his feet last night & had a good nights sleep. It was tight work getting to office thro the snow....

February 13.... It was a very heavy fall of snow—said to measure 6 inches. I did not kindle a fire expecting to go back. I went to Millers fire & waited till the mail was opened. It snowed very hard during my stay there. After I had started to come home, Tidmore having delayed thro all of 2 mo's stopped me to go back to the office to pay me a bale of cotton. I bought it & credited on his notes. Watson & I played Bezique last night—he beat 2 Rubbers 4 out of 5 games....

February 17. Tuesday.... Watson came up and sat with me in the office. Jones & others came in. After dinner we went to see McRary. Last night we played Bezique. He beat me 4 to 2. We are invited to day to dine with the Bishop [Wilmer] at Charley Wallers. I declined as we are expecting company—Mrs Shepard and Miss Jackson. Got a postal from Graham at New Orleans—says it is a much bigger thing than he supposed. he had got the draft on Copp paid. Gen Gordon is dead....[29]

---

[29] General Charles Gordon, a hero of the British Empire, was sent back to rescue the isolated British garrisons in 1884. Betrayed by his Egyptian lieutenant, who opened the gates to the forces of Mohammed Ahmad, Gordon was shot dead in the streets. Two days later, the English army of relief reached Khartoum, but it was too late.

February 19. Ash Wednesday. Ther 36° 25° It was a cloudy cold unpleasant day. Wilmer preached twice. Congs small. I went with Watson in the morning and Liz at night. Mary Avery came home with Liz & stayed all night. Watson & I went to depot to meet Mr Reed his uncle but he was not on the train. It turned very cold last night & we had a bright night & sunrise....

In early March, Grover Cleveland and Thomas Hendricks were inaugurated as president and vice president of the United States. At last, the Democratic Party was back in power.

March 4. Wednesday..... To day is the day for Cleaveland's Inauguration. Much good luck to him. The ordeal is a fearful one. We had no cards last night....

March 5.... Mr Cleaveland & Hendricks were inaugurated I suppose.... We got no cotton news. It is off in Liv. 6 1/16....

March 6. Friday.... There is great gladness over Cleaveland's inauguration—Grant is placed on retired list. No getting clear of him yet. The national Hog.

March 7. Saturday.... We got Cabinet as sent in by Cleaveland.—Thos F. Bayard [Delaware], Sec of State, Whitney N.Y. Navy, Endicott, Mass., War, Manning N.Y., Treas., Vilas, Wisconsin, P[ost].M[aster] Genl, Garland [Arkansas] Atty General, Lamar [Mississippi] Sec of Interior....

March 8. Sunday.... Cleaveland's cabinet has been confirmed. The long agony is over & a Democratic President is at the helm.

Benners became uneasy over the possibility of a war between England and Russia. He especially worried that the price of cotton would be affected by such a conflict.

March 12. Thursday.... There is uneasiness felt at the prospect of a war between England and Russia—about Afg[h]anistan. First peach blooms reported yesterday—a few. Mr W consulted Dr Peterson—provided a tonic. Cotton is off a little—War news affects it....

March 14. Saturday.... War cloud increases. Mr Gladstone replied to questions that situation was not improved. Cotton & stocks have declined—M 10 1/4 Selma....

March 27. Friday.... The War news from England is threatening—25000 militia called for in England. It has affected Cotton & Stocks....

March 28. Saturday.... War news from Europe very threatening. Vegetation is coming on rapidly. Cotton feels effect of war news—declined 1/16 recpts are expected 6,000,000—I still have 6 bales....

March 29. Sunday.... The day was cloudy and threatening—and in the afternoon a rain preceded by thunder & lightning came up & I rode home in the [omni]bus last night. We played Bezique. I beat 5 straight games & W. 2. Miss Ella & I quit even. She gave Graham a game of Logomachy[30] which is quite entertaining. The news from Europe continues very threatening. England has sent an ultimatum to Russia & is making great preparations. Cotton declined 1/8 in Selma & Montgomery.

March 30. Monday.... There is no light breaking yet on the War question—provisions are rising & cotton falling—very great consequences hang on the war or no war....

March 31.... The prospect of a European war depresses cotton and raises provisions....

There were persistent reports of Grant's ill health in the spring of 1885. On 26 March, Benners first refers to Grant's health—"Gen Grant's condition is not supposed to have improved any—he has cancer of the tongue. "For the next few months, Benners followed Grant's deteriorating condition.

April 1.... There was a rumor of death of Gen Grant, it proved untrue tho he is very ill. Mr Watson is quite complaining with his head. After supper we went to Col Harveys. There is more hope of peace from foreign dispatches. The French have had a reverse in China....

---

[30] Logomachy or War of Words, a card game published by F. A. Wright Co. in 1874.

April 2. Thursday.... Mr Snedecor got a loan to go to N. Orleans. European news is more pacific. French ministry have resigned. Chinese have whipped the French pretty badly.... Selma 10 3/8 could get a 1/8 over quotations. Trees are putting out beautifully. Flowering peach is splendid. Grant is reported better....

April 3. Friday.... Another very pleasant day. Marshal[l] finished planting in the field—and it rained last night about 12M. It ought to come right up. Jenny got home on the train. Liz, Graham, Ella & I met her & walked home together. Annie Cobbs also came. Mary Avery met her. I was surprised on opening my window to see the mock orange tree in full bloom. I never saw so sudden a bloom. Gen Grant is reported to be dying....

April 9. Thursday.... Last night Fanny, Liz & Ella went with Graham to hear two women hold forth on Temperance. Brook[s] wife was one He made a few remarks and they took up a collection. Our habits & ways are being yankeeised.... Grant is supposed to be dying.

April 10. Friday.... We had no company. Played Bezique with Watson. We each made two games. After supper Watson & Fanny & Liz went to [T. B.] Randolphs. Liz got letter from Willie. He postpones his visit to next summer. Grant still survives—is reported a little better. Peace is reported between China & France—news between England and Russia more threatening again. Cotton panicky in Liv....

April 17.... We had the pleasure of meeting Jenny from New Orleans at the depot—Mary Avery, Annie Cobbs, Charlotte Ellerby & Sally Pasteur came along—all greatly delighted.... Jenny brought some fine Bananas & oranges & a nice pattern for a silk dress—Liz is making two dresses for her. She returns on Monday. Grant is related better. he says he will get well....

April 18. Saturday.... Graham went with Ella & Liz to concert last night. Jenny declined, had seen and heard so much. Mr Brooks & Harry Hawn performers. W & I walked towards depot.... Grant is reported better—A vast amt of Twaddle is telegraphed about him.—

Benners's health worsened in May, but he remained active despite the pain. On 11 May, he complained—"My dyspepia is right bad." He began to take more quinine, which had become a daily necessity. His friend C. L. Stickney had not been well either.

May 9.... I had a bad night—nightmare—took Dwights cholera mixture. No cotton news.

May 10.... Fanny & Liz got off to New Orleans on the train last night, 9.10 P.M. Yesterday before dinner Miss Maria Lewis called & said she was going with her brother Hardin & would be glad if Liz would go too & I persuaded Fanny too so last night Miss Lewis called & took Liz & I went in bus with Fanny. Card this A.M. from Liz at Akron—she got there all right & would leave in 20 min. Graham & I are alone....

May 11. Monday. Ther 63° 56° Another cool bright day. I missed Liz & Fanny very much. I read service and a sermon. Isaac came to dinner—in afternoon Tom Stickney called in carriage for me to go with him to see Mr C.L.S. He is suffering very much from a carbuncle on his neck he has had over two weeks.... My dyspepsia is right bad. We are still in the dirt & mortar at home. Not cleaned up yet.

May 14. Thursday.... Card from Liz from N. Orleans—she is delighted [and is] much pleased with Haverly Hotel—good rooms—went to grounds on the steamboat Clinton. It was Alabama day. Fireworks were superb. Had rooms on the wing cleaned out & windows washed in parlor. John Cobbs came round to play Bezique. I slept in my own room last night.... The discomfort of white washing & plastering is very great and dirt & dust & mortar are everywhere.... The roses are very beautiful and the mult[i]flora at the corner of the house has bloomed beautifully thro the coating of dust & mortar from the bricks of the chimney—Like virtue shining thro the vicious atmosphere surrounding....

May 17. Sunday.... Liz returned from N[ew] O[rleans] exposition on the train. Maria Lewis & Randolph came with her. Fanny concluded to wait till Tuesday. I was not expecting Liz. she got home before I had the house cleaned up. Abe Sheldon & Marshal Thornton came for rations & to borrow money. Liz was delighted with her visit to N.O. and had much to tell about it. I played backgammon with Liz last night. I am feeling feeble & dyspeptic....

May 23. Saturday. Ther 76° 72° A cloudy day with a smart shower of rain about 11 oclock. Much harder up town than at my house. It was clear & cloudy by turns. A very dull day. Had a pain in my breast. Miss Mary Avery said Mr Cobbs asked me to read on sunday (Whit-sunday). We had no company for dinner....

May 31. Sunday. Ther 76° 68° A very slight drizzle before dinner, fair before night & bright moonlight. I rode in hack to train to meet Mag & the children but they failed to arrive. Liz & Graham also went down. I returned in hack to office. We expected them to dinner. I presume they continue to spend a day or so in N.O. as trains made connection. Eborn & his wife came from Livingston on it. The street was almost blockaded in front of W. D. Lees by an oak which had been blown down the evening before from C. E. Wallers lot. I had a bad spell about dinner time and after—got some powders prescribed by Dr Peterson....

June 1. Monday.... I went to depot & met Mag & children—they missed connection in New Orleans, stayed there one night & all night at Akron. They are all well and I was very glad to see them. Mrs Brown, Mary Hatch & Martha Benners came from Kornegays about the same time. There were a good many callers in evening. Jones's, Roulhacs, Randolphs, Mr Erwin, Hatty Clarck and Col Harvey & wife, & Mr Ivey Lewis at night. Russia has accepted English proposals & peace is assured for present. It was Trinity Sunday and I attended twice.... I wrote to Alfred in the evening informing him of the arrival of his family. Dr Peterson gave me a prescription of Pepsin & Bismuth & also quinine. I think it made me feel better—But I am far from well....

June 3. Wednesday.... I felt unwell all day—took quinine. I had all the company of previous day. I wrote to Watson & Willie & Jenny. We rec'd very pretty photograph from her. There seems to be no doubt of the peace news. Cotton steady, good demand in Liv. It has been injured in low places & where dirt has washed over it. I felt very unwell last evening. I am taking bismuth & pepsin and quinine. Victor Hugo's funeral came off in Pantheon in Paris on Monday 1st June....

Benners continued to record events in Europe and India. Prime Minister Gladstone lost a vote in the House of Commons and resigned. Inexperienced in matters of foreign policy, he had waited too long to save the British forces of General Gordon at Khartoum. His replacement was Lord Salisbury.

June 11. Thursday.... Ministry in England have been defeated in the Commons and Mr Gladstone & cabinet have resigned. The immediate question was on the Budget in which the tax on Beer & Whisky was increased. Great excitement prevails & war talk is again indulged. Cotton declines & securities. We have nice vegetables. Corn, cabbage, beans, potatoes, cucumbers, squashes, onions. Plums are plenty & dewberries—Have seen no peaches....

June 13.... The English news is very interesting. Mr G[ladstone] has resigned—Queen has requested him to withdraw it. A case of yellow fever reported at Gretna near New Orleans—a 2 year old child died. Cholera increasing in Spain....

June 14. Sunday.... Gus is complaining with headache. I was very weak & blue. No letters from my children. Marshal called to get money to get express. Earl of Salisbury has taken Gladstone's place. I think it is a strange fact that a small tax on beer & whisky should work such results, & so largely affect the world....

June 17.... Got scantling[31] from Shacke[l]ford for George to fix the fence—poor stuff. The cotton is very grassy & prospect very poor. Liz & I & Graham played backgammon last night. I beat her & he beat me. Marquis of Salisbury has accepted Mr Gladstone's place. No letters from abroad. Liz has finished Jenny's graduating dress.... I took quinine yesterday & felt better. Cotton down.

June 18. Thursday.... Liz got Jenny's dress done and sent it by Express to her & I enclosed $5 in a letter to get her slippers & Gloves. George Washington is working on the garden fence & gates....

June 19. Friday.... Fanny had Ben Hilliard ploughing the cotton—it is very grassy. The price is going down. 11 1/2 in N.Y. 5 3/4 in Liv. No

---

[31] Scantling—small piece of lumber (as an upright piece used in framing).

quotations from Selma. Bartholdi statue has arrived.[32] There has been an increase of the cholera in Spain. The Marquis of Salisbury has not yet announced his cabinet. Russia will again become dangerous to the world's peace....

Though he was feeling poorly Augustus Benners still decided to attend Jenny's graduation in Montgomery. It was a special day for her and the family.

June 25. Thursday Ther 82° 78° A pleasant day yesterday, no rain. On Monday 22 inst. I went with Liz to Montgomery to Jenny's Commencement. At Selma we rode in Hack to Mr Somervilles & got dinner. The weather was the hottest I have felt and I was quite unwell. At 4.20 we left for Montg'y and got there at 7.15. Took Liz & baggage in hack to Hamner Hall & returned to exchange. Got a room 214, washed off & went to supper—felt better and enjoyed my supper. had a good night's rest undisturbed & next morning after breakfast walked to the Capital & Govt House, saw Gov Watts,[33] Judge Brickell & Dawson, went to Govt house on my way back. it is quite pretentious. Booker Supt of Internal Revenue for Ala has his office here. On my return to Exchange got a hack & went to ride with Liz. Stopped at the Capital, saw Judge Stone [or Stowe] he is 73 years old & is looking well & vigorous—said he had been restored to health by using quinine & capsicum 5 months, 2 grs of former & 1/2 gr of latter. We rode around some and called for Jenny at McDonald's open house. After dinner I got in hack & called for Jenny & Liz to take a ride on Perry St. It threatened rain and was not so pleasant in consequence. I carried Liz & Jenny to the Hall, and after supper went to McDonalds opera house. The lower part was crowded—and the exhibition of the girls on the stage was very pretty. I staid till after Jenny read her composition "one may smile & smile & be a villain." I could not hear one word. I came to my room & had a good night's sleep & the next morning sent a hack for Liz & Jenny & I walked to the depot. There was a crowd there. Jenny & Liz & the

---

[32] Frederic Auguste Bartholdi, sculptor of the Statue of Liberty. The statue arrived in New York harbor in June 1885 on board the French frigate *Isere*.

[33] Thomas H. Watts was governor of Alabama from 1863 to 1865.

baggage soon arrived, and at 8.15 we started for Selma. Annie Cobbs came along. We got to Selma at 12.15. The girls remained at Depot & got lunch from the waiting woman. I went to town in St. cars, got some apples, peaches & candy and returned in St cars to Depot. Liz saved me some Lunch which I enjoyed—got the girls some lemons and left at 2.20. got home about 5.30 and rode home in the omnibus. heard that Graham got the 2nd prize, a very handsome book, Authors of Wit & Humor....

In the last six weeks of his life, Benners suffered from pain but kept abreast of national and international affairs. He noted that the strike of cab drivers in Chicago was finally over, that "Indians are murdering citizens in Kansas," that there was a stir of anger in London over the sale of girls for immoral purposes, and that Russia and England were again talking about war. He continued to worry about the price of cotton, although there were fewer entries about cotton than in earlier years. He constantly worried about his children and their lives. Ed was never far from his thought: "My heart bleeds for him."

July 1.... Salisbury has become premier and matters are again looking critical with Russia. Matters look very unsettled & complicated. Cotton is very depressed tho recpts continue to fall off. My crop is very poor from want of work.... We have corn squash cucumbers potatoes onions cabbage beans & okra. Peaches are nothing. a few figs on the trees not yet ripe. Grapes look promising....

July 10. Friday.... Car drivers strike at Chicago is over. Cleaveland, O. still disturbed. Indians are murdering citizens in Kansas. Jenny went with Ben Vail in buggy to party at Carter Randolphs. Got home about 2 A.M. about 20 people there. It was a Eucre party. Cotton reported firm in N.Y. at 10 1/2.

July 11. Saturday. Ther 80° 78° It was one of the warmest days we've had, Ther 94° dinner time. There was a very promising cloud came up after dinner with prospect of wind & rain—there was very acceptable rain but quite light—it rained a long time & did much good.

Ther fell 10 degrees. Not a good day with me. Jack[34] was reported for spanking a negro boy. No company. Helpless do nothings. Great stir in London on licentiousness. sale of girls for immoral purposes. Pall Mall Gazette is at the head of the Movement. Cotton firm N.Y. 10 1/2 Mid.

July 12. Sunday. Ther 80° 76° A pretty warm day with clouds in the evening promising rain—but there was only a very light sprinkle. Jack was tried before the mayor for spanking a little black boy who called him a jackass—small business. I had to pay his fine & costs 4.75. Fanny hired Alice Royal's horse & vehicle and went in the morning to Kornegay's. Graham & Gus & Allen went with her. I had to decline reading to day on account of bad cold & hoarseness. The excitement in London about Pall Mall gazette exposures is great....

July 15. Wednesday.... I had a bad night. Waked at 2 & staid awake some time. I am very weak & out of sorts. There was a trial going on in the court house before the mayor for a fight at the African Methodist church, about a woman. The worms are in many places south of us.... Jenny & Graham are invited to a lawn party at Mr George Erwins to night....

July 17. Friday.... I am sorely puzzled what to do with my folks—I am much depressed—It seems like all things are against me. Ed is poor fellow, my heavy affliction—his health is not good, no prospect of improvement....

The entries in the last two weeks of his life made numerous references to Grant's death and efforts to find a suitable place for his burial. Benners considered these efforts an example of "vulgarity & bad taste." Ironically, both Grant and Benners had been in poor health at the same time. However, Grant died first on 23 July; Benners outlived him by fifteen days.

July 24. Friday.... We all hands were invited by Mrs Harvey to breakfast with her & went at 7 o'clock. We numbered 9 in all—had a nice breakfast and pleasant time.... Gen Grant is reported to have died yesterday morning at 8 oclock at Mt McGregor....

---

[34] Jack Morris. a freedman, was hired by Benners on January 5, 1885 for $4.50 a month as a house servant and handyman.

July 25. Saturday.... We heard of the death of Gen Grant. He died July 23, 85. Very extravagant demonstrations are being made over it. Cleaveland sent Mrs G. letter of sympathy. Southern cities are also many of them very demonstrative because at Appomatox he returned their horses to Confeds & treated Lee with great courtesy. Nil de mortius millenum....[35]

July 26. Sunday.... Col Jones & Mrs Nelson & her child spent the day with us. We had frozen peaches & milk, grapes, peaches & apples & melons. They left about 6 P.M. The burial of Gen Grant is the subject mainly occupying public attention—he desired that his wife when she dies should be buried by his side and Central Park New-York has been proffered & accepted....

July 27. Monday.... The proposal to bury Grant in Central Park is unfavorably criticised.

July 30. Thursday.... Grant it is said is to be buried at Riverside park—vulgarity & bad taste is conspicuous....

August 2. Sunday.... Grants funeral is the engrossing topic with papers....

The last few days of his life were active—he sold Walker Place and went to several church services, but he was unhappy that Liz was going to Dallas to visit Alfred. He had great difficulty parting with her. "What shall I do—she is housekeeper," he wrote.

August 5. Wednesday. Ther 82° 76° The weather was more moderate yesterday. No rain or sign of it. Pleasant night. Col Jones took dinner. I was quite uncomfortable at dinner time and feel badly this morning. Liz leaves this evening with Mag for Texas. What shall I do—she is housekeeper. I shall miss them very much. I thought they had better wait till later. I am perplexed about the others, what to do with them. God help me. Perhaps it will turn out well. I wrote to Alfred about his deed sent to Seay.

---

[35] No fame beyond the grave.

August 6. Thursday. Ther 82° 76° A pleasanter temperature. Ther 88° Col Jones & Pride took dinner with us & we were in a state of confusion & excitement all day—preparing for Mag & family to leave for Texas & also Liz. There were many callers. They rode in Randolphs carriage to the depot & Graham & Pride & I went in the Hack and they got a fair start at 8.03 P.M. for Dallas. Mr Stollenwerck was on the train bringing a young lady who wanted to go to Texas with Mag. I was nearly sick all the evening parting with Liz was a great trial. I dread Texas. It was still enough when I got home.

August 7. Friday. Ther 86° 82° A very hot day. Ther over 92°. I had an unpleasant time. Stomach uncomfortable. Of course it was very quiet at home—so many having left. Fanny presided at the table. I did not come to town after dinner. Graham & I & Jenny & I played Backgammon. I slept very well. No news from the travelers. Liz was to have sent back my R.R. ticket but it did not come. I called at Harveys in evening. Grants corpse has reached New York and is lying in state at City Hall. Cholera is very bad in Spain & in France.

Augustus Benners died this day of apoplexy [*a stroke*].
Signed H. Graham Benners

Bibliography

Barney, William L. *The Road to Secession: A New Perspective on the Old South*. New York: Praeger Publishers, 1972.

Barney, William L. *The Secessionist Impulse: Alabama and Mississippi in 1860*. Princeton NJ: Princeton University Press, 1974.

Benners, Alfred Hatch. *Slavery and Its Results*. Macon GA: The J. W. Burke Company, 1923.

Biographical Directory of the American Congress, 1774–1949. Washington, DC: US Government Printing Office, 1950.

Boatner, Mark, III. *Civil War Dictionary*. New York: David McKay Co., Inc., 1959.

Bowman, John S. *Civil War Almanac*. New York: Gallery Books, division of W. H. Smith Publishers, Inc., 1983.

Brazy, Martha Jane. "An American Planter: Slavery, Entrepreneurship and Identity in the Life of Stephen Duncan, 1787–1867." Ph.D. diss., Duke University, 1998.

Bridgwater, William, and Seymour Kurtz, editors. *The Columbia Encyclopedia*, 3rd edition. New York/London: Columbia University Press, 1963.

Cobbs, Nicholas H., Jr. "Alabama's 'Wonder of the Earth.'" Presidential address, Alabama Historical Association, Selma, AL, 16 April 1994.

Curb, Randall, editor. *Historic Hale County*. Greensboro AL: The Preservation Committee of the Alabama Reunion, 1989, printed by the *Greensboro Watchman*, 1989.

Dalzell, Robert F., Jr. *Enterprising Elite: The Boston Associates and the World They Made*. New York/London: W. W. Norton & Co., 1987.

Divine, Robert A., et al. *America Past and Present*. New York: Longman, 1999.

Dorman, Lewy. *Party Politics in Alabama, from 1850 through 1860*. Historical and Patriotic Series. Montgomery: Alabama State Department of Archives and History, 1935. Reprint, Tuscaloosa AL: University of Alabama Press, 1995.

DuBose, John Witherspoon. *Alabama's Tragic Decade, Ten Years of Alabama 1865–1874*. Edited by James K. Greer. Birmingham AL: Webb Book Company, 1940.

Fleming, Walter L. *Civil War and Reconstruction in Alabama*. New York: Columbia University Press, 1905. Reprint, Gloucester MA: Peter Smith, 1949.

Foner, Eric. *Reconstruction, America's Unfinished Revolution*. New York: Harper & Row Publishers, 1988.

Garrett, William. *Reminiscences of Public Men in Alabama for Thirty Years*. Alanta: Plantation Publishing Company's Press, 1872.

Going, Allen J. *Bourbon Democracy in Alabama 1874–1890*. University: University of Alabama Press, 1951.
Hall, John C. "When Stars Fell on Alabama." *Alabama Heritage*, no. 55 (Winter 2000).
Hoogenbloom, Ari. *The Presidency of Rutherford B. Hayes*. Lawrence: University Press of Kansas, 1988.
Hoole, W. M. Stanley, editor. *Reconstruction in West Alabama*. Tuscaloosa AL: Confederate Publishing Co., 1959.
Hubbs, Guy W. "Guarding Greensboro, A Confederate Company and the Making of a Southern Community." Ph.D diss., University of Alabama, 1999.
Kestenbaum, Lawrence. *The Political Graveyard*, Ann Arbor MI [politicalgraveyard.com].
Kronk, Gary W. *Cometography: A Catalog of Comets*, volume 2, 1800–1899. Cambridge/New York: Cambridge University Press UK, 2004.
Kytle, Jack, and Luther Clark, editors. *Alabama: A Guide to the Deep South*. New York: Richard R. Smith, 1941.
Liestman, Daniel. "Chinese Laborers in Reconstruction Alabama." *Alabama Heritage*, no. 8 (Spring 1988).
Long, E. B., with Barbara Long. *The Civil War Day by Day, and Almanac, 1861–1865*. Garden City NY: Doubleday Press, 1971.
Lonn, Ella. *Reconstruction in Louisiana after 1868*. New York: G. P. Putnam's Sons, 1918. Reprint, New York: Russell & Russell, 1967.
McPherson, James M. *Ordeal by Fire: The Civil War and Reconstruction*. New York: McGraw-Hill, 2001.
McWhiney, Grady, Warner O. Moore, and Robert E. Pace, editors. *Fear God and Walk Humbly, the Agricultural Journal of James Mallory, 1843–1877*. Tuscaloosa: University of Alabama Press, 1997.
Mellown, Robert O. "Mental Health and Moral Architecture." *Alabama Heritage*, no. 32 (Spring 1994).
Murrin, John M. et al. *Liberty, Equality, Power, A History of the American People*. New York: Harcourt Brace & Co., 1996.
Polakoff, Keith Ian. *Politics of Inertia: The Election of 1876 and the End of Reconstruction*. Baton Rouge: Louisiana State University Press, 1973.
Randall, James G., and David Donald. *Civil War and Reconstruction*. Lexington MA: D. C. Heath & Co., 1969.
Rawick, George P., editor. *The American Slave: A Composite Autobiography*, vol. 1, Supplement, Series 2. Westport CT/London: Greenwood Press, 1979.
Report of Committee of the Senate of the United States for Second Session of the Forty-fourth Congress, 1876–1877. Washington, DC: US Government Printing Office, 1877.
Rogers, William Warren, Jr. *Confederate Home Front, Montgomery during the Civil War*. Tuscaloosa: University of Alabama Press, 1999.
Rogers, William Warren, et.al. *Alabama, The History of a Deep South State*. Tuscaloosa: University of Alabama Press, 1994.

Schweikert, Larry. *Banking in the American South*. Baton Rouge: Louisiana State University Press, 1987.

Scott, Paul G. "The Family Benners." College Park GA: self-published family genealogy, 1990.

Scruggs, J. H., Jr. *Alabama Steamboats 1819–1869*. Self-published, 1953.

Sellers, James Benson. *The Prohibition Movement in Alabama: 1702–1943*. Chapel Hill: University of North Carolina Press, 1943.

Snedecor, V. Gayle. *A Directory of Greene County for 1855–6*, Mobile AL: Strickland & Co., 1856. Edited and indexed by Franklin Shackelford Moseley, Eutaw AL: *The Greene County Democrat*, 1957.

Staudenraus, P. J., editor. *The Secession Crisis, 1860–1861*. The Berkeley Series in American History. Edited by Charles Sellers. Chicago: Rand McNally & Co., 1963.

Sulzby, James F. Jr. *Historic Alabama Hotels and Resorts*. Tuscaloosa: University of Alabama Press, 1960.

Taylor, Joe Gray. *Louisiana Reconstructed, 1863–1877*. Baton Rouge: Louisiana State Press, 1974.

Tharin, W. C. *A Directory of Marengo County for 1860–61*. Linden AL: Farrow & Dennett, 1861.

United States, Luke P. Poland, and John Scott. 1872. *Report of the Joint Select Committee to inquire into the condition of affairs in the late insurrection states, so far as regards the execution of the laws, and safety of the lives and property of the citizens of the United States and Testimony taken*. Washington, D.C.: US Government Printing Office, 42nd Congress, 2nd session, H.R. doc. no. 22, serial set 1536.

US Census records, 1850, 1860, 1870 Alabama population schedules, National Archives Micropublication.

Warren, Alfred P., and Sara B. Warren. *Something of Pride: An Historical Novel of the Hatch House*. Self-published, 1999.

Wiggins, Sarah W. *The Scalawag in Alabama Politics, 1865–1881*. Tuscaloosa: University of Alabama Press, 1977.

Wooster, Ralph A. *The Secession Conventions of the South*. Princeton: Princeton University Press, 1962.

Yerby, William Edward, *History of Greensboro, Alabama from Its Earliest Settlement*. Montgomery AL: The Paragon Press, 1908.

Index

Abe (sharecropper), 303-4, 332
absentee ballots, 71
Adams, Orren (sharecropper), 303
Aggy (slave), 32-33, 81, 90, 116
Alabama constitutional conventions, 12, 142, 143, 225-29; fighting in, 101, 126, 134, 135-36; legislature, 9-10, 25-31, 35-37, 71-73, 91-92, 109n 106, 111-12, 128, 203-4; readmission of, 142-43, 146; state elections, 25-31, 172, 203-4, 237
Alfred (slave), 116, 127
American party, 41
amnesty, postwar, 11, 139, 141, 183
Amy (freedwoman), 156
Anderson, James A., 28
Anderson, Robert J., 57, 58
Anne (slave), 75
Ann (slave), 116
Anthony (slave), 87, 116
Antietam, battle of, 9, 89-90
Appomattox Courthouse, 10, 136-37
Arcola plantation, 16
Arlington Cemetery, 249
Arthur, Chester A., 296, 297-98, 299-300, 300-301, 304, 312
Atkins, John, 154, 216-17, 218
Atlanta, campaign for, 122-26, 127
Austro-Prussian war, 148
Avery, Mary, 175, 224, 266, 309-11, 314, 321-22, 331, 333

Badger, George Edmund, 151
ballots, absentee, 71
Banister, Rev. Mr., 101
banks, failures of, 42-43, 195-96, 201-4, 207-8, 231, 257, 267; Freedman's Savings and Trust, 213; legislation regarding, 9, 71-73, 211-12, 214
Barry, A. P., 30
Batchelor, Frances, 5, 50-51
Batie, Lizzie. *see* Beatty, Lizzie
Bayard, Thomas Francis, 301, 329
Bayol, Edward, 310
Beattie, Lizzie. *see* Beatty, Lizzie
Beatty, Lizzie, 180, 207, 274, 275
Beecher, Henry Ward, 195-96, 313
Benners, Alfred Hatch, biography of, 17; education of, 163, 197
first child of, 183; legal practice, 170, 208, 304; mother's death and, 291-94; planter, 188, 190-93, 195-96, 198-200, 202; in Texas, 220-21, 268, 287, 300, 304
Benners, Annie LeVert (Poellnitz), 19
Benners, Augusta Edwena, 46
Benners, Augustus, biography of, 4-16, 23-24
Benners, Augustus (grandchild), 183, 185, 199, 283, 321, 334
Benners, Augustus (son), 19, 33-34
Benners, Charles, 19, 114, 142
Benners, Edward Graham (brother), 5-7, 16-17, 38, 44-49, 155, 286, 290-91
Benners, Edward Graham (son), biography of, 13, 18; farming efforts of, 206-8, 210, 214, 217, 220, 225-26, 231, 234, 238, 241 jury duty, 261; mental illness of, 279-

82, 287-88, 290, 296, 310-11, 337
Benners, Eleanor (Davidson), 18
Benners, Elizabeth. *see* Benners, Liz
Benners, Elizabeth L. (later Willis), 82, 144-45
Benners, Evalina Rowe (Tomlinson), 82n 36
Benners, Fanny (daughter), biography of, 17; church and, 175, 287; death of parents and, 14, 294-95, 339; flag presentation by, 67; running of household, 258, 267, 334; skating rink and, 311; travels of, 49, 111, 167, 172-73, 176-79, 224, 332
Benners, Fanny (sister), 37-38, 50
Benners, Frances (Batchelor), 5, 50-51
Benners, Graham, biography of, 19; companion to father, 296, 332; death of parents and, 292, 294-95, 338-39; Ed and, 279; education of, 307, 314; first snow, 173; second prize, 336; skating rink and, 311, 314
Benners, Gus. *see* Benners, Augustus (son)
Benners, Hamilton Graham (Graham). *see* Benners, Graham
Benners, Helen (Donaldson), 17, 46, 293
Benners, Henry, 46, 155, 163, 165
Benners, Isaac, 279, 280-81, 305, 311, 332
Benners, James Marbury, 19, 54
Benners, Jane (Hatch), biography of, 16; death of, 14, 290-92; family network of, 23; mourning over, 291-94, 304-5; nursing of father, 223, 277-78; travels of, 146-47, 163, 224, 282-84, 286, 289-92
Benners, Jane (Jenny), biography of, 18-19; birth of, 148

death of parents and, 294-95, 339; education of, 15, 313-14, 331, 335-36
Benners, Jenny. *see* Benners, Jane (Jenny)
Benners, John, 19, 104-5, 121, 123, 136
Benners, Liz, biography of, 18; entertainments of, 162, 179-80, 259, 311, 314; graduation speech by, 197; housekeeping of, 14, 338; travels of, 224, 332, 338-39; walks with father, 294-95
Benners, Lucas, 19, 54-56
Benners, Lucas Jacob IV, 5
Benners, Lucas Jacob V, 82n 36
Benners, Margaret Erwin (granddaughter), 299
Benners, Margaret (Jones), 17, 180, 183, 333, 338-39
Benners, Martha, 333
Benners, William Haywood (Willie), biography of, 18; birth of, 53-54; concerns over, 13-14, 209, 279, 298, 306; education of, 264; insurance job, 304, 307, 310, 321; travels of, 186, 282-83
Bentonville, battle of, 135
Big Hannah (slave), 85, 116
Big Wash (slave), 32n 14, 116
Bill (slave), 85, 90, 115
Black, Fred (sharecropper), 287
Black Belt, 44n 28, 65n 8
Blackford, William T., 232
Black Republicans. *see* Republican party
blacks. *see* freedmen
Blaine, James G., 14, 234-35, 247, 255, 284, 296-97, 312-13, 323-25
Bland-Allison act, 266, 267
blockade, U.S., 73-74
Blount Springs AL, 54-56, 168-69, 214-15, 236-38, 274-75, 306

Index

Blunt, Jeff, 293, 305
Bonaparte (slave), 39
bonds, county officials, 219-20
Borden family, 40-41
Boyd (overseer), 40
Bray, Caswell S., 39
Breen, Robert F., 191-92
Bristow, Benjamin H., 235
Britain. *see* England
Brown, Benjamin Gratz, 188
Bryan (slave), 98, 116, 124
Bryce, Peter, 280-82
Buchanan, James, 8, 41, 52
Bull Run, battles of, 9, 68-69, 87-88
Burge family, 209
Burke (sharecropper), 269, 303-4
Burke (slave), 64, 110, 115, 127
Bush, Jacob J., 146

Caldwell, Tod R., 186
Canebrake, the, 65n 8
Caroline (slave), 98, 111, 114, 116, 124-25
Carpenter, Matthew Hale, 213
Carver, Pullman, 29
Castilla (slave), 116, 122
Caswell, Fort, 93-94
catfish industry, 65n 8
Celia (slave), 55, 89, 111, 115, 116, 117
Centennial, U.S., 236
Central City Insurance Company, 176
certified checks, payment by, 201-3
Chadwick, William (sharecropper), 308
Chamberlain, D. H., 246-47, 260
Chancellorsville, battle of, 101
Chapman, Henry (sharecropper), 293, 303, 308, 327
Charles (slave), 32, 91, 113, 116, 119
Charleston, attacks on, 95, 109, 132
Chattanooga, fighting at, 110-11, 112-13
Cheatham, Benjamin, 131
Cheney Place plantation, 7, 145-46
Chicago IL, 178, 336
Chickamauga, battle of, 109-11
children, Benners, 17-19. *see also individual children*
Chiles, Jim (sharecropper), 241, 256, 268, 300, 320, 327
cholera scare, 195-98
Christina (slave), 116
church. *see* Episcopal Church
civil rights bills, 11, 147-48, 213-14, 221-22
Civil War, Benners and, 9-10
Clark, T. Crawford, 67
Clayton, Powell, 312
Cleveland, Grover, 14, 315, 323-25, 329, 337
Cobbs, Addison, 100
Cobbs, Annie, 313, 331, 336
Cobbs, John, 310-11, 332
Cobbs, Nicholas Hamner, 21
Cobbs, Richard Hooker, 21, 127, 175, 185, 278, 280-81, 290, 310-11
Cockrell, William E., 251
Cold Harbor, battle of, 122-23
Coleman, Wiley, 27, 30-31, 118, 128, 143, 154-55, 270
Colorado, admission of, 149
comets, sightings of, 53, 67, 294-96, 298
Compromise of 1850, 8
Confederate money. *see* money, paper
confiscation acts, postwar, 143
Congress, U.S., 11-12, 249-53, 300-301
conscription. *see* draft, Federal
Conservative party. *see* Democratic & Conservative conventions
constitutional conventions, 12, 142, 143, 166, 167-68, 225-29

Cook, A. T. (sharecropper), 303-4
Cook, J. D., 307
Corinth, fighting around, 79-80, 83, 85, 90
cotton, confiscation of, 143; price of, 13, 42-43, 263-69, 273, 276, 305-9, 329-30, 336-37; theft of, 141; war subscription, 66-68, 71, 193-95; worm, 186-87, 198-200, 238, 273, 275, 298
Cowin family, 101, 142, 306
crisis, banking. *see* banks
Criswell, Sam, 290
Croom, Isaac, 20, 94
Cuba, Americans executed in, 204-5
Currency Bill of 1874, 211-12
Currency Tax, Confederate, 114-15
Curry, Jabez L. M., 35
Custer, George Armstrong, 236
Czar Alexander II, murder of, 285

Daves family, 21, 49, 51, 192, 194, 254
David (house servant), 265, 267
Davidson, Eleanor (later Benners), 18
Davis, David, 301
Davis, Jefferson, 68-70, 130, 135, 139
Davis, Richard, 257
Delia (freedwoman), 140, 146
Delia (slave), 11, 119, 124
Democratic & Conservative Conventions, 11-12, 171-72, 184, 225-28, 233-34, 269-72
Democratic party, 11-12, 41-42, 96, 188-89, 216-19, 225-29, 235, 237-55, 276, 313-15, 323-25, 329
dentist, trip to, 315-23
Dick (slave), 114, 116
Dilse. *see* Dilsy (slave)
Dils (slave), 116
Dilsy (slave), 115, 119
diphtheria epidemic, 201
Diver (slave), 127

Donaldson, Fort. *see* Donelson, Fort
Donaldson, Helen (later Benners), 17, 46, 293
Donelson, Fort, 75-77
Dorman, Amasa M, 99, 103
Dorman, Willie, 277
Douglass, Frederick, 256-57
draft, Federal, 96-97
Drake (overseer), 127-29, 138-39
Dred (slave), 73
Drew, George Franklin, 247
DuBois family, 99, 288
Duskin, George M., 188-89, 204, 229, 256

Ed (freedman), 144-45, 156, 166-67
Edmond (freedman), 167
Ed (slave), 55, 73, 75, 93-94, 103, 109, 113, 115-19, 122-23, 125-27
Edwards, John, 116, 273, 303
Edward (slave). *see* Ed (slave)
elections, congressional, 153-54, 217-19, 276; municipal, 205, 209; presidential, 41-42, 57, 127, 182-84, 188-89, 312-15, 323-25, 329; state, 25-31, 172, 203-4, 237
elections, Senate committee on, 12-13, 249-53
electoral votes, presidential, 12-13, 241-55
Eli (sharecropper), 303
Elisha (slave), 116, 121-22
Ellen (slave), 33
Elliah (slave), 117
Ellsworth, Elmer, 65
Emily (slave), 32
Emline (freedwoman), 146, 155, 156, 167
Emline (slave), 55, 87, 113, 116-17, 122, 124
Emma (cook), 153
England, Civil War and, 86, 99; cotton and, 268-69, 329-30;

elections in, 334-35; Russia and, 263-65, 266-69, 273, 336-37
Enrollment Act, Federal, 97
Episcopal Church, 22, 100-101, 175, 176-77, 182-83, 187, 193, 206
Etheridge, Emerson, 68
Europe, CSA and, 83-84, 86, 95, 99, 130-31, 133
Extortion Bill, 9-10, 91-92

Federal troops. *see* troops, Federal
Female Academy, Greensboro, 22, 162
Fenian Brotherhood, 150
Ferry, Thomas White, 230, 250
Fillmore, Millard, 8, 41, 210
fire, Greensboro, 232
fire company, Greensboro, 175
Fisher, Fort, 129-30
Florida, CSS, 89
force bill, 222
Forrest, Nathan Bedford, 101, 136, 205
forts. *see specific forts*
Fourteenth Amendment, 149-50
France, CSA and, 83-84, 86, 95, 133
Frances, Little. *see* Little Frances (slave)
Frances (slave), 115, 116, 122, 125
Franco-Prussian war, 172-73
Frank (slave), 39, 115
Franky (slave), 90
Freedman's Savings and Trust Company, 213
freedmen. *see also* slaves; emancipation celebration, 260, 268, 311; emigration of, 207; judicial system and, 143-44, 207, 210-11, 269; labor system and, 138-39, 140, 144, 146, 155, 156, 167; legislation regarding, 147-50, 149-50; political participation of, 172, 188-89, 203-4, 214, 218,

226-27, 229, 238-39, 250-51, 312; poverty of, 293; railroad excursion for, 200; sharecropping and, 303-4, 305-8, 327; unrest surrounding, 150, 163, 205, 215, 238, 248; voter registration and, 165-66
Freedmen's Bureau, 11, 140
Freemasons, 21-22, 257, 261
Frémont, John C., 8, 41
friends, Benners's, 19-21. *see also individual friends*

Gaines, Fort, 126
Garfield, James, 14, 283-84, 295-300
Garner, Hannah, 263
George (freedman), 139, 257-58
George (slave), 91, 107, 110, 113, 116, 119, 127
Georgia, fighting in, 109-11, 120, 122-27, 129-31
Germany, attack on Emperor of, 272
Gettysburg, battle of, 107
Gladstone, William Ewart, 334
Godfrey (slave), 115, 124-25
Gordon, Charles, 328, 334
Gordon, John Brown, 257
Grange, the, 222, 226
Grant, Ulysses S., 182, 184, 187-89, 191, 225, 230, 239, 245-46, 248, 299, 304, 329, 330-31, 338-39
Grant, Wash, 223, 256, 269, 275, 300, 303, 306, 327. *see also* Wash (slave)
Greeley, Horace, 182, 183, 184, 188-89
Green, James, 163, 189, 218
Greene County, division of, 155, 157-58
Greene Springs School, Havana, 22, 28
Greensboro Female Academy, 22, 162

Greensboro Guards, 19, 59, 65, 84, 90n 52, 101, 142
Greensboro Temperance Society. *see* temperance movement
Grigg, Loyd, 300
Griggs, James E., 159, 202
Grist, Ross (sharecropper), 305-6, 327
Groce (sharecropper), 145, 153
Grow, Galusha Aaron, 67-68
Guards, Greensboro. *see* Greensboro Guards
Guiteau, Charles, 295-97, 300-301, 304
Gus (slave), 116

habeas corpus, suspension of, 114-15
Hagins, Julia (later Mellown), 205n 85
Hale, Stephen, 66, 84
Hale County, 157-58, 159-60, 166, 189
Hall, Gus, 230
Hamilton, Jesse, 144, 209
Hampton, Wade, 246-47, 255, 258-59, 260
Hancock, Winfield, 14, 234-36, 283
hands. *see* slaves
Hannah, Big. *see* Big Hannah (slave)
Hannah (slave), 69, 93, 111, 112, 116
Haralson, Jeremiah, 239, 243, 251
Hardaway, William R., 29, 30
Hardy, Aquilla, 29
Harpers Ferry, 66
Harris, George W., 250, 251
Harry (slave), 116, 127
Harvey, John G., 20, 22, 155, 295
Hatch, Alfred, 14, 16, 23, 30n 12, 49, 94, 165-66, 171, 193-95, 202, 223, 274, 276-78
Hatch, Alfred P., 16, 125, 224, 306
Hatch, Benjamin Francis, 16, 152, 278

Hatch, Caroline, 16, 150, 160, 166, 169-70
Hatch, C. W., 118, 143-44, 168, 203-4, 206
Hatch, Elizabeth Blount (Vail), 16
Hatch, Evalina (Lena), 16
Hatch, Jane. *see* Benners, Jane (Hatch)
Hatch, Lemuel, 16
Hatch, Lemuel D., Col., 193-95
Hatch, Lemuel Durant, Rev., 34, 64, 154
Hatch, Lena, 16
Hatch, Mary, 16, 154, 292
Hatch, Parker. *see* Hatch, Alfred P.
Hatch, Victoria (Jones) Walker, 16, 292
Hawkes, Francis H., 27, 30-31
Hawks, Frank, 40
Hayes, Rutherford B., 12-13, 234-35, 241-55, 256-58, 270, 272
Hays, Charles, 218
Haywood family, 21, 49-50, 109, 196-97, 256, 295, 327
Hendon, Benjamin F., 37
Hendon, W. T., 30-31, 68
Hendricks, Thomas A., 235-36, 240-43, 315, 329
Henry, Fort, 75
Henry, William (slave), 39, 81, 116, 127
Henry (sharecropper), 303
Henry (slave), 98, 107, 113, 116, 127
Herndon, Thomas H., 111, 184, 188
Herran, John (overseer), butchering duties, 74, 92, 93, 94, 113, 145; cotton theft and, 141; disciplinary duties, 113; harvest duties, 69, 89, 102, 104, 105, 110, 143; hauling duties, 65; marketing duties, 111; planting duties, 59, 95, 100, 103; terms of employment, 70, 76, 91, 107, 113, 140; tool repair by, 101

Herrin. *see* Herran, John (overseer)
Hicks, Tilman, 210
Hilliard, Ben (sharecropper), 334
Hobson, Richmond Pearson, 19, 314
Holcroft (sharecropper), 306
Huckabee family, 27-29, 31-32, 44, 113
Huggins, Jacob, 109, 122, 271
Hunt, R. S., 27, 29, 31
Hutchinson family, 67, 159

immunization, 92
impeachment, presidential, 166
Impressment Act, Confederate, 98. *see also* provisions, impressment of
inflation, war and, 9, 74, 85, 90, 97, 111, 118-19, 127, 132, 137
inflation bill. *see* Currency Bill of 1874
Inge family, 21, 27, 30-31, 110, 205
Ireland, unrest in, 301
Isaiah (slave), 116, 121

Jackson, Fort, 81-82
Jackson, James, 65
Jackson, Reuben H., 117
Jacob (slave), 39
Jane (slave), 115, 125
Jay Cooke & Co., 201
Jeffries, A. S., 143, 288, 301-2
Jemison, Henry, 145-46
Jenny (freedwoman), 140, 146
Jenny (slave), 11, 55
Jim (sharecropper), 259, 303
Jim (slave), 116
Joe (slave), 39, 116
John Edwards (slave). *see* Edwards, John
Johnson, Andrew, 11, 147-48
Johnston, Joseph, 83-84, 104-6, 108-9, 123-25, 222
Jolly, Arnold, 29-30
Jones, Allen C., 19, 22, 65, 306

Jones, Catherine, 306
Jones, Eliza J. (Withers), 212
Jones, George, 254, 258
Jones, Margaret (later Benners). *see* Benners, Margaret (Jones)
Jones, Wesley, 265, 290, 327
Jones, William (sharecropper), 327

Keating Lake. *see* Keyton Lake
Kellogg, William P., 215
Kelly's Ford, battle of, 98-99
Kentucky, fighting in, 88-89
Keyton Lake, 64-65
Khartoum, siege of, 327, 328, 334
Kirksy (sharecropper), 153
Kit (freedman), 146, 156, 169, 257, 264-65
Kit (slave), 55, 75, 87, 88n 49, 106, 115, 118, 121, 122, 125, 127
Knight, M. C., 216-17
Kornegay, Caroline (Carrie), 300
Kornegay family, 21
labor, plantation. *see* freedmen; sharecropping; slaves

Lathrop, C. A., 202
Laura (slave), 115, 122
law practice. *see* legal practice
Lee, Tom, 303
legal practice, 11, 23-24, 43-44, 151
legislature, Alabama, 9-10, 25-31, 35-37, 71-73, 91-92, 109n 106, 111-12, 128, 203-4
Leonid meteor shower, 53
LeVert, Cornelius (sharecropper), 300
Lewis, David P., 189, 238
Lewis, Ivey, 314, 333
Lewis (freedman), 139
Lewis (slave), 32, 85, 98, 114, 115, 123, 127
Liberal Republican party, 182, 183, 184, 188-89

Liberty, Statue of, 335
Liddy (cook), 290
Liddy (slave), 116
Lincoln, Abraham, 8-10, 57-59, 68, 87, 96-97, 130, 133-34
Lindsay, R. B., 172, 184
liquor laws. *see* temperance movement
Lishe. *see* Elisha (slave)
Little Bighorn, battle of, 236
Little Frances (slave), 81, 98, 116
Little Tom (slave), 98, 99
Little Wash (slave), 32n 14, 85
Little William (slave), 124
loan, Confederate cotton. *see* subscription, cotton
Logomachy, 330
Long, Rebecca (later Jones), 19
Lorrain glass, 317
Louisiana, 119, 120, 241, 255, 258-59, 261
Lydia (slave), 33
Lynch, John, 312
Lyon, Nathaniel, 67
Lyon family, 59, 194-95, 271

Manassas, battles of, 9, 68-69, 87-88
Manuel (sharecropper), 308, 327
Margaret (slave), 33, 39, 93, 112
Maria (freedwoman), 169
Maria (slave), 116
Marshall (sharecropper). *see* Thornton, Marshall (sharecropper)
Mary (freedwoman), 167
Mary (slave), 55, 99, 111, 114, 115, 116, 117
Mason-Slidell affair, 73-74
Math (sharecropper), 284, 303
Math (slave), 116
May, James T., 45
May, Milton, 79
Mayfield, J. O. K., 39

May (slave), 39
McAllister, Fort, 96
McCrary, David F., 154, 285, 328
McEnery, John, 215
Melissa (slave), 39
Mellown, David Ewing, 205n 85
Mellown, Julia (Hagins), 205n 85
Mellown property, 13, 205-6, 207, 305-9
Memminger, Christopher, 71
Memphis, capture of, 85
Merrimac, 78
Merriman, Augustus S., 186
meteor showers, 53
Military bill, Confederate, 114-15
Military bill, Reconstruction. *see* Reconstruction legislation
Miller, William (Billy), 29
Milly (slave), 73, 115, 116, 122
Mississippi, fighting in, 79-80, 83, 85, 90, 113-14
Mobile, defense of, 96, 126, 134
Mobile Mutual Insurance Company, 156
Modoc War, 193, 195
molasses. *see* sugar cane
money, paper, 71-73, 97, 118, 119, 137
moon, eclipse of, 147, 294
Moore, Andrew B., 139
Moore, Frank (sharecropper), 263
Moore, John W., 166
Moore, Pauldo (sharecropper), 246, 269, 284, 303
Moore, Sydenham, 8, 20-21, 59, 66, 84, 86, 312
Morca (slave), 85, 116
Morgan, Fort, 59, 89, 126
Morgan, John Tyler, 179-80, 197, 238, 255, 257
Morris, Jack (hired hand), 337
Moultrie, Fort, 57, 95n 61
mower, patent hay, 202

murders, 40, 216-17, 277
Murphy, William M., 7, 37-38

Nancy (slave), 44, 117
Nashville, loss of, 76-77
National Union convention, 152-53
Ned (freedman), 148, 155
Ned (slave), 37, 55, 111, 114, 116, 127
Negroes. *see* freedmen
Nelson, A. Sidney, 161
Nelson, John, 202, 207
New Bern NC, 49-52, 82
New England, travel to, 176-79, 315-23
New Orleans LA, 81-82, 215
Nicholls, Francis T., 255, 258-59, 261
Nick (sharecropper), 257-58
Nick (slave), 116
Nigger bill. *see* slaves, Confederate arming of
Northampton MA, 176-79, 315-23
Norwood, William M., 94
Nutting, Samuel, 122
Oak Grove Academy. *see* Avery, Mary
Oliver, Gus, 248
Orris (slave), 39
Osborn, Thomas C., 34, 121, 142, 198
overseers, Benners's. *see individual overseers*
Owen, Stephen D., 112-13

Palmer, B. D., 39
Panic of 1873, 201-4, 207-8
Paris Green (wormkiller), 198-200
Parker. *see* Hatch, Alfred P.
Parnell, Charles Stewart, 301
Parsons, Lewis E., 141, 143
Pasteur family, 260, 269, 314, 331
Patrons of Husbandry, 222, 226
Pauldo (sharecropper), 269, 284, 303

Paul (slave), 85, 98, 107, 116, 127
peace talks, North-South, 130, 134, 136-37, 138
Peck, Sophia (later Watson), 20
Pemberton, Fort, 97, 98-99
Pensy (slave), 91
Perry Insurance & Trust Company, 151-52
Perry (sharecropper), 145, 151
Petersburg, campaign for, 122-24, 131, 136
Peter (slave), 116, 117, 123, 127
Peterson, Bat, 45
Peterson, F. M., 217, 333
Phillip, Fort. *see* St. Phillip, Fort
Phillis (slave), 39, 85, 93, 112
Pickens family, 146, 193, 210, 307, 308
Pillow, Fort, 85, 119
Pitts (overseer), 32
Planters and Merchants Insurance Company, 152
Planters Insurance Company, 10, 20, 129-30
Poellnitz, Annie LeVert (later Benners), 19
politics, involvement in; Alabama legislature, 9-10, 25-31, 35-37; Alabama legislature (Confederate), 71-73, 91-92, 103-5, 109n 106, 111-12, 128; Democratic & Conservative conventions, 171-72, 184, 225-28, 233-34, 269-72; division of Greene County, 157-58; during Reconstruction, 11-13; Senate elections committee, 249-53; switch to Democratic party, 41-42
Polk, Leonidas, 45, 122
Pollard, Charles Teed, 183
Port Hudson, fighting at, 96, 97, 98, 99, 104, 105, 107

Potter resolution, 270, 272, 273
Potts, John (slave), 115, 125, 127
practice, law. *see* legal practice
presidential elections, 41-42, 57, 127, 182-84, 188-89, 312-15, 323-25, 329
prices, war. *see* inflation, war and
Priscy (slave), 70, 75, 85, 115, 116, 125
Privileges and Elections, Senate Committee on, 12-13, 249-53
Produce Loan Act, Confederate, 66n 11, 194n 76
provisions, impressment of, 98, 102, 114, 120, 121, 130, 138
Pulaski, Fort, 81

Quigley, 256n 148. *see also* Republican party

race. *see* freedmen; segregation; unrest, racial
radicals. *see* Republican party
railroads, arrival in Greensboro, 172-73; attendance at Directors' convention, 184-85, 188; excursion for blacks on, 200; flooding and, 286-87; Grange and, 222n 118; Nathan Bedford Forrest and, 205; travel by, 49-52, 176, 182-83, 188, 199, 206, 272-73; yellow fever and, 275
Ramey, A. Rodolf, 118
Randolph family, 94, 100, 153, 191, 314, 336
Rapier, James T., 239, 243
Ravesies, A. H., 141
Reconstruction, Benners and, 10-13
Reconstruction legislation, 11, 158-60, 161, 167
rents, property. *see* sharecropping
representation, southern, 147-50. *see also* Union, readmission to

Republican party, 11-12, 41, 58-59, 153-54, 172, 182-83, 187-89, 204, 234, 312-13, 323-25
Rhoda, (freedwoman), 11, 140, 146
Rhodes (sharecropper), 303, 327
Ridgway, Bradley H., 30
Roanoke Island, capture of, 74-75
Roulhac, Thomas, 21, 174-75, 209, 230, 271, 277, 283, 301-2
Russo-Turkish war, 261-62, 263-65, 266-69, 273

Salina (house servant), 156, 162
Salisbury, Marquis of, 334-35, 336
San Stefano, Treaty of, 266-69
Savannah, attacks on, 95-96, 129-30
scantling, 334n 31
Scarborough (overseer), 115, 117, 119, 121
Scarff, W. D. C., 306
schools, Greensboro, 22
Scip (slave), 109
Scott family, 206
screw pulverizer, 146, 289
Seay, Thomas, 198, 237, 253, 270, 315
secession, southern, 8, 57, 58-59
segregation, 48, 192, 214, 222
Senate, U.S., 12, 249-53, 300-301
Seven Days Battle, 86n 45
Seven Pines, battle of, 84
Seven Weeks War, 148
Seymour, Horatio, 103
sharecropping, 13, 15, 145, 145-46, 151, 153, 220, 263-64, 300, 303-4, 305-8, 308-9, 326-27
Sharpsburg, battle of, 9, 89-90
Sheldon, Abe (sharecropper), 303-4, 332
Shelley, Charles M., 239, 240, 243
Shenandoah Valley, fighting in, 85, 134
Sherman, William Tecumseh, 10,

129-30, 312
Sherman's bill. *see* Reconstruction
  legislation
Shiloh, battle of, 79-80
shorts, milling, 119
silver bill, 266-67
Silvey (slave), 39
Sip (slave), 44
skating rink, 311, 314
Slavery and Its Results (Benners), 17
slaves. *see also* freedmen; *individual
  slaves;* Confederate arming of,
  131, 135; conscription of, 107;
  discipline of, 64, 113, 124;
  freedmen's contracts and, 11,
  140, 146; freeing of, 41-42, 59n 7,
  130, 138-39; list of, 115-17;
  nomenclature of, 31;
  nonfraternization with, 48;
  provisions to, 64, 85, 111, 114,
  119; taxes on, 91-92; trade in, 39,
  42, 93, 112; travel with, 55
Slidell, John, 73-74
Smaw, William R., 190
Smith, Henry, 257
Smith, Hilliard (overseer), 32, 33
Smith, L. H., 307, 308
Sons of Temperance, Greensboro, 23
South Carolina, 95, 109, 130-34,
  246-47, 255, 258-59, 260
Southern University, Greensboro, 23
Spain, war with foreshadowed, 204-5,
  208
Star of the West, 58
state elections, Alabama, 25-31, 172,
  203-4, 237
Statue of Liberty, 335
steamboat, travel by, 44-49
Steel, S. N., 93
Stickney, C. L., 21, 271, 274, 287,
  296, 332
Stickney, Richard, 154, 226, 310, 327
Stockton, Daniel D., 154

Stokes (sharecropper), 327
Stollenwerck family, 150, 156, 199,
  201, 308
Stowe, Harriet Beecher, 195-96
St. Phillip, Fort, 82
Stringfellow, I. E., 303
subscription, cotton, 66-68, 71, 193-
  95
substitutes, conscription and, 112
sugar cane, 100, 104, 107, 109, 110,
  126-27
Sumner, Charles, 210, 213
Sumter, Fort, 57n 38, 58, 95n 61,
  109n 106
Sunbeam, horse, 11, 102, 120, 138
supplemental Reconstruction act, 161
surrender, Confederate, 10, 136-37,
  138
Susan (slave), 90, 115
suspension, bank. *see* banks

Tallman, James A., 100, 122
taxes, 9-10, 91-92, 209
Taylor, Buck (sharecropper), 303
Taylor, Zachary, death of, 8, 25
temperance movement, 22-23, 25-31,
  95, 327, 331
tenant farming. *see* sharecropping
Tennessee, fighting in, 95, 107, 110-
  11, 112-13, 118, 119, 127, 129-30
Territorial bill. *see* Reconstruction
  legislation
Thornton, Marshall (sharecropper),
  251, 295, 331, 332, 334
Thurman, Allen G., 315
Tilden, Samuel, 12, 235-36, 240-43,
  247-48
Tomlinson, Evalina Rowe (later
  Benners), 82n 36
Tom (slave), 59, 116, 122
Tom White (slave). *see* White, Tom
  (slave)
travel: to Alabama legislature, 91-92,

109, 111-12, 128; to Blount
  Springs, 54-56, 168-69, 214-15,
  236-38, 274-75; to Confederate
  Congress, 59; to Fish River, 169-
  70; to Hunstville, 175; to Mobile,
  146-47, 151, 152, 170, 176, 185-
  86, 199; to Montgomery, 155,
  171-72, 271-72; to New Orleans,
  167; to Northampton, 176-79,
  315-23; to North Carolina, 49-
  51; by railroad, 176, 182-83, 188;
  to Texas, 44-49; to Washington
  DC, 51-52, 249-53
Trice, William T., 231
troops, Federal, 11, 13, 239, 258n
  152, 259-60, 261-62
Tunstall family, 146, 173, 271, 304,
  315
Turpin, John, 19, 271
Tutwiler, Henry, 22, 28

Union, readmission to, 142, 143, 146,
  147-50
Union convention, National, 152-53
unrest, racial, 163, 205, 215, 238, 248

vacations. *see* travel
vaccination, 92
Vail family, 21, 34, 308, 336
Vallandigham, Clement, 103
Van Dorn, Earl, 101
veto, first override of, 147-48
Vicksburg, siege of, 85, 94-100, 102-
  8
violence, racial. *see* unrest, racial
Virgil (freedman), 140, 146
Virgil (slave), 11, 33, 44, 55, 86, 93
Virginia, CSS, 78
Virginia theater, Civil War. *see*
  individual battles
Virginius, Steamer, 204, 207-8
voter registration, Reconstruction,
  165-66

Walker, John T., 216-17
Walker, Lawrence W., 145-46
Walker, Mary, 305, 311, 313-14
Walker, Victoria Jones (later Hatch),
  16, 292
Walker Place plantation, 7, 301, 303-
  4, 338
Wallace, Ed (sharecropper), 303
Waller, C. E. (Charley), 21, 175,
  197-98, 216, 270
Waller, Robert B., 66, 67, 261
Walton, John W., 86, 155
Want (freedman), 144
Want (slave), 116, 123, 124, 127
Ward, Alfred, 84, 101
war prices. *see* inflation, war and
Wash, Big. *see* Big Wash (slave)
Wash, Little. *see* Little Wash (slave)
Washington, George (sharecropper),
  334
Washington's birthday, 76-77, 209,
  265
Wash (slave), 32, 115, 123. *see also*
  Grant, Wash
Watson, Fred, 230
Watson, Henry, 19-20, 105, 176-80,
  190-91, 204-5, 258-59, 309, 315-
  23, 328-31
Watson, Sereno, 318-19
Watson, Sophia (Peck), 20
Watts, John, 246n 137
Watts, Thomas H., 335
Webb, Henry, 21, 79-80
Webb, James D., 21, 27, 29-31, 35-
  37, 44, 65n 9, 109-10
Webb, James E., 155, 163, 253, 257,
  312, 315
Webb, J. H. Y., 21, 271
Webb, William P., 21, 30, 39, 118,
  143, 198
Weller, Elliah, 163
Wemyss, J. A., 29, 78, 148, 152, 160,

257, 293-94
Wheeler, William A., 235
Whig party, 25-31, 41
Whiskey ring, Grant and, 230
White, Tom (slave), 75, 98, 113, 116, 128
Wilderness, battle of the, 120
Williams, Ness, 290
William (slave), 75, 116
Williamson, Jim, 277
Willis, Elizabeth L. (Benners), 82, 144-45
Wilson, Cephas L. (Ceph), 29-30
Wilson, Henry, 188, 230
Wilson, William B., 100
Windsor (slave), 73, 115, 116, 125
Withers, Eliza J. (later Jones), 212
Withers, Robert W, 44n 28
Witherspoon, T. F., 64, 169
worm, cotton, 186-87, 198-200, 238, 273, 275, 298
Wright, George Grover, 256
Wright (slave), 98, 107, 110, 116
Wymes, J. A.. *see* Wemyss, J. A.
Wynne, Charles, Sr., 309

yellow fever epidemic, 201, 202-3, 274-76
Yerby, Miles Hassell, 22
Yorktown VA, 83, 301
Young, W. B., 188, 203-4, 271

About the Editors

Glenn M. Linden is an associate professor of history at Southern Methodist University in Dallas, Texas, where he has taught since 1968. He holds a Ph.D. in history from the University of Washington. He has edited two books, *Voices from the Gathering Storm* (2001) and *Voices from the Reconstruction Years, 1865–1877* (1999), and was co-editor of *Voices from the House Divided: The United States Civil War as Personal Experience* (1995) and *Politics or Principle: Congressional Voting in Congress on the Civil War Amendments and Pro-Negro Measures 1838–1869* (1976).

Virginia Linden has a bachelor's degree from the University of Washington and a master of arts in sculpture from New Mexico State University in Las Cruces, New Mexico. She has worked with her husband on all of his books: editing, researching, and preparing the manuscripts.